Accountability in Public Policy Partnerships

Accountability in Public Policy Partnerships

Julia Steets
Associate Director, Global Public Policy Institute, Germany

First published 2010 by
PALGRAVE MACMILLAN

Palgrave Macmillan in the UK is an imprint of Macmillan Publishers Limited, registered in England, company number 785998, of Houndmills, Basingstoke, Hampshire RG21 6XS.

Palgrave Macmillan in the US is a division of St Martin's Press LLC, 175 Fifth Avenue, New York, NY 10010.

Palgrave Macmillan is the global academic imprint of the above companies and has companies and representatives throughout the world.

Palgrave® and Macmillan® are registered trademarks in the United States, the United Kingdom, Europe and other countries.

ISBN 978–0–230–23897–8   hardback

This book is printed on paper suitable for recycling and made from fully managed and sustained forest sources. Logging, pulping and manufacturing processes are expected to conform to the environmental regulations of the country of origin.

A catalogue record for this book is available from the British Library.

Library of Congress Cataloging-in-Publication Data

Steets, Julia, 1975–
    Accountability in public policy partnerships / Julia Steets.
        p. cm.
    ISBN 978–0–230–23897–8 (hardback)
    1. Public-private sector cooperation. 2. Government accountability.   I. Title.
    HD3871.S74 2010
    352.3'4—dc22

                                                                                2010027560

10   9   8   7   6   5   4   3   2   1
19   18   17   16   15   14   13   12   11   10

Printed and bound in Great Britain by
CPI Antony Rowe, Chippenham and Eastbourne

Contents

List of Figures and Tables

Figures

Tables

Preface

This book is about public policy partnerships and their accountability and its theme derives from my work for the Global Public Policy Institute (GPPi). At the institute, we have been following, analysing and debating the rise of public policy partnerships and their implications for global governance over many years. Time and again, we returned to questions of accountability. What effects do partnerships have on existing accountability relationships? How can partnerships themselves be held accountable? Answering these questions seemed central to any debate relating to partnerships, yet difficult since the necessary concepts were not sufficiently developed. Within the context of my doctoral dissertation, submitted to the University of Erfurt in late 2007 under the title 'Defining Accountability Standards for Public Policy Partnerships', I therefore set out to develop a concept and model of accountability that would help us understand, assess and guide the development of partnerships. Since partnerships include public, business and civil society actors and are active in very different areas, I quickly found myself building a generally applicable accountability model. I hope that the thoughts developed in this book will be helpful for those working with partnerships and of interest for those thinking about accountability.

Naming all individuals who supported me during the research and writing phases or provided critical inputs would be impossible. My special thanks go first and foremost to Prof. Dr. Dietmar Herz, my supervisor, as well as Prof. Dr. Frank Ettrich, who acted as secondary supervisor. I would also like to thank Martin Sprott, Bernd Siebenhüner, Angelika Steets, Andreas Blätte, Thorsten Benner, Jan Martin Witte and Jenny Scharrer for their critical and supportive feedback and Kristina Thomsen for her support in revising and adapting the manuscript.

Julia Steets
Ambach

List of Acronyms

4C	Common Code for the Coffee Community
AICPA	American Institute of Certified Public Accountants
BGB	Bürgerliches Gesetzbuch
BPD	Business Partners for Development, now also known as Building Partnerships for Development
CEO	Chief Executive Officer
CFO	Chief Financial Officer
CSD	Commission on Sustainable Development
CSR	Corporate Social Responsibility
DALYs	Disability-Adjusted Life Years
DESA	United Nations Division for Sustainable Development
DFID	Department for International Development (UK)
DKV	Deutscher Kaffeeverband/German Coffee Association
DOTS	Directly Observed Therapy, Short-Course (a treatment strategy for TB)
ECOSOC	United Nations Economic and Social Council
EITI	Extractive Industries Transparency Initiative
ESCB	European System of Central Banks
ESMAP	Energy Sector Management Assistance Program (World Bank)
EU	European Union
FAO	United Nations Food and Agriculture Organization
FASB	Financial Accounting Standards Board (US)
FDA	Food and Drug Administration (US)
FOCJ	Functional, Overlapping, Competing Jurisdictions
FRSs	Financial Reporting Standards
FRSSE	Financial Reporting Standard for Smaller Entities
GAAP	Generally Accepted Accounted Practices
GAIN	Global Alliance for Improved Nutrition
GAO	Government Accountability Office, formerly: General Accounting Office (US)
GAVI	Global Alliance for Vaccines and Immunisation
GRI	Global Reporting Initiative
GTZ	Deutsche Gesellschaft für Technische Zusammenarbeit (Germany)
GVEP	Global Village Energy Partnership
GWP	Global Water Partnership
IAASB	International Auditing and Assurance Standards Board
IASB	International Accounting Standards Board

ICANN	Internet Corporation for Assigned Names and Numbers
IFAC	International Federation of Accountants
IFRS	International Financial Reporting Standard
IGO	Intergovernmental Organisation
ILO	International Labour Organization
IMF	International Monetary Fund
INGO	International Non-Governmental Organisation
INTOSAI	International Organization of Supreme Audit Institutions
IP	Internet Protocol
IPSASB	International Public Sector Accounting Standards Board
IRS	Internal Revenue Service (US)
ISA	International Standard on Auditing
ISEAL	International Social and Environmental Accreditation and Labelling Alliance
ISO	International Organization for Standardization
IUCN	The World Conservation Union
MAD	Multiple Accountabilities Disorder
MDGs	Millennium Development Goals
MSC	Marine Stewardship Council
NAO	National Audit Office (UK)
NCVO	National Council for Voluntary Organisations (UK)
NGO	Non-Governmental Organisation
NPO	Non-Profit Organisation
OECD	Organisation for Economic Co-Operation and Development
OMB	Executive Office of the President, Office of Management and Budget (US)
PCFV	Partnership for Clean Fuels and Vehicles
PM	Performance Measurement
PMs	Performance Measures
PPP	Public Private Partnership
RBM	Roll Back Malaria
REEEP	Renewable Energy and Energy Efficiency Partnership
SSAPs	Statements of Standard Accounting Practice
SIDA	Styrelsen för Internationellt Utvecklingssamarbete/Swedish International Development Cooperation Agency
SMEs	Small and Medium Enterprises
SORP	Statement of Recommended Practice
TB	Tuberculosis
TNC	Transnational Corporation
USAID	United States Agency for International Development
UN	United Nations
UNDP	United Nations Development Programme
UNEP	United Nations Environment Programme
UNICEF	United Nations Children's Fund

VENRO	Verband Entwicklungspolitik deutscher Nichtregierungs-organisationen
WCD	World Commission on Dams
WHO	World Health Organization
WSSD	World Summit on Sustainable Development
WTO	World Trade Organization
WWF	World Wide Fund for Nature

1
Introduction

1.1 Accountability – a fuzzy concept and its importance for partnerships

Accountability. Oh no, I don't know that I can. [...] I guess some of us, when we think of that [...] word we understand the importance of checks and balances. We understand that there are some things that – where accountability is near instantaneous, and that there are other things where there are grey areas and it's much less difficult. But what it means, very simply, is to – to me, anyway – is that people understandably look to individuals, who have responsibilities, to be accountable for the conduct of those responsibilities. [...] you need to put in place a series of things that hold people reasonably accountable for their actions, and people, I think, expect that.

US Secretary of State Donald Rumsfeld when asked about how he would define accountability (Council on Foreign Relations, 2004)

'Accountability' has become a prominent political catchword. The term serves as a rallying cry for civil society organisations aiming to control the actions of governments, international organisations and corporations,[1] and is used by those who want to create a positive image for their organisation[2] as well as those attacking their opponents for irresponsible behaviour.

Yet – as is often the case with political buzzwords – Donald Rumsfeld is not the only one who finds it difficult to put his finger on what exactly the term means. As Mark Bovens put it so aptly:

As a concept, however, 'public accountability' is rather elusive. It is a hurrahword, like 'learning,' 'responsibility,' or 'solidarity' – nobody can be against it. It is one of those evocative political words that can be used to patch up a rambling argument, to evoke an image of trustworthiness, fidelity, and justice, or to keep critics at bay.

(Bovens, 2005, p. 182)[3]

1

In addition, understandings about accountability vary between the public, private and civil society sectors,[4] adding to the conceptual confusion. Governments and public administrations, the business sector and increasingly also the non-profit sector each have their own distinct accountability traditions.

The discourse and practice of accountability in the public sector, for example, has developed in the context of representative democracy. Democratic governments around the world have espoused the same basic institutional structure, comprising a legislative, an independent judiciary and an executive. Each of these institutions has a range of typical accountability mechanisms. These mechanisms either allow for direct citizen control or work through a system of checks and balances.[5]

Corporate accountability in its classical form has three distinct layers. Firstly, societies use legal and fiscal rules and their enforcement to hold corporations accountable for conforming to social norms and contributing to social goals. Secondly, consumers use market mechanisms to create accountability for product quality and price. Thirdly, owners use a variety of mechanisms treated in the corporate governance literature to induce managers to maximise returns.

Questions of accountability of non-profit organisations have gained prominence concurrent with the recent rise in power of these organisations. But while the debate has intensified, it is far from reaching a consensus. It is not only disputed who NGOs should become more accountable to or for what but also whether more accountability is desirable at all. In addition, the debate has largely remained theoretical and many of the recommendations have not (yet?) been translated into practice. Currently, NGOs are mainly accountable to public authorities, their donors and their members.

Most contributions to the literature on accountability are specific to one of these sectors, even though increasing efforts were made over recent years to apply the concepts and experiences from one sector to another. Reflecting the fact that accountability arrangements are often highly complex, many contributions focus on specific subgroups of agents and individual accountability mechanisms.[6]

In the debate about partnerships, the issue of accountability is particularly salient. Partnerships are cooperative arrangements between international institutions, governments, corporations and civil society organisations to address pressing local and international policy problems.[7] As the ability of traditional nation states to address complex questions has increasingly come under question and as states are transforming, partnerships have emerged in many areas as a promising mechanism for defining and implementing complex and controversial policies. Partnerships now address urgent problems ranging from regulating the technical aspects of the Internet to enhancing the social responsibility of companies and providing remedies to global health crises. Prominent examples of partnerships at the global level include the Global Reporting Initiative (GRI),[8] a partnership that develops and disseminates standards to guide the sustainability reporting practices of companies and other organisations, and the Global Fund to Fight AIDS, Tuberculosis and Malaria,[9] a global initiative to raise additional resources for the fight against these diseases.[10]

Since partnerships routinely include actors from the public, corporate and civil society sectors, we cannot simply rely on any one established accountability system. Defining concepts and effective mechanisms of accountability is therefore even more complex for partnerships than for more traditional institutions. This complexity renders partnerships an interesting object of study for analysing different understandings, implications and new developments of accountability. A focus on partnership accountability also has the potential to generate insights for the discourse on the accountability of other institutions.

Moreover, most principled objections against partnerships are based on concerns about accountability. These criticisms imply that by shifting policy decisions to partnerships, governments can circumvent control by their domestic constituencies and international institutions can weaken control by member states.[11]

Corporations for their part are accused of using partnerships to improve their reputation without significantly changing their management and operational practices.[12] Thus they evade public pressure for moving towards more sustainable practices and counteract the drive for binding regulations.[13] At the same time, shareholders may criticise companies for their partnership activities because they are costly and (at least in the short term) inefficient.

NGOs or other civil society organisations, finally, can be seen as risking, being co-opted and losing their critical edge by participating in cross-sectoral partnerships. Moreover, large NGOs that have the capacity to partner with other institutions may be tempted to claim they represent constituencies that do not actually have any influence over the NGO's policies and activities.[14]

These critiques have a common denominator. They fear that partnerships reduce the accountability of the participating organisations without creating alternative accountability mechanisms.[15] If validated, these critiques would seriously undermine the credibility and legitimacy of partnerships as a mechanism to address public policy problems.[16] This has also been recognised by the supporters of partnerships. In unison with many partnership critics, many of them now demand that partnerships should become (more) accountable.[17]

But, for the most part, the demand for accountability has remained general. It is rarely explained why exactly partnerships should be accountable, let alone what this would entail in practice.[18] Acar and Robertson confirm this gap in the literature and debate: 'The question of accountability in multi-organizational networks and partnerships has not been adequately addressed in the literature' (Acar and Robertson, 2004, p. 332).

Given how central the question of accountability is to the success of the partnership approach to public policy, a carefully differentiated conceptual and normative understanding of partnership accountability is critical.

1.2   Purpose and structure

This study aims to add to our conceptual and normative understanding of accountability by providing a unified model of accountability that can, beyond partnerships, also be applied to more traditional accountability debates in the public, private and civil society sectors. Moreover, its purpose is to add to the debate on and practice of partnerships by defining concrete and consistent standards for partnership accountability.[19]

Both 'partnership' and 'accountability' are political buzzwords. As such, they lack clear and broadly accepted definitions. To avoid building normative castles on conceptual quicksand, this book takes five steps for defining accountability standards for partnerships. These steps and the corresponding chapter numbers are illustrated in Figure 1.1.

- Defining terms and clarifying concepts:
  To prepare the ground for empirical analysis and normative reflections on partnership accountability, this study begins with a discussion of the two terms at the centre of enquiry.

  Chapter 2 proposes a working definition of the term 'partnership' that will be used throughout the study. To clarify exactly what the term denotes, it is compared and contrasted with other definitions and related concepts, namely networks and corporatism.

  To provide a clear understanding of the term 'accountability', the same chapter traces this concept to its theoretical roots in principal–agent

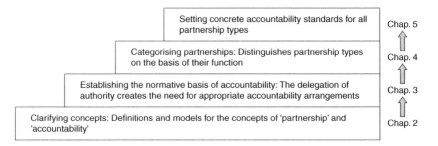

Figure 1.1   Structure of the argument

theory. It proposes a basic model illustrating the general workings of accountability relationships and analyses what this means in practice. The chapter also explores the contradictions between different kinds of accountability, underlining the fact that organisations need to choose carefully which accountability arrangements to adopt.

- Establishing the normative core of accountability:
  Having delineated the subject of this study, Chapter 3 begins the normative enquiry. It asks what gives the concept of accountability its normative impetus or why we believe that organisations ought to be accountable.
  To answer these questions, the chapter begins with a review of the relevant literature. Several different justifications for accountability have been proposed in different fields, but none of them is found fully satisfactory. Therefore, the study goes on to develop its own argument. This alternative account is based on mainstream ideas in legal, political and economic theory, as well as liberal political and moral philosophy. It suggests that it is the delegation of authority – be it explicit or implicit, ex-ante, ex-post or hypothetical – that creates the need for appropriate accountability arrangements. The chapter then takes the normative argument further. It asks which properties determine when an accountability arrangement is appropriate. Based on the argument that the need for accountability is grounded in delegation, it makes the case that an organisation's function is key for deciding which type of accountability the organisation should espouse.

- Categorisation:
  The abstract principles developed in Chapter 3 need to be applied to the reality of partnerships. Chapter 4 relies on a range of partnership examples and clusters them into four categories, distinguished by their main function.

- Defining concrete accountability standards for different partnership types:
  Chapter 5 develops concrete accountability standards for each of the four groups of partnerships. The chapter first takes the main function of each partnership group and analyses what authority is needed to exercise that function. To determine necessary accountability principles and standards, it then refers to and adapts standard accountability practices and commonly accepted normative expectations relating to accountability in functionally similar organisations.

2
The Concepts of Partnerships and Accountability

Before launching into normative reflections on accountability in Chapter 3, this chapter develops a basic understanding of the central terms around which this book is structured and sketches the necessary background and context for locating the debate.

2.1 Partnerships

Nowadays, partnerships are everywhere. Visit the website of any major international institution, government, large corporation and – increasingly – non-governmental organisation (NGO) and you will most likely find some information about this organisation's partnership programmes or philosophy. Similarly, if you participate in a conference on governance issues or global public policy[1] problems, the odds that 'partnerships' will be on the agenda are good.[2]

As mentioned in the Introduction, partnerships today address a wide range of issues. As a result, the term 'partnership' is nearly ubiquitous. It is used to describe many different and often contradictory phenomena.[3] To be able to use the term in a social scientific context, this section defines its essential characteristics and distinguishes it from other concepts, namely networks and corporatism.

2.1.1 Definition

For the purposes of this book, 'partnership' is defined in an ideal typical way[4] as a voluntary cooperative arrangement

- between organisations from the public, private and/or civil society sectors. The public sector includes public institutions at the local, regional, national and inter- or supranational level. The private sector includes small- and medium sized, as well as large and trans- or multinational companies. Civil society organisations can range from local, community-based organisations to large, transnational development initiatives.

- that display a certain degree of institutionalisation. While partnerships are often dynamic in their composition and working methods and don't need to follow a uniform or standardised institutional model, they must show a minimum of formality. This minimum includes a clear understanding of who the partners are, some regular form of consultation and agreed decision-making procedures.
- that have common, non-hierarchical decision-making procedures and share risks and responsibilities. Different organisations cooperating on an equal footing and determining policies and action plans jointly is what transforms any working relationship into a partnership. Of course, that does not mean that partnerships know no power differentials between their partner organisations or that decision-making procedures cannot in any way reflect these differences. But for a cooperative relationship to be a partnership, all partner institutions have to be involved in a significant way in the taking of important decisions. This also implies that partner organisations share risks and responsibilities involved in the partnership.
- whose purpose is to address a public policy issue. Partnerships are of interest in the context of political science insofar as they work to achieve a societal goal and thus complement or substitute the work of governmental actors. This criterion, however, is not a very strict one, since many governments have been liberal in defining what constitutes a public policy issue.

In brief, 'partnership' is defined as a voluntary cooperative arrangement, involving public, private and/or civil society organisations that is formalised with common, non-hierarchical decision-making procedures and that addresses a public policy issue.

At the global level, partnerships address a broad range of issues. The Partnership for Clean Fuels and Vehicles (PCFV), for example, aims at reducing air pollution caused by vehicles in developing countries. The Internet Corporation for Assigned Names and Numbers (ICANN) regulates the technical elements of the Internet's name and numbering systems in order to preserve the operational stability of the system and promote competition. The Extractive Industries Transparency Initiative (EITI) aims to increase transparency and accountability to ensure that the revenues derived from extractive industries contribute to sustainable development and poverty reduction. The Global Alliance for Improved Nutrition (GAIN) seeks to reduce malnutrition of populations at risk through the fortification of staple foods and other strategies, and the Common Code for the Coffee Community (4C) promotes sustainability in the production, processing and trading of mainstream coffee by compiling and promoting relevant standards.

The definition employed here shares some common traits but also displays significant differences with some other definitions of partnerships employed in a social scientific or practical-political context.

The Political Declaration of the WSSD in Johannesburg, which was so instrumental in promoting the concept of partnership by including it as an official, 'type II', outcome of the summit, contains no more than the following:

> We recognize that sustainable development requires a long-term perspective and broad-based participation in policy formulation, decision-making and implementation at all levels. As social partners, we will continue to work for stable partnerships with all major groups, respecting the independent, important roles of each of them.
>
> (World Summit on Sustainable Development, 2002a, § 26)

The Johannesburg Plan of Implementation that was adopted along with the political declaration is slightly more detailed in that it specifies the involvement of 'major groups' in partnerships. At the same time, it constricts the definition to include only cooperative arrangements focusing on policy implementation (rather than policy definition, for example) in the area of sustainable development.

> [T]he implementation should involve all relevant actors through partnerships, especially between Governments of the North and South, on the one hand, and between Governments and major groups, on the other, to achieve the widely shared goals of sustainable development. As reflected in the Monterrey Consensus, such partnerships are key to pursuing sustainable development in a globalizing world.
>
> (World Summit on Sustainable Development, 2002b, § 3)

This definition of partnerships and the subsequent work of the UN are, however, based on a more detailed description of criteria for partnerships. The criteria were developed in the run-up to WSSD and endorsed in the decision of the eleventh meeting of the Commission on Sustainable Development. Like the definition proposed here, they recognise partnerships as voluntary, multi-stakeholder initiatives. But they only focus on initiatives designed to contribute to the implementation of internationally agreed development goals and include a range of normative criteria, such as that partnerships should pursue an integrated approach to sustainable development, display a sectoral and geographical balance and be designed in a transparent and accountable manner.[5]

The WSSD's focus on cooperation in order to achieve a public policy goal is echoed in the political science literature, for example, in Börzel and Risse, who focus on partnerships that transcend national borders:

> Transnational PPPs [public-private partnerships] would then be institutionalized cooperative relationships between public actors (both governments

and international organizations) and private actors beyond the nation-state for governance purposes, [i.e. for] the making and implementation of norms and rules for the provision of goods and services that are considered as binding by members of the international community.

(Börzel and Risse, 2005, p. 199)

By contrast, the Food and Drug Administration (FDA), a US government agency that actively encourages 'partnering with the private sector', sees partnerships as a predominantly commercial relationship and therefore includes only financial restrictions in its definition:

> For example, a public/private partnership could be an arrangement whereby a contractor or third party develops and operates a system which is beneficial to the FDA and others and charges the cost of the service to users. Revenue generated by the system would be expended by the contractor or third party to maintain and improve the system.
>
> (United States Food and Drug Administration, 2004, p. 1)

In a similar vein, the German government's definition of partnerships focuses on co-financing mechanisms – mainly in the context of development policies.

> We take 'public private partnerships' to be development partnerships with the private sector. Partnerships consist of projects that are co-financed by corporations and development agencies.
>
> (Gesellschaft für Technische Zusammenarbeit, 2004)
> (Author's translation)[6]

A comparable emphasis on the financial aspects of a partnership appears, for example, in Lindner and Rosenau – though they focus more on traditional contracting-out models, where the government plays the role of the financier that pays the private sector to provide public services, rather than the user-fee or co-financing models emphasised above by the governments:

> [We generalise] the partnership notion to include almost any combination of public funding and private provision of services for public purposes.
>
> (Linder and Rosenau, 2000, p. 7)

In some respects, then, the definition of 'partnerships' proposed here is narrower than other definitions in use (most notably with respect to the common decision-making criterion), while in others it is wider than at least some others (e.g. on the type of actors involved or the purposes pursued by the partnership).

While these definitions differ from one another in various respects, they all belong to the same emerging discourse that places partnerships in the context of a public policy or governance context. As such, they have a significantly different understanding of the term than a standard dictionary definition such as Merriam-Webster's that defines 'partnership' as a legal term.

> [A partnership is] a legal relation existing between two or more persons contractually associated as joint principals in a business, or a relationship resembling a legal partnership and usually involving close cooperation between parties having specified and joint rights and responsibilities.
>
> (Merriam-Webster, 2004, entry for 'partnership')

2.1.2 Partnerships between networks and corporatism

While the term 'partnership' is by now much used in political practice and analysis, there is no extended theoretical work establishing a theory of policy partnerships. Networks and corporatism, by contrast, are concepts or models with a much longer and more refined theoretical pedigree. Both terms deal with modes of policymaking that include actors from the private and/or civil society sectors and have been applied to the study of partnerships. This section provides a brief summary of both traditions of thought and explains the overlaps and differences as compared to the partnership concept used here.

2.1.2.1 *Corporatism*

Corporatism is a political system that provides for a legal representation of different industrial, economic and professional groups and their inclusion in political decision-making processes.[7] Early proponents of corporatist political structures such as Adam Müller saw corporatism as a way to transform class conflict into class cooperation. Fascist economic theory and practice drew heavily on this concept, contributing to the negative associations made with the term today.[8]

Are partnerships between governmental organisations, corporations and civil society organisations, then, just a revival of corporatist structures under a new guise? This, in fact, is one of the more powerful criticisms that have been directed against proposed and existing partnerships.[9]

Some significant parallels exist between corporatism and partnerships that warrant a careful analysis of the arguments made and evidence collected in the literature about corporatism. First, corporatism, like partnerships, is about including organised interests in the policymaking process. As a consequence, the participation of individuals in the political process takes a setback in both arrangements – an argument that is particularly important for partnerships operating at the national or local level. At the same time, this means that in both cases the participation of groups can be regulated, thereby potentially minimising existing inequalities of access to people in power.

Second, some thinkers such as John Ralston Saul have described corporatism as a system in which organised elites get to influence the policy process at the expense of ordinary citizens.[10] The same argument has been debated with respect to NGOs.[11] For the question whether NGOs are an elite project, one should certainly differentiate between different types of civil society organisations, for example, between large and established institutions operating at an international level such as Amnesty International and small, community-based organisations. But when analysing partnerships between governmental organisations, corporations and civil society groups, one must bear in mind that large NGOs possess far greater visibility and resources for engaging in high-profile partnerships than grassroots organisations.[12]

Finally, both partnerships and corporatist solutions can have their most positive impact in policy areas rife with conflict. Addressing these conflicts through cooperative approaches does not only mitigate social unrest, it also improves compliance with the decisions taken. This aspect becomes the more important, the weaker the central control mechanisms of the political system in question are.

But there are also important differences between these two concepts. First, corporatist political systems normally only include labour and business interests and focus on macroeconomic policy decisions. Partnerships can include these, but are rarely restricted to them. Rather, partnerships can cover the entire spectrum of policy issues. In each case, they will gather those groups that can affect the outcome and contribute to solving the problem addressed. Thus, for example, the World Commission on Dams (WCD) was composed of representatives of governments interested in large dam projects, companies specialised in building these large projects and civil society groups representing those affected by the dams, who were previously often engaged in violent protests against the dam projects.[13]

Second, the groups included in corporatist governance structures tend to be highly centralised, with business as well as labour organisations representing entire sectors. Partnerships, by contrast, often include small community-based organisations representing one very specific section of society or individual businesses whose operations have an impact on the goals of the partnership.

Finally, corporatism is a system that usually operates in the context of a national political system.[14] As such, its decision-making structures ultimately depend on the authority of the state. This can, but does not have to, lead to hierarchical decision-making procedures in corporatist institutions. Partnerships also work at the inter- or transnational level. While partnerships thus often operate 'in the shadow of hierarchy',[15] their decision-making processes by definition have to be non-hierarchical. Therefore only those corporatist arrangements with common and non-hierarchical decision-making procedures would qualify as partnerships.

2.1.2.2 Networks

Networks are the subject of an impressive body of literature in anthropology, sociology, political science and economics. Naturally, these studies contain a broad variety of approaches, themes and focal points. When trying to establish how networks relate to partnerships, it is useful to distinguish three modes of network research: network analysis, network theories or models and networks as empirical phenomena.

As an analytical approach, network analysis had an early precursor in the sociological work of Georg Simmel[16] around the turn of the last century. It developed into a more widespread and coherent approach in sociology and anthropology[17] in the 1970s and has further developed since. In essence, network analysis is an approach to social enquiry that focuses on the interactions between individuals or organisations. To understand certain dynamics or outcomes, it typically maps the links and exchanges between different actors, often using complex mathematical and statistical tools. Based on patterns of interaction or the position of different actors in the network, situations can be classified.[18]

In political science, policy network analysis is closely associated with the notion of 'governance'.[19] Governance theories and approaches often take the diminished capability of central government to govern using traditional methods as their point of departure[20] and focus on ways of steering by political authorities.[21] Over recent years, a vast body of literature discussing the concept of governance and applying network approaches to policy analysis has developed. Yet the cumulative insights derived from the governance debate seem limited and network analysis as an analytical approach has serious shortcomings.[22] Moreover, a network approach is ill suited for achieving the purposes of the present enquiry, namely, to develop accountability standards for partnerships. Therefore, this study does not adopt a network approach to social analysis.

Network theory, by contrast, is mainly concerned with explaining why networks emerge, how they operate and what impact they have on social interactions. An important source of network theory is transaction cost analysis. It posits that firms choose that organisational form which allows them to minimise their transaction costs in the production and marketing process. Thus they can either rely on the market, on hierarchies (i.e. the vertical integration of suppliers) or networks of known and trusted firms to secure needed inputs and sell their products.[23] Unfortunately, 'network theory' does not constitute a coherent body of work[24] generating a consistent set of assumptions and hypotheses. While some specific network theories may offer interesting insights relating to the emergence and operations of partnerships, they are unlikely to contribute much to the question of how accountable partnerships should be.

Finally, the term 'network' is used as an empirical category. Since the applications of network analysis and theories are extremely broad, so are the descriptions of what constitutes an actual network. Delimitating the fuzzy notion of 'partnership' from the equally ill-defined notion of 'network' can therefore seem a futile task.[25] Yet when concentrating on policy networks, two broad approaches can be distinguished. Most authors employ a broad definition of networks, which encompasses all non-hierarchical forms of linkages among actors involved in the policy process. This can range from entirely informal and fluid arrangements with no fixed decision-making procedures to highly formalised corporatist structures or intergovernmental policy-coordination mechanisms.[26] What these arrangements have in common is that the actors are mutually dependent on each other for solving the problem at hand and seek to coordinate their activities to that aim.[27]

As represented in Figure 2.1, if this wide definition of networks is used, partnerships can be understood as a specific form of network. A possible conceptual alternative to 'partnership' would therefore be 'institutionalised network'. But, apart from the heavy and often problematic theoretical baggage referred to above, the concept of 'network' also has a narrow definition with connotations that do not fit the subject of this investigation well. Take, for example, Grahame Thompson's definition of networks:

> Networks have often been considered as above all 'informal' practices of coordination. They rely upon direct personal contact. They tend to be localized as a result, or confined to a particular clearly defined group with similar concerns, interests or aspirations. Such that they display a systematic orientation, these work through attributes like loyalty and

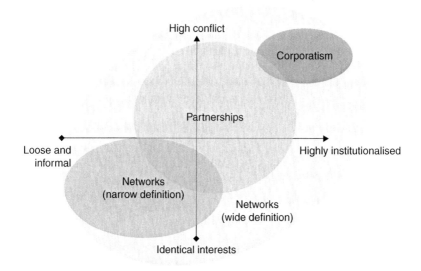

Figure 2.1   Partnerships, networks and corporatism

trust rather than administrative orders or prices. [...] Governance of an activity is achieved through the identity of a common purpose or interest, for which all will work for a collective result. These tend towards a 'flat' organizational structure, where at least there is a lot of formal equality between the participants (though there may actually be significant real differences of power and authority in practice).

(Thompson, 2003, pp. 30–1)

This description suggests that networks arise among actors with similar interests and therefore only need a low degree of institutionalisation to coordinate their activities. Partnerships, by contrast, often form among actors with strongly diverging interests. To find cooperative solutions which benefit all participants, clearer rules and decision-making procedures as well as stronger commitments by the partner organisations are required. It is due to these connotations of extremely loose structures, identity of interest and the dominance of trust and loyalty[28] that the term 'partnership' is preferred here over 'institutionalised networks'.

2.2   Accountability

As indicated in the opening pages of this book, the concept of accountability is highly complex. Yet accountability does have a specific core meaning. This section proposes a general, 'core' definition of accountability, clarifies the concept by asking the questions 'who is accountable, to whom, for what, how and why?' and explores some of the general problems and dilemmas of accountability.

2.2.1   Defining the 'core' of accountability

A standard dictionary definition of accountability reads as follows:

> [Accountability is] the quality or state of being accountable; *especially*: an obligation or willingness to accept responsibility or to account for one's actions.
>
> (Merriam-Webster, 2004, entry for 'accountability',
emphasis original)

That definition contains two central elements: the notion of responsibility and that of accounting for something. The original meaning of 'to account', in turn, is the 'reckoning of money received and paid' (Douglas-Harper, entry for 'account'). Accounting, then, primarily refers to the keeping and transmitting of information. This meaning is reflected in our understanding of 'accountants', that is, professional bookkeepers. In this context 'accounting' is neutral, in the sense that it only implies an accurate reporting of facts, not an evaluation of these facts.

When we say 'to account for', though, the term has a different connotation. According to an etymological dictionary, it was around 1700 that the term started to be used in the sense of 'explaining' and 'answering for money held in trust'.[29] This is where the 'responsibility' part of the definition stems from. People entrust their money to others, who accept the responsibility to deal with it according to the terms agreed. 'Accounting for', then, means not only transmitting accurate information about the use of that money but also explaining whether the money was handled as agreed.

From the perspective of an actor (often termed the 'agent'), then, 'accountability' means:

- providing accurate information about one's activities or behaviour;
- evaluating that behaviour with reference to certain standards, rules or expectations;
- thereby recognising one's obligations and accepting responsibility for one's actions.

But accountability always involves a second side, since it is a concept that refers to the relationship between at least two actors. In the dictionary's example, the other side are the people who entrusted their money to somebody else (often termed the 'principal'). They are only prepared to delegate control over their property to an agent if they can trust that the agent will honour his obligations and act in their best interest. To be able to hold the agent accountable for doing so, the principals need sufficient information about the agent's behaviour. They also need to maintain some leverage over the agent, that is, the ability to impose positive or negative sanctions. In a working accountability relationship, the principal's ability to impose sanctions and the agent's anticipation of these sanctions are sufficient to control the agent's behaviour.

From the perspective of the principal, then, accountability is a mechanism to ensure that the agent does not abuse his authority and acts in the best interest of the principal. It is at this point that the concepts of accountability and legitimacy intersect. Where a principal has access to sufficient accountability mechanisms, he is likely to regard the agent's exercise of authority as legitimate. Because of this connection, many authors writing from a political background have a habit of mentioning both terms in the same breath and of using them almost interchangeably.[30] Yet the concepts are different and it is important to be aware of their distinctions.

'Legitimacy' is a term used in political science to designate a situation in which citizens accept the authority of the government and are therefore prepared to comply with its policies.[31] In his early treatment of the subject, Max Weber emphasised that legitimacy can have several sources, including tradition and charisma, as well as the formal correctness and legality of the act of ruling.[32] In the context of today's democratic discourse, it is more

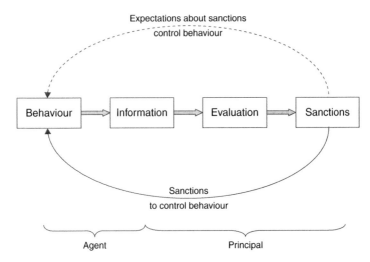

Figure 2.2   Accountability

commonplace to acknowledge that legitimacy can derive from the use of appropriate inputs or processes, as well as the achievement of desirable outputs or results.[33] In a democratic understanding of governance, appropriate accountability arrangements create input accountability.[34] But legitimacy can also derive from the effectiveness or efficiency of an organisation in achieving results, which does not require a similar accountability relationship.

The basic mechanism of accountability is represented in Figure 2.2. An agent behaves within the context of a certain set of obligations and expectations.[35] Information about this behaviour can either be provided by the agent herself or demanded and generated by the principal. The principal then evaluates this information and applies positive or negative sanctions accordingly. Insofar as the agent can anticipate this reaction, she can adapt her behaviour to avoid negative sanctions.

In the previous paragraphs, I have used the terms 'principal' and 'agent' to designate the accountability holder and holdee respectively. The terms derive from principal–agent theory, an important theoretical construct in economics. The theory was originally designed to analyse the relationship between the owners and managers of companies. Over time, this reasoning has been applied to a wide array of situations, relaxing some of the stricter assumptions of the economic formulations of the theory.

In an early paper on the problems arising in principal–agent arrangements, Stephen Ross defined the basic relationship as follows:

[A]n agency relationship has arisen between two (or more) parties when one, designated as the agent, acts for, on behalf of, or as a representative for the other, designated the principal, in a particular domain of decision problems.

(Ross, 1973, p. 134)

The theory assumes that both parties are autonomous actors and rational agents who want to maximise their expected utility. In most cases the principal's utility function differs from the agent's utility function, and that's where the problem starts. The agent does not automatically act in the best interest of the principal. Since the activity takes place in an environment containing unpredictable developments which cannot be influenced by the agent, not all aspects of the agent's behaviour can be predetermined in detail. In addition, the relationship involves an information asymmetry because the agent will always be better informed about his activities than the principal.[36]

Because of these three elements – diverging goals, a situation of uncertainty and information asymmetry – a principal–agent relationship brings disadvantages to the parties involved. These so-called agency costs arise either from the efforts needed to make the agent act in the best interest of the principal or from the loss incurred if the agent's activities diverge from the outcome preferred by the principal.[37]

To limit the negative impacts of principal–agent relationships – or, in other words, to improve the accountability of the agent to the principal – economists have focused their attention on two aspects of the relationship: the definition of sanctions and incentives to align the interests of agent and principal and the provision of information to reduce the principal's monitoring costs. In a business context, solutions usually involve remuneration schemes for managers linking their income to company profits and strictly regulated and audited financial reporting mechanisms.

Economists working on principal–agent theory early on stressed the possibilities of expanding their reasoning to other social or political relations. Thus, Jensen and Meckling noted:

> Before moving on, however, it is worthwhile to point out the generality of the agency problem. The problem of inducing an 'agent' to behave as if he were maximizing the 'principal's' welfare is quite general. It exists in all organizations and in all cooperative efforts – at every level of management in firms, in universities, in mutual companies, in cooperatives, in governmental authorities and bureaus, in unions, and in relationships normally classified as agency relationships such as those common in the performing arts and the market for real estate. The development of theories to explain the form which agency costs take in each of these situations (where the contractual relations differ significantly), and how and why they are born will lead to a rich theory of organizations which is now lacking in economics and the social sciences generally.
>
> (Jensen and Meckling, 1976, p. 313)[38]

Particularly political scientists focusing on democratic accountability have taken up this suggestion and have applied the insights derived from economic analysis to political processes. In many cases they have also adopted the focus on sanctions/incentives and the provision of information. Thus Andreas Schedler defines political accountability as follows:

> [T]he notion of political accountability carries two basic connotations: answerability, the obligation of public officials to inform about and to explain what they are doing; and enforcement, the capacity of accounting agencies to impose sanctions on powerholders who have violated their public duties.
>
> (Schedler, 1999, p. 14)

Similarly, Robert Keohane, who develops a concept of accountability for inter- and transnational politics, proposes this definition:

> Accountability refers to relationships in which principals have the ability to demand answers from agents to questions about their proposed or past behavior, to discern that behavior, and to impose sanctions on agents in the event that they regard the behavior as unsatisfactory.
>
> (Keohane, 2002b, p. 3)

In the original formulation of principal–agent theory in economics, a number of assumptions generated a clear framework which allowed analysts to focus on how to strengthen accountability. Most cases are based on a contract which clearly defines the principal and the agent. What the agent is accountable for also tends to be uncontested. It is to maximise the principal's expected utility, usually defined in financial terms. Finally, while different types of sanctions and incentives do exist, the main focus in economic relationships is on monetary rewards or sanctions.

All of those parameters, however, have become contested and problematic. Within economics, stakeholder theories, for example, demand recognition of other stakeholder groups as principals, thus also changing what the agent is held accountable for.[39] When applying the concepts of principal–agent theory to wider social or political situations, the definition of agent and principal changes, as well as the aspects for which the agent is accountable and the sanctions and incentives used to strengthen accountability.

2.2.2 Who is accountable, to whom, for what and how?

To characterise any given accountability relationship, it is useful to begin by clarifying the parameters outlined above: Who is the agent? Who are the principal(s)? For what is the agent accountable? and How is this accountability created or strengthened?[40] Without exploring any specific answers, this section sketches the general scope of these questions.

2.2.2.1 Defining the agent

In the example used above for defining the core of accountability, an accountability relationship was created by one party entrusting money to another. If the agent that is thus created is an individual, it is obvious who can be held accountable for the correct use of the funds. In modern societies, though, many aspects of our political, economic and social lives are dominated by organisations. When it comes to holding organisations accountable, the question of who exactly is accountable can turn into a major problem.

The basic dilemma has been coined the 'problem of many hands' by Dennis Thompson. In an essay analysing responsibility in politics, he defines the problem as follows:

> Because many different officials contribute in many ways to decisions and policies of government, it is difficult even in principle to identify who is morally responsible for political outcomes. This is what I call the problem of many hands.
>
> (Thompson, 1980, p. 905)

If a process is too complex to identify individual contributions to specific outcomes, then holding individuals accountable for undesirable outcomes becomes difficult. As a result, individuals as well as organisations as a whole in many instances manage to escape blame and avoid accountability.[41] This also undermines the preventive function of accountability, encouraging irresponsible behaviour.

Given the far-reaching impact of organisations on modern societies, strategies to address the problem of who can be held accountable are very important. Mark Bovens, for example, distinguishes four different solutions to the problem, each with its own pragmatic and normative advantages and shortcomings.

In systems of *corporate accountability*, organisations as independent entities are treated like persons. Most legal systems recognise organisations as 'legal persons', that is, as the bearers of rights and responsibilities. This approach makes it easy to identify the agent and can ensure that the organisation is held to account for its misconduct even when the individuals originally responsible for these decisions are no longer present.[42] Mechanisms relying on corporate accountability can be problematic because organisations often do not behave rationally (hence undermining the preventive function of accountability); because lack of external insight makes control difficult; because organisations can dissolve to escape accountability; and because sanctions can affect people who are not responsible for the misconduct (Bovens, 1998, Chapter 5).

The three remaining solutions are different varieties of holding individuals within organisations to account for corporate conduct. A common form is *hierarchical accountability*. Each official in an organisation is accountable to his superior and the individual at the top of the organisation is held accountable for the behaviour of the organisation as a whole. Again, this model presents a very clear and easy-to-apply solution to the problem of many hands. Problems arise when the leaders of organisations lack adequate information and control over all activities of the organisation. In these cases, hierarchical accountability only has a limited preventive and educational effect on the organisation[43] (Bovens, 1998, Chapter 6).

Another solution is *collective accountability*, that is, a system in which each individual member of a group or organisation is held to account for the actions of the collective. This mechanism is certainly very effective in ensuring that individuals are held to account and might have a strong preventive effect. At the same time, most individuals identify as members of specific groups and might feel individually responsible for group conduct. Yet enforcing sanctions to implement collective accountability clearly contradicts fundamental principles of the rule of law and of Western conceptions of morality. The application of collective form of accountability in formalised accountability relations is therefore very rare[44] (Bovens, 1998, Chapter 7).

Finally, models of *individual accountability* seek to identify the exact contribution of a person to an outcome and hold her accountable accordingly. This solution corresponds most closely to the normative principles underlying democratic societies but is fully affected by the problem of many hands. To overcome this problem, organisations can, for example, clarify who bears what responsibility and improve the transparency of working processes (Bovens, 1998, Chapter 8).

Since each of these approaches has advantages and shortcomings, Bovens suggests applying a mix of accountability mechanisms depending on the situation. The question of who is held accountable thus remains contested. The problem is exacerbated by the fact that many of the most pressing contemporary public policy problems are influenced by a host of different institutions, groups and individuals. When speaking about the problems that partnerships are designed to address, the problem of many hands therefore applies not only within organisations but also for the multitude of organisations involved.

2.2.2.2 Defining the principal(s)

A politically even more controversial question than who is the agent is the definition of the relevant principal(s). In most cases, multiple actors are recognised or are struggling to be recognised as principals. In businesses, for example, shareholders are broadly accepted as having the right to hold management to account, but in many cases we also see customers, employees and suppliers making accountability claims. Similarly, leading public officials in democracies are accountable to parliament as well as to independent financial agencies controlling the use of public funds and to the general public via the media.

The existence of multiple principals raises two problems. Firstly, as we have seen above when defining agency costs, monitoring the agent is costly for the principal. If multiple or fragmented principals exist,[45] a collective action problem arises since no single actor has an incentive to bear the costs of providing information that could be used by all principals to monitor the activities of the agent.[46]

The second, more intractable problem lies in the fact that different principals have different, potentially conflicting criteria for judging the agent's conduct. Thus shareholders hold managers accountable for high returns on investment, employees for high salaries, good working conditions and job security, while customers emphasise low prices and high product quality.[47] Similarly, public officials are held to account for producing outcomes by the media and public, while financial oversight committees demand accountability for the correct use of funds.[48]

Agents can use the existence of multiple principals to avoid accountability.[49] But they can also accept the complex task of assigning priorities among principals and balancing their various claims. R. Edward Freeman in his argument to adopt a stakeholder theory of the firm – which is no other than to recognise other stakeholders as co-principals on an equal footing as shareholders – described the scope of the challenge confronting managers:

> The task of management in today's corporation is akin to that of King Solomon [...] management must keep the relationships among stakeholders in balance.
>
> (Freeman, 2001, p. 44)

All partnerships face a range of different principals. Depending on the formality of their accountability claims, we can generally distinguish three levels of accountability holders: legal and fiscal authorities, formal principals and informal principals. The different layers are illustrated in Figure 2.3.

Figure 2.3   Layers of principals

Legal and fiscal authorities: The level of accountability with the strictest and most formalised definition of both obligations for agents and sanctions in case of their violation is to legal and fiscal authorities. In the debate about institutions that act at the transnational or international level, legal and fiscal accountability is often neglected, because there is no all-encompassing international legal code or court system. Yet almost all institutions are located and operate on national territories and are thereby bound by their respective rules and regulations.[50] Multinational corporations, for example, despite their power have to abide by the rules of the countries they operate in. Integrated international markets and financial systems do, however, allow them to choose which national regulatory and enforcement system they want to be subject to. This can put corporations in a strong position when they lobby for changes in national rule systems.

Formal principals: The next level of accountability is that defined by contracts or other means of formal delegation. In these cases, contracts, statutes or briefs establish who transfers what authority to whom. Thus they clearly define the identity of both principal and agent, as well as the obligations of the agent and sanctions that apply in case of non-compliance. As a result, formal accountability relationships tend to be uncontested in principle. Disputes may arise over the details of honouring obligations or the application of sanctions but not the existence of an accountability relationship itself. Examples for such principal–agent situations include the relationship between company owners and managers, between elected governments and their ministers as well as their delegations in international organisations and between civil society organisations and their members or donors.

Informal principals: A third level of accountability is based on the informal, implicit or hypothetical delegation of authority. As argued in greater detail in section 3.2.3, organisations often assume authority without explicit prior authorisation. In these cases, those who originally or rightfully hold the authority now exercised by the organisation have a claim to accountability. The lack of formality means, however, that these claims are often contested.

In practice, the relative power of groups or individuals often determines whether they can hold an agent accountable. Establishing clear criteria for determining who should be recognised as a principal is nevertheless important, not least because legitimacy itself has become a currency of power in a globalised world.

2.2.2.3 What are agents accountable for?

Accountability was defined above in the context of a principal–agent relationship. This makes it easy to define what an agent is accountable for in abstract terms. Agents are accountable for using the authority given to them in a way that fulfils the principal's expectations. When somebody entrusts the management of resources to somebody else, for example, she probably expects the agent to use those resources efficiently and effectively to achieve the agreed goal.

But principal–agent relationships can take on very different forms. In addition, any single agent can be subject to the accountability demands of a variety of principals. It is therefore impossible to describe all the possible aspects an agent can be held to account for in concrete terms. Generally speaking, though, agents are held accountable for the way they handle resources, for their compliance with rules and procedures and for the outcomes they produce.

Accountability for finances: Financial accountability could be subsumed under the other two headings relating to processes and outcomes, but it deserves to be treated separately because it is so central both to our understanding of accountability[51] and to the workings of organisations.

Agents can be held accountable for three different aspects of the way they handle resources. Firstly, it can concern the sources of an agent's financial and other means. Whoever provides an organisation with resources gains influence over it. This can make the agent dependent and corrupt its impartiality. Public agencies, many civil society organisations and institutions involved in evaluation and monitoring are thus often held accountable for the sources of their funds.[52]

Secondly, agents are accountable for using their resources efficiently and effectively. Those who provide an organisation with resources usually want to ensure the agent uses them in the best way for reaching the desired goals. In the private sector, return on investment is a common measure for establishing whether resources were well used. In the public and civil society sectors, similar measures are usually more difficult to find.

Thirdly, the way an agent handles resources can be under scrutiny. Because efficiency and effectiveness are often hard to measure in public agencies and civil society organisations, more weight tends to be attached to the rules and processes for managing resources. Thus donors and public agencies often predetermine in great detail which resources can be allocated for what purpose and agents are held accountable for following those rules. The key to proper financial management – professional bookkeeping and accounting, combined with adequate reporting – though, is expected of organisations in all three sectors.

Accountability for finances can create considerable conflicts and dilemmas. Firstly, different principals often have different views on what resources should be spent on. Company managers, for example, can be pressured by shareholders to deliver maximum dividends. Employees may favour higher wages; consumers usually opt for lower prices and NGOs lobby for a greater share of resources to be invested, for example, in environmental protection.

Secondly, the three aspects of financial accountability are not necessarily compatible. An environmental NGO that rejects contributions from oil companies to maintain its independence, for example, may be unable to reach its goals because of a lack of resources. Similarly, professional and accurate accounting and reporting is costly and can divert resources away from other purposes. And strict and detailed rules on how to handle resources can curtail the flexibility of agents to such an extent that their efficiency suffers. As further discussed in section 2.3, organisations must therefore carefully determine which aspects of accountability they want to stress.

Accountability for compliance with rules and processes: Another general aspect that agents are held accountable for is their compliance with rules and procedures. Rules and predefined procedures serve to control the behaviour of agents. They can do so by directly protecting the interests of others. Companies, for example, in many countries have to pay their employees minimum wages and are restricted in their rights to fire them. Other rules and processes are components of accountability mechanisms. They make it easier for principals to enforce their accountability claims. An example of this is the right of workers to unionise or to participate in the management of the company. Principals are often interested in enforcing compliance with these rules and processes because it allows them to create effective accountability for their other interests.

The rules and processes regulating the behaviour of agents can be defined by governmental authorities in laws, regulations and fiscal rules. But they can also be determined by principals. When a new agency is created, for example, the founding institutions create a statute and by-laws determining the agency's mandate and governance. Common types of rules and processes that agents are expected to follow include:

- Legal and fiscal rules: The rules and processes prescribed for organisations are complex and vary between countries as well as between different organisational forms. They pertain, for example, to the requirements for registration or incorporation, the treatment of employees or competitive practices. Compliance with these rules can be enforced by national judicial systems. Where judicial systems work well, accountability for compliance with legal and fiscal rules is therefore high.
- Decision-making procedures: Another important set of rules and prescribed procedures covers the way organisations make decisions. This includes regulations on which body can take which decisions by what decision rule, as well as who needs to be included or consulted and who is bound by the decision. Decision rules can be important mechanisms to strengthen accountability. They help determine who bears what responsibility for a certain outcome and allow those principals who are included in the process to articulate their preferences directly. Irrespective of the outcome of a decision, principals therefore often hold agents accountable for following the correct procedures when taking decisions.

Which decision-making procedures are set for an organisation is highly dependent on context. The requirements are often stricter for the public than the private sector and more demanding for taking strategic decisions than for implementing them. A standard that all types of organisations can be held accountable for is due diligence.[53] Principals demand due diligence from managers and bankers in investment decisions. But the public also holds public agencies and NGOs accountable for 'not doing their homework properly'. Thus Greenpeace, after the Brent Spar campaign, as well as the Bush administration in the follow-up to the invasion of Iraq experienced a sharp drop in public support.[54]

- Transparency: A final crucial set of rules and regulations determines what information an organisation has to provide to whom. As we have seen in the definition of accountability above, access to reliable and useful information is essential to any accountability mechanism. Transparency requirements therefore figure prominently in the rules and procedures laid down for organisations[55] and principals are often keen to enforce compliance with these rules. The rules regulate not only what needs to be communicated but also determine requirements for the quality of information. Many organisations, for example, are obliged to conform to strict standards in their accounting and reporting, and must have their accounts and activities verified by independent auditors.[56]

Accountability for results: Perhaps the most obvious aspect that organisations are held to account for are the outcomes or results of their work. This includes firstly which goals an organisation pursues. Take, for example, an advocacy NGO that claims to represent the interests of indigenous people and seeks to stop the construction of a dam on their behalf. The group of indigenous people may actually disagree and try to hold the NGO accountable for its goals. Similarly, citizens hold governments accountable for the goals they pursue by endorsing or rejecting proposed policies in elections.

Secondly, accountability for results can refer to the way in which an organisation achieves its aims. The main question here is whether the organisation is efficient in its operations. Consumers, for example, can hold companies accountable for efficiency by choosing products that, at similar quality, are offered at a cheaper price. Comparison is more difficult in the public and civil society sectors. But donors, for example, increasingly use measures like the ratio of overhead costs to total budget as shorthand for efficiency.

Finally, principals can focus on the quality of results. Is the organisation effective and successful in reaching the goals it set for itself? A government that was voted in on the promise to reduce unemployment, for example, may lose subsequent elections if it fails to deliver effective results. Similarly, a research institution can quickly lose its reputation as well as funding if its results fail to live up to scientific standards, just as a professional auditor will find himself in court and out of business if his results are not accurate and impartial.

In practice, creating accountability for the efficiency and quality of results is often difficult. The chief reason for this is that some outcomes are much easier to evaluate than others. Thus, it is much easier to judge the financial returns of an investment than to measure the social or environmental effects of an investment decision, policy or civil society campaign. As a result, accountability for easy-to-measure results often takes precedence over accountability for more fuzzy kinds of results, or accountability for easily evaluated procedural aspects dominate outcome accountability. As Robert Behn argued persuasively for accountability in the political sector, this can lead to serious shortcomings in the overall workings of a political system (Behn, 2001).

2.2.2.4 How is accountability created or strengthened?

The definition of accountability proposed above contained a description of the basic mechanism through which accountability works. An agent behaves in a certain way. Information about these activities is used by the principal to evaluate the agent's behaviour. Depending on whether or not the behaviour conforms to the principal's expectations, she will apply sanctions to control the agent's activities, thus establishing what could be termed 'retroactive accountability'. If the agent can anticipate this reaction, the expectation of sanctions influences his actions, hence generating 'proactive' or 'preventive accountability'.[57]

Accountability can go wrong at each of these four steps: Firstly, the effects of the agent's behaviour can be unclear.[58] Secondly, the information available to the principal can be biased or insufficient for an appropriate evaluation. Thirdly, accountability can fail if the expectations of the principal or principals are unclear or contradictory. Finally, the principal might not possess sufficient means for sanctioning the agent or his threat to use those sanctions may not be credible enough to preventively change the agent's behaviour.

Mechanisms to create or strengthen accountability, then, are measures that address any of these issues.[59] Since an accountability system is only as strong as its weakest point,[60] effective accountability strategies address all four areas at the same time, or focus on the area with the greatest shortcomings.

Clarifying the agent's contributions and responsibilities: There are two situations in which the effects of an agent's behaviour are unclear: Firstly, the activities and responsibilities of an actor may be well known, but the consequences of these actions are not. Many environmental problems, for example, are causally extremely complex and scientifically disputed. Apart from improving the scientific evidence relating to the problem, accountability can be improved if very specific behavioural goals are defined based on existing evidence. This happened, for example, in the area of climate change, where the Kyoto Protocol defined specific targets for the reduction of CO_2 emissions. These are now used to either make companies reduce their emissions or pay for additional emission rights.

Secondly, this lack of clarity can occur when the agent's responsibilities are unclear. The obvious remedy here is to assign responsibilities and tasks more clearly. While the agents must retain flexibility to react to unexpected developments, a clearly defined mandate is important to establish account-ability within an organisation, and also when different groups or institutions cooperate to reach a joint goal.

Improving the provision of information: As we have seen above, information asymmetry is one of the major drivers of agency costs. Correspondingly, transparency, or the availability of correct and useful information, is a central precondition for accountability.[61] The issues relating to transparency include the scope, source, quality, credibility, formats and associated costs of information:

Generally, principals want information on anything they hold the agent accountable for. This can refer to an organisation's finances, its operating procedures and internal governance, as well as the outcomes produced in different areas. The challenge for any organisation is to find the right balance between the necessary scope and degree of detail in reports and their usability. In addition, certain aspects of an organisation's work might be subject to legitimate confidentiality requirements, such as, for example, the takeover plans of a company.

Information can be generated by both the agent and the principal. In both cases, the quality of information is crucial and different types of reporting and auditing standards are used to guarantee quality. When it is the agent who makes information available, he often encounters credibility problems. These are most commonly addressed through external verification.[62] When the principal generates the necessary information, credibility can also be an issue (e.g. Greenpeace's Brent Spar episode), but in addition, the question of how sources of information are protected and how the agent deals with information requests are salient.[63]

Another important aspect concerns the format in which information is transmitted. To be useful, the format must fit the needs of the respective audience. Thus while publications of English language annual reports on the Internet might be appropriate for satisfying the information needs of Western NGOs, they might not be accessible to local communities in the developing world. Here, signs, billboards or public discussions in the local language might be necessary to convey information effectively.

Finally, the costs of providing and using information have to be considered. Providing detailed reports and evaluations of an organisation's activities can be highly complex and requires specialised skills and staff time. From the perspective of an agent, bearing this cost is only worthwhile if it serves to avert sanctions. For principals, particularly when they are fragmented, generating information can lead to a collective action problem. Stock markets have solved this problem by specifying disclosure requirements for listed companies and by employing rating agencies to provide additional information and evaluate available data.

Clarifying the principal's expectations: To create a strong accountability relationship it is also crucial that the principal's expectations be clearly defined and articulated. Clearly defined and, where possible, operationalised expectations form the basis for evaluating the agent's behaviour.

In many cases, the expectations and demands of a principal are ill defined. This can be the case in situations involving formal delegation. Even where a contract defines the principal–agent relationship, the tasks and achievements expected of the agent can be too broad to provide any practical guidance.[64] But a lack in clarity is even more frequent in informal accountability relationships such as between consumers and producers or civil society groups and political institutions. Here, expectations are often not articulated at all or are unclear and subject to change.

When the principal is a fragmented and dispersed group of individuals or organisations, formulating precise expectations presents a formidable challenge that might require the installation of a centralised spokesperson. The task is easier when the principal is an individual or a coherent group or institution. Here, the scope for improvement is often large, particularly in the political sphere. Yet a fundamental tension will always remain between the desire to define precise steps and responsibilities in a mandate and leaving the agent with a sufficient degree of freedom to react to unforeseen developments.[65]

The case becomes even more complex when different principals with diverging interests and expectations exist. As Robert Keohane pointed out, this can be abused by agents to avoid accountability.[66] The flipside of this coin is that those agents who do not want to escape accountability and are confronted with multiple, conflicting expectations can find it impossible to do justice to all principals.[67] Despite their best intentions, they can be subject to sanctions from various sides. To avoid sanctions, the agent can create transparency about which expectations exist and how she balances or prioritises them, hoping for understanding and approval from the principals. Alternatively, she can attempt to make the principals (or at least some of them) to agree on a coherent set of objectives among themselves. Companies conducting multi-stakeholder dialogues, for example, can use this forum for either of the two strategies of explaining and creating transparency or developing a consensus among stakeholders.

Strengthening sanctions and incentives: The ability to impose negative or positive sanctions is the ultimate means through which principals control the agent's behaviour. The types of sanctions available to different groups or individuals vary considerably in their nature and their salience to the agent. They include:[68]

- Legal and fiscal sanctions: Organisations, even if they work on a transnational or international level, are bound by the laws and regulations of the country they operate in. Legal and fiscal systems around the world define very explicit rules for the behaviour of individuals and corporate actors, as well as the sanctions to be applied in case of their breach. Both the content of these rules and sanctions and the degree of their enforcement vary significantly between countries. Well-functioning legal and fiscal systems can impose tough sanctions and can therefore be very effective in creating accountability. This accountability, though, is usually limited in scope, sanctioning only outright transgressions of norms.
- Elections: In democratic political systems, elections are commonly used as sanctions to ensure the political leadership respects the preferences of the people.[69] Elections are also used within many organisations or cooperative bodies to make elected officials accountable to their electorate.
- Disciplinary measures: In hierarchical organisations, superiors can usually resort to disciplinary measures for holding their staff to account for their actions. These can be quasi-legal (as is the case in military organisations) or result in pay-cuts, changes in the job description or dismissal.
- Financial incentives: While legal sanctions, elections and disciplinary measures have a strong impact on agents, financial incentives and sanctions can be more easily fine-tuned and thus allow for a more differentiated form of accountability. Financial sanctions are used to hold both individuals and organisations to account. Thus managers' salaries are often linked to the company's performance, consumers and investors can exert pressure through their market decisions and donors often link their contributions to specific demands.
- Withdrawal and voluntary compliance: A potent sanctioning mechanism for those who might not have formal or financial means to influence an organisation or process is the option to stop participating in it[70] or fail to comply with its resolutions. To be effective, the actor who denies participation or compliance must be critical to the issue at hand. Thus, for example, the refusal of the US to participate in international agreements like the Kyoto Protocol seriously affects its effectiveness. Similarly, the quantity of individuals leaving the GDR prior to the fall of the Berlin Wall seriously undermined the state's legitimacy. In the corporate sector, the operations of a company can be threatened if many employees quit their jobs or lay down their work in strikes. At the international level, where no centralised enforcement mechanism exists, the necessity to achieve voluntary compliance with norms and resolutions is one of the key levers for groups demanding the consideration of their interests, hence creating accountability for inclusion.

- Reputation: A more subtle and diffuse type of sanction relates to an individual's or an organisation's reputation. The opinions held by relevant groups about an organisation or individual matter since they influence their ability to operate. Reputation affects, among others, who want to work for, engage with or vote for the actor and how seriously products or ideas are taken.[71]
- Protest and violence: Finally, all those who feel they do not possess sufficient alternative sanctions to hold an agent accountable can resort to protests or even violence to make their claims heard. From the so-called Monday demonstrations against labour market reforms in Germany, via the street protests against the World Trade Organization's (WTO) policies in Seattle to acts of sabotage and violence against oil firms operating in the Nigerian Delta region, it is particularly those who feel excluded and marginalised who resort to protests and violence to create accountability.

With such a broad array of potential sanctions available, two main strategies exist to strengthen accountability based on sanctions. Firstly, institutional structures can be changed to give specific principals access to new kinds of sanctions. This can mean the creation of entities organising collective action to increase the sanctioning potential, such as trade unions or NGOs giving voice to marginalised groups. Or it can mean the inclusion of groups in decision-making processes, as is the case when corporations conduct multi-stakeholder dialogues or when the UN grants NGOs official status in its negotiations.[72] The latter process is often an attempt to change available sanctioning mechanisms from those that work crudely and *ex-post facto* like protests and violence to more differentiated ones that are better suited to creating proactive or preventive accountability such as elections or participation in decision-making processes.

Secondly, the accountability effect of existing sanctions can be strengthened by improving their enforcement. Better enforcement not only allows stronger retroactive accountability but thereby also makes the threat of sanctions more credible, thus enhancing preventive accountability. One way to make the enforcement of sanctions more reliable is the creation or strengthening of enforcement institutions, such as state prosecution offices, disciplinary committees in institutions or control and evaluation units in donor organisations. Another way is to make sanctions more immediate and link them more directly to the agent's behaviour. Thus, for example, managers' salaries are now often directly tied to company performance. This means that sanctions and rewards are triggered automatically.

2.2.2.5 When is the agent interested in strengthening accountability?

We have now seen how accountability can be created or strengthened at each of the four steps involved in the basic accountability mechanism. Measures to improve accountability can be taken by both sides, the principal(s) and the agent. While it seems obvious why principals want to create strong accountability (namely to align the agent's behaviour as much as possible with their own interests and goals), it might not be so clear why an agent might be interested in strengthening his own accountability.

Indeed, Keohane suggests that 'Opportunistic agents will seek to design institutional arrangements that only nominally control their behavior' (Keohane, 2002b, p. 14). Similarly, Robert Behn argues that agents have a very clear view on accountability which does not make it sound like a desirable outcome: 'Those whom we want to hold accountable have a clear understanding of what accountability means: accountability means punishment' (Behn, 2001, p. 3).

Yet there are clear instances in which agents do take measures to make themselves more accountable. Of course, these actions can be taken in response to or anticipation of pressure for reform. But it can also be in the agent's interest to actively push for improved accountability. Jensen describes this in his early definition of agency costs:

> In addition in situations it will pay the *agent* to expend resources (bonding costs) to guarantee that he will not take certain actions which would harm the principal or to ensure that the principal will be compensated if he does take such actions.
>
> (Jensen and Meckling, 1976, p. 5, emphasis original)

Figure 2.4 illustrates the motivation of principal and agent in creating or strengthening accountability.[73] The situation is presented as a simple game involving two steps. Agent A can either pursue his own or the principal's interest. Principal P can either apply sanctions to A or not. The payoff structure (payoff A, payoff P) shows that the optimal outcome from the perspective of the agent is 'pursue A's interests' and 'no sanction'. The principal,

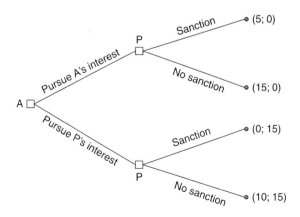

Figure 2.4 The principal's and agent's interest in accountability

by contrast, has a strong preference for the agent to pursue P's interests. Therefore, the principal has an interest in making the threat of sanctions credible enough to induce A to choose 'pursue P's interests'.

From the perspective of the agent, the situation is slightly more complex. His first instinct is probably to try to weaken accountability so that he can pursue his own interests without incurring any sanctions. Two considerations, however, can change this calculus. Firstly, the principal is probably only willing to engage in this game at all or to play it again if she sees a reasonable chance that the agent will pursue P's interests. As long as the agent derives a greater benefit from playing than from not playing, he has an interest in making a credible commitment not to abuse his authority, that is, in strengthening accountability.[74] Secondly, the agent also has a strong motivation to avoid a situation where he does his best to act in the principal's interests, but gets sanctioned nevertheless. He can reduce this risk by demanding that the principal clearly articulates her expectations and preferences and by ensuring that the principal receives adequate information about the agent's behaviour. In this sense, too, the agent can be interested in strengthening the accountability relationship.

2.2.3 The accountability dilemma

The term 'accountability' carries overwhelmingly positive connotations. Many therefore assume that it is simply a case of 'the more, the better'.[75] This is particularly the case in the international sphere, where researchers and activists now increasingly come to see mechanisms to strengthen the accountability of different organisations as a means to balance the democratic deficit of global institutions.[76]

While accountability does play an important role in making the operations and policies of influential actors more responsive to the needs and interests of those affected, it is not always a case of 'the more, the better'. In Mark Boven's words, 'Public accountability may be a good thing, but we can certainly have too much of it' (Bovens, 2005, p. 194).

Accountability relationships can have negative impacts in three main respects. Firstly, principals can hold agents accountable according to multiple, sometimes even contradictory standards. Where this is the case, accountability demands can have a paralysing effect on organisations. In addition, even well-intentioned agents will find it impossible to fulfil all expectations at once and face undeserved sanctions. Jonathan Koppell has described organisations trying to satisfy various conflicting accountability demands as suffering from a 'multiple accountabilities disorder' (MAD). In his experience, such situations are likely to undermine the overall accountability of an organisation: 'Rather than satisfying all conceptions of accountability, the MAD-afflicted organization often satisfies none' (Koppell, 2005, p. 99).

Secondly, accountability mechanisms generate costs. Creating transparency and monitoring activities, for example, requires substantial efforts on the part of the principal as well as the agent. Where sanctions are imposed, they further reduce the benefits of at least one of the sides involved.

Thirdly, excessive accountability can hamper flexibility and innovation. When accountability means strict control, this constricts the agent's flexibility and ability to react to events and new developments. This means that the agent may not be able to act and to use resources as efficiently as he otherwise could. In addition, the threat of strong sanctions may lead many agents to act more cautiously and avoid taking risks. Risk taking, however, is essential for developing innovative solutions to problems.

Accountability can thus involve both benefits and negative consequences.[77] In the literature, opinions about the overall effect of accountability on performance diverge. First, there is a range of authors who see a positive effect. Thus, for example, Melvin Dubnick quotes numerous sources and describes the 'promise of performance' as follows:

> According to proponents of accountability-centered reforms, enhanced accountability will (among other things) result in [...] improvements in the quality of government services.
>
> (Dubnick, 2003, p. 1)

This view is contradicted by those who see a conflict between accountability and performance. Peter Self described this dilemma as a central one:

> [T]he tensions between the requirements of responsibility or 'accountability' and those of effective executive action can reasonably be described as the classic dilemma of public administration.
>
> (Quoted in Behn, 2001, p. 11)

Alnoor Ebrahim makes a similar claim for non-profit organisations (NPOs). He contends that

> for NPOs and nongovernmental organizations (NGOs) involved in activities of complex social development and poverty alleviation, too much accountability can hinder them in achieving their missions.
>
> (Ebrahim, 2005, p. 56)

This last quote already indicates that authors searching for an answer to the question of whether accountability enhances or hinders performance that is valid across the board may be misguided. Many researchers reject the assumption that accountability has either necessarily positive or always negative consequences. Aucoin and Heintzman, for example, argue that

> [p]itting accountability against performance does not, in our view, address the issue in the most constructive manner. [...] Improving accountability

arrangements does not necessarily improve performance, but the proposition that there can be improved performance in the absence of improved accountability is a proposition that cannot be sustained.

(Aucoin and Heintzman, 2000, p. 54)

Similarly, Melvin Dubnick comes to the conclusion that

we cannot and should not continue to rely on the assumed relationship between accountability and performance [namely, that accountability improves performance].

(Dubnick, 2003, p. 40)

Rather than trying to solve the question of whether or not accountability enhances performance once and for all, researchers should therefore concentrate on determining under which circumstances which types of accountability have an overall positive effect on the situation. Robert Behn's book *Rethinking Democratic Accountability* is a good example for such an approach. He develops detailed proposals for shifting accountability in public administration from accountability for finances and fairness to more accountability for performance (Behn, 2001). This book hopes to make a contribution in a similar vein. It develops an abstract framework for defining what type of accountability is appropriate for which kind of organisation and develops concrete standards indicating which groups of partnerships should adopt which accountability measures.

2.3 Partnership accountability

Partnerships as cooperative governance mechanisms and the concepts and practices of accountability each on their own raise sufficient research puzzles to fill volumes. What is it, then, that makes accountability important for partnerships and why do partnerships create particularly challenging questions for accountability?

This section focuses on the special nature of partnership accountability in terms of the salience of accountability to partnerships, the specific acuteness of accountability trade-offs and the distinctive complexity of developing accountability concepts and mechanisms for partnerships.

2.3.1 Political salience

Accountability is important for any organisation that influences the lives of individuals. Yet in the debate about partnerships involving actors from the public, corporate and civil society sectors, the issue is particularly salient. As argued in the introduction to this book, most principled objections against partnerships are based on concerns about accountability.

Fears run deep that we cannot hold to account remote powers whose actions have far-reaching impacts on our lives. This is especially the case in societies accustomed to liberal-democratic political arrangements, which at least theoretically grant their citizens extensive controls over government operations. Take for instance the intense debate about the 'democratic deficit' of the European Union. It shows how sensitively people react when their governments surrender authority to less directly accountable institutions.[78] By agreeing to common decision-making procedures, partners also delegate some authority to partnerships. This stretches the accountability links to the partners' original accountability holders and thus weakens their control over outcomes. If the partnership does not have appropriate accountability mechanisms in place to compensate for this accountability loss, a political backlash against its activities can be expected.

At the same time, partnerships are often created to address accountability problems of the partner organisations. The focus here is less the absolute level of accountability than to whom organisations are accountable. Reformers often demand greater inclusiveness and accountability to various stakeholder groups from government, international organisations and corporations. Partnerships are one avenue for achieving just this. By giving important stakeholder groups a say in decisions, partnerships can create more accountability.[79] Partnerships thus present challenges to established forms of accountability, yet promise more accountability to new principals.

Beyond that, reflections about partnership accountability have a special relevance now because most partnerships are still relatively young, in particular those launched during or in the aftermath of the 2002 World Summit on Sustainable Development. It is now that standards for their internal governance structures, reporting requirements, transparency and other accountability mechanisms are being defined – yet most actors are still lacking the necessary experience with partnerships to take informed decisions on these issues.

If we take other institutional developments as an indicator, we can observe that accountability systems are typically reformed or strengthened *after* they failed, that is, in response to disasters and scandals. Thus the scandals that led to the resignation of the European Commission (EC) under Jacques Santer triggered important reforms concerning the transparency of EC procedures and the powers of control of the European Parliament.[80] Similarly, the mismanagement and accounting problems leading to the spectacular collapse of numerous companies like Enron encouraged corporate governance reforms in the US.[81] While these changes will hopefully help prevent similar problems in the future, the damage in terms of losses of financial resources and trust was done.

Research leading to a better understanding of the types, mechanisms, trade-offs and minimum requirements of partnership accountability could contribute to the preventive installation of adequate accountability mechanisms. This would give partnerships the chance to develop good governance structures without experiencing disastrous failures.

2.3.2 Importance of trade-offs

As discussed above, accountability can be strengthened by addressing the clarity of the agent's responsibilities, the flow of information, the clarity of the principal's expectations and criteria for evaluation or the availability of sanctions. Each element in the accountability chain, though, has its downside:

- Very clearly demarcated responsibilities of individual actors make it more difficult to adapt to changed circumstances and might prevent these actors from focusing on the big picture;
- providing information that is timely, accurate and fits the needs of different principals is labour-intense and creates substantial costs, thus diverting resources away from other uses;
- operationalising principals' expectations is fraught with difficulties and can deflect attention away from broader goals and defining common expectations of different principals can be a lengthy, if not impossible, process;
- strong sanctions diminish the readiness to assume risks, while giving many stakeholders access to new sanctions by including them can make decision-making processes very cumbersome.

The arguments mentioned so far apply to all actors that are accountable to someone. But just as the issue of accountability is especially relevant for partnerships, so are the trade-offs. Firstly, partnerships in many cases are not strongly institutionalised. Designed at least in part as an alternative to overly bureaucratised and inefficient traditional institutions, partnerships are a particularly valuable tool of governance when they remain flexible. This means that the risk of losing the ability to adapt quickly to new developments is especially high for partnerships.

Secondly, the provision of timely, relevant and accurate information presents bigger problems to new than to established institutions. When institutions are in the early stages of their development, they typically have few staff members and very constrained resources. That makes it difficult to spare the necessary time and money for providing information. In addition, young institutions change at a faster pace than old ones, making it more difficult to keep information up to date. Since the fashion of cross-sector partnerships is a relatively recent phenomenon, most partnerships are still young, making the costs of providing information relatively high.[82]

The third point relates to the difficulties that arise when different principals pursue diverging goals. The interests of different accountability holders rarely converge. Yet for most other types of institutions it is possible to prioritise these interests depending on the strength of the sanctions the principals have at their disposal.[83] Partnerships by definition include actors from the public sector, businesses and/or civil society as partners. This means that groups with potentially widely diverging interests belong to the innermost layer of accountability holders and enjoy roughly equal status. Problems of conflicting goals can therefore not be solved by prioritising one principal's issues over the others. Partnerships either have to resolve the conflict by reconciling interests and finding compromises – often a long and burdensome process – or ignore it at the risk of making meaningful partnership activities impossible.

Finally, sanctions work most effectively if they work preventively. For an agent to be able to adapt his behaviour preventively, he must be in a position to anticipate under what conditions which sanctions will be applied. This is unproblematic where a partnership explicitly defines these sanctions (e.g. by linking the salaries of partnership managers to performance or by deciding that the executive board has to be regularly approved through elections). For many other issues, however, expectations are shaped by different corporate or national cultures. Thus both the rules and the likelihood of their enforcement can vary significantly between national legal systems as well as between partner organisations. This can result in a lack of clarity about sanctions and thereby undermine their effectiveness as means of prevention.

2.3.3 Complexity

Finally, as argued in the Introduction, defining concepts and effective mechanisms of accountability is even more complex for partnerships than for more traditional institutions. This complexity – together with the salience of the topic and the enhanced relevance of trade-offs – makes it important to arrive at a clear empirical, analytical and normative understanding of partnership accountability.

More specifically, the complexity stems from two major factors. Firstly, partnerships engage in a broad variety of activities, ranging from advocacy and awareness raising, generating information and verifying compliance, setting norms and standards to funding or coordinating policy implementation. As will be argued in Chapter 3, partnerships ought to embrace different accountability arrangements depending on what functions they exercise. Between the various partnership types, there are significant, albeit inconsistent, variations in accountability.

Secondly, understanding and evaluating partnership accountability is complex because accountability concepts and mechanisms have so far been developed mostly for traditional institutions. The accountability traditions of democratic governments, international organisations, corporations and civil society organisations differ significantly.[84] Since partnerships include actors from and perform the functions of several of these organisations, we need to define standards for partnerships that take these differences into account. This will be the subject of the normative inquiry in the following chapters.

3
Why Organisations Ought to be Accountable

Why do organisations generally, including partnerships, need appropriate accountability mechanisms? For many this may seem like asking 'why should individuals behave morally?' so obvious seems the normative content of accountability. As argued in the Introduction, the moral appeal of the concept of accountability is so strong that it has become a rallying cry for partnership critics. If the charge that partnerships are unaccountable can be substantiated, this would seriously undermine the partnership approach to public policy.

It may be because accountability is a 'hurrahword' (Bovens, 2005, p. 182) that it is rarely discussed why we actually see it as a 'good'. Without a clea r normative basis, however, there is bound to be confusion over what accountability means in practice. Note, for example, that our accountability expectations differ significantly depending on the kind of institution concerned. Thus an accountable government needs democratic elections, an informed public, effective parliamentary control systems and transparency on decision making and the budget. An advocacy NGO, by contrast, may be expected to be transparent about the sources of its funds and their allocation, but not necessarily to be democratic in its operations. Mulgan and Uhr confirm these differences in expectations when they write:

> Although the term 'accountability' is fundamental to governance discourse, expectations of accountability vary quite markedly with different institutional and community perspectives.
>
> (Mulgan and Uhr, 2000, p. 1)

Faced with these variations, some analysts propose to abandon accountability as a normative principle. Brown and Moore, for example, propose to treat

> accountability not as an abstract, fixed moral ideal, but instead as a strategic idea. [... In this conception,] instead of there being one right answer of how best to structure accountability, one gives a contingent answer.
>
> (Brown and Moore, 2001, p. 2)

This, however, is throwing the baby out with the bathwater.[1] Rather than giving up on accountability as a norm because it has different practical manifestations, we need to investigate what the normative basis of accountability is. This will provide us with a firmer ground for formulating consistent accountability demands.

This chapter aims to clarify why organisations need appropriate accountability mechanisms. It first conducts a literature review to identify which justifications for accountability are commonly given. Finding the main justifications for accountability lacking, it then proposes an alternative argument which grounds the demand for accountability in delegation.

3.1   Major justifications for accountability

This section reviews the literature directly concerned with interorganisational partnerships as well as arguments proposed in the broader global governance literature – and, where applicable, their intellectual roots in other disciplines. The latter was included because the partnerships analysed here operate at the international or global level and can be seen as part of the emerging system of global governance. In this literature, three main types of arguments have been proposed: consequentialist justifications for accountability, arguments derived from stakeholder theory and claims based on power and democracy.

3.1.1 Consequentialist justifications

Many authors argue that organisations should be accountable because this has positive effects. Most often, they claim that appropriate accountability arrangements enhance an organisation's effectiveness. Pauline Vaillancourt Rosenau, for example, claims that 'Public-private policy partnerships must be accountable if they are to fulfill policy objectives successfully' (Vaillancourt Rosenau, 1999, p. 19).

Without further explanation or differentiation, this claim is puzzling. As discussed in section 2.2.1, strong accountability arrangements can have serious practical downsides. Establishing accountability processes can create significant direct costs and strict accountability regimes can hamper flexibility and reduce the agent's willingness to accept risks. Therefore, in Thomas Risse's words, 'improving accountability as such does not insure the effectiveness of governance arrangements' (Risse, 2006, p. 186). Many authors thus explain how accountability is linked to effectiveness or efficiency. But accounts of what this link actually is vary.

Kovach, Neligan and Burall, for example, argue that accountability entails greater participation. Participation leads to better-informed decisions that affected groups are more likely to comply with. Thus accountability can make interventions more effective. For them,

[i]n the end, accountability boils down to two things. To justice [...]. And to efficiency; the involvement of people in the decisions that affect them leads to better decisions being made in the longer term.

(Kovach et al. 2003, p. 1)

Others argue that the value of accountability lies in its potential to increase the level of trust in a political system. Trust reduces transaction costs and thereby enables institutions to work more efficiently.[2] Margaret Gordon, for example, claims that

[p]ublic trust in government is important to public officials because it is central to the receiving of support for the creation and implementation of public policies, and subsequently for effective, cooperative compliance. [...] Information that serves to make the actions of public officials transparent to the public improves government accountability and enhances the public's trust.

(Gordon, 2000, p. 297)[3]

Yet others see accountability as a key element of legitimacy.[4] For a system of governance, legitimacy is key, because it encourages voluntary compliance and cooperation. This way, accountability makes governance mechanisms more effective and more efficient. Robert Keohane, for example, argues that without adequate accountability in a democratic era

those who are being governed will regard processes of governance as illegitimate, and will tend to withhold their allegiance. Without significant accountability, political systems are unlikely to yield either justice or stability.

(Keohane, 2002b, p. 13)

Due to its practical drawbacks, more accountability certainly does not always create more effectiveness. The consequentialist case for accountability, then, can only be that the right type and right level of accountability increase effectiveness. The main arguments provided in the literature, however, do not explain coherently which type and which level of accountability are appropriate.

In addition, a consequentialist justification is always contingent and does not acknowledge the inherent value of a concept or practice. It has often been argued, for example, that authoritarianism is a more efficient form of government than democracy.[5] One could defend democracy by arguing that this is factually incorrect. A more effective defence, however, would claim that democracy has a value in itself because it is based on the rights of individuals.

In the case of accountability, emphasising its positive effects may be a good tactic for convincing institutions to strengthen their accountability mechanisms. But it renders the concept rather arbitrary. Take, for example, Brown and Moore who see accountability as 'a strategic idea to be formulated and acted upon by an INGO [international NGO] with the goal of better understanding and achieving its strategic purposes' (Brown and Moore, 2001, p. 2).

If accountability serves to achieve something else, then an institution can always opt for alternative instruments promising the same results. Most straightforwardly, a partnership could argue, for example, that it can implement its programmes more efficiently and effectively if it eschews lengthy debates and costly participation.[6] The same holds for the more sophisticated arguments, such as the one promoting accountability because it enhances legitimacy. As argued earlier, legitimacy can derive from sources other than accountability and only input-based legitimacy requires adequate accountability, not output-based legitimacy.

3.1.2 Power and stakeholder theory

The most common non-consequentialist claim for accountability is based on power. If institutions affect the lives of others, so the argument goes, they should be accountable to them. Accountability mechanisms are safeguards against the abuse of power. Peter Spiro asserts this connection very explicitly: 'Wherever power is exercised, questions of accountability are appropriately posed. One can never assume that power will be deployed in a responsible manner' (Spiro, 2002, p. 162).

More implicitly, many others are making a similar argument. Kovach, Neligan and Burall, for example, base their claim for more accountability of intergovernmental organisations (IGOs), transnational corporations (TNCs) and NGOs on the following account:

> All three types of organisations [IGOs, TNCs and NGOs] have the power to affect the lives of millions of people throughout the world. [...] The people and communities affected by all three groups of organisation [*sic*] are making ever-louder claims for increased power to hold them to account. [... People have a] right to have a say in decisions that affect them.
>
> (Kovach et al. 2003, p. 1)

The claim that power requires accountability has some intuitive appeal. This is why the argument is frequently used by campaigners. But without further justification, the underlying normative logic is not immediately clear. On what basis do people claim that powerful institutions should be accountable?

For corporations, the argument has been developed most extensively in stakeholder theory. A stakeholder, in the original definition of R. Edward Freeman, is 'any group or individual who is affected by or can affect the achievement of an organization's objectives' (Freeman, 1984, p. 5). The normative claim is that stakeholder groups should have a say in important decisions of the institutions they are affected by. Again, in Freeman's words,

> each of these stakeholder groups has a right not to be treated as a means to some end, and therefore must participate in determining the future direction of the firm in which they have a stake.
>
> (Freeman, 2001, p. 39)

What Freeman is advocating is much more than just consulting stakeholders before taking decisions. He envisages a system in which the claims of other stakeholder groups have the same weight as the interests of shareholders. The goal of his theory is to replace 'the notion that managers have a duty to stockholders with the concept that managers bear a fiduciary relationship to stakeholders' (Freeman, 2001, p. 39).

Kenneth Goodpaster calls this the 'multi-fiduciary stakeholder synthesis' and explains that this would involve

> a management team processing stakeholder information by giving the same care to the interests of, say, employees, customers, and local communities as to the economic interests of stockholders. [... And] all stakeholders are treated by management as having equally important interests, deserving joint 'maximization'.
>
> (Goodpaster, 2002, p. 53)

Stakeholder theory thus falls clearly into the category of arguments justifying accountability on the basis of power. Stakeholders include those who are influenced by a company's activities.[7] They are said to have a right to be included in decision making, which means that the company has the corresponding duty to establish an accountability mechanism working through participation.

Many advocates of stakeholder theory simply assert that there is a moral basis for this claim, rather than argue for it.[8] As his last quote indicates, however, Freeman does make the normative argument and bases his claims on a Kantian deontological approach to ethics.[9] According to this approach, acts are ethical when they are guided by considerations of rights and duties, not consequences.[10] For Kant, the defining characteristic of humans is their capacity to reason. Reason enables humans to transcend their desires, make ethical judgements and act accordingly. This free will gives humans dignity and constitutes their unconditional worth.

Respect for the unconditional value of individuals is the basis for Kant's moral system. From it he derives the 'categorical imperative', the general rule to which ethical behaviour and norms must conform. In one of its formulations, the categorical imperative demands that we treat other humans as ends in themselves and not merely as means to other ends.[11]

Applying this to corporations, Evan and Freeman conclude that companies have a duty to respect the legitimate rights of others to determine their own freedom and to accept responsibility for their effects on others (Evan and Freeman, 1988). So far their argument does not go beyond claiming that managers have the same moral obligations to their fellow human beings as everybody else. But they take the claim a step further by translating the moral obligation into an institutional requirement. According to them, managers are not only morally required to take stakeholder interests into account but they should guarantee this by making themselves institutionally accountable to them.[12] To come back to Freeman's original articulation of the claim, stakeholders 'must participate in determining the future direction of the firm in which they have a stake' (Freeman, 2001, p. 39).

Stakeholder theory was developed to justify the moral obligations and institutional requirements of companies. The argument, however, can be applied to all types of institutions. In fact, the stakeholder concept is now also widely used in debates about political institutions and NGOs.[13]

There are, however, serious problems in stakeholder theory and the kind of institutional environment that would be created by its consistent application. Firstly, the normative claim made by stakeholder theory itself has been vigorously attacked on moral grounds. Milton Friedman's journalistic defence in 1970 of the shareholder approach to business has by now become famous. He argues that a manager has no fiduciary responsibility to other stakeholders. Rather he

> has direct responsibility to his employers. That responsibility is to conduct the business in accordance with their desires, which generally will be to make as much money as possible while conforming to the basic rules of the society, both those embodied in law and those embodied in ethical custom.
>
> (Friedman, 2002, p. 33)

Friedman bases his claims on a theory of property rights derived from John Locke and follows Adam Smith in his description of the socially beneficent effects of the market. He argues that if managers took the interests of other stakeholders into account and deviated from maximising profits as their sole goal, it would imply that they were spending other people's money on a social purpose of their own choosing. This, however, would amount to the same as taxing other people and deciding how that tax should be spent. In doing so, managers would usurp the role of government and violate essential democratic principles designed to protect individual liberties: elections as the mechanism to choose representatives and the separation of powers. As a result, not just economic freedom but political freedom as well would be undermined.[14]

Secondly, even if we do not contest the basic normative claim made by stakeholder theory, its consistent translation into institutional practice would create serious practical problems. Following Freeman's argument quoted above, stakeholder theory requires that all stakeholders must participate in determining the future direction of the firm. Implementing this demand would not only generate serious costs, given that stakeholder groups pursue very different interests, it would also make it extremely difficult to take any decisions. Kenneth Goodpaster has articulated this objection for businesses. He argues that adopting a multi-fiduciary stakeholder approach would 'blur [...] traditional goals in terms of entrepreneurial risk-taking [and] push [...] decision making towards paralysis because of the dilemmas posed by divided loyalties' (Goodpaster, 2002, p. 56).

Thirdly, these institutional consequences would contradict some of the basic philosophical tenets underpinning the moral case for stakeholder theory. The creation of encompassing accountability systems would create something approaching total control. Total control may be an effective way to ensure that nobody violates ethical norms and that all behave according to the categorical imperative. At the same time, though, it would eliminate freedom. Individuals would no longer be in a position to make moral judgements and follow their free will in acting accordingly. Respect for humans' capacity to reason and their free will are, however, the starting point for Kant's ethical theory. Demanding institutional control mechanisms for all moral requirements derived from the categorical imperative thus undermines the very philosophical basis on which stakeholder theory is built.

Current practice in the protection of stakeholder rights reflects the fact that a *consistent* application of stakeholder theory would create substantial problems. Over the last century or so liberal democratic societies have increasingly enshrined the protection of certain stakeholder rights in law. Freeman, in fact, used these legal developments as support for his argument that stakeholder theory should replace shareholder theories of the firm. He argues that

> the result of such changes in the legal system can be viewed as giving some rights to those groups that have a claim on the firm, for example, customers, suppliers, employees, local communities, stockholders, and management.
>
> (Freeman, 2001, p. 40)

In some cases legal regulations do not only protect specific rights of stakeholders but strengthen their ability to hold managers or corporations accountable. Workers in liberal democracies, for example, have the right to unionise, which strengthens their bargaining position in relation to management. In some countries, they even have the right to be represented on the company board. The position of consumers is strengthened, for example, by rules demanding companies to publish the ingredients of products. And many local communities assert their right to influence companies' activities by keeping a tight grip on planning permissions.

But these examples also show that the main demand of stakeholder theory, namely that stakeholders have a right to participate in decision making, is not being implemented consistently. Firstly, the stakeholder groups mentioned by Freeman are granted access to very different accountability mechanisms. Only very few apart from shareholders and managers are recognised to have a direct right to 'determine the future direction of the company' by being represented on the board. In Germany, Austria and the Scandinavian countries, for example, only employees have a right to representation.[15] In countries that are closer to the Anglo-American tradition, not even employee representation is recognised.

Secondly, some stakeholder groups are not granted access to any accountability mechanisms at all. Take the employees of a competitor for instance. They are clearly stakeholders because the company's policies affect the position of its competitors, which in turn influences the prospects of the competitors' employees. Despite their status as stakeholders, their right to hold the company to account is not recognised in any major legal system. Similarly, the rights of communities that don't live in the immediate neighbourhood of a company are not usually protected by law.

Different stakeholder groups are thus treated differently in both practice and discourse. Stakeholder theory claims that institutions should be accountable to all those who are influenced by a company or can influence it. This logic contains two options for differentiating between stakeholders: by the degree of influence they wield over the company or by the degree to which they are influenced by it. Neither version, however, provides a sufficient explanation for why stakeholders should get access to different kinds of accountability mechanisms.

The first option was later pursued, for example, by the original proponents of stakeholder theory. Edward Freeman and David Reed propose to recognise not only 'stakeholders in the wider sense' as defined earlier but also 'stakeholders in the narrow sense'. The latter are defined as 'Any identifiable group or individual on which the organization is dependent for its survival' (Freeman and Reed, 1983, p. 91).[16]

This distinction based on the power of stakeholders generates results that are practically less problematic and provide a better match to current practice than the original formulation. But the match is not perfect. Even using the narrow definition, competitors must be recognised as stakeholders and the demand that they should have a right to hold an organisation to account is not widely supported. More importantly, though, the distinction itself cannot be justified when stakeholder theory is taken to be non-instrumental and normative. If stakeholder theory demands accountability mechanisms out of respect for the rights of others, why should powerless actors be less worthy of protection than powerful ones?[17]

The alternative is to distinguish stakeholder groups on the basis of the degree of influence an organisation wields over them. This version is much less problematic on a normative level. At the same time, however, it can only justify convincingly that the level of stakeholder involvement should vary with the degree of being influenced. Why, though, should customers, for example, mainly exercise their right to accountability through consumer choice and access to information, communities through their right to set binding rules and regulations and employees through direct representation in decision-making organs?

Stakeholder theory, then, convincingly argues why individuals – including managers – have moral responsibilities towards the people they influence. But it is contested whether they have a duty to actively promote the interests of all those they influence and whether their responsibilities should translate into accountability mechanisms.[18] In addition, even differentiated versions of stakeholder theory cannot account for why different stakeholder groups should get access to different kinds of accountability mechanisms.

3.1.3 Power and the democratic deficit

In the political realm, demands for accountability are also often based upon power or influence. Usually, though, the argument does not refer to stakeholder theory but is linked to the concept of democracy.

Take, for example, the claims articulated by Woods and Narlikar. They demand more accountability for the WTO, the IMF and the World Bank on the following grounds:

> [D]ecisions and policies taken at the international level are increasingly affecting groups and people within states. Where previously these people could hold their national governments to account for policies, they must now look to international institutions where the decisions are being made. The question therefore arises: to whom are these institutions accountable and are they accountable to those whom they directly affect?
>
> (Woods and Narlikar, 2001, p. 569)

The argument thus is that influence has shifted from national governments to international institutions and that this creates a legitimate demand for more accountability. In the wider academic debate, two schools of thought have developed this argument in greater detail: democratic theorists and researchers concerned with global governance.

Most democratic theory is concerned with the conditions and institutional forms of democracy within nation states.[19] But, as some democratic theorists note, the ability of nation states to govern themselves is being eroded. This erosion constitutes a serious threat to the democratic norm of self-rule. Relatively early on, Karl Kaiser stated this threat with some urgency:

> Transnational relations and other multinational processes seriously threaten democratic control of foreign policy, particularly in advanced industrialised societies. The intermeshing of decisionmaking across national frontiers and the growing multinationalization of formerly domestic issues are inherently incompatible with the traditional framework of democratic control.
>
> (Kaiser, 1971, p. 706)

David Held, a leading contemporary contributor to democratic theory, further elaborates that the principle of majority rule within nation states is threatened from two sides: citizens are affected by decisions taken in other states and international institutions increasingly assume decision-making powers. According to him, problems for democracy arise

> because many of the decisions of 'a majority' or, more accurately, its representatives, affect (or potentially affect) not only their communities but citizens in other communities as well. [... And problems arise] from decisions made by quasi-regional or quasi-supranational organizations such as the European Union (EU), the North Atlantic Treaty Organization (NATO) or the International Monetary Fund (IMF). For these decisions can also diminish the range of decisions open to given national 'majorities'. The idea of a community that rightly governs itself and determines its own future – an idea at the very heart of the democratic polity – is today, accordingly, problematic.
>
> (Held, 1996, pp. 337–8)[20]

At this point, scholars of global governance join the debate. These scholars usually have a different starting point. They observe that various forms of governance exist beyond the nation state. These governance systems rarely take the form of a traditional government, but exercise some similar functions. Extrapolating democratic theory from its domestic context, they often argue that global governance therefore needs to be democratic.

The most intensive debate has emerged in the context of the European Union (EU), a prime example of a strong supranational and intergovernmental regime. In some policy areas, the EU can adopt binding policy decisions by majority vote. Much more explicitly than other international institutions, the European Union thus curtails the autonomy of nation states. Many critics have argued that relative to its influence, the democratic credentials of the EU are too weak. They have coined the concept of the 'democratic deficit' to describe this state of affairs.[21]

While the EU has attracted most attention, analysts have extended the critique to other international organisations or the system of global governance in general. Favourite targets for diagnosing a democratic deficit and demanding institutional reform are the global financial institutions,[22] the United Nations[23] and other intergovernmental institutions or processes.[24] But the demand for more democracy does not stop with intergovernmental institutions. Rather, many scholars and political analysts extend it to all organisations contributing to global governance.[25]

The Commission on Global Governance, a panel of eminent persons initiated by Willy Brandt, recognises NGOs, citizens' movements, transnational corporations and capital markets along with intergovernmental institutions and processes as part of the system of global governance. In its influential, but controversial report 'Our Global Neighbourhood' it demands that

> adequate governance mechanisms [...] must be more inclusive and participatory – that is, more democratic – than in the past. [...] This vision of global governance can only flourish, however, if it is based on a strong commitment to principles of equity and democracy grounded in civil society.
>
> (Commission on Global Governance, 1995, Chapter 1)

This amounts to a general demand for democracy or democratic accountability for all influential institutions. Echoing Peter Spiro's comment quoted above, Held and Koenig-Archibugi express this in a very concise way: 'there is agreement among democrats that wherever power is exercised there should be mechanisms of accountability' (Held and Koenig-Archibugi, 2004, p. 125).

Faced with the erosion of national autonomy and the increasing influence of international institutions, there appears to be a rough consensus that more democracy is needed.[26] How this is to be achieved in practice, however, is highly controversial. It would be beyond the scope of this book to portray even just the major proposals in detail or to analyse their advantages and criticisms. The following paragraphs therefore only sketch some of the main approaches. What is important is that they all advocate the creation of stronger accountability, though they have very different mechanisms in mind.

One possibility for safeguarding democracy is to limit the influence of global forces and to reassert national autonomy. Some leading thinkers doubt that intergovernmental institutions – let alone transnational corporations, NGOs or partnerships – can ever be democratic. Robert Dahl, for example, the most respected and vocal sceptic in this regard, doubts that citizens can ever exercise effective control over international organisations. Nevertheless he acknowledges that international institutions can be necessary and useful. He only cautions against seeing the decline of national and local governments as unavoidable:

> In weighing the desirability of bureaucratic bargaining systems in international organizations, the *costs to democracy* should be clearly indicated and taken into account. [...] Supporters of democracy should resist the argument that a great decline in the capacity of national and subnational units to govern themselves is inevitable because globalization is inevitable.
>
> (Dahl, 1999, p. 34, emphasis original)

Other intellectuals and activists take the argument further and demand strict limits to the influence of international regimes and actors. This, so the argument goes, would reassert the sovereignty and autonomy of nation states and thus safeguard democracy. The argument has, for example, been en vogue among neo-conservatives in the US. An influential group of scholars dubbed 'the new sovereigntists' argue that America should defend its sovereignty and refuse to sign core international treaties.[27] Jeremy Rabkin, for example, argues that

> [b]ecause the United States is fully sovereign, it can determine for itself what its Constitution will require. And the Constitution necessarily requires that sovereignty be safeguarded so that the Constitution itself can be secure.
>
> (Quoted in Spiro, 2000)

This logic has proved influential in the US where policymakers have refused to support new international regimes from the Kyoto Protocol to the establishment of the International Criminal Court. But most American analysts are aware that a genuine limitation of global forces would be very costly for powerful states like the US and probably impossible for weaker nations. A rollback of globalisation and the abolishment of certain international institutions are therefore only advocated by some of the most radical anti-globalisation movements and lack scholarly support.

Rather than limiting global forces, most scholars propose to strengthen democracy by making international actors more accountable. In Joseph Stiglitz' words, economic globalisation has outpaced political globalisation, requiring the strengthening and democratisation of global political institutions:

> There are too many problems – trade, capital, the environment – that can be dealt with only at the global level. But while the nation-state has been weakened, there has yet to be created at the international level the kinds of democratic global institutions that can deal effectively with the problems globalization has created.
>
> (Stiglitz, 2006, p. 21)

Proposals cover a continuum between the creation of a democratic world state and the increased use of existing accountability mechanisms. Some advocate revolution to reach their goals, whereas others hope for political evolution. And while most scholars make a prescriptive case for their proposed solution, some believe that the developments they sketch are inevitable.

Alexander Wendt, for example, suggests not only that the creation of a world state with a monopoly on the legitimate use of organised violence is desirable but believes that it will be the natural outcome of the dynamics inherent in the current 'anarchical society' of sovereign states (Wendt, 2003). Immanuel Wallerstein also believes that the current international system faces a fundamental transformation based on its inherent tensions and dialectic forces. He, however, predicts that sovereign states will 'wither away' and pave the way for world socialism (Wallerstein, 1984).

Less radical but still far reaching are proposals that don't envisage the creation of a fully blown world state but of certain elements of world government. Falk and Strauss, for example, suggest the installation of a global parliament. This parliament would be elected by popular vote and would be in a position to adopt laws binding on all international actors. In addition, it would supervise the implementation of existing international laws and provide democratic oversight over institutions like the IMF, the WTO or the World Bank (Falk and Strauss, 2001). Similarly, Otfried Höffe proposes the creation of a minimal world republic. This federal construction would complement the system of sovereign states and work in accordance with the principle of subsidiarity (Höffe, 1999).

All of the proposals just mentioned seek to remedy the current democratic deficit of global governance by creating democratic institutions at the global level. Thereby, citizens and their representatives gain new means to hold powerful institutions to account and to participate in decision-making processes. In part, this is also how a number of proposals that envisage a system of multiple, overlapping jurisdictions would address the democratic deficit. In addition, however, these systems would rely on increased competition between systems or levels of governance to generate stronger accountability.

In a 'cosmopolitan democracy', for example, various levels of governance would coexist. Depending on their scope, problems would be tackled either at the local, state, interstate, regional or global level. A world constitutional court would adjudicate conflicts over the allocation of authority between these levels (Archibugi, 2004).[28] At each level, non-trivially affected people would participate in the decision-making process (Held, 2004). In a similar vein, Eichenberger and Frey have proposed the concept of 'FOCJ': Functional, Overlapping, Competing Jurisdictions. Key to their model is that there are not only various levels of jurisdiction but that different jurisdictions compete for providing the same 'governmental goods'. Democratic control and competition are the accountability mechanisms ensuring justice and efficiency (Eichenberger and Frey, 2002).

Yet another set of proposals accepts the current institutional structure as it is and suggests strengthening its democratic accountability mechanisms. For most writers, this would entail an expansion of the possibilities for participation. Civil society organisations or NGOs already play an increasingly influential role in international politics.[29] Many analysts believe that increased NGO participation in international organisations could provide the key for creating more democratic accountability. Jan Aart Scholte, for example, argues that NGOs could help reduce the democratic deficit of global governance, both through their activism and their participation in international organisations (Scholte, 2002). Others, however, are sceptical about the legitimacy and representative nature of NGOs.[30] Stutzer and Frey therefore present an alternative for increasing popular participation. They advocate giving groups of citizens chosen through a process of random selection direct voting rights in important decisions and control over leaders of international organisations (Stutzer and Frey, 2005).

Finally, some authors see attempts to increase the democratic accountability of international actors as unrealistic. Instead, they propose to rely on a broader variety of accountability mechanisms. Keohane and Nye, for example, suggest that next to electoral accountability, there can be 'hierarchical accountability', 'legal accountability', 'reputational accountability' and 'market accountability'. Faced with the realities of the current international system, they propose to strengthen its overall accountability by focusing on and fostering these different kinds of accountability:

> Rather than offer a counsel of despair, we argue for more imagination in conceptualizing, and more emphasis on operationalizing, different types of accountability. It is better to devise pluralist forms of accountability than to bewail the 'democratic deficit'.
>
> (Keohane and Nye, 2001, p. 8)

To cut a very long debate short, scholars of different backgrounds and ideological convictions propose strengthening accountability mechanisms to counter the democratic deficit of global governance. To achieve this they propose reasserting the authority of nation states, creating a world state or at least the functional institutions of a cosmopolitan democracy, increasing participation in international organisations or relying on varied forms of accountability – and this list could be extended further.

The number of authors writing in this vein indicates that the argument that influence creates a legitimate demand for accountability gains sway when couched in terms of democracy. But the vast discrepancies in the recommendations derived from this also suggest that the argument is problematic. Two aspects in particular fail to convince when a general requirement for accountability for all influential actors is derived from the norm of democracy:

Firstly, it is not clear why *all* institutions should have *democratic* accountability. Many propose extending the possibilities for participation at the international level as a realistic way of bridging the democratic deficit. This, however, runs into the same practical difficulties as the demands derived from stakeholder theory. Even when based on a democratic foundation, we have to agree with Robert Keohane's assessment that 'Merely being affected cannot be sufficient to create a valid claim. If it were, virtually nothing could ever be done, since there would be so many requirements for consultation, and even veto points' (Keohane, 2002a, p. 15).

In addition, the requirement of democratic accountability for all institutions does not really follow from the logic of the democratic deficit argument. Even in the domestic context, the norm of democracy only requires that citizens elect a parliament. The main role of parliaments is to set rules and to control the executive. Transferring this to the international level, it would seem appropriate to demand democratic accountability of institutions exercising similar functions, that is, rule setting.[31] But it is not evident why actors contributing to global governance in other ways should also be democratically accountable.

A closer look at the proposals introduced above reveals that many authors would probably not oppose this limitation. They often start their argument with the problem that the increasing influence of different actors in global governance creates a democratic deficit. This suggests that their proposals for more democratic accountability would apply to all actors involved in global governance. But their concrete examples are most often concerned with rule-setting institutions. This is obviously the case for those advocating the creation of a world state or a world parliament. It is also true for proponents of cosmopolitan democracy and 'FOCJ' who speak of the creation of 'jurisdictions' at different levels. And it also applies to many authors proposing increased participation. Their favourite examples for concrete reforms are all involved in defining norms and rules: the European Union, the United Nations and the international financial institutions, in so far as they set rules for international trade or for the internal macroeconomic policies of states.[32]

Secondly, where the use of different forms of accountability is proposed, it remains unclear *which* institutions ought to have *what kind* of accountability. A 'pluralistic system of accountability' (Benner et al., 2004) avoids the first problem just discussed. If various types of accountability are considered, it becomes much easier to see how they can apply to all actors involved in global governance. Transnational corporations for instance are clearly subject to market accountability, whereas NGOs are often subject to reputational accountability. It is also plausible that the application of these different accountability mechanisms can be diversified. In the 'FOCJ' proposal, for example, various jurisdictions would compete for providing 'governmental goods'. This amounts to the creation of market-based accountability for governmental institutions. It is very difficult, however, to use this 'pluralistic system of accountability' as a normative concept. It shows how accountability *could* be created, but not how it *should* be created.

A justification of accountability based on power and democracy, then, relies on a more solid normative basis than consequentialist and stakeholder arguments. As in the case of stakeholder theory, however, the translation of the moral claim into institutional practice is problematic. Analysts supporting this line of reasoning either demand democratic accountability for all kinds of institutions, which is neither logically convincing nor practicable, or they allow for various forms of accountability but are not in a position to indicate when which kind of accountability should be in place.

3.2 The alternative: Justifying accountability through delegation

Another way to justify the demand for accountability is through delegation and authorisation. As discussed in section 2.2.1, the concept of accountability is closely linked to the idea of delegation. 'To be accountable' originally meant to 'answer for money held in trust'. This section argues that the link between accountability and delegation is not just etymological and definitional. Rather, delegation also forms the normative core of the concept of accountability.

The argument based on delegation intersects and overlaps with instrumental, stakeholder and democratic approaches in various instances. The basic claim, however, is different and leads to a more stringent and differentiated assessment of the accountability requirements of different organisations. This approach is therefore better suited as the basis for developing accountability standards for partnerships.

The claim that delegation demands the creation of appropriate accountability mechanisms is developed in three steps. Firstly, it is argued that delegation creates a duty for the agent to act in the best interest of the principal. Then, the case is made that in institutional settings only appropriate accountability mechanisms can guarantee respect for the principals' interests and autonomy. Finally, it is maintained that the argument holds not only for explicit forms of delegation but also for implicit, ex-post and hypothetical delegation.

3.2.1 Delegation and the duty to act in the best interest of the principal

It is widely accepted as a norm that individuals or organisations acting on behalf of others have a duty to act in their best interest. This is reflected in different legal and philosophical traditions.

The first philosophical and legal principle supporting the obligation to promote principals' interests is the *duty to keep promises and honour contracts*. Delegation is often formal and its terms and conditions are enshrined in a contract. To establish a partnership, for example, different organisations may sign a memorandum of understanding defining the authority, structure, tasks and goals of the partnership. In this constitutional contract, the partners define their expectations and interests. The partnership then has an obligation to fulfil its mandate because it has agreed to do so in a contract.

Promise keeping is a central norm in Western moral philosophy that is reflected in most legal systems around the world. In Holly Smith's words: 'For centuries it has been a mainstay of European and American moral thought that keeping promises – and the allied activity of upholding contracts – is one of the most important requirements of morality' (Smith, 1997, p. 153).

In David Hume's sceptical tradition, promise keeping is seen as a very useful social practice enabling, for example, the division of labour. Since it is in everyone's interest to protect promise keeping as a social institution, breaking one's promises is morally bad (Hume, 1969). Based on very different assumptions, rationalist philosophers arrive at the same conclusion. In John Rawls' formulation, the principle of fairness demands that if you benefit from a social practice, you ought to adhere to it yourself (Rawls, 1971). It has also been argued that promises create a moral obligation in themselves and not just because they are a useful and just social practice. Thomas Scanlon, for example, reasons that promise breaking is morally wrong because it disappoints expectations and can lead to losses for other parties who acted on these expectations (Scanlon, 1990).[33]

Reflecting this broad moral agreement, most societies have enshrined the duty to uphold contracts in law. Partnership officials are therefore bound by moral standards and law to act in the interests of their principals in so far as these are expressed in a mutual contract. If the obligation to act in the principal's interest were only founded on contract, however, it would be very limited. Contracts can never provide a full and detailed definition of the principal's interests. Even when adhering to the terms defined in the contract, agents have significant autonomy and discretion. In addition, many instances of delegation are not formalised in a contract.

Independent of any contractual obligations, there is a wider norm demanding that agents promote the interests of their principals. This norm finds various expressions in legal practice and reasoning. In common law countries, for example, it is enacted through the concept of *fiduciary obligations*. A fiduciary relationship exists when one person acts on behalf of another, has significant discretion and by exercising this discretion can affect the interests of the principal. Typical fiduciary relationships include that between agent and principal, director and corporation, guardian and ward, lawyer and client, partner and fellow partner and trustee and trust beneficiary.[34] A fiduciary relationship generates the obligation that the fiduciary act in the principal's best interest:

> If a person in a particular relationship with another is subject to a fiduciary obligation, that person (the fiduciary) must be loyal to the interest of the other person (the beneficiary). The fiduciary's duties go beyond mere fairness and honesty; they oblige him to act to further the beneficiary's best interests.
>
> (DeMott, 1988, p. 882)

More specifically, the evolving common law practice in this area demands that fiduciaries have no conflict of interest with their fiduciary duty, do not accept different fiduciary duties that conflict with each other and do not profit from their position.[35] The purpose of these rules is to create a basic protection against the abuse of delegated authority:

> The need to control discretion has been a justification for the imposition of the harsh rule concerning fiduciaries since the beginning. [...] The desirability of deterring the fiduciary from using his discretion except for the benefit of the principal or beneficiary is often mentioned in subsequent judgements, and this aspect is also enshrined in the prohibition against allowing a conflict of interest and duty.
>
> (Weinrib, 1975, p. 4)

The concept of fiduciary obligations was introduced by the English courts of equity and has since been developed through case law in common law countries. As such, the concept has no direct equivalent in civil law countries. The norm that agents should act in the best interest of their principals nevertheless finds expression in civil law systems. Lacking general regulations on fiduciary duties, most civil law countries have instead developed more specific rules governing individual fiduciary relationships. A comprehensive analysis of these rules is impossible here – on the one hand because many different relationships are at stake and on the other because there are infinite variations between civil law countries. A few examples must therefore suffice to indicate that the norm that agents should act in the best interest of their principals also pervades systems of civil law.

The German institution of *Treuhand*, for example, covers the trustee – trust beneficiary relationship. Stefan Grundmann argues that most civil law jurisdictions have functionally equivalent institutions to trust and *Treuhand* which are all characterised by the fact that the 'trustee administers the assets for the benefit of the settlor' (Grundmann, 1999, p. 414).[36] The fiduciary relationship between guardian and ward corresponds to the German *Vormundschaft*. According to the Bürgerliches Gesetzbuch (BGB), a *Vormund* is obliged to care for and represent the ward and his assets (BGB, 2006, §§ 1793 and 1796). When the interests of the ward conflict with those of the guardian, a court can withdraw the *Vormund's* authorities. The Roman principle of *negotiorum gestio* also exists in many civil law countries. It covers instances of ex-post delegation and decrees that a previously unauthorised agent cannot demand remuneration for his services to avoid conflict of interest.[37]

The norm that those who act on behalf of others have a duty to promote their principals' interests is not only prominent in legal thinking and practice but also in political theory. In fact, it lies at the heart of *liberal democratic thought*.

Liberal democracy has its intellectual roots in the Enlightenment. Rather than accepting government as God given, philosophers of the Enlightenment were searching for ways to legitimise political authority rationally. The most prominent school of thought uses the concept of a social contract to do so. While there is a huge diversity between social contract thinkers,[38] they usually start with describing or imagining a state of nature. In the pre-social state of nature, humans are born free and equal and this endows them with a set of natural rights. This, however, also leads to pervasive conflict – be it because the human instinct for self-preservation inevitably creates competition and conflict over scarce resources[39] or because social interactions corrupt humans and make them selfish and competitive.[40] In any case, conflict challenges humans to use their capacity to reason to overcome the state of nature. They conclude a social contract and establish society and/or political authority.

What are the implications for the government thus created? Using the same intellectual construct, contract theorists have arrived at fundamentally different answers to this question. Thomas Hobbes famously argued that life in the state of nature was a constant war of all against all, violating natural law. To ensure 'their own preservation' and 'a more contented life thereby' (Hobbes, 1909, Chapter XVII), all individuals permanently transfer their liberties to a central institution, the Leviathan. The Leviathan is created through this contract but is not himself a party to the contract. Therefore, and because it is necessary to establish security, argues Hobbes, his authority is absolute and cannot be revoked.

Another version of the social contract justifying absolutist rule is that of Jean-Jacques Rousseau. Very much concerned with preserving individual liberty, Rousseau's individuals in the state of nature only enter a contract of association, not one of submission. They square the circle and gain a system of government while preserving their liberty by ruling themselves. The resulting doctrine of popular sovereignty nevertheless creates absolute power. Embodying the *volonté générale*, the sovereign holds indivisible, inalienable and unlimited authority.[41] Both Hobbes and Rousseau thus arrive at a somewhat paradoxical conclusion. They assume that individuals are born free, equal and rational, yet voluntarily create a sovereign with unlimited power who is under no obligation to respect individual rights. It may be because of this inherent contradiction that another version of social contract theory has become much more widely accepted.[42] Similar to Hobbes and Rousseau, John Locke argues that conflict prevailing in the state of nature threatens individuals' liberty and property. And since humans are rational, they can be presumed to agree to the establishment of a central authority to determine rules and adjudicate their application. But according to Locke, this consent is only imaginable if the government fulfils the purpose for which it was established, namely to protect liberty and property. The social contract therefore limits the sovereign's authority and creates an obligation for him to act in the interest of his subjects. In Locke's words:

> [Y]et it being only with an intention in every one the better to preserve himself, his liberty and property; (for no rational creature can be supposed to change his condition with an intention to be worse) the power of the society, or legislative constituted by them, can never be supposed to extend farther, than the common good; but is obliged to secure every one's property, by providing against those three defects above mentioned, that made the state of nature so unsafe and uneasy.
>
> (Locke, 1690, Chapter IX, §131)[43]

This key argument in John Locke's political theory thus embodies the norm that agents (in this case the government) have a duty to promote the interests of their principals (the citizens). The claim is central to our current normative understanding of politics. Locke stands at the beginning of a strong tradition of liberal and constitutional thought. Of course, neither social contract theories nor the doctrine of liberal democracy have remained without their critics,[44] but since at least the eighteenth century, they have become dominant in Europe and America. David Held, for example, describes at once the significance of John Locke as one of the first exponents of the liberal tradition and recognises the centrality of this school of thought:

> Locke [...] signals the clear beginnings of the liberal constitutionalist tradition, which became the dominant thread in the changing fabric of European and American politics from the eighteenth century.
>
> (Held, 1996, p. 74)

Boucher and Kelly also emphasise the importance of the social contract tradition for contemporary politics: They write that it

> is also clear that the ideal of political life as an agreement on fair terms of association between individuals who have a recognized status as free and equal is a moral ideal that has a very deep resonance in modern culture,

and it is one that has proved a great inspiration to those who do not enjoy the recognition of that status.

(Boucher and Kelly, 1994, p. 29)

And while this philosophical tradition originated and developed in 'the West',[45] liberal democracy has come to enjoy broad support as a normative ideal throughout the world.[46] Amartya Sen emphasises this point in an essay on the universality of democracy as a value:

> While democracy is not yet universally practiced, nor indeed uniformly accepted, in the general climate of world opinion, democratic govern-ance has now achieved the status of being taken to be generally right.
>
> (Sen, 1999, p. 5)

3.2.2 Delegation and the need for appropriate accountability mechanisms

The norm that delegation creates a duty for the agent to act in the best inter-est of his principal, then, is well established in philosophy and legal think-ing. It is argued in this section that the need for appropriate accountability mechanisms in institutional settings involving delegation follows quite directly from this norm. Before further developing this thought, however, an important objection has to be considered. What happens when the norm is rejected?

The main branch of thought rejecting the norm that agents have a moral duty to act in the best interest of their principals is economics. This is sig-nificant since economic principal–agent theory forms the main basis for our understanding of accountability. Interestingly, despite the differences in philosophical assumptions, economists arrive at the same institutional conclusions. They also argue that appropriate accountability mechanisms are necessary. Before returning to our main argument, let us therefore briefly consider the economic case for accountability.

Economists following the tradition of Adam Smith agree with many moral and political philosophers that humans are free and rational beings. But, while many moral philosophers condemn self-interested behaviour, econo-mists accept it. More than that, they believe that self-interest gives rise to the division of labour and trade and thereby vastly increases the wealth and well-being of societies. Adam Smith famously described this as an effect of the 'invisible hand':

> Every individual [...] generally, indeed, neither intends to promote the public interest, nor knows how much he is promoting it. [...H]e intends only his own gain, and he is in this, as in many other cases, led by an invisible hand to promote an end which was no part of his intention.

Nor is it always the worse for the society that it was no part of it. By pursuing his own interest he frequently promotes that of the society more effectually than when he really intends to promote it.

(Smith, 1904, Book IV, Chapter 2, §9)[47]

Even in a principal–agent relationship, economists would therefore expect agents to act in their own self-interest. But while economists would not, in general, condemn this behaviour as immoral, they would also see it as problematic. Because the interests of owners and managers diverge, owners must expect a loss when they delegate management authority. Adam Smith describes the problem for joint stock companies, where ownership is divided and control over managers weak:

The directors of such companies, however, being the managers rather of other people's money than of their own, it cannot well be expected, that they should watch over it with the same anxious vigilance with which the partners in a private copartnery frequently watch over their own. Like the stewards of a rich man, they are apt to consider attention to small matters as not for their master's honour, and very easily give themselves a dispensation from having it. Negligence and profusion, therefore, must always prevail, more or less, in the management of the affairs of such a company.

(Smith, 1904, Book V, Chapter 1, §107)

First and foremost, this loss affects the owners and stockholders of companies. But it also reduces the overall wealth of society because it implies an inefficient allocation and use of resources. Seen from a utilitarian perspective – which most economists share – the efficiency loss created by delegation is therefore not only economically but also morally bad.[48] Most economists would probably reject demands for accountability based on the claim that agents have a moral duty to act in the best interest of their principal.[49] But they do demand the creation of adequate accountability mechanisms because it can limit the efficiency loss inherent in delegation.[50]

The economic justification for accountability also contains the criteria for establishing what 'appropriate' accountability mechanisms are. The goal is to minimise the loss incurred from delegation. Not only does the self-interested behaviour of agents generate costs but the creation of accountability as well. Principals have to invest in incentives for the agent and monitor the agent's behaviour. Agents incur so-called bonding costs trying to assure the principals that they will act in their interests. 'Agency loss', the overall loss from delegation, thus comprises incentive and monitoring costs, bonding costs and the remaining loss resulting from diverging interests.[51] An ideal accountability arrangement is one that minimises the combined agency loss.

It is reassuring that the school of thought that rejects the basic assumption underlying the argument for accountability presented here arrives at similar conclusions regarding the need for accountability mechanisms. Ultimately, however, the economic argument is a consequentialist one. It demands accountability because, and as long as, it increases efficiency. As discussed in section 3.1.1, consequentialist arguments can neither provide a solid defence of accountability, nor can they account for the inherent value we tend to attach to accountability. A more stringent demand for accountability can be derived from the rights of principals and the corresponding duty of agents to act in their best interest.

Let us thus return to our main argument. We have established that agents have a duty to act in the best interest of their principals. How, then, does this lead to the demand for appropriate accountability mechanisms? Accountability creates control over agents. Since agents cannot always be trusted to respect their duties, accountability mechanisms are necessary to prevent the abuse of authority and to protect the principals' rights.

The argument is so well established in political philosophy[52] that it is only rarely made explicit. John Locke, for example, seems to perceive no need to argue why the duty of the government to act in the interests of the governed requires certain institutional practices. As if it were self-evident, he simply claims that because government should protect the interests of citizens, it has to respect and promote the rule of law:

> And so whoever has the legislative or supreme power of any common-wealth, is bound to govern by established standing laws, promulgated and known to the people, and not by extemporary decrees; by indifferent and upright judges, who are to decide controversies by those laws; and to employ the force of the community at home, only in the execution of such laws, or abroad to prevent or redress foreign injuries, and secure the community from inroads and invasion. And all this to be directed to no other end, but the peace, safety, and public good of the people.
>
> (Locke, 1690, Chapter IX, section 131)

The rationale behind this and other demands for procedural and substantial controls on government activities is quite simple. Humans are assumed to be fallible and corruptible. There is therefore always a risk that those who are put in a position to govern over others will abuse their authority and violate the rights of the governed. A 'good' form of government is therefore one that has effective accountability mechanisms in place to prevent this from happening. Most famously and eloquently, James Madison has articulated this connection:

> If men were angels, no government would be necessary. If angels were to govern men, neither external nor internal controls on government

would be necessary. In framing a government which is to be administered by men over men, the great difficulty lies in this: you must first enable the government to control the governed; and in the next place oblige it to control itself. A dependence on the people is, no doubt, the primary control on the government; but experience has taught mankind the necessity of auxiliary precautions.

(Hamilton et al. 1992, Federalist No. 51)

Next to periodic elections, Madison proposed 'checks and balances' between different government departments as effective mechanisms of control. His claim that governments need to be controlled has been accepted by most subsequent political thinkers. The bulk of the debate has not centred on whether or not accountability is necessary but on which accountability mechanisms are most effective. Standard debates in the normative and comparative political science literature, for example, tackle questions such as which electoral system best enables citizens to express their preferences and control parliament and the executive; how elements of direct democracy can strengthen citizen control; whether federal or centralised, presidential or parliamentary systems are best suited to create accountability while allowing for an effective system of government; and what role independent government agencies play to strengthen or weaken accountability.[53]

More recently, the tone of this debate has changed. Rather than exploring how the public sector can be controlled most effectively, a range of authors now focus on the negative side effects of existing accountability mechanisms. The predominantly procedural controls, so the argument goes, stifle creativity and discourage public officials from taking risks. As a result, public services are often inefficient. Despite this critique, however, these authors do not simply demand the abolition of existing accountability structures. Rather, they advocate the adoption of different kinds of accountability mechanisms. The New Public Management literature,[54] which is at the forefront of this debate, for example, demands replacing procedural accountability with accountability for outcomes. Christopher Pollitt summarises the New Public Management proposals as follows:

Responsibility is to be decentralized, targets – not procedures – are to become the key focus for public officials, costs will be cut, bureaucracy eliminated, standards raised, and service to the citizen-customer thrust to the foreground of concern.

(Pollitt, 1995, p. 203)

Even among the critics of the standard accountability arrangements of governments it is thus widely accepted that a 'good' form of government is an accountable one because this protects citizen rights and ensures that officials respect their duty to act in the best interest of citizens. Molly Beutz even goes so far as to suggest that the consensus on the desirability of accountability is so great that democracy is most appropriately defined in terms of accountability:

> Focusing on accountability provides the basis for a functional vision of democracy that both attends to questions of social and material equality and structural change and can be applied in a variety of contexts. A vision of democracy as accountability is more robust than a purely procedural definition because it attends to important substantive goals. At the same time, however, it avoids the necessity of a priori agreement on the substantive ends to be achieved by leaving those decisions in the hands of those who are in the best position to make them.
>
> (Beutz, 2003, p. 405)[55]

It is understandable why the concern with accountability is so central in political thinking. After all, citizens do not just delegate any authority but the authority to define and enforce the rules by which a society lives. This makes the transfer of authority very far reaching and potentially difficult to reverse.[56]

But the argument also applies to other spheres. It is true for all kinds of institutions that a 'good' institutional set-up is one that effectively protects rights and encourages ethical behaviour. For institutions involving delegation this means that the 'ideal' institutional form includes accountability mechanisms that effectively protect the principals' rights. Both the legal practice in liberal democracies and a plethora of additional, voluntary governance codes reflect this normative consensus.

Earlier, in the section on stakeholder theory, it was discussed that in many countries companies are required by law to have certain accountability mechanisms. Legal rules determine standards among others for organisational structures, procedures and the transparency of companies and other organisations. How strict these standards are depends on the nature of the organisation and differs from country to country. Under German law, for example, all companies are required to maintain correct books and publish annual results. Medium and large companies additionally have to conduct professional audits and have to allow worker representation (Handelsgesetzbuch §§ 238–325, Mitbestimmungsgesetz). The governance requirements are also usually much stricter for public companies. In the US, for example, the Sarbanes-Oxley Act of 2002 applies only to publicly traded companies. It demands that companies evaluate and disclose their internal control systems, establish independent audit committees and that chief executive officers (CEOs) and chief financial officers (CFOs) swear by oath that their accounts are correct.[57]

Over recent years, these legal regulations have been supplemented by a veritable flood of voluntary governance codes. For companies, for example, Holly Gregory has compiled a 'partial listing of corporate governance guidelines and codes of best practice' for developed markets that includes over 100 such codes (Gregory, 2001). For non-profit organisations, the NGO Independent Sector publishes a compendium of standards, codes and principles that lists over 60 examples applicable in the US.[58] These codes are published by intergovernmental organisations, governments, professional associations and social groups and vary significantly in scope and strictness.[59] The application of these codes is usually voluntary. Nevertheless their number and spread shows that the normative consensus that 'good' organisations need accountability mechanisms is widespread.

Earlier in the chapter stakeholder theorists were criticised for using these laws and emerging regulations to support their claim that all stakeholders should have the right to participate in determining a company's future. In what way, then, is the argument made here different? Firstly, the claim here is that there is a normative consensus that organisations need appropriate accountability mechanisms, not that all groups should be allowed to participate in decision making. What exactly counts as 'appropriate' will be analysed in greater detail at the end of this chapter. Secondly, a closer look at the exact requirements made by law and voluntary codes reveals that only those stakeholder groups that are principals, that is, those who delegate some form of authority to an organisation, are included in accountability arrangements.

To illustrate this, let's return to the example of a public company. An operating company has various forms of authority delegated to it. Investors delegate the right to manage their money to the company. Local communities or governments authorise it to operate on their territory. Employees give it the authority to determine under what conditions they work. Consumers, finally, by buying the company's products, authorise it to take over a specific segment in the division of labour. Laws also protect the rights of other groups. Competitors, for example, are shielded from unfair competition by anti-trust and anti-dumping legislation. But only the groups delegating authority to the company are recognised to have a right to accountability. Thus most governance codes are concerned with issues that enable shareholders to control managers. Local communities are included in the planning process, workers have the right to unionise or sit on the company's board and consumers at least get some rights to information so they can take informed decisions. Competitors, suppliers or non-local communities that are affected by the company's activities, by contrast, are not granted any rights that would enable them to hold the company to account.

Accountability mechanisms, then, are designed to prevent the abuse of authority and protect the rights of principals. Appropriate accountability arrangements are therefore an integral part of what constitutes a 'good' institutional set-up. This is the normative core of the concept of accountability and the main reason why we cherish accountability as something good.

The argument leaves one potential loophole. What if people are not as fallible and corruptible as James Madison and the political thinkers following him assumed? Would accountability mechanisms not be superfluous if agents were less prone to abuse their authority? The answer is no. Even where agents have the best intentions, accountability mechanisms are necessary because individuals are autonomous and determine their preferences and conceptions of the good individually. Agents can therefore not simply assume they know their principals' interests. As illustrated in the basic model of accountability presented in section 2.2.1, accountability is not only about evaluating the agent, accountability mechanisms can also enable principals to articulate their preferences by formulating a mandate, through consultations or by sanctioning agents who get it wrong. Even well-intentioned agents therefore need appropriate accountability arrangements.

As already alluded to earlier, a core assumption in liberal philosophy is that humans are by their nature free and rational. The concept of human autonomy, which derives from the Greek 'autonomos' or 'self-ruling', encompasses exactly these two elements.[60] Firstly, humans are autonomous in the sense that they are independent of others. And secondly, humans are autonomous because they are rational. Rather than blindly following their passions, their capacity to reason enables humans to develop moral and ethical norms and to act according to them.[61]

The term 'autonomy' can refer to the capability, actual ability, the right or the value of self-government.[62] Philosophers also disagree on what it means exactly for an individual to act autonomously.[63] All accounts, however, at least agree that individuals have the capacity to form their own understanding of what is good and to pursue this in their actions. Autonomy in this sense is an essential human characteristic that deserves respect.

Liberal philosophers have used the demand for respect for human autonomy to justify a range of different norms. A prominent argument is that respect for autonomy renders most instances of paternalism illegitimate.[64] Autonomy has also been used to defend the right to free speech, the right to vote, the right to be free from taxation for redistributive purposes, as well as the right to contraception, abortion, association and religion.[65] While the value of autonomy tends to go undisputed, it is controversial which specific rights can be derived from it.[66]

The argument put forward here should be much less controversial. If autonomy means that individuals have the capacity to form their own conceptions of the good, this implies that they determine their preferences and interests individually. Without communication or observation, it is therefore difficult if not impossible for outsiders to determine what exactly the preferences of an individual are. The assertion that preferences are specific to individuals is widely accepted. Mainstream economic theory, for example, sees preferences as individually determined and builds its rational choice models[67] around that assumption.[68]

If preferences are intrinsically determined by individuals, it implies that agents can never fully anticipate the preferences of their principals. If they really want to live up to their duty and act in the best interest of their principals, agents need some mechanisms to determine what these interests are.

Depending on their nature, accountability arrangements can contribute to a clarification of the principals' interests in at least three different ways. Firstly, some accountability mechanisms enable principals to express their preferences by formulating a mandate at the outset of the exercise of delegated authority. Secondly, accountability mechanisms can enable principals to provide feedback on the agent's ongoing performance. Finally, all accountability mechanisms include an element of sanction or reward. This enables principals to signal after the fact whether or not they agree with the agent's performance. Democratic elections are a good example for an accountability mechanism that fulfils two of these functions. They formulate a mandate for incoming politicians and sanction incumbent officials.[69] Opinion polls or midterm elections are an example for an ongoing feedback mechanism.

In addition to preventing the abuse of authority and protecting the rights of principals, accountability mechanisms thus provide principals with an opportunity to articulate their preferences and interests and to protect their autonomy. Irrespective of whether an agent is well intentioned or not, a good institutional set-up requires appropriate accountability arrangements.

3.2.3 Ex-post and hypothetical delegation

> Any accountability relationship [...] always presupposes some delegated authority.
>
> (Löffler, 2000, p. 15)

It has been argued that delegation is not only an important defining characteristic of accountability but that it also lies at the heart of the normative content of the concept. What exactly, though, is meant by delegation? Does the argument only apply to instances of explicit and formal delegation or also to other situations? This section argues that it is also valid for implicit, ex-post and hypothetical delegation.[70]

When individuals or organisations delegate authority, they can do so explicitly, implicitly or hypothetically, as well as before or after the agent engages in any activities. The classical and most easily recognisable form of delegation is explicit and ex-ante. It occurs when somebody formally entrusts an agent with a certain authority and the agent subsequently acts on this authority. Most partnerships are created through an act of explicit and ex-ante delegation. The founding partner organisations take the decision to set up a partnership and define its mandate. WCD, for instance, was formally set up by a stakeholder workshop convened by the World Bank and the World Conservation Union (IUCN). Its authority and tasks were defined to include a review of the development effectiveness of large dams and their alternatives, as well as the development of internationally acceptable criteria, guidelines and standards for large dams (World Commission on Dams,

2000, p. 28). All major activities of the commission thereafter – the creation of a knowledge base, deliberations and negotiations among commissioners and communication and awareness raising – served to achieve these goals.

The ex-ante delegation of authority can also be implicit. Here, the transfer of authority can be inferred from somebody's behaviour and the agent subsequently bases his action on this implicit or inferred delegation. Take a simple example: before getting on a bus, I hand my suitcase to the driver who stores it in the luggage compartment. By handing over my luggage, I implicitly confer the authority and responsibility to look after my luggage on the bus company. Within the realm of partnerships, implicit ex-ante delegation could happen, for example, when the Roll Back Malaria Partnership (RBM) collects signatures for a petition on malaria.[71] By signing the petition, individuals indicate not only their support for a specific issue but also their acceptance that RBM will speak on their behalf on this issue.

When authority is transferred before the agent takes action, it is usually easy to recognise the act of delegation. Often, though, no prior authorisation takes place. Many organisations acting for or on behalf of others simply usurp the authority to do so and define their own mandates.

One set of organisations, for example, receive appropriate initial authorisation, but over time, they expand their activities beyond the original mandate. Critics have coined the term 'mission creep' to describe this expansion of responsibilities. In international politics, the charge of mission creep is most frequently levelled against international financial institutions like the IMF. The IMF was originally set up to act as a lender of last resort to promote the stability of the international exchange rate system. Over time, however, the IMF has also come to extend loans to countries for various different reasons. It has especially been criticised because it attaches conditionalities to its loans and thus influences the domestic economic policies of the borrower countries.[72]

Another group of organisations lacks appropriate formal authorisation. They have been given a mandate and respect it in their activities, yet those who defined the original mandate had no or only partial authority to do so. Many partnerships fall under this category as they are initiated by a small group of relevant stakeholders, while their activities aspire to be more broadly applicable. The Common Code for the Coffee Community (4C), for example, was founded by only two organisations, GTZ and the Deutscher Kaffee-Verband.[73] Its mandate is to develop a code for sustainability in the production, processing and trading of mainstream coffee. The code aspires to be applicable at the global level and to be accepted as binding by all organisations dealing with coffee. Similarly, GRI was founded by CERES, an NGO. It set itself the goal to develop and disseminate standards to guide the sustainability reporting practices of companies and other organisations. None of the organisations that – as GRI hoped – would later accept these standards as binding for themselves authorised GRI to assume this task.

Organisations acting without appropriate prior authorisation are not, however, necessarily illegitimate. Authority can also be delegated retrospectively or agents can act as if they were properly authorised. Ex-post authorisation can be explicit. Affected parties can, for example, formally ratify an organisation's mandate by joining at a later stage. Thus states joining the European Union have to accept the *acquis communautaire* and delegate the authority to legislate in all areas that have already been integrated. Similarly, new partner organisations typically have to formally endorse the partnership's mandate. When a range of important coffee processing and trading companies as well as producers' associations joined the 4C initiative, they formally acknowledged its authority to develop a sustainability code.

Ex-post delegation can also occur implicitly. In some instances, we can infer from the behaviour of an organisation that it has retrospectively accepted the delegation of authority. Take GRI as an example. The initiative boasts that by the end of 2005, 750 organisations were using the GRI guidelines as the basis for their sustainability reporting (Global Reporting Initiative, 2006a, p. 4). Even though they have not formally joined the partnership, these organisations implicitly accept the GRI's authority to develop guidelines by using them. In other cases, even the failure to protest can be interpreted as implicit ex-post delegation. Voigt and Salzberger, for example, do this for the delegation of legislative powers in domestic democratic systems:

> [Whenever collective decision-making powers] that are not constitutionally assigned to a body other than the legislature are in fact being exercised by such a body, this can be regarded as a delegation of legislative powers. [... This includes] *Ex post* delegation, which occurs when another organ performed decision-making and the legislature refrains from reversing (or positively affirming) the decision.
> (Voigt and Salzberger, 2002, p. 292, emphasis original)

Finally, delegation can be hypothetical. In this case, the organisation does not intend to achieve real authorisation. To determine a legitimate course of action, it nevertheless tries to imagine what the principals would or ought to consent to. Organisations promoting animal rights, acting on behalf of severely mentally handicapped people or the rights of small children, for example, can rely on hypothetical delegation to guide their activities. For governments, Hanna Pitkin was one of the first to explicitly name hypothetical consent as a criterion for legitimate authority. She explains the 'doctrine of hypothetical consent' as follows:

> For a legitimate government, a true authority, one whose subjects are obligated to obey it, emerges as one to which they *ought to consent*, quite apart from whether they have done so.
> (Pitkin, 1965, p. 999, emphasis original)

Hypothetical and ex-post delegation play a particularly important role in circumstances where prior authorisation is difficult, costly or impossible to achieve. At the international level, for example, the lack of an established political system and the existence of a very broad range of actors with different interests make it hard to organise consensus.[74] Many areas of political concern would never be addressed if ex-ante delegation were always required. The system of international law, for example, could only come into existence through implicit and ex-post consent.[75] Organisations acting without proper authorisation can therefore play a constructive part in international politics and other similar areas.

The frequency and impact of organisations acting without ex-ante authorisation make it all the more important to define institutional criteria for their legitimacy. Where organisations act without appropriate authorisation, a simple criterion applies. They usurp authority unless they intend to achieve ex-post authorisation, or, where this is not possible, act as if the necessary authority had been delegated to them.

This has important implications for our discussion of accountability. Even where no explicit prior act of delegation has taken place, legitimate agents have the obligation to act in the best interest of their future or hypothetical principals. Therefore, a good institutional set-up under these conditions requires that agents identify their principals and create appropriate accountability mechanisms to them.

There is, however, a significant difference between ex-post and ex-ante delegation. Ex-post delegation means that principals – at least in theory – reserve the right to accept or reject the activities of the agent and thereby to grant or deny retrospective authorisation. This links the argument back to power and effectiveness. In some cases, the agents become so powerful that the principals do not actually have the freedom to choose whether or not they agree to ex-post delegation. Take the IMF, for example. Borrower countries are typically in an economically difficult position that makes them dependent on extended or new IMF loans. This forces them to accept conditionalities and does not allow them to freely decide whether or not they want to accept the IMF's authority to impose such conditions. In situations like this, appropriate accountability mechanisms remain necessary to protect the principals' rights.

In other cases, no such power asymmetries prevent principals from exercising their freedom of choice. Here, accountability, while in theory still based on the principals' rights, in practice becomes more a question of effectiveness. The principals' rights are automatically protected as principals can reject the agent's activities. But accountability remains important when seen from the agent's perspective. The agent's efforts are in vain if they are not accepted by the relevant principals. Appropriate accountability mechanisms provide the agent with a better understanding of the principals' real preferences. They also assure principals that their interests are taken seriously and thereby increase the principals' sense of ownership and perception of legitimacy. This makes principals more likely to support or comply with the results generated by the partnership and thus grant ex-post authorisation.[76] This way, accountability becomes an important tool for increasing effectiveness.

Both GRI and the 4C initiative illustrate these mechanisms. Both partnerships define rules or guidelines in order to change the behaviour of organisations. Their success thus depends on whether or not relevant actors accept the proposed rules and act accordingly. It may be for that reason why both initiatives have opted to structure themselves as partnerships. By turning their key prospective principals into partner organisations, they make themselves accountable to them.

Deriving a requirement for appropriate accountability arrangements from ex-post or hypothetical delegation is also a widespread and broadly accepted practice in other disciplines. It has been argued here that the normative core of the concept of accountability is based on the rights of principals that are created through delegation. Earlier, we found that the rights of principals are recognised in today's major legal systems and that they are a central element in liberal democratic thought. Closer examination of these legal norms and philosophical arguments shows that both also cover instances of ex-post and hypothetical delegation.

First, the legal regulations. Most domestic legal systems have elaborate rules covering instances of explicit delegation. Cases in which agents act without prior authorisation are an exception from the rule. Under certain conditions, though, ex-post and hypothetical delegation are recognised. Where they are, the agents are considered to have the same or, if anything, stricter obligations towards the principal than in instances of explicit ex-ante delegation.

Under German law, for example, 'mission creep' is covered by § 665 BGB. It states that agents can only diverge from their original mandate if they can assume that the principal would consent to this if he knew about the circumstances. In addition, the agent is required to inform the principal about this change and should wait for a reply, unless action is necessary to avert danger. The BGB also regulates the actions of unauthorised agents. It clearly states that agents have to respect the real or hypothetical interests of the principal and have the same obligations as authorised agents:

> If somebody acts on behalf of somebody else without being authorised by him or without otherwise having the right to do so, he must act in the way required by the interest of the principal as defined by his real or assumed will. [...] Otherwise, the duties of an authorised agent as defined in §§ 666–8 apply to the agent.
>
> (BGB, 2006, §§ 677 and 681) (Author's rough translation)[77]

Interestingly, in German law and other civil law systems, hypothetical delegation also creates obligations for the principal. Following the Roman principle of *negotiorum gestio*, unauthorised agents are not allowed to make a profit from their activities, but they are entitled to receive compensation for the damages they incur.[78] Common law countries are often more restrictive in this respect. The obligation for the restitution of damages and costs is recognised more rarely, thus providing even stronger protection of the rights of principals.[79]

Another legal institution recognising hypothetical and ex-post delegation is prominent in common law countries. As already discussed,[80] the concept of fiduciary obligations is key to regulating principal–agent relationships. It creates protections to ensure the agent uses his discretionary power beneficently. The concept also covers situations in which the principal has not authorised the agent to act on his behalf, as, for example, the relationship between a guardian and a ward. In this case, fiduciary obligations apply and demand that the agent act in a way that would meet the ward's approval if he had the capacity to consider the situation or that he will accept once he has achieved the ability to do so.

Admittedly, most legal systems only recognise ex-post or hypothetical delegation under relatively strict conditions. But where it is recognised, the agents are considered to have the same or more far-reaching obligations as in instances of explicit ex-ante delegation. In normative philosophy, ex-post and particularly hypothetical delegation enjoy a much stronger standing than in legal practice. The most prominent rights-based approaches in political and moral philosophy rely on hypothetical consent as the basis for their arguments.

Social contract theory was introduced here as a cornerstone of liberal thought. Early proponents of the theory such as Hobbes, Rousseau and Locke described the pre-social state of nature and the process leading to the formation of societies as part of their argument. Many critics read these parts as an interpretation of history and attacked the philosophers on the ground that their reading of history was unrealistic.[81] Robert Filmer, for example, argued that individuals were not actually born free and equal as assumed by the contractarians. Instead, Filmer contends, humans are born into pre-existing authority structures and have a natural obligation to respect the authority of their fathers. On this account, individuals cannot transfer their right to self-rule to a ruler because they do not have it in the first place.[82] David Hume rejects Filmer's patriarchalism, but also doubts the realism of the social contract. He argues that the existing governments he knows are actually founded on usurpation or conquest, not the consent of the governed. To those arguing that the original contract was concluded in ancient history when humans first grouped in societies, he counters that such historical agreement cannot be binding for governments or citizens today:

> But the contract, on which government is founded, is said to be the original contract, and consequently may be supposed too old to fall under

the knowledge of the present generation. If the agreement, by which savage men first associated and conjoined their force, be here meant, this is acknowledged to be real; but being so ancient, and being obliterated by a thousand changes of government and princes, it cannot now be supposed to retain any authority. [...] But besides that this supposes the consent of the fathers to bind the children, even to the most remote generations, (which republican writers will never allow) besides this, I say, it is not justified by history or experience, in any age or country of the world.

(Hume, 1994, p. 190)

Even among the early contract thinkers, though, the social contract was often understood as a mental construct rather than historical fact. John Locke, for example, does make repeated efforts to find real life examples for his contract argument. But at the same time, he argues that moral principles cannot be derived from history. Rather, it is from reason and through reason that moral norms are discovered:[83]

[A]t best an argument from what has been, to what should of right be, has no great force [...]. But to conclude, reason being plain on our side, that men are naturally free, and the examples of history shewing, that the governments of the world, that were begun in peace, had their beginning laid on that foundation, and were made by the consent of the people; there can be little room for doubt, either where the right is, or what has been the opinion, or practice of mankind, about the first erecting of governments.

(Locke, 1690, Book 2, Chapter VIII, §§ 103–4)

In modern political and moral philosophy, the social contract remains central. Modern contractarians have given up all pretence about the historicity of the contract. Instead, they rely explicitly on hypothetical models of consent and delegation to derive the principles of morality as well as criteria for the legitimacy of government. Fred D'Agostino, for example, stresses this point:

In its modern guises, contract approaches are not intended as accounts of the historical origins of current social arrangements, but, instead, as answers to, or frameworks for answering, questions about legitimacy and political obligation.

(D'Agostino, 2006)

In moral philosophy, for instance, thinkers writing in the tradition of Immanuel Kant use a hypothetical contract to derive the principles of morality. Kantian contract thinkers argue that individuals can determine what it right and what is wrong by doing a thought experiment. Would rational individuals agree to the norm underlying or the reasons given for an activity? If they would, the activity is morally acceptable, but if they would not, the activity is morally wrong. Kant expresses this principle in the first formulation of the categorical imperative: 'handle nur nach derjenigen Maxime, durch die du zugleich wollen kannst, daß sie ein allgemeines Gesetz werde' (Kant, 1996/1786, p. 68).[84]

John Rawls, the most famous contemporary Kantian philosopher, tries to make this thought experiment more impartial. He demands that individuals ignore their actual situation while considering the same question. To achieve this, individuals must make the morality test from an 'original position' or behind a 'veil of ignorance' disguising their real current position:

> [T]he principles of justice for the basic structure of society are the object of the original agreement. They are the principles that free and rational persons concerned to further their own interests would accept in an initial position of equality [...]. Among the essential features of this situation is that no one knows his place in society, his class position or social status, nor does any one know his fortune in the distribution of natural assets and abilities, his intelligence, strength, and the like. [...] The principles of justice are chosen behind a veil of ignorance.
>
> (Rawls, 1971, pp. 11–12)

For Thomas Scanlon, a wrong action similarly is one that 'I could not justify to others on grounds I could expect them to accept' (Scanlon, 1998, p. 4). Also seeking to include a criterion of impartiality, this leads him to describe judgements about right and wrong as 'judgments about what would be permitted by principles that could not reasonably by rejected, by people who were moved to find principles for the general regulation of the behavior of others' (Scanlon, 1998, p. 4).

The contract argument in this form involves hypothetical consent. Kantian contractarians are typically concerned with establishing the legitimacy of specific norms and actions. The contract they are using therefore tends to involve the direct hypothetical consent of individuals to moral or legal norms and principles. Only rarely do moral contract thinkers consider the legitimacy of institutions. But where they do, they tend to follow the logic of their moral argument and rejoin the political social contract tradition based on Locke's writings.

Kant, for example, treats the question of what good political institutions ought to look like only fleetingly.[85] According to him, humans need to live in societies ruled by law to realise their innate capabilities. Government is necessary because humans are not purely governed by reason but sometimes also follow their animal-like instincts, violating the freedom of others. Government enforcing obedience to just laws is thus necessary to protect the freedom of all. Kant realises that this poses a dilemma because rulers are also fallible humans prone to succumbing to their instincts. While perfectly just rule is impossible, Kant's theory demands that humans seek to approach it – presumably by creating accountability mechanisms that prevent the abuse of authority and protect the rights of the hypothetical principals:

> The head of state should be just in himself, and yet a human. This task is therefore the most difficult of all; its complete achievement is impossible: humans are made from such twisted material, that nothing totally straight can be built from it. Nature only demands us to approach the idea.
>
> (Kant, 1996a, p. 316) (Author's rough translation)[86]

For contemporary thinkers using a social contract argument, Ann Cudd confirms that most moral contractarians are also political contractarians, though she does not see this link as a necessary one: 'There is no necessity for a contractarian about political theory to be a contractarian about moral theory, although most contemporary contractarians are both' (Cudd, 2006).

Accordingly, most social contract thinkers agree that legitimate institutions are those that rational individuals could or would consent to. In other words, institutions need to be set up as if individuals had delegated the necessary authority to them or so that they will delegate this authority retrospectively.[87] Social contract thinkers thus base their influential arguments on models involving hypothetical consent or delegation.

But social contract theory has not remained undisputed. As indicated, Filmer and Hume criticised the realism of the social contract. Hypothetical contracts have also created intense debate. Communitarians following in the footsteps of Georg Wilhelm Friedrich Hegel, for example, doubt that humans can be thought of as independent of their communities. They posit that individuals can only develop their potential and capacities within a community and that it is therefore only in the context of a community that individuals can be said to be free and have rights. Even hypothetically, the idea of a social contract to establish a political or moral community therefore makes no sense.[88] Marxists claim that individuals are shaped by the material conditions they live in. They argue that material exploitation and alienation first need to be overcome before individuals can enjoy freedom. It is only after the revolution that individuals can found a genuine human community allowing them to achieve their full potential.[89] Feminists, finally, criticise social contract thinkers for ignoring the 'sexual contract' that precedes the social contract and subjects women to the authority of men, for implicitly giving the 'free and equal individuals' (white) male characteristics and for ignoring the morality of care.[90]

These and other criticisms present serious challenges for social contract theories. Contractarians have particular difficulties in countering the argument that humans are shaped by society. Because they are so deeply embedded in concrete social structures, it is questionable whether social contract thought experiments can create impartial judgements.[91] But this critique is much less damaging for the argument on accountability proposed here. It acknowledges that individuals are socially embedded and pursue particular interests. In fact it is because humans have different conceptions of the good and different interests that appropriate accountability structures are necessary. Recall that hypothetical or ex-post delegation creates an obligation for the agent to act in the best interest of his principals. Accountability structures are necessary to prevent the abuse of authority and to enable the autonomous principals to articulate their specific interests and preferences. The communitarian, Marxist and feminist critiques may thus be problematic for social contract theorists, but they attack other assumptions made by contractarians and do not question the construct of hypothetical consent or delegation itself.

There is, however, another challenge against the social contract that is more directly relevant to the argument proposed here. An important number of thinkers deny that a hypothetical contract can be binding. Ronald Dworkin, for example, argues that

> hypothetical contracts do not supply an independent argument for the fairness of enforcing their terms. A hypothetical contract is not simply a pale form of an actual contract; it is no contract at all. [... I]t may be that I would have agreed to any number of [...] rules if I had been asked in advance [...]. It does not follow that these rules may be enforced against me if I have not, in fact, agreed to them.
>
> (Dworkin, 1973, p. 501)[92]

Contract thinkers have reacted in different ways to this charge. Rawls argues that even if hypothetical agreements cannot bind, the concept of the original position is significant because it describes the conditions under which individuals agree on a political conception of justice that we consider fair (Rawls, 1993, pp. 24–7). Similarly, Thomas Scanlon is prepared to admit that hypothetical consent is mainly used as a heuristic device or a metaphor to help unearth what we believe is 'reasonable' or 'just'. Other contractarians including Jeffrey Paul, Samuel Freeman, Brian Barry, Gerald Gaus, Christopher Morris and James Fishkin agree with Dworkin that a hypothetical contract may not be binding. Nevertheless they argue that it has argumentative force as a justification for specific norms.[93] Cynthia Stark suggests distinguishing between a contract that is morally binding and one that is enforceable. She proposes that a hypothetical contract is binding in the sense that it justifies moral principles and gives individuals reasons why they should comply with these norms. But she argues that hypothetical consent is not sufficient for justifying governmental enforcement of these norms (Stark, 2000).

The dispute on whether or not or to what degree a hypothetical contract can be considered as binding cannot be resolved here. But neither does it need to be resolved for the argument on accountability. Critics question only whether social contracts can be binding on individuals, by creating either political obligations or specific norms. They do not, however, protest when the social contract is used to argue for a limited government that has an obligation to promote the interests of its citizens and needs accountability mechanisms to ensure this.

Where does this difference stem from? Hypothetical contracts can have different structures with implications for the standing of the parties involved. Consider first a contract à la Rawls or Kant that justifies norms. Its hypothetical members are the same individuals who would then be bound by the norm. In that sense, the contract is symmetrical, and in this case, its binding force is disputed. In political theory, it is more common to deal with contracts that involve both individuals and a government. Here, the contract is asymmetrical. Individuals conclude a hypothetical contract conferring authority on a government. The government assumes this authority consciously and explicitly. While the individuals thus grant their consent only hypothetically, the government actually agrees to the delegation contract. As a result, it is controversial whether the individuals can be considered bound by the contract. But, as long as we believe that individuals are autonomous and have certain rights, it is beyond dispute that the government incurs certain obligations through its involvement in the social contract.

In the argument on accountability presented here, we are concerned with real, ex-post and hypothetical delegation. If the contract establishing these principal–agent relationships is hypothetical, it is asymmetrical. Just like the government in the example above, the agent assumes authority that originally belongs to individuals or other institutions. If the agent acts legitimately, it does not rob others of their rightful authority, but becomes party to a delegation contract. Again, the consent of the agent to this contract can be considered real, whereas the consent of the principals is hypothetical. Even when no actual delegation takes place, the agent is bound by the same obligations as an agent who was properly authorised.[94]

Assuming that individuals are autonomous and endowed with certain rights, this leaves us with the following conclusion: delegation of authority creates an obligation for the agent to promote the interests of the principals. Appropriate accountability mechanisms are necessary to prevent the abuse of authority and to protect the principals' autonomy. An agent acting without prior authorisation can only be legitimate if she acts as if the authority had been delegated to her or so that it will be delegated later on. Hypothetical and ex-post delegation may not be binding for principals but create the same obligations for agents as real delegation. A good institutional set up therefore involves appropriate accountability mechanisms protecting the rights of those who originally held the authority now exercised by the organisation.

3.3 The advantages of justifying accountability through delegation

The argument based on delegation proposed here intersects and overlaps in various ways with the other justifications of accountability sketched at the outset of this chapter. In what ways, then, does it differ from and how does it improve on alternative accounts? Put very briefly, it provides a theoretical basis for accountability that at the same time creates a firmer normative basis and leads to more differentiated practical results.

Let's recapitulate in slightly greater detail. Three main existing approaches to justifying accountability were found in the literature relevant to partnerships. The claims based on a consequentialist logic, on stakeholder theory or on arguments derived from democracy were found open to criticism on different levels. An important recurring problem was that the arguments either relied on a weak normative basis or that their political demands did not follow from their main normative case.

Thus consequentialist arguments only demand accountability if and in so far as it promotes another good, such as efficiency or effectiveness. In doing so, accountability is not recognised as a value in itself. The demand for accountability remains contingent and accountability can be replaced by other mechanisms if they produce the same result.

Stakeholder theory, at least in its original formulation by Edward Freeman, stands on much firmer philosophical grounds. Based on an account of individual rights, it provides a strong – though disputed – case for why managers ought to act morally and consider the effects of their decisions on others. As argued above, though, the theory becomes more problematic when it is used to justify demands for accountability mechanisms. The claim that all stakeholders ought to be included in decision making is not widely accepted or reflected in social practices. Moreover, a consistent realisation of these demands would contradict the philosophical principles the argument is built on.

Democratic theory, finally, makes a philosophically sound and widely accepted claim that governments ought to have democratic accountability mechanisms. Researchers have extended the democratic argument to other situations. To remedy a democratic deficit or to create a legitimate system of global governance, they demand the extension of accountability mechanisms to all influential organisations. As argued earlier, however, the democratic logic does not really back a call for democratic accountability for all institutions. And where more differentiated accountability mechanisms are proposed, the theory provides no guidelines for determining which accountability mechanisms should apply to which organisations.

The argument based on delegation presented here provides a clearer justification for accountability as well as a firm normative basis for its claims. Firstly, like stakeholder and democratic theory, it relies on a rights-based philosophical approach, emphasising the value of individual autonomy. As a result, the normative power of the argument is stronger than that of consequentialist justifications.

There is, however, an exception to this. Where delegation is ex-post and the principals can genuinely choose whether or not to grant authorisation after the fact, the argument relapses into a consequentialist one.[95] In this case accountability is not necessary to protect rights but only to enhance the effectiveness of an organisation's work. But even in this instance, the argument based on delegation does not create a normatively less powerful demand for accountability than stakeholder and democratic theory. Rather, like them, it claims that accountability is a matter of right only where an institution wields significant power. Beyond this, it provides a coherent account of when accountability is (also) a matter of expedience, namely, when organisations need ex-post approval and support to be successful.

Secondly, delegation avoids some of the theoretical problems of stakeholder theory. The basic claim is that delegation creates an obligation for agents to promote the interests of their principals. This, together with the need to protect the autonomy of principals, justifies the demand for appropriate accountability mechanisms. This claim is much more widely accepted in the social sciences and more broadly reflected in social practices than the case made by stakeholder theory that all those influenced by somebody's actions have a claim to accountability. Moreover, as will become clear in Chapter 5, the concrete demands derived from delegation do not create the kind of total accountability that a consistent application of stakeholder theory would. Thus the application of the theory does not undermine the philosophical principles it is built on.

Finally, like the democratic deficit and global governance arguments, the case based on delegation builds on the strong normative foundations of democratic theory. But rather than directly extending democratic theory to other institutional settings, delegation makes the analogy at a more abstract level. All organisations rely on some form of delegated authority. Therefore, they all need appropriate accountability mechanisms, but these do not necessarily have to involve democratic accountability. This way, the delegation argument applies the principles of democratic theory more consistently to other spheres.

Another important criticism against existing justifications concerns their ability to generate differentiated demands for accountability. The existing consequentialist, stakeholder or democracy arguments either lead to a general, undifferentiated claim for accountability or provide no basis for establishing which situation requires what kind of accountability mechanisms.

Consequentialist arguments, for example, do allow for the application of different accountability mechanisms. If accountability is necessary to achieve other goals, organisations should choose the mechanisms that best promote these goals. But rather than providing a normative case for the adoption of specific accountability mechanisms, it is left to each organisation to figure out which arrangement best suits it. Diversity and flexibility thus come at the cost of arbitrariness.

Stakeholder theory in its original formulation recognises all groups that are influenced by or can influence an organisation as stakeholders. Apart from the degree of influence, it contains no criterion allowing for a differentiation between stakeholders. As a consequence, the same kind of accountability is demanded for all stakeholder groups. This, however, does not clearly correspond to widely held moral convictions as expressed by laws, regulations and the demands of accountability activists.

Arguments based on democratic theory, finally, either demand democratic accountability for all or recognise different possible accountability mechanisms without providing guidance on how and why to apply them. The accountability demands derived from delegation, by contrast, are more differentiated in two respects. On the one hand, delegation recognises a smaller group as legitimate accountability holders than stakeholder and democratic theory. Only those who originally or rightfully hold the authority exercised by an institution have a right to access to accountability mechanisms. This excludes a number of groups who are only influenced by an organisation. On the other hand, within this smaller group, delegation allows for a variety of accountability mechanisms and provides criteria for their application. What authority is delegated determines which accountability mechanisms are appropriate. How exactly this works and which authority requires which accountability type is discussed in the next section.

3.4   Form should follow function

Wherever authority is delegated, appropriate accountability mechanisms are necessary. What, though, counts as an 'adequate' or 'appropriate' accountability arrangement for the wide variety of partnerships?

To date, there are only few initiatives or organisations that define explicit accountability standards applicable to partnerships. The few that exist – like the Global Accountability Index of the NGO One World Trust[96] – propose to apply the same standards to companies, the public sector, civil society and, by implication, to all forms of partnerships. Most existing governance and accountability standards, however, refer to a much more limited group of organisations. This can be companies, civil society organisations and public agencies or even more specific groups, such as the extractive industries, educational institutions or health care providers.[97] These standards define very different accountability requirements depending on the type of organisation they address. At the same time, they usually fail to define a more general principle that would explain why different standards are valid under different circumstances. Without such a principle, however, it is difficult to apply the standards to new situations such as partnerships.

This section establishes a general criterion for determining when an accountability arrangement is appropriate. It argues that concrete accountability requirements depend on the organisation's function. Function determines which accountability mechanisms are appropriate.

If delegation makes accountability necessary, it also establishes which accountability mechanisms are appropriate. What authority is delegated affects what the agent is accountable for. Different mechanisms are suited for creating accountability for different aspects. An organisation's function indicates what authority has been, will be or is assumed to have been delegated to it. Therefore, function determines which accountability mechanisms are appropriate. This, in a nutshell, is why form should follow function in partnership accountability.

The previous section established that agents need adequate accountability arrangements because they exercise authority that originally or rightfully belongs to somebody else. This argument already includes a general definition of what the agent is accountable for. Agents are accountable for exercising their authority in a way that corresponds to the interests of the original authority holders (the principals).[98]

Principal–agent relationships, though, can involve the delegation of different kinds of authority. It can be, for example, the authority to manage property, the authority to set rules and standards or the authority to generate information or knowledge. What exactly the agent is accountable for, then, depends to an important degree on what authority has been delegated. Thus property managers are typically accountable for generating high returns. Legislators are accountable for adopting policies that promote the interests of society and for creating rules that are implemented in a fair and impartial manner. Monitoring agencies or scientific institutions, finally, are accountable for generating accurate and high-quality information or knowledge.[99]

To create or strengthen the accountability of organisations, a variety of concrete mechanisms can be employed. They can range from elections, participation rights and process rules to performance evaluation and incentive packages. In any given situation, those mechanisms are appropriate that are likely to strengthen accountability for the relevant issue area. Accurate accounting and reporting combined with sanctions or incentives, for example, are well suited for creating accountability for financial results. Elections, opinion polls and direct participation, by contrast, are better suited for enabling individuals to articulate their preferences and process rules can help to ensure that rules are implemented in a fair and impartial way. The participation of independent experts and compliance with quality standards, in turn, are safeguards for accurate and high-quality information or knowledge.

These brief examples show that the adequacy of an accountability arrangement to an important degree depends on the nature of authority that is delegated. As discussed in the previous section, the notion of delegation used here is wide. It includes not only explicit and ex-ante delegation but also implicit, hypothetical and ex-post delegation. This means that what counts for evaluating an accountability arrangement is not just what authority has been formally delegated. Rather, it depends on the authority an organisation actually exercises and thus on what function is fulfils. Therefore, organisational function is key to judging what accountability arrangements are appropriate under what circumstances. It is in this sense that the dogma of 'form follows function'[100] applies to partnership accountability.

4
Partnerships in Practice

It was established in the previous chapter that an organisation's accountability arrangements should depend on its function. What functions, though, do partnerships fulfil? This chapter proposes a functional classification of partnerships and outlines some of the main variations in partnership accountability.

4.1 Partnership types ...

Partnerships come in many guises. They differ from each other in many respects. Correspondingly, partnerships can be classified in many different ways. Criteria that have been used or could be used for the categorisation[1] of partnerships include:

- Composition:[2] In section 2.1.1, partnerships were defined as cooperative arrangements between public, private and civil society sectors. Depending on who participates, we can differentiate between business-government, business-NGO, NGO-government and tri-sectoral partnerships. By the same token, we can distinguish local, national and international partnerships. Another option would be to classify partnerships according to the type of organisation leading or convening the partnership.
- Size: The number of organisations participating in a partnership can vary widely. This could be used as the basis for a distinction, for example, between bilateral, trilateral, small, medium and large partnerships.
- Reach: Partnerships differ in their ambitions and can try to address local, national, regional or global problems.
- Field of activity:[3] Another possibility is to distinguish partnerships according to the issue area they seek to address. A classification based on this criterion would include, for example, health, education, water and forestry partnerships.
- Governance:[4] Partnerships also vary in the institutional form and governance structure they choose. This includes, for example, largely

informal partnerships, partnerships that are run by one leading partner organisation and partnerships that are incorporated as independent entities.

- Degree of involvement:[5] Many partnerships aim at involving other organisations in the work of a core partner. For these partnerships, a significant criterion is how strongly and in which areas the other partner organisations get involved.

- Relationship between the partner organisations:[6] One important determinant for the relationship between partner organisations is the difference in their power status. At the extremes of the spectrum would be horizontal partnerships (with all partners enjoying equal status) and hierarchical partnerships (though really hierarchical forms of cooperation would no longer count as a 'partnership'). Another important dimension is the degree of prevailing conflict. At one extreme, all partner organisations have identical interests so that the partnership merely serves to coordinate activities. At the other end, partner organisations start with opposing interests and use the partnership to negotiate compromises.

- Reason of engagement of the main partner organisation(s):[7] Organisations have different motives for engaging in partnerships and this can serve as a basis for categorising partnerships. Governments, for example, can enter into partnerships to gain access to additional resources, to induce voluntary compliance with regulations by private actors, to increase their legitimacy and responsiveness or to manage conflicts between different parties. Corporations can join partnerships for philanthropic reasons, to improve their reputation, to motivate staff or to manage risks. And NGOs, finally, can be motivated by a desire to influence relevant decisions by partner organisations, increase their leverage by joining forces with others or to receive resources.

- Function: Finally, partnerships can be classified according to their contribution to a public policy problem. This is the approach chosen here, which is discussed in greater detail below.

If partnerships can be classified according to all these and probably more criteria, why choose a categorisation based on partnership function? To be valid and useful, a classification needs to be well defined and consistent and rest on criteria that are relevant to the subject under scrutiny.[8] If this study aimed, for example, at uncovering why different parties engage in partnerships, then a classification linked to partnership composition or the reason of engagement of the main partner organisations would be appropriate.

Here, the research interest is to develop standards for partnership accountability. As argued in the preceding chapter, concrete accountability requirements depend on organisational function, defined in terms of the relevant authority transferred to or assumed by partnerships. Therefore, a classification based on partnership function is appropriate for this study.

A number of other political scientists have also proposed functional classifications of partnerships. Often, these researchers approach partnerships from the perspective of global governance. Thus their primary research interest is to analyse how governance is exercised at the international or global level and what contribution partnerships make.

In their analysis of 'global public policy networks', Reinicke and Deng, for example, distinguish six partnership functions: placing issues on the agenda, negotiating and setting standards and regulations, developing and disseminating knowledge, making and deepening markets, implementing ideas and decisions and closing the participatory gap (Reinicke and Deng, 2000, pp. 25–55). In a later publication on partnerships between the UN and business, Witte and Reinicke differentiate four functions: advocacy, developing norms and standards, sharing and coordinating resources and expertise and harnessing markets for development (Witte and Reinicke, 2005, p. 8). Inge Kaul, in a publication for UNDP, lists seven functional purposes, including trading comparative advantage, exploring new products and markets, improving market inefficiencies by developing and disseminating norms and standards, expanding markets into new countries and to new consumer groups, brokering special market deals, encouraging innovation and research and development and pulling together all available forces and resources to respond to a pressing global challenge (Kaul, 2006, p. 223).

Even these few examples of classifications based on partnership function show significant variations in the number and kinds of categories created. In part, this is due to different definitions of what constitutes a partnership. But in part it is also due to the fact that the identification of functions is influenced by the researchers' perspective. With an underlying interest in finding out what authority is delegated to or assumed by partnerships, the four following functional partnership types can be identified: advocacy and awareness raising, rule setting and regulation, policy implementation and information-generating partnerships. These categories can also accommodate the functions uncovered by the researchers just cited.[9] While there is no reason to suspect that the following list is not exhaustive, further empirical evidence could lead to the discovery of additional functions. This would, however, not invalidate the present reflections but require extending the analysis to the newly discovered functional groups.

4.1.1 Advocacy and awareness-raising partnerships

Many partnerships require only basic forms of authority to operate. At a minimum, this includes a licence to operate granted by the country of incorporation or the host agency(ies) and the authority to manage operational resources. The partnerships operating on the basis of minimal authority include those whose main function is to engage in advocacy activities, to raise awareness, to collect and disseminate information or to offer a platform for coordinating the activities of partner organisations.

Advocacy and awareness-raising partnerships are formed because their members hope they can draw attention to a policy problem more effectively when they join forces. Those engaging in advocacy lobby other policymaking institutions, such as governments or intergovernmental organisations, to change their policies. The Partnership for Clean Fuels and Vehicles (PCFV), for example, which was launched during the World Summit on Sustainable Development in 2002 by a group of automobile and fuel companies, environmental NGOs, international organisations, government agencies and research organisations, tries to convince governments to introduce and implement stricter regulations in order to achieve greater use of cleaner gasoline and vehicle technology.[10]

Other partnerships focus more on awareness raising to achieve their policy goals. In that case, they target their efforts directly at those whose behaviour they want to change. A good example for this is the Global Public–Private Partnership for Handwashing with Soap, which campaigns to convince people to regularly wash their hands with soap to reduce diarrhoeal diseases.[11]

To facilitate the exchange of information and to encourage learning across institutional boundaries, many partnerships collect and disseminate relevant information. Very often, the collection and dissemination of information is part of or supports a partnership's advocacy or awareness-raising activities. The Extractive Industries Transparency Initiative (EITI), whose goals are to increase accountability to ensure that revenues derived from extractive industries contribute to sustainable development, for example, maintains on its website a collection of materials from other organisations relating to transparency and the extractive industries.[12]

The collection of information can also serve to facilitate coordination. Especially at the international level, important policy problems are often addressed by a multitude of different actors. This fragmentation can lead to overlaps as well as contradictions and result in inefficiencies. A number of partnerships present themselves as platforms facilitating the coordination between various actors.[13] RBM, a partnership aiming to provide a coordinated international approach to fighting malaria, for instance, encourages local as well as international actors to coordinate their activities. Similarly, the Global Water Partnership (GWP), which was created in 1996 by the World Bank, UNDP and SIDA in order to promote and support sustainable water management, encourages diverse actors to build local and regional coalitions with the goal of achieving integrated water resources management.[14]

4.1.2 Rule setting and regulation partnerships

In many areas, especially at the international level, no binding rules or regulations exist. A range of partnerships has been created to address this regulatory gap. They develop norms, standards and codes of behaviour for specific fields of activity. In the absence of a global executive, compliance with these norms is usually voluntary. Nevertheless the partnerships usually aim at achieving widespread compliance. In this sense, they exercise a quasi-legislative function and assume the corresponding authority. One example for a rule-setting partnership is the WCD. When conflicts relating to the construction of large dams escalated, the commission was convened to develop generally accepted standards for the construction and running of large dams, based on a common assessment of their effectiveness for development. While not considered binding, the standards are now used as a reference point by different stakeholder groups affected by dams. Another example is the Internet Corporation for Assigned Names and Numbers (ICANN).[15] ICANN is the coordination body for the domain name system of the Internet. It regulates the technical elements of the Internet's name and numbering systems in order to preserve the operational stability of the system and promote competition. While it lacks the backing and status of a world government, its regulations are considered authoritative by the concerned communities.

Not all partnerships operating with rules and standards, though, are genuine rule-setting or regulation partnerships. Rather than creating new norms and codes, some simply advocate and create incentives for compliance with broadly accepted existing standards. The 4C initiative, for example, is an advocacy partnership that may be confused with a rule-setting partnership. It encourages coffee producers and traders to comply with a set of norms that are derived from major conventions, resolutions or guidelines of the United Nations, the International Labour Organization (ILO), the Organisation for Economic Co-Operation and Development (OECD), or from conservation legislation.

4.1.3 Policy implementation partnerships

Yet other partnerships have formed around pressing development issues and seek to address them directly. Real implementation partnerships mobilise significant resources and allocate them for implementing policies. By contributing funds or other resources, other organisations or individuals explicitly authorise the partnership to manage and allocate these resources. The Global Alliance for Improved Nutrition (GAIN), a joint initiative of international organisations, bilateral donors, industry representatives, NGOs and private foundations to reduce malnutrition of populations at risk, for example, has over 60 million US\$ at its disposal for grants, technical assistance and start-up investments.[16] The GAVI Alliance, launched in 2000 as the 'Global Alliance for Vaccines and Immunisation' by a group of governments, donors, health organisations, NGOs, companies and research institutions to increase the rate of vaccinations among children, has an annual budget of 600 to 800 million US\$ to support the development of new vaccines and the immunisation of populations in need.[17]

Other partnerships can only spend resources at a much lower level. As a complement to their advocacy and awareness work, they engage in what has been labelled 'implementation support' earlier. They offer selected support services to facilitate the implementation of the policies they promote. The Global Village Energy Partnership (GVEP), whose goal is to improve access to modern energy services for the poor, for instance, provides training to entrepreneurs and financial intermediaries.[18] Another good example is the Renewable Energy and Energy Efficiency Partnership (REEEP), a global partnership between over 200 organisations, business and non-profits to expand the development of renewable energy.[19] REEEP provides training to financial institutions and sometimes seeds funding for the establishment of funds for energy projects.

4.1.4 Information-generating partnerships

Finally, there is a set of partnerships tasked with generating information on behalf of others. Where information is disputed or multiple agents face a collective action problem in generating it, partnerships can contribute to the solution of public policy problems by providing it. This can refer to different kinds of information. In the case of the WCD, for instance, the partnership was called upon to provide an impartial assessment of the effects of a controversial practice. The Marine Stewardship Council, an initiative to improve the health of the world's oceans and create a sustainable global seafood market, by contrast, verifies and certifies the compliance of businesses with its principles and code of conduct.[20]

4.2   ... and their accountability arrangements

The remainder of this section outlines some of the main variations in partnership accountability.

4.2.1 Legal and fiscal accountability arrangements

The partnerships mentioned above operate at the international or global level. This does not mean, however, that they operate in a regulatory void. Rather, they operate within different and usually across several concrete legal and fiscal systems. Like all other individuals and corporate bodies, partnerships and their staff can be held accountable through the systems of criminal and civil law of their countries of origin and operation. Where individuals enjoy diplomatic status, they are mainly held accountable through their home country's legal system. Beyond this common criminal and civil legal accountability, however, there are significant variations concerning their legal status.

Firstly, partnerships can be incorporated as independent entities. Through incorporation, they become subject to the special legal and fiscal rules of their host country. The rules and regulations depend on the one hand on which country the partnership is incorporated in. On the other hand, they depend on what kind of incorporation the partnership chooses. Among the case examples, incorporation as some type of non-profit organisation or foundation is most common. Thus, for example, GRI operates as a foundation under Dutch law, ICANN is a non-profit, public benefit corporation incorporated in California, REEEP is an international NGO under Austrian jurisdiction and the 4C initiative is a membership organisation under Swiss law. With this status, these partnerships are exempt from taxes and can often receive tax-deductible donations. In exchange, they have to demonstrate that they pursue a charitable objective and submit regular financial and activity reports.

Some of the partnerships incorporated as independent organisations enjoy special status. Thus, for example, GWP is now operating as an intergovernmental organisation in Sweden and the Global Fund is recognised by the Swiss government as having international personality. The special status confers privileges and immunities on the partnership and its staff and thus reduces legal and fiscal accountability to the host state.

Secondly, partnerships can opt for a semi-institutionalised form. Rather than enjoying independent legal personality, partnerships can be coordinated by a secretariat hosted by a third organisation. In that case, legal and fiscal accountability are channelled through the host organisation. The staff members of the secretariat are then usually employed by the host organisation and are subject to its internal rules and regulations. With the other partnership bodies lacking corporate legal standing, the secretariat is usually responsible for financial management and represents the partnership in relation to external parties. This constellation thus often confers more responsibility and influence on the secretariat than other governance options. In PCFV, for example, the secretariat assumes most of the legal and fiscal accountability. PCFV is coordinated by a clearing house hosted by UNEP. The other partner organisations explicitly reject legal reliability for partnership activities. In many cases, arrangements like this also reflect the dominant commitment of one of the core partners. Thus it is no coincidence that the EITI secretariat was for a long time hosted by DFID[21] and the secretariats of RBM and the Global Partnership to Stop TB,[22] a partnership including over 500 partners from all sectors aiming to eliminate tuberculosis as a public health problem by 2050, are coordinated by WHO.

Finally, some partnerships have even more informal arrangements than that. Rather than having one official secretariat responsible for finances and contractual relations, partnerships can be run by informal management teams. In these cases, the partnership as an entity has no legal and fiscal accountability. Instead, all participating individuals are held accountable through their own organisations. With the secretarial functions distributed among various organisations, moreover, it is difficult to assign clear responsibilities and create formal accountability. The Partnership for Handwashing with Soap, for example, is managed by an informal coordination team composed of members of the World Bank and the Water and Sanitation

Program. Similarly, the secretariat of the Voluntary Principles on Security and Human Rights in the Extractive Industries partnership, a joint initiative of almost 30 governments, companies and NGOs, is split between two host organisations.[23]

4.2.2 Financial accountability

Financial accountability is a crucial component in any accountability arrangement. Firstly, appropriate financial procedures prevent basic forms of abuse, such as corruption and fraud. Secondly, as the old proverb points out, 'he who pays the piper calls the tune': Control over finances permits influence over many substantive decisions. This is why, for example, the power of parliaments to approve budgets counts as an important criterion for democratic governance.

Financial accountability has different facets to it and the case examples analysed here show variations along all of these dimensions. A first aspect concerns the question of how strongly an organisation depends on its financiers. De facto, the presence of a single dominant donor implies more dependence than reliance on a broad range of different financial sources. GAIN, for example, strongly depends on an individual donor. Around 70 per cent of the resources committed for its first five years of operations were contributed by the Gates Foundation. This is in stark contrast to initiatives that seek to protect their independence by relying on as broad a financial basis as possible. ICANN, for instance, is financed through fees contributed by members. Similarly, the 4C initiative has recently been transformed into a membership organisation.

The standing of donors is also influenced by the partnerships' formal arrangements. Some organisations reserve special positions for important donors, whereas others explicitly avoid this. REEEP, for example, belongs to the former category. All organisations contributing at least €70,000 per year are given a seat on the finance committee, which oversees the partnership's financial activities. Similarly, GAVI grants major donors permanent membership on the GAVI Board. GRI, by contrast, stresses its formal independence from donors. It explicitly states in its main governance documents that 'A contribution does not allow any special role in the governance of the Foundation [or] any special access to information separate from what is available to others' (Global Reporting Initiative, 2002a, Art. 25.2).

A second important question relates to who takes financial decisions and authorises the organisation's budget. In partnerships with strong member control, for example, the general assembly or meeting of partners can have the authority to approve work plans and budgets. Among the partnerships reviewed here, only PCFV follows this model.

It is more common for the partnership board to exercise financial oversight and control. In RBM, for example, the work programmes and budgets are prepared by the secretariat and require board approval. In many cases, boards are supported by or delegate financial decisions entirely to independent committees. Thus, for example, the foundation board of the Global Fund takes funding decisions based on recommendations by a technical review panel. Similarly, an independent proposal review panel prepares funding decisions for the GAIN board. In the GAVI Alliance, a special, independent fund board, made up of eminent persons, bears fiduciary responsibility.

As already mentioned, another set of partnerships gives donors a special role in their governance, including financial oversight and control. Finally, very informal partnerships sometimes have no formal, centralised budget process. Partnership activities are either financed one-by-one by individual partner organisations or the secretariat or coordination team takes financial decisions. The Handwashing with Soap initiative, for example, has no formal governance rules for deciding on financial matters. In GVEP, before its incorporation as GVEP International, the secretariat had fiduciary responsibility.

A third important issue relates to the procedures for accounting, auditing and reporting on finances. All organisations entrusted with managing non-trivial resources have processes in place for accounting for their use. Since most partnerships have non-profit status or are part of public or non-profit organisations, they are subject to relatively strict accounting requirements. The partnerships surveyed in this book differ in two main respects.

Firstly, they differ strongly in the scope and detail of the financial data they report publicly. At one extreme are partnerships publishing no financial data at all, like the Voluntary Principles or the Handwashing with Soap initiative. At the middle of the spectrum are partnerships like the WCD, which publishes details about the sources of its funds, but not their allocation, or RBM, which accounts for the finances of individual projects, but not the partnership as a whole. At the other end of the transparency spectrum are initiatives like GWP or the Global Fund. They regularly publish comprehensive data detailing both financial contributions and expenditures.

In addition, partnerships differ in whether or not they undergo an independent, external audit. Initiatives like PCFV, for example, are relatively transparent about their financial situation. With an annual budget of significantly less than a million US$, however, it employs no external auditors. For partnerships with larger budgets, by contrast, professional audits are standard practice.

4.2.3 Elements of process accountability

'Process accountability' is shorthand for the way decision making and implementation processes make an organisation accountable to members and external stakeholders. Partnerships differ markedly concerning the degree to which they create accountability to stakeholders through governance processes. Process accountability can be created through inclusion, representative composition, member control, possibilities for external participation and transparency.

The first crucial aspect to consider in relation to a partnership's process accountability is its inclusiveness. Who can join the partnership as a member and under what conditions? The most inclusive partnerships among the case examples are those engaged in advocacy and awareness raising. Often, like GWP or GVEP, they are open to all those who share the partnership's mission and objectives. In other cases, membership is tied to conditions. Thus, for example, organisations joining the Stop TB partnership have to commit to measures contributing to the fight against tuberculosis. The 4C initiative demands that corporate partners score an average 'yellow' on the common code principles and engage in a process of continuous improvement. Yet other partnerships are closed to new members. The WCD, for example, was set up by a workshop convened by IUCN and the World Bank. In reaction to protests, the initial reference group was expanded. Despite this, the initiative never defined criteria or processes for accepting new members.

A second important feature concerns how representative a partnership and its bodies are. To ensure an adequate representation of different interests, some partnerships define a specific stakeholder composition for their decision-making bodies. The Global Fund, for instance, reserves a fixed number of seats on its board for donors, recipient countries, affected communities, NGOs, companies, foundations and operating partners. Other broad coalitions like GWP have no predetermined stakeholder composition.

Thirdly, inclusion is not only a question of who can become a member and how representative partnership bodies are but also of how much influence members have over partnership decisions. The case examples differ strongly on this count as well. Some partnerships involve their partner organisations directly in defining policies. GRI, for example, demands of all its members to participate at least once every three years in a working group. The working groups are responsible for revising the GRI reporting guidelines, which form the heart of the initiative. In others, members play an authorising and supervisory role. The PCFV meeting of partners, for instance, approves work programmes and budgets and hears regular reports on activities. Often, this role is linked to the authority to select the partnership board or executive committee. GVEP members, for example, formally have the authority to select the majority of the partnership's board members, but only by accepting a slate of candidates. In a final group of partnerships, members do not have much influence on the decision-making process. In the Stop TB partnership, for example, partner organisations only have an advisory and consultative role.

Accountability to stakeholders, however, cannot only be created through membership. An alternative is to create meaningful opportunities for external stakeholders to participate in partnership governance. Stakeholder inputs can be solicited to determine the strategic direction of a partnership, but also to take very concrete decisions. Among the case examples, the partnerships with the most proactive stance towards involving external stakeholders are

ICANN and the WCD. In the case of ICANN, all affected or concerned parties, be they organisations or individuals, can submit comments on proposed regulatory changes, demand the reconsideration of existing policies, trigger an independent review or use the ombudsman to articulate their interests and concerns. The WCD solicited the inputs of a broad range of stakeholders when creating its knowledge base. This included on-site meetings, regional consultations, Internet conferences and fora, as well as public submissions. A final important element of process accountability is transparency. The availability of accurate, relevant and timely information is crucial because it enables members and external stakeholders to evaluate the performance of the partnership. Therefore, as depicted in the model of accountability in section 2.2.1, information is an essential building block for creating accountability. In addition, access to information is a precondition for the active participation of external stakeholders and partners in the governance and decision making of partnerships.

Different kinds of information are relevant in this respect. Firstly, transparency about the governance and working processes used by partnerships is important. Information on who plays what role and has what kind of authority in a partnership makes it possible to assign responsibility for performance to individuals or organisations. It also enables interested groups to understand their possibilities for participation. Secondly, financial transparency is significant. Openness about the sources of funds used by a partnership allows gauging its independence. Transparency on the allocation of funds is key for avoiding fraud and provides the basis for assessing performance. Finally, information about the activities of partnerships is critical. A detailed account of past engagements is essential for evaluating the agent's work. Openness about upcoming decisions and actions, in turn, promotes active participation.

On all three fronts, partnerships can create different degrees of transparency. At one extreme are partnerships that publish no or little information about their governance, finances and work and are reluctant to make this information available even on request. Among the case examples presented here, the Voluntary Principles are the least transparent. There is barely any information about the partnership and its workings available online or in other publications. Requests for additional information were well received, but did not provide any significant new insights. Most of the partnerships included in the case examples provide relatively far-reaching disclosure through their website and printed publications such as annual reports. A small group spearheaded by ICANN proactively disseminates relevant information to enhance public participation.

4.2.4 Accountability for outcomes

Partnerships are created by their partners in order to achieve some public goal – be it the fair and smooth running of the Internet or the effective prevention and treatment of diseases like AIDS, malaria and tuberculosis. The accountability mechanisms discussed so far, however, do not focus directly on outcomes. Rather, they are mainly designed to prevent fraud and the abuse of authority and to allow different groups to influence partnership decisions. Which mechanisms, then, are used to ensure that partnerships work efficiently and effectively towards achieving their goals?

In creating accountability for outcomes, partnerships and their principals face a major difficulty. For organisations providing public goods, it is often very difficult and complex to assess performance. Firstly, this is because partnerships do not have obvious and measurable targets that would be comparable, for example, to a company's financial bottom line. Instead, partnerships and their principals have to translate their general goals into measurable objectives. Secondly, partnerships usually seek to address issues that result from a complex interplay of factors. This often makes it very hard to establish what impact can be attributed to a particular organisation.

Creating the conditions for assessing a partnership's performance and evaluating its impact is therefore no easy feat. Faced with these problems, some partnerships reviewed here eschew attempts to create accountability for outcomes altogether. Thus, for example, EITI has no concrete targets for its work. It also lacks mechanisms to verify whether member organisations comply with its recommendations. Other partnerships, by contrast, invest significant efforts to assess their performance and impact. This includes setting precise targets, assessing the partnership's outputs and impact and linking performance assessments to sanctions and incentives.

Many partnerships define precise targets for their work. REEEP, for example, translates its priorities into measurable aims such as 'remove the barriers of investment in at least two countries', 'establish at least one functioning fund' or 'build a database of at least 1000 experts'.[24] This makes it easy to assess whether or not the partnership has reached its immediate goals. But there are two major problems with quantitative output targets like this.

Firstly, they provide little information about the quality of the outputs and do not show whether the organisation was efficient in its operations. If REEEP manages to build a database listing 1000 experts, for example, this does not tell us whether the database is well designed, or whether REEEP built the best database for the available resources. To evaluate quality and efficiency, some partnerships rely on comprehensive external reviews of their performance. The Handwashing with Soap partnership, for example, commissioned a review of its strategy, activities and organisation.[25]

Secondly, it is often difficult to link immediate outputs to impact. To remain with the REEEP example, does the database really trigger more investment in renewable energy and energy efficiency? Some partnerships therefore also define impact targets for their work. RBM, for example, set itself goals in terms of malaria prevention and treatment. According to the Abuja Declaration, the aim was to reach 60 per cent of those infected with diagnosis and treatment within 24 hours of the onset of symptoms and to provide 60 per cent of those at risk with effective preventative measures by 2005.[26]

To turn impact targets into an effective accountability tool, a system for measuring changes relating to the public policy problem addressed must be in place. In the case of RBM, the partnership regularly publishes the World Malaria Report. The report assesses the global prevalence of malaria as well as treatment and prevention coverage and thus allows the tracking of progress.

Where partnerships rely on intermediaries for implementing activities, assessing their achievements becomes key to creating outcome accountability. The Global Fund has developed very strong policies in this respect. To achieve 'performance based grant making', it negotiates indicators of success and reporting requirements with each recipient country. Each funded project annually submits a progress report and undergoes an external audit. Where the administrative capacity to conduct those is missing, the fund provides capacity-building measures.

Assessing a partnership's performance is only the first step in creating accountability for outcomes. To be effective, the assessment should be linked to sanctions or incentives. At one level, these can be directed at partnership managers and staff. None of the partnerships described above has a differentiated incentive package for managers that would be comparable to those used in companies. Even so, the threat of dismissal and the promise of a salary increase or promotion related to performance assessments can be effective as sanctions or incentives.

At a second level, the sanctions and incentives can aim at implementing organisations. Partnerships like the Global Fund provide financial resources to other organisations promising to contribute to the fights against AIDS, tuberculosis and malaria. Its sanctions in case of bad performance are clearly spelled out. Only those recipients who can demonstrate progress in reaching their targets receive future disbursements of funds.

At a third level, effective sanctions and incentives can apply to the partnership as a whole. Most partnerships depend in some way on the support of others. Advocacy and awareness partnerships need the endorsement of other actors to be able to state their claim forcefully. Implementation partnerships can usually only work if they can convince donors to commit substantial resources. And all partnerships need to cover their operational costs. Demonstrating that the partnership is effective and efficient in reaching its goals is one of the key factors for attracting new supporters and retaining old ones. In some cases, the continued support of external parties, especially donors, is explicitly linked to good performance.

The partnerships surveyed here, then, rely most commonly on self-defined targets, evaluations as well as incentives and sanctions to create accountability for outcomes. Outside the realm of partnerships, another mechanism of outcome accountability is prominent. Companies are mainly held accountable for operating efficiently by the market. In a market setting, consumers or clients choose between the products and services offered by competing organisations. These organisations depend financially on customer demand. By choosing the best products or services for the best price, consumers thus automatically create accountability for outcomes.

Most of the partnerships described above do not work through the market. They are usually donor financed and if they offer services, they do so in a non-competitive environment. The few exceptions to this among the case examples are often imperfect. Thus, ICANN charges fees for its services. Accountability to its 'customers', however, remains limited because ICANN holds an undisputed monopoly in regulating the Internet. The 4C initiative is also in the process of becoming more dependent on market mechanisms. It has transformed itself into a membership organisation and seeks to cover its core costs through membership fees. Since other organisations have alternatives to belonging to the 4C initiative, it operates under more competitive conditions.

These incipient market mechanisms do allow 'clients' at least in part to hold partnerships accountable for their performance. But this can also be problematic when the interests of the 'customers' conflict with the partnership's original goals. The 4C initiative, for example, wants companies to conform to certain sustainability standards in their behaviour. Conceivably, companies have an interest in reaping the reputational benefits of complying with the common code, but want to avoid strict standards or real behavioural changes.

4.2.5 Accountability through independence and professionalism

Performance evaluation and market mechanisms serve to create accountability for efficiency and effectiveness. For the work of some organisations, however, efficiency and effectiveness are not the only or the most relevant criteria. For partnerships tasked with generating information, for example, the quality and objectivity of the outcomes is more important. This is true for partnerships seeking to establish accurate knowledge, as well as for partnerships verifying the compliance of third parties with norms and standards. Neither quantitative measures of success, nor customer demand are usually adequate means for creating accountability for quality and objectivity.

Instead, partnerships rely on independence and professionalism to create confidence in the information they provide. The WCD, for example, organised broad and diverse participation to ensure the objectivity of its knowledge base. The 4C initiative separates the compliance verification mechanisms from its main work. It relies on independent auditors to verify the activities of its members. To ensure their professionalism, auditors have to fulfil 4C standards and be accredited by the initiative. Similarly, MSC uses independent auditors to verify compliance with its standards. Auditors are accredited through a professional accreditation organisation.

4.2.6 Overview over partnerships and their main accountability arrangements

Table 4.1 provides an overview over the partnerships mentioned above, indicating their main functions (where partnerships have more than one dominant function, they are listed several times) and their most important accountability arrangements.

The categorisation of the partnerships and the description of their accountability arrangements are rough. Nevertheless this overview unveils certain patterns. The group of advocacy and awareness-raising partnerships is the largest and shows the greatest diversity with respect to accountability. Relatively many partnerships in this group have generally weak formal accountability arrangements. Many are also intent on creating financial accountability, while exceptions emphasise process and outcome accountability.

Table 4.1 Partnership functions and accountability arrangements

Function	Examples by main function(s)	Main accountability focus
Advocacy awareness raising collection and dissemination of information coordination	Partnership for Clean Fuels and Vehicles	Financial accountability to partners
	Extractive Industries Transparency Initiative	Financial accountability to donors and increasing accountability to stakeholders
	Global Partnership to Stop TB	Mixed accountability with emphasis on accountability for outcomes
	Global Village Energy Partnership	Some financial accountability
	The Global Public–Private Partnership for Handwashing with Soap	Incipient accountability for outcomes
	Renewable Energy and Energy Efficiency Partnership	Financial accountability to donors; accountability for outcomes
	Common Code for the Coffee Community	Financial accountability, independence and professionalism in compliance verification
	Global Water Partnership	Financial accountability to donors
	Roll Back Malaria	Process accountability to partners; accountability for outcomes

(Continued)

96

Table 4.1 Continued

Function	Examples by main function(s)	Main accountability focus
Rule setting regulation	Global Reporting Initiative	Process accountability to stakeholders
	Internet Corporation for Assigned Names and Numbers	Process accountability to stakeholders
	Extractive Industries Transparency Initiative	Financial accountability to donors and increasing accountability to stakeholders
	Voluntary Principles on Security and Human Rights in the Extractive Industries	Little formal accountability
	World Commission on Dams	Process accountability to stakeholders; independence
	Marine Stewardship Council	Process accountability in rule setting; independence and professionalism in verification
Policy implementation implementation support	Global Alliance for Improved Nutrition	Financial accountability; accountability for outcomes
	Global Partnership to Stop TB	Mixed accountability with emphasis on accountability for outcomes
	Global Alliance for Vaccines and Immunisation	Financial accountability to donors; accountability for outcomes
	Roll Back Malaria	Process accountability to partners; accountability for outcomes
	The Global Fund to Fight AIDS, Tuberculosis and Malaria	Financial accountability; accountability for outcomes
Generation of information compliance verification	Marine Stewardship Council	Process accountability in rule setting; independence and professionalism in verification
	World Commission on Dams	Process accountability to stakeholders; independence
	Common Code for the Coffee Community	Financial accountability, independence and professionalism in compliance verification

Some of the partnerships engaged in regulating the activities of others or setting norms and standards also display few formal accountability mechanisms. The clear majority of them, however, focus on process accountability. Often, they have adopted very complex work processes that allow for or actively solicit the participation of a diverse group of external stakeholders. Implementation partnerships overwhelmingly emphasise a combination of financial accountability and accountability for outcomes. Usually, this includes very detailed and externally audited reports on the sources and allocation of funds. Most often, it also includes sophisticated analyses or tools to measure the outputs and/or impact of the partnership's activities.

Partnerships generating information or verifying compliance, finally, tend to stress independence and professionalism in their work. In the case of the WCD, the inclusion of external stakeholders is used to ensure professionalism and objectivity in the creation of knowledge. MSC and the 4C initiative have programmes to verify the compliance of companies with their standards. It is noticeable that both partnerships separate compliance verification from their other activities and underline the professionalism and independence of the verification process.

In the previous chapters, the argument was made that, seen from a normative standpoint, accountability requirements should depend on organisational function. This chapter clustered the partnerships into four categories, depending on their main function: advocacy and awareness raising, rule setting and regulation, implementation and information generation. It also examined which accountability arrangements were espoused by the partnerships. Great differences were found between individual partnerships, both in how strong their overall accountability was and in what aspects of accountability they emphasised. When grouped by function, it became apparent that – with the exception of the advocacy, awareness raising and coordination group – partnerships with similar functions tended to focus on similar elements of accountability.

These emerging, but imperfect, empirical patterns add two messages to the discussion here. Firstly, they confirm that the argument proposed here is rooted in broadly held normative convictions. While the demand that accountability arrangements should depend on organisational function has not previously been made explicit, the incipient practice of partnership accountability displays variations that are consistent with this claim. This demonstrates that the logic implicit in existing normative discourses is compelling and has an intuitive appeal.

Secondly, however, the overview underlines the need for developing explicit accountability standards for partnerships. The patterns linking partnership function to accountability focus are far from perfect. Moreover, even partnerships emphasising the same aspects of accountability can vary strongly in the strength and quality of accountability they create. To enable differentiated external assessments and to guide partnerships in their development of accountability systems, a consistent translation into practice of the normative principles introduced earlier is therefore necessary.

In Chapter 3, the implications of widely held normative assumptions for the concept of accountability were made explicit. Two steps remain to be taken. Firstly, it needs to be determined which accountability focus is adequate for which type of partnerships. Secondly, concrete criteria and standards need to be defined for each aspect of accountability. Both elements are the subject of debate in the next chapter.

5
Concrete Partnership Accountability Standards

In Chapter 3, it was argued that accountability arrangements should depend on organisational function. In Chapter 4, it was shown that depending on their main function, four different groups of partnerships can be distinguished. Which kind of accountability should each of these groups concentrate on? And which standards do partnerships need to live up to in order to create a sufficient level of accountability?

This chapter takes each functional group of partnerships in turn and establishes which accountability standards it, as well as other organisations with similar functions, should fulfil.

5.1 Advocacy and awareness-raising partnerships: Basic standards for all partnerships

The first group of partnerships identified above includes those whose main purpose is to promote certain issues through advocacy and awareness campaigns. Often, these partnerships also collect and disseminate relevant information and offer a platform for the coordination of the activities and programmes of members.

As indicated above, these partnerships only require basic forms of authority to operate. They are basic in the sense that they are a precondition for any partnership to work. Partnerships exercising functions other than advocacy and awareness raising demand other forms of authority in addition to this basic set. All partnerships should therefore comply with the accountability standards developed here for advocacy and awareness-raising partnerships, in addition to their more specific requirements. The common basis for all partnership types includes three forms of delegated or assumed authority.

Firstly, partnerships need the authority to exist and operate. Who grants this authority depends on the formal constitution of the partnership. Partnerships can be incorporated and have independent legal status. In this case, the country of incorporation determines the rules and conditions for registration. Most countries have stricter rules for organisations that are granted exemptions from taxes.[1] Partnerships that are not incorporated as independent entities derive their authority to operate from their founding members and the institution(s) hosting the partnership secretariat. Thus the host organisation, often in cooperation with the founding partners, can determine which rules and procedures apply to the partnership.

Secondly, partnerships need to acquire authority over the necessary operational resources. For their financial needs they can rely on a variety of sources. Some draw on an initial endowment to support their ongoing activities, others use contributions from members, individual or institutional donations or, in rare exceptions, revenues from commercial engagements. In addition, partnerships often rely on volunteer staff time, as well as office space and equipment contributed by partner organisations.

Thirdly, partnerships require the support of partner organisations or members. Even where they do not contribute financial or other resources, partners are important because they express support for the partnership and its mission through their membership. This kind of support is especially important for advocacy and awareness-raising partnerships. Their members usually have to explicitly endorse the partnership's goals by signing up to its mission statement. The more individuals and organisations do so, the more forcefully an advocacy and awareness-raising partnership can promote its cause. Supportive partner or member organisations are also more likely to contribute relevant information to the partnership, to take up knowledge and information disseminated by the partnership and to accept the partnership's proposals for coordinating member activities.

As depicted in Figure 5.1, the basic forms of authority required by partnerships – the licence to operate, authority over operational resources and support by partner organisations – give rise to three basic forms of accountability. All types of partnerships should at a minimum be subject to procedures and mechanisms to ensure accountability for complying with relevant rules and regulations, to create financial accountability and to generate accountability for working towards the partnership's mission.

Many NGOs are functionally similar to advocacy and awareness-raising partnerships. While NGOs do engage in many different kinds of activities,[2] advocacy and awareness raising as well as the collection and dissemination of information and the provision of platforms for coordination are often core components of NGO work.[3] While developing concrete accountability standards for advocacy and awareness-raising partnerships, we can therefore draw on broadly accepted and established governance and accountability standards for NGOs.

5.1.1 Accountability for complying with relevant rules and regulations

Rules are designed to regulate behaviour. They serve to prevent individuals and organisations from abusing their authority and violating the rights of others.

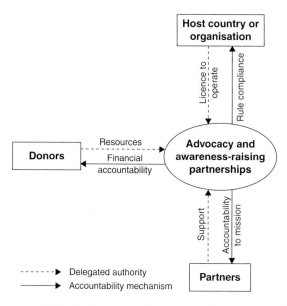

Figure 5.1 Accountability of advocacy and awareness-raising partnerships

Because societies, host institutions and partner organisations grant them the right to operate, partnerships have a duty to ensure they comply with the relevant rules and regulations. These rules are defined by various kinds of institutions and are often linked to different accountability mechanisms.

Firstly, partnerships exercise their activities in specific countries. Wherever they operate, local civil and criminal laws apply. Compliance with civil and criminal legislation is enforced by local court systems. Their efficiency in creating accountability for compliance with laws varies between countries. In well-governed societies with an established tradition of the rule of law, compliance tends to be relatively widespread, even though individual violations can go undetected or remain unpunished. In countries with weak legal systems and rampant corruption, by contrast, illegal behaviour may be common and legal accountability often remains low.

Secondly, many partnerships choose to incorporate or register themselves as independent legal entities. Incorporation and registration usually take place in individual countries and are linked to specific rules and regulations for the chosen form of organisation. It is most common for partnerships to seek registration as tax-exempt organisations or charities. Among the partnerships presented earlier, for example, GRI is incorporated as a Dutch foundation, ICANN is a non-profit, public benefit corporation in California, GAIN is a Swiss foundation, GVEP International is recognised as a charity in the UK, REEEP is an international NGO in Austria, the 4C initiative a Swiss association, the Global Fund a Swiss foundation and MSC an NGO recognised as a charity in the UK and with non-profit status in the US. While the exact stipulations vary from country to country, partnerships have to fulfil specific criteria to be recognised as a charity or tax-exempt organisation. This usually includes the requirement to promote an accepted public good, to adopt certain standards relating to the governance of the organisation and to submit regular reports on activities and finances.[4]

The authority to register organisations and to recognise them as charitable or tax-exempt can be vested in different institutions. In some countries, the tax authorities are responsible, in others it is a branch of the judiciary, a government ministry or an independent commission. Irrespective of their institutional identity, these authorities can hold partnerships accountable for complying with the rules linked to registration. Thus if they are not satisfied with the institutional design and purpose of the organisation at the outset, they have the authority to deny registration or recognition.[5] Moreover, these institutions usually demand regular and standardised reports on the partnership's financial situation and activities. If the partnership fails to comply with this stipulation or if its reports reveal an infraction of other rules, the organisation's charitable status can be revoked. Some charity commissions or registration offices can, in addition, supervise or audit registered organisations in greater detail. If properly applied, these options allow registration offices significant control over partnerships.

Thirdly, partnerships that are not registered as independent legal entities are usually hosted by other organisations. In most cases, one or several of the core partner organisations assume this role. EITI, for example, is hosted by the Norwegian Government, Stop TB and RBM by WHO and GAVI by UNICEF. It also occurs, though it seems to be less common, that external organisations are entrusted with this task. The Voluntary Principles, for instance, have a secretariat hosted jointly by the International Business Leaders Forum and Business for Social Responsibility. The host organisations, especially if they are large and established, have detailed rules governing their operations. Intergovernmental organisations such as UNICEF or WHO are usually free to determine what these rules are. Others, like the International Business Leaders Forum, are themselves registered as charities and must therefore comply with the applicable national rules. However the rules may be defined, a partnership that is hosted by a third organisation thereby becomes subject to its internal rules and regulations.

The mechanisms available for enforcing the internal rules of host organisations vary widely. As *ultima ratio*, host organisations can terminate their cooperation with the partnership. In addition, more established organisations often have internal disciplinary measures to enforce compliance with their rules. These can include complaints procedures, as well as internal evaluations, audits and disciplinary sanctions. The WHO, for example, has a system of internal controls under the auspices of its director general that includes the review, evaluation and monitoring of all its operations and activities.[6]

The institutional set-up of the host organisation is thus an important determinant for the effectiveness of its rules as an accountability mechanism for
partnerships. Another important factor is whether the partnership is hosted
by one or several institutions. With more than one host organisation, responsibilities are split and more difficult to assign and it is potentially unclear
which rules apply in which situation.

Finally, internal rules and processes can support and complement these
external and externally enforced rules. Partner organisations usually determine internal rules in the mutual agreement setting up a partnership, in
the partnership's statutes or by-laws, in the terms of reference for individual
partnership bodies or in a code of conduct for partnership staff. These documents usually define the partnership's mission, goals, targets and values; the
composition, function and responsibilities of the various partnership bodies;
work processes for taking decisions, accounting, reporting and auditing; as
well as rules governing conflicts of interest or other standards for the behaviour of staff members. The by-laws of the Global Fund, for instance, specify
the partnership's mission and goals, as well as the purpose, composition,
function, responsibilities and working methods for each partnership body. In
addition, the partnership has adopted an ethics and conflict of interest policy
that, for example, defines standards of conduct for contacts with members of
the Global Fund involved in funding decisions.[7]

Partnerships can take various steps to make internal rules effective as
accountability mechanisms. Firstly, the rules, processes and responsibilities
need to be explicit, clear and known to those concerned. This implies that
internal rules and regulations should be available in written form, should
cover the most important aspects of the organisation's work and should be
communicated adequately to all staff members and partners.

Broadly recognised governance requirements for NGOs also emphasise this
point. Thus, for example, the International Center for Not-for-Profit Law identifies as a generally accepted international practice that national laws require
non-profits to submit their governance arrangements with registration and
may require rules on conflicts of interest.[8] The Panel on Accountability and
Governance in the Voluntary Sector proposes that boards adopt 'a code of
ethical conduct and an effective monitoring and complaints procedure' as
well as 'a framework for internal regulations, including a constitution and
bylaws' (Panel on Accountability and Governance in the Voluntary Sector,
1999, p. 29). Similarly, the International Non Governmental Organisations'
Accountability Charter stresses that organisations should have 'written procedures covering the appointment, responsibilities and terms of members
of the governing body, and preventing and managing conflicts of interest'
(International Non Governmental Organisations, 2006, p. 4). The Handbook
on NGO Governance goes into greater detail and suggests that the basic
documents of an NGO should include the name of governing body(ies), their
relation to other organisational entities, the basic responsibilities and powers

of different bodies, the duties of individual board members, the minimum number of board members, membership rules, terms of office, number of meetings per year, the method of convening meetings, decision-making procedures and conflict of interest provisions.[9]

Secondly, partnerships need effective oversight to ensure compliance with internal rules. The main responsibility for exercising oversight lies with a formal board or a group of partner organisations exercising board functions. What enables boards or their functional equivalents to fulfil this task effectively? There is a broad literature addressing this question relating to non-profit organisations, which often draws on the more established literature on corporate governance. Researchers reviewing this literature have found it diverse and conclude that 'there is no consensus about an ideal way of governing nonprofit organizations' (Bradshaw et al., 1998, p. 11).

Despite this lack of consensus, most recommendations and codes cover a limited range of recurring themes.[10] They usually contain measures intended to ensure that board members know their responsibilities and the processes used to exercise oversight. This includes, for example, recommendations that board responsibilities should be clearly defined, standard practices should be described in board manuals and new board members should get an orientation or training. Another group of suggestions aims at creating the preconditions for board members to exercise effective oversight by focusing on their skills and the information available to them. This comprises proposals to select board members with an adequate mix of skills, to ensure they work actively to acquire information about the organisation's activities and that they receive adequate activity and financial reports. A final set of propositions is concerned with the willingness of board members to fulfil their duties. This includes, for example, recommendations to make attendance of board meetings mandatory, to ensure the independence of board members and to create regulations governing conflicts of interest.

Finally, partnership oversight bodies need to be in a position to apply sanctions or incentives to enforce compliance with internal rules. Partnership boards or their functional equivalents can often rely on the following sanctions: Most boards have the authority to accept and control financial and activity reports and to approve future work plans and budgets for the partnership. This means that they can require additional or changed reports and they can veto activities that seem to run counter to internal rules or the partnership's mission. Partnership boards also often hold the authority to appoint and dismiss the partnership's CEO or manager. Thus they can react to suspected misconduct by firing the responsible manager. Finally, core partner organisations, which are often represented on the board, can sanction insufficient compliance with internal rules by withdrawing their support from the partnership.[11]

The first pillar of accountability for partnerships is compliance with relevant rules and regulations. Partnerships have little influence over many important factors shaping the effectiveness of external rules and their enforcement systems. They have little bearing, for example, on the quality of national regulatory systems and the reliability of courts in host and operating countries. Likewise, partnerships can rarely influence the quality of governance arrangements of host organisations. But, as the preceding discussion has shown, partnerships can take a range of steps to increase their accountability for complying with relevant external and internal rules and regulations. These measures are the concrete accountability standards that all partnerships, including advocacy and awareness-raising partnerships, should comply with. They include the following elements.

5.1.1.1 Choose a well-governed host organisation

Partnerships usually determine where they want to operate based on their mission and goals, rather than accountability considerations. But they have greater flexibility in choosing their host organisation. For this decision, issues relating to accountability should be strongly considered.

If a partnership incorporates itself as an independent legal entity, for example, it should seek incorporation in a country that has well-defined legal and fiscal rules for private organisations. The host country should also have a well-established and well-functioning legal system and low levels of corruption. Among the case examples, all independently incorporated partnerships heed this advice. They are incorporated in the Netherlands, the US, Switzerland, the UK, Austria or Sweden.

Instead of incorporation, partnerships can also opt for a secretariat or coordinating mechanism hosted by a third organisation. Arrangements like this can create equally strong accountability for complying with relevant rules and regulations if a few principles are respected when choosing the host organisation. Firstly, partnerships should decide on one host organisation, rather than two or more. Where more than one organisation act as hosts, it becomes more difficult to assign responsibilities and determine whose rules apply under which circumstances. Secondly, the organisation chosen as host should itself be incorporated in a well-governed country and/or have a well-established and well-functioning internal governance system. Most of the partnerships contained in the case examples are hosted by intergovernmental organisations such as UNEP, WHO or UNICEF.

Partnerships can also be managed by largely informal coordination teams, usually made up of founding partner organisations. The Handwashing with Soap partnership, for instance, is organised by a coordination team from the World Bank and the Water and Sanitation Program, as well as through working groups involving various partner organisations. Arrangements like these diffuse accountability for complying with relevant rules. With various international partners cooperating, it is neither clear which national laws apply to the activities of the partnership, nor can a clear host institution be identified.

Instead of informal coordination teams, partnerships should therefore either incorporate or choose an organisation to host their secretariat.

5.1.1.2 Adopt clear internal rules

In addition to external rules and regulations defined by host countries or organisations, the founding members of a partnership can define internal rules and processes. Internal regulations are important to ensure that the partnership operates in the way and for the goals intended by the founding partners. Internal rules can also be an additional means for ensuring compliance with external norms.

To establish an effective set of internal rules, partnerships should conform to the following principles:

- Partnerships should state their internal rules, processes and governance arrangements clearly and in writing.
- Internal rules should cover the central elements of the partnership's governance, including all of the partnership's bodies, committees or working groups, detailing their authorities, roles and responsibilities; the processes for taking decisions and reporting on activities and finances; and the ethical standards and values guiding the partnership's work.
- Partnerships should also take measures to ensure that all those concerned, especially members of the oversight body, know the rules and their responsibilities. Basic steps to achieve this include making the rules and procedures easily available and providing new staff and board members with an introduction or training on the rules.

5.1.1.3 Create an effective oversight body with the ability to apply sanctions

In a final important step to create accountability for complying with relevant rules and regulations, partnerships should create an effective internal oversight body. This board or committee monitors whether or not the partnership and its staff comply with relevant rules. Its role is important because it creates awareness about the rules, can have a preventive effect and can uncover and rectify cases of non-compliance or abuse.

Partnerships can take a number of steps to establish an effective internal oversight mechanism:

- Partnerships must clearly assign the responsibility to exercise oversight to one of their bodies or committees, such as the partnership board. When defining these institutional arrangements, partnerships should make sure that the oversight function is clearly separated from management responsibilities. This increases the likelihood that the oversight body will act as an institutional check on partnership management.

• Partnerships should ensure that members of the oversight body clearly understand their responsibilities. Next to choosing committed individuals to serve on the oversight body, partnerships can support this by highlighting oversight duties during the recruitment process and providing members with written or oral instructions and good practice examples on implementation.

• Partnerships should also make sure that members of the oversight body are in a position to exercise their responsibilities properly. This requires on the one hand that board members have the necessary skills and expertise. Important skills include expert knowledge relating to the thematic focus of the partnership, a good understanding of the legal and regulatory environment for the partnership's work and experience in accounting, reporting and evaluation practices. Individual members do not have to cover all of these areas of expertise, but the oversight body as a whole should. On the other hand, this entails that other partnership bodies supply the oversight body with relevant, timely and accurate information. Oversight bodies should have the formal authority to receive and approve annual financial and activity reports and get regular updates from partnership management. Staff members reporting instances of malpractice can be another important source of information. Policies offering protection to so-called whistleblowers can further encourage a good information flow to the oversight body.

• Effective oversight also depends on the willingness of board members to exercise their responsibilities adequately. Ultimately, their willingness to act lies in the hands of individual board members, but partnerships can take some measures to support them. The first crucial step is to select individuals suited for this task to serve as members of the oversight body. Board members should have high personal integrity and be committed to their role. Members of the oversight body should also be independent, that is, they should not be closely related to management, and the board as a whole should either be neutral or represent the interests of all major stakeholders. Partnerships should also define a policy on conflicts of interest and implement it for their board members.

• Finally, partnerships should give their oversight bodies the authority to apply sanctions. With the means to enforce their conclusions, oversight bodies are both more likely to take their own task seriously and to be taken seriously by other members and bodies of the partnership. The authority and responsibility for accepting annual activity and financial reports is key in this regard. It ensures that the partnership provides members of the oversight body with relevant information and allows the oversight body to demand additional information. This right should be coupled with the authority to sanction management. One possible instrument is the power to accept future work plans and budgets. While this provides the oversight body with significant clout, it can also blur the boundaries between management and oversight and undermine the independence of the oversight body. Another, less problematic, possibility is to give the oversight body the authority to hire (potentially subject to a veto of the host organisation) and fire partnership managers.

5.1.2 Financial accountability

Institutions or individuals delegate the authority to manage and allocate resources to partnerships. Partnerships, in turn, delegate this authority to their managers and responsible staff members. These instances of delegation give rise to a legitimate demand for financial accountability. Since all partnerships need resources to be able to operate, basic financial accountability is expected of all of them.

In practice, accountability for finances involves various levels. Those who provide the partnership with resources have the most obvious claim for financial accountability. Most partnerships rely predominantly on contributions from partners or external donors. Some, like ICANN also demand fees for the services they provide. Advocacy and awareness-raising partnerships, however, do not usually offer goods or services. The following paragraphs therefore only consider the role of donors – be they partner organisations or external donors – as providers of funds.

Donors have various possibilities for ensuring that their funds are used in the way they intended. Most commonly, the contributions of large donors are linked to specific reporting requirements. They determine when partnerships need to report on their activities and financial decisions. This can range from quarterly or annual to project-related reports. In addition, donors often prescribe the format to be used for reporting. For partnerships depending on various donors all working with different formats, this can create a significant workload and costs.

Donors can also tie their contributions to specific activities or areas. MSC, for example, reports that of the total donations of £2,283,894 it received in 2006, £740,148 were restricted in their use (Marine Stewardship Council, 2006, p. 21). Similarly, REEEP received €876,533 in general donations in the financial year 2005–6, and €5,177,228 in donations related to specific projects (Renewable Energy and Energy Efficiency Partnership, 2006, p. 39). Tied contributions allow donors to influence relatively directly how their money is spent. At the same time, however, they restrict the flexibility of the recipient organisation and can thus undermine its ability to react to unforeseen circumstances and allocate resources in the most efficient way.[12]

While most of the partnerships surveyed here rely mainly on large institutional donors, some also seek contributions from individuals. Thus, for example, the Stop TB partnership, the Global Fund and MSC all solicit individual donations. Small-scale individual donors cannot negotiate the same conditions to their contributions as large donors. Like them, however, they can refuse to donate or discontinue their support. To strengthen the trust of individual donors, these partnerships are therefore likely to create transparency relating to their use of resources. Sometimes, they even allow individual donors to select particular activities they want to invest in.

Another possible donor model that partnerships could rely on is that of a foundation or trust. In this model, donors provide the partnership with a large initial endowment which finances ongoing operations. While none of the case examples analysed here can draw on such an endowment, this would have important implications for the partnership's financial accountability. The main difference to other donor-based financial models is that donors provide all funds upfront. This means that they cannot use the threat to discontinue funding as a sanction. Even more than agreements with large regular donors, the terms connected to an endowment are likely to define very specifically what activities can be supported with the funds and which procedures the partnership needs to comply with when taking decisions.

On a second level, partnerships are held accountable for finances by their host states or other host organisations. Two different rationales can be at work here. In one set of cases, the host organisation also plays the role of a donor. This is the case, for example, when states recognise partnerships as charities or tax-exempt institutions. As discussed above, this status usually restricts the range of permissible activities and is linked to special reporting requirements.

In another set of cases, host organisations do not act as donors. Instead, they use their authority to grant partnerships the 'licence to operate' and include rules on financial accounting and reporting as part of their overall rules and regulations. The Global Partnership to Stop TB, for example, is hosted by WHO. As part of its role as a host, WHO is responsible for financial administration. While the coordinating board takes decisions with financial implications, WHO can veto those on administrative grounds.

On a third level, partnerships further delegate the authority over resources internally. Thus, in a typical set-up such as the one chosen by GAIN, donors provide the partnership with resources. Internally, the partnership board bears fiduciary responsibility. It approves the partnership's annual work plan and budget, receives and approves activity and financial reports and appoints the executive director of the secretariat. The executive director appoints further staff members and delegates operational authority to allocate and account for financial resources to them. Internal rules and procedures on the handling, accounting and reporting of finances, linked to internal oversight mechanisms, can help to ensure that financial accountability is created at this level as well.

Financial accountability, then, is created at various levels. As with accountability for complying with relevant rules and regulations, partnerships cannot freely determine all relevant parameters at all of these levels. In order to ensure an adequate level of financial accountability, advocacy and awareness-raising partnerships, as well as partnerships fulfilling other functions, should adopt the following basic accountability standards relating to finances.

5.1.2.1 Adopt a system of internal financial controls

Internal controls are the first step towards establishing financial accountability. They include policies and processes designed to manage the risk of fraud and misappropriation. They serve to ensure that resources are used as intended and that they are accounted for properly.

A standard set of basic internal control measures are generally accepted as good practice for any kind of organisation handling resources. For NGOs, these basic standards have been articulated, for example, by the Charity Commission for England and Wales, by Mango, a non-profit organisation working to improve the financial management of NGOs, and by the Office of New York's Attorney General.[13] The recommendations issued by these as well as other institutions contain broadly similar components and are subject to little controversy.

Advocacy and awareness-raising partnerships, as well as other types of partnerships, should adopt the key elements of these standards. They include the following measures:

- Partnerships should have a clear internal delegation of responsibilities relating to resources. Ideally in a written format, the authorities to receive payments, authorise expenditures, maintain accounts, oversee accounting processes and prepare and approve budgets should be clearly assigned to individual staff or board members. It is also important to ensure that the assigned individuals have the necessary skills and qualifications to exercise their respective responsibilities.
- When assigning the various responsibilities, partnerships should ensure that key duties are separated and a system of checks and balances is established. Thus, for example, a single individual should not be responsible at the same time for processing complete transactions and recording them. Similarly, accounts should not be controlled by the person responsible for recording transactions in the first place. Moreover, significant expenditures should require the approval and signatures of more than one individual.
- To enable oversight and control over their activities, partnerships should operate on the basis of budgets and financial plans. Regular reconciliations between the planned budget and actual incomes and expenditures as well as reconciliations between partnership records and actual cash, property and bank deposits should be carried out.
- Finally, partnerships should adopt controls for cash and other assets. Cash and valuables should, for example, be kept in a safe place to which general access is restricted. Partnerships should keep a register of assets with

individual reference numbers for objects. Receipts should be issued for money received and expenditures should be supported by documentation. In addition, partnerships should reduce cash transactions to a minimum and adopt policies to safeguard investments and fixed assets.

5.1.2.2 Adopt accounting and reporting policies complying with donor demands and generating reliable, relevant, comparable and understandable information

Adequate accounting and reporting policies are a further element of a system of internal financial controls. They are the cornerstones of financial accountability to internal as well as external principals.

A partnership's accounting system tracks incomes, expenditures and changes in assets. It enables those responsible to uncover instances of fraud and misappropriation. Reports are based on the data generated by the accounting system. They collect and present relevant information in a systematic manner. They usually cover not only the organisation's finances but also its activities and achievements. Reports thus serve to assess the financial situation of a partnership. They allow analysing whether spending decisions and activities conform to the partnership's policies and relevant external rules. Importantly, they also help establish what the partnership has achieved and how efficiently it works.

Which criteria, though, do accounting and reporting policies need to comply with to create a true and fair view of an organisation? There is a general consensus that the generated information must be relevant, reliable, comparable and understandable. These criteria were defined by the International Accounting Standards Board (IASB).[14] The IASB is an independent, private organisation based in London, leading efforts to create internationally recognised accounting and reporting standards. It issues the International Financial Reporting Standards (IFRS). These standards are not automatically binding but are adopted by an increasing number of countries. Thus, for example, the European Union endorses many IFRSs and incorporates them into European law.

The standards defined by IASB mainly apply to corporations and there is no equivalent body setting standards for NGOs that could be applied to advocacy and awareness-raising partnerships.[15] In the absence of international standards specifically designed for NGOs, many see the UK Charity Commission's Statement of Recommended Practice (SORP) on Accounting and Reporting for Charities as an important reference document. The statement reflects the same general principles of relevance, reliability, comparability and understandability (Charity Commission for England and Wales, 2005, p. 10).

These general principles are relatively abstract. How can they be translated into practice? Answering this question requires consideration for a broad array of specific and often complex issues. Without going into too much detail, the following paragraphs discuss which specific standards are emerging for the accounting practices of non-profit organisations. They then discuss requirements for reports to internal governing bodies, donors and public authorities.

Relevant and broadly accepted criteria for the accounting practices of non-profit organisations, which can be applied to advocacy and awareness-raising partnerships, have been defined in several documents. Firstly, as already mentioned, the UK Charity Commission's SORP on Accounting and Reporting for Charities is a widely used reference document. It often refers to principles laid down by the UK Financial Reporting Council and its Accounting Standards Board. This body defines Statements of Standard Accounting Practice (SSAPs) and Financial Reporting Standards (FRSs), most of which also apply to NGOs or charities.[16] Secondly, due to the large number of non-profit organisations registered in or financed by the US, the Generally Accepted Accounting Practices (GAAP) in force there also enjoys wide recognition. The main institution defining GAAP for charities in the US is the Financial Accounting Standards Board (FASB). Its statements 93, 116, 117, 124 and 136 set down important accounting practices.[17]

These documents contain an emerging consensus on accounting rules that are specific to non-profit organisations and go beyond or deviate from generic good accounting practices:

- Non-profit organisations should distinguish their incomes and assets depending on whether or not their use has been restricted by donors. They should also include certain in-kind contributions of services as incomes.[18]
- Non-profits should account separately for expenses related to their mission or function and those amounting to overhead costs.[19]
- Non-profit organisations should also, like companies, report the gains and losses made on assets and investments. In doing so, they should report assets and investments at their fair value and take account of depreciation.[20]

Detailed and broadly accepted accounting standards, then, have been defined for charitable organisations and NGOs. Since advocacy and awareness-raising partnerships are functionally similar to non-profit organisations, they should comply with these accounting standards.

Based on the information generated through the accounting system, partnerships should also prepare regular financial and activity reports. The authority over financial resources allowing a partnership to cover its operational costs is often delegated by various parties. Partnerships should therefore issue reports at different levels, including reports to internal supervisory bodies, reports to donors and reports to host organisations or fiscal authorities. To date, only few broadly accepted standards for those reports have emerged. The issue is further complicated by the fact that requirements differ depending on the addressees and the purposes pursued by individual reports.

Firstly, partnerships should prepare internal reports for their governing bodies, such as partnership boards or meetings of core partners. As already discussed, it is broadly accepted as a standard of good governance for non-profit organisations that boards or their functional equivalents bear fiduciary responsibility. Boards usually take strategic decisions but delegate the task of managing and allocating resources to the organisations' management and staff. They exercise control by approving work-plans and budgets and by receiving regular reports. There are no commonly accepted standards defining criteria for these internal reports. Beyond the basic requisite that reports should be accurate and understandable, however, the purpose of board reports dictates some necessary conditions:

- Internal reports should be frequent and be made available regularly before the supervisory body convenes.
- Partnership boards or equivalent bodies exercise control through their approval of work-plans and budgets. Internal reports should therefore provide the necessary information to allow for an accurate comparison between those documents and the partnership's actual activities, incomes and expenditures.
- Internal reports should also support the supervisory body in its strategic planning role. To this aim, they should include information on projected future financial developments, the financial implications of key decisions and the relative effectiveness and efficiency of individual programmes and activities.

Secondly, partnerships should submit regular reports to their donors. The partnerships described in the case examples rely mainly on the financial and other contributions of donors to cover their operational expenses. The reports should enable donors to assess whether the partnership has fulfilled potential conditions attached to the contributions. Moreover, they should allow donors to establish whether or not the resources were used, and were used efficiently, to achieve the intended purposes. Which format these reports take and whether commonly accepted standards for their content exist depends on the type of donor involved.

States represent one important kind of donor. Governments can sponsor partnerships as well as other organisations directly. In terms of creating standard reporting requirements, however, their role as indirect donors or supporters is more important. As discussed earlier, many partnerships are incorporated as independent legal entities and enjoy the status of tax-exempt charities or non-profit organisations. As such, they face special reporting requirements defined by state authorities. Because of their widespread application, these requirements often turn into more generally used parameters for external reporting. This is especially the case where other donors demand similar information or where the official reports are openly accessible and are used as a basis for assessing non-profit organisations.

Due to the large number of charities registered there, the annual reports requested by the Internal Revenue Service (IRS) of the US Department of the Treasury are seen as an important model for official reports.[21] In the US, all registered charities with annual revenues exceeding US$25,000 must file a completed IRS form 990 every year.[22] On this form, non-profits have to report their revenues, expenses (differentiating between programme expenses, administrative costs, fund-raising expenses and payments to affiliates) and changes in their net assets. Moreover, they have to provide balance sheets, details on functional expenses, lists of key current and former staff members, directors and trustees and discuss their activities and achievements. Following a regulation of 1999, non-profits have to make the three most recent IRS filings available to anyone interested upon request.[23] With IRS data publicly available, it has become an important source of information for NGO assessments. GuideStar, for example, is an organisation collecting information on non-profit organisations and rating their accountability. It relies heavily on data derived from IRS form 990.[24]

The reporting requirements in other important host states for non-profit organisations including partnerships tend to be broadly similar. In the UK, charities with an annual income exceeding £10,000 must file an annual return with the Charity Commission.[25] What information charities need to include depends on their size. With revenues below £250,000, they need to list their total incomes and expenditures, the contact details of trustees and a summary of their activities. Above £250,000, charities need to include further details on fund-raising, benefits for trustees, properties, relations to connected trading companies and instances of misappropriation. If revenues exceed £1 million, charities have to include a 'summary information return', which differentiates income by sources and contains additional information on aims, strategy, activities and achievements, as well as programme expenditures, governance and future plans. Through the Charity Commission's website, all filed reports are publicly accessible and they are used by agencies like GuideStar UK to evaluate organisations.[26]

For partnerships incorporated as tax-exempt institutions or charities, then, official annual returns are an important element of financial accountability. Filing these reports is not optional. To fulfil their reporting duty adequately, partnerships should:

- Incorporate important reporting parameters into their accounting system from the outset. If the official annual return requires, for example, to distinguish between different types of incomes and expenditures, only an accounting system that mirrors these criteria can deliver the necessary information.

- Complete all required sections of the report and verify the accuracy of the data.
- Prepare and file reports in a timely manner.
- Make copies of the report available to interested parties, preferably by posting it on the Internet.

Institutional and individual contributors are another important kind of donor. Among the partnerships surveyed for this book, most rely on governments, multilateral institutions, corporations and foundations as their main donors.

Large donors tend to attach conditions, including specific reporting requirements, to their contributions. Problems can arise when partnerships depend on a range of large donors, each imposing different reporting conditions. To reduce the resulting administrative burden, partnerships can try to negotiate with donors to achieve a harmonisation of reporting requirements. This could, for example, involve a convergence of standards around the criteria for official annual returns.[27]

Some partnerships, such as Stop TB for example, also solicit individual contributions. In this case, partnerships need to be more proactive for providing adequate reports to donors. Small individual donors may not be powerful enough to set their own reporting rules, but they do have a right to receive adequate information on how their funds are spent. In addition, they can sanction organisations violating this right by refusing future support. Partnerships should therefore publish regular reports for small donors of their own accord.

The most relevant and broadly accepted existing standards for public annual reports of advocacy and awareness-raising partnerships are again those contained in the UK Charity Commission's SORP on Accounting and Reporting by Charities.[28] According to this document, an annual report should contain reference and administrative details for the charity, its trustees and advisors; information on the organisation's structure, governance and management; a statement of its objectives and activities; an analysis of its achievements and performance; a financial review; as well as an explanation of future plans (Charity Commission for England and Wales, 2005, pp. 7–9). For the summarised financial statements, the commission specifies that they should contain information on both financial activities and the balance sheet, that they ought to be consistent with statutory accounts and that they should not be misleading either through omission or inappropriate amalgamation.

Regarding their reports to direct donors, advocacy and awareness-raising partnerships should therefore comply with the following principles:

- Comply with the reporting requirements set by large donors or negotiate those terms.

- Partnerships relying on or intending to reach small individual donors should in addition publish an annual report containing accurate and not misleading summary financial information and describing the organisation's activities and achievements.

Thirdly and finally, partnerships must report to their host organisations. In this case, the demand for financial accountability is not based on financial support. Rather, it is part of the general rules and regulations that host organisations can attach to the licence to operate. Partnerships can, for example, be incorporated as independent legal entities without receiving indirect state support through tax exemption. The local fiscal authorities will nevertheless demand detailed annual financial reports to determine the organisation's tax burden and to verify its compliance with other rules. Similarly, partnerships hosted by a third organisation usually have to report regularly on their activities and finances. Again, the reports serve to establish whether the partnership complies with internal rules and regulations. Moreover, the reports deliver necessary information to host organisations enabling them to fulfil their reporting duties.

To strengthen their financial accountability through adequate reporting to host organisations, partnerships should ensure they follow relevant rules and regulations as described in section 5.1.1.

5.1.2.3 Conduct independent audits for large partnerships

Financial audits work to control an organisation's accounting and reporting practices.[29] They involve internal or external professionals assessing the fairness of financial statements and their compliance with GAAP or the IFRS. Auditors do not usually verify an organisation's accounts in all their detail. Instead, they most often use a sampling technique to test accounting practices.

Independent, external financial audits provide the strongest assurance that financial statements are fair. External auditors have to fulfil strict professional qualification criteria.[30] Commissioning an external audit can therefore incur significant costs.[31] Regulations determining audit requirements often differ depending on the kind of organisation concerned. Thus it is common that publicly traded companies are generally required to have independent audits. Private companies below a certain financial turnover threshold are usually exempt from audit requirements.[32] For NGOs and non-profit organisations, audit regulations vary strongly even among leading Western countries. Over recent years, however, a trend has been emerging to make audits obligatory for large NGOs exceeding specified financial thresholds.[33]

In the UK, for example, charities whose gross income exceeds £500,000 or charities with a gross income over £100,000 and assets exceeding £2.8 million must commission an independent audit.[34] In the US, organisations receiving federal or state grants of US$500,000 or more must have an independent audit.[35] So far, non-profits that do not rely on major government grants are not subject to an audit requirement. An important recent panel, though, was encouraged by leaders of the US Senate Finance Committee to propose reforms to strengthen the governance and accountability of the non-profit sector. In its final report, the panel recommends the introduction of external audits for non-profit organisations with total annual revenues exceeding US$1 million.[36]

The practice of demanding obligatory audits has not been consistently implemented in other countries. Despite this, evaluation agencies focusing on NGOs have adopted the standard. The Standards for Charitable Accountability of the BBB Wise Giving Alliance, for example, states that organisations with an annual gross income of over US$250,000 should have an external audit (BBB Wise Giving Alliance, 2003, §11). Moreover, many larger NGOs recognise their obligation to provide audited financial statements. In their Accountability Charter, for example, a range of international NGOs commit to attaching audit results to the financial data they present in annual reports (International Non Governmental Organisations, 2006, p. 4).[37]

Since there is an emerging consensus that non-profit organisations with substantial revenues should undergo independent audits, the same standard should apply to advocacy and awareness raising as well as other partnerships. Defining a financial threshold after which the standard applies is necessarily somewhat arbitrary. For NGOs, the revenue threshold is often between €500,000 and 1 million. For private companies, though, audit exceptions can apply up to a turnover of €8.8 million. The threshold chosen here presents a relatively conservative limit because the consensus on audit requirements is still emerging and not yet firmly established. Therefore, and due to the high costs of audits, only partnerships with annual budgets exceeding €5 million should be subject to independent, external audits to strengthen financial accountability.

To be effective, audits have to fulfil certain principles. The most basic requirement is that only professional and independent auditors should conduct audits. As for accounting, other, more detailed auditing standards have been defined by various professional and regulatory bodies. At the international level, a crucial rule-setting institution is the International Federation of Accountants (IFAC) and its International Auditing and Assurance Standards Board (IAASB). It sets the International Standards on Auditing (ISAs). ISA 200, for example, defines the 'objective and general principles governing an audit of financial statements' and applies to audits in all sectors.[38] It requires auditors to comply with the IFAC Code of Ethics for Professional Accountants (International Federation of Accountants' Ethics Committee, 2005), to adopt an attitude of professional scepticism, to reduce audit risk, to obtain reasonable assurance that financial statements are free from material misstatements and to determine whether the financial reporting framework adopted by the organisation under scrutiny is acceptable (International Federation of Accountants, 2007, pp. 213–29).[39] Audits on the financial statements of partnerships should comply with relevant international and national auditing standards.

In summary, partnerships should observe the following principles relating to audits:

- Partnerships with annual budgets exceeding €5 million should submit their financial statements to professional, independent audits.
- The audits should comply with applicable ISAs, as well as relevant additional national regulations.
- Audit results should be published together with the audited financial statements.

5.1.3 Accountability for working towards the partnership's mission

Finally, advocacy and awareness-raising partnerships need the general support of partners or members to be able to work effectively. 'General support' is a more diffuse notion than either the granting of a licence to operate or the delegation of authority over operational resources. It is therefore also less immediately clear which kind of accountability demand follows from the granting of support.

The lack of clarity stems from two factors. Firstly, general support can manifest itself in different ways depending on the orientation of the partnership. Partnerships like PCFV focus mainly on advocacy campaigns to influence important decision makers. Support in this case means that partners subscribe to this call and grant the partnership the authority to speak on their behalf when advancing its claims. Partnerships like REEEP aim to serve as information hubs. Here, active support implies that partners supply their information to the partnership and use and integrate the information offered by the partnership in their work. Advocacy and awareness-raising partnerships can also emphasise their role as coordinators, as does, for example, RBM. In that case, support entails that partners accept the authority of RBM to propose modalities for coordination.

Secondly, partner organisations can have very different motives for joining or supporting partnerships. Businesses, for example, are often interested in showing good corporate citizenship, increasing their reputation or improving their investment markets. Governments and intergovernmental organisations may be driven by a desire to mobilise additional resources, by the urge to demonstrate leadership or by the wish to develop more effective approaches to problem solving. NGOs, in turn, can in addition be motivated by the desire to gain influence over key decisions.[40] These different motives give rise to different expectations of what partnerships should deliver. Partner organisations will therefore hold a partnership to account by either continuing or withdrawing their support depending on different performance criteria.

Despite these variations, support is in all cases closely linked to partnership mission. As described above, the partnership's mission strongly influences what support entails in practice. Moreover, the partnership's mission usually serves as a common denominator for all partner organisations. These organisations are presumably only willing to join a particular partnership with its specific mission if they believe that this meets their expectations. Both, a company trying to enhance its reputation and a government seeking new ways to address public policy problems, for example, can only achieve their objectives if the partnership works successfully towards its own goals.

In exchange for the general support of their partners and members, advocacy and awareness-raising partnerships should therefore be accountable for working towards achieving their mission. To create this kind of accountability, partnerships should follow some basic standards in their work:

5.1.3.1 Define a clear mission

An obvious and necessary precondition for making partnerships accountable to their mission is to have a clearly defined and understood mission. Writing down a clear and meaningful mission statement is not always an easy task. The challenge is to define a goal and vision that is broad and flexible enough to integrate various actors with potentially very different interests and to allow the partnership to adapt flexibly to changing circumstances. At the same time, however, the mission statement should be specific enough to have meaning for partners and supporters and to be able to guide strategic planning and programming.

The Stop TB partnership provides a good example for the required level of specificity of mission statements. The partnership pursues the strategic goal of eliminating tuberculosis as a public health problem and achieving a world free of TB. In this quest, it defines its mission as follows:

> To ensure that every TB patient has access to effective diagnosis, treatment and cure; To stop the transmission of TB; To reduce the inequitable social and economic toll of TB; To develop and implement new preventive, diagnostic and therapeutic tools and strategies to stop TB.
> (http://www.stoptb.org/stop_tb_initiative/#vmg,
> last accessed 27 August 2009)

To ensure their mission is clear, meaningful and relevant, partnerships should adhere to the following principles:[41]

- Partnerships should adopt mission statements that are specific enough to provide guidance for their strategic planning and the development of programmes and activities.

- Mission statements should be published in a prominent position in publications and reference documents and should be known to the partnerships' key stakeholders.
- To increase the mission statement's practical relevance and ensure that it is and continues to be backed by partner organisations, partnerships should periodically discuss and review their missions.

5.1.3.2 Orient partnership activities along the mission

Once a partnership has created a clear and meaningful mission statement, the next challenge is to ensure its relevance to the partnership's activities. Accountability to mission implies that the mission statement plays a central role in the planning and work of a partnership. This can be achieved if the following principles are respected:

- Partnerships should not conduct any major activities that are unrelated to their mission. Instead, all important elements of their work programmes should promote their mission.
- Mission statements should guide the strategic planning of partnerships. Using a results chain or logical framework approach,[42] partnerships should identify which courses of action are likely to contribute to achieving their mission and select them accordingly.
- To make the rationale behind their work programmes transparent, partnerships should also structure their activity reports around their mission. These reports should contain an explanation of how the partnership's main efforts are intended to contribute to the mission. Moreover, activity reports should portray the partnership's achievements, the obstacles it encountered and the consequences it drew from past experiences.

5.1.3.3 Employ resources efficiently in pursuit of the mission

Finally, an organisation intent on creating accountability for working towards its mission needs to demonstrate that it uses its resources efficiently in pursuing its goals. Measuring efficiency in organisations addressing public policy problems is notoriously difficult, because they have no clearly defined bottom line and address complex issues.[43]

Most efforts to evaluate the efficiency of public policy programmes rely on benchmarks. Benchmarking is a technique originally developed by companies. It involves identifying the best competitor and using that organisation's performance as a yardstick.[44] Benchmarking can be a useful tool for assessing the relative efficiency of partnerships or other organisations working in the same field. It could be used, for example, to compare the efficiency of the Global Fund, RBM and other health providers in fighting malaria. Benchmarking, however, cannot usually serve to establish detailed efficiency criteria that would be applicable to organisations working in different fields.

The efficiency standards defined here for advocacy and awareness-raising partnerships therefore have to remain very general. They include the following basic principles and criteria:

- Partnerships should define priorities for the allocation of scarce resources depending on how efficiently the various possible activities contribute to the achievement of the partnership's mission.[45] To create a reliable basis for these decisions, partnership boards or management should encourage evaluations of ongoing programmes.
- Partnerships should control their costs related to administration and fund-raising and ensure that the clear majority of their resources is spent on programme activities. Following a broadly accepted benchmark for NGOs, partnerships should at the very least allocate 65 per cent of their total funds to activities designed to directly contribute to mission achievement.[46]

5.1.4 Summary of standards

Table 5.1 contains a summary of relevant accountability standards for advocacy and awareness-raising partnerships.

Table 5.1 Accountability standards for advocacy and awareness-raising partnerships

Accountability principles	Accountability standards	Practical steps
Compliance with rules and regulations	Choose a well-governed host organisation	Incorporate as an independent legal entity in a country with well-defined rules for private organisations and a well-established and functioning legal system
		Or choose one organisation to host the partnership, which is itself well governed
	Adopt clear internal rules	Clearly define internal rules, processes and governance arrangements
		Rules cover roles and responsibilities of partnership bodies, decision-making procedures, reporting requirements and ethical standards
		Ensure that internal rules are known to all those concerned, especially the oversight body

(Continued)

122

Table 5.1 Continued

Accountability principles	Accountability standards	Practical steps
	Create an effective oversight body with the ability to apply sanctions	Clearly assign responsibility for oversight to one body or committee and separate it from management responsibility
		Ensure members of the oversight body understand their responsibilities by choosing committed individuals, emphasising responsibilities during recruitment and offering information
		Ensure that members of the oversight body have the necessary skills and expertise and are adequately supplied with information, including through whistle-blower protection
		Select independent individuals with strong personal integrity to serve on the oversight body and adopt a conflict of interest policy
		Enable members of the oversight body to apply sanctions and incentives
Financial accountability	Adopt a system of internal financial controls	Clearly delegate internal responsibilities for resources
		Separate key duties and install a system of checks and balances
		Operate on the basis of budgets and financial plans
		Adopt controls for cash and other assets
	Adopt accounting policies generating reliable, relevant, comparable and understandable information	Distinguish incomes and assets depending on whether or not their use has been restricted by donors
		Account separately for expenses related to mission/function and overhead costs
		Report gains and losses made on assets and investments, using their fair value and accounting for depreciation

123

Table 5.1 Continued

Accountability principles	Accountability standards	Practical steps
	Adopt reporting practices generating reliable, relevant, comparable and understandable information and complying with donor demands	Internal reports should be available before board meetings, enable a comparison between budgets, work-plans and actual activities and enable strategic planning
		Incorporate reporting requirements in the accounting system, file complete and accurate returns on time and make them publicly available on request
		Reports to donors should comply with the conditions set by large donors; partnerships relying on small, individual donors should publish annual reports including a financial review and information on activities and achievements
	Conduct independent audits for large partnerships	Partnerships with annual budgets exceeding €5 million should undergo professional, independent audits
		Audits should comply with relevant ISAs and national regulations
		Audit results should be published alongside financial statements
Accountability for working towards the partnership's mission	Define a clear mission	Mission statements should be specific enough to guide strategic planning and programming
		Publish mission statements prominently and ensure it is understood by stakeholders
		Periodically discuss and review mission statements
	Orient activities along the mission	Do not conduct any major activities unrelated to partnership mission
		Use mission statements as a guide to strategic planning
		Structure activity reports around the mission
	Employ resources efficiently in pursuit of the mission	Define priorities based on mission-related efficiency and evaluate ongoing programmes
		Control overhead costs and ensure they do not exceed 35 per cent of total revenues

5.2   Standards for rule setting and regulation partnerships

A second group of partnerships comprises those engaged in defining new rules, standards or regulations for specific policy areas or groups of organisations. GRI, for example, develops standards and guidelines for sustainability reporting, ICANN regulates important aspects of the Internet, WCD has created criteria for decisions relating to the building of large dams, MSC developed rules for sustainable fisheries, EITI has proposed standards on transparency in the extractive industries and the Voluntary Principles created guidelines for the security arrangements of companies.

In all those cases, compliance with the proposed rules or regulations is ultimately voluntary. The partnerships chosen as case examples here all operate at the international level. Thus they work outside the realm of nation states and their rule-making and rule-enforcement systems. The proposed norms do also not enjoy the status of international law. To be considered as binding under international law, governments either have to back norms through explicit agreement or through consistent customary practice.[47] The partnerships analysed here, however, usually only include a very limited number of governments, their rules have not (yet) become common state practice and do often not address states but companies or other organisations.[48]

Yet the rules and regulations defined by partnerships are not always and not necessarily non-binding. Partnerships can, for example, involve private actors in the decision-making processes of official norm-setting institutions, such as national parliaments or international conventions. The results of the work of these partnerships are immediately incorporated into national or international law and are therefore binding. In addition, even voluntary rules set by partnerships can assume a de facto binding character when the affected stakeholders depend strongly on the partnership.

The rules and regulations defined by partnerships are thus very often, but not necessarily, non-binding. What does this imply for the authority delegated to or assumed by rule-setting partnerships? As discussed in detail in section 3.2.3, especially organisations operating at the inter- or transnational level often lack prior authorisation. Instead, they rely on ex-post or even hypothetical delegation to legitimise their activities. Most of the rule-setting partnerships under scrutiny here operate in the hope that as many relevant actors as possible will comply voluntarily with the proposed rules and thus accept them as binding for themselves. In order to achieve this kind of ex-post authorisation, rule-setting partnerships should therefore adopt the same accountability arrangements as if they had the authority to determine binding rules.

What, then, are the accountability principles linked to the authority to set binding rules? Building on respect for the principle of autonomy, the authority to determine rules requires democratic accountability. Rule-setting partnerships should therefore focus on creating democratic accountability to

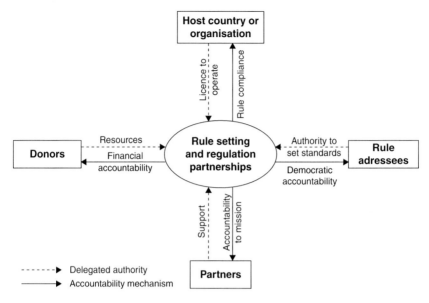

Figure 5.2   Accountability of rule setting and regulation partnerships

those delegating the authority to establish rules. This accountability focus, in addition to the basic accountability standards defined in the previous section, is depicted in Figure 5.2.

5.2.1 Applying democratic accountability standards to rule-setting partnerships

Because of their concentration on developing new rules and regulations for certain areas or groups of actors, rule-setting partnerships should espouse democratic accountability mechanisms. The traditional field for the application of democratic accountability is the public sector. Rule-setting partnerships assume functions resembling most closely those of the legislative. Parliaments are typically held accountable by a combination of elections, supplementary mechanisms to involve citizens, rules and a system of checks and balances.

Partnerships operate in a very different institutional environment than traditional legislative bodies. Therefore, the mechanisms used to create legislative accountability should not be applied directly to rule-setting partnerships. Rather, legislative accountability mechanisms fulfil various purposes. The accountability arrangements that rule-setting partnerships should adopt do not necessarily have to take the exact same form, but they must achieve the same effects as parliamentary accountability mechanisms.

Legislative accountability pursues two major aims: to give those affected by legislation a say in the decision-making process and to avoid the abuse of legislative authority. Individual democratic polities emphasise different elements, but tend to use a common set of mechanisms to achieve these ends.

To achieve the inclusion of citizens in the legislative process, most democratic countries rely on regular parliamentary elections, as well as elements of direct democracy. Supplementary accountability mechanisms strengthen the provision of information to citizens, for example through transparent governance processes, the work of the media and the opposition. Another set of supplementary tools provides citizens with additional means to articulate their interests. They include official consultation processes, opinion polls, interpretations of the 'public mood' created by the media, as well as interest groups, protests, lobby activities, petitions and the use of public complaints procedures.

In order to avoid the abuse of legislative authority, democracies typically rely on rules and systems of checks and balances. Constitutional rules, for instance, safeguard fundamental rights and delimit the authority of parliaments. Procedural rules, moreover, determine the formalities and ensure that decisions are taken in a transparent manner. Through checks and balances, both the executive and the judiciary have certain possibilities to control legislative actions. This puts them in a position to prevent or counter potential abuses of legislative authority.

Fulfilling their responsibility to be democratically accountable, rule-setting partnerships should adopt accountability arrangements that are functionally equivalent to legislative accountability. In other words, they should adopt accountability mechanisms that allow for the effective participation of those affected by the rules and that prevent an abuse of the partnership's authority.

5.2.2   Accountability through participation

Giving those affected an influence over decision-making processes has long been accepted as a hallmark of democracy. More recently, the principle has also been recognised as important for many organisations working at the trans- or international level, especially those focusing on development.[49] For organisations defining rules, guidelines or standards, two sets of international standards exist. The International Organization for Standardization (ISO), which is very influential since its standards are often translated into binding rules, has published a guide outlining procedures and participation rules for standard-setting bodies.[50] Building on this document, but taking the criteria much further, the International Social and Environmental Accreditation and Labelling Alliance (ISEAL) has produced a code of good practice for organisations setting social and environmental standards.[51]

For international organisations and NGOs not involved in setting rules and regulations, similar standards for the inclusion of affected stakeholders have not been defined. Since the practice enjoys great popularity, however, numerous handbooks, 'how-to'-guides and studies on the effectiveness of individual techniques have been published.[52]

In the following paragraphs, democratic accountability standards for rule-setting partnerships are proposed. They are either derived from general democratic principles, the ISO and ISEAL codes or draw on broadly accepted practices of participation. The standards cover two main areas: formal avenues for participation and inclusion and the provision and dissemination of information.

5.2.2.1 Create formal possibilities for participation and inclusion

The first and most obvious step for giving those affected a say in the deliberations and decisions of rule-setting partnerships is to create formal avenues for participation. Partnerships can choose between various options of how to include stakeholders. Each model has its own problems and advantages. Which alternative is most effective and best suited to the situation depends, among other factors, on how many groups or individuals need to be included and on how strongly those groups are organised.

As a first alternative, partnerships can include stakeholder representatives in their formal governance structures. The WCD, for example, emphasised the multi-stakeholder composition of its central decision-making bodies. The 12-member commission itself took the most important decisions and approved the text of the report, containing standards and principles for the building of large dams. The commission was selected by a multi-stakeholder working group to represent various stakeholder groups, including governments, project-affected people, NGOs, people's movements, the dam-construction industry, export credit agencies, private investors and the international development community.[53] Moreover, the commission relied strongly on the WCD Stakeholder Forum as a sounding board and advisory group. This forum was made up of 68 members, including the participants of the original multi-stakeholder workshop, as well as additional members that were granted access to make the forum more inclusive.

Including stakeholders in the decision-making bodies of partnerships strangthens their democratic accountability. Through their direct involvement, stakeholder representatives have immediate control over the outcomes of the rule-setting process. This model corresponds most closely to the traditional democratic paradigm, where citizens tend to elect the members of parliament. Instead of citizens, partnerships include stakeholders. In principle, this appears to be a fitting equivalent since both citizens and stakeholders are those affected by legislation. Moreover, the inclusion of multiple stakeholders is congenial to the idea of partnerships. Many favour this form of governance arrangement precisely because it allows for the involvement of various groups on an equal footing. Finally, this model also offers pragmatic advantages. Because participation is channelled through representatives, the number of individuals involved in the governing bodies stays limited. This means that decision-making processes remain manageable, both logistically and financially.

At the same time, however, the inclusion of stakeholder representatives raises a number of serious problems. In traditional democratic polities, citizens tend to be clearly defined as all individuals of a certain age holding the country's nationality.[54] Stakeholder groups, by contrast, have to be defined individually for each project or organisation.[55] This raises the critical question of who is recognised as a stakeholder and who takes this decision. The WCD, for example, while renowned for its high degree of democratic legitimacy, has been criticised for disregarding women and populations living downstream of dams as significant stakeholder groups.[56]

Another basic democratic principle that can turn problematic when applied to 'stakeholder democracy' is the 'one person, one vote' rule. Should all stakeholder groups have an equal number of representatives? If not, which criteria should be applied to weigh the influence of individual groups? Their size? The degree to which they are influenced by the rules? This is another aspect that was criticised about the work of the WCD. It operated on the assumption that all identified stakeholder interests should be treated as equally important and legitimate. Klaus Dingwerth sees this as a general problem of stakeholder approaches: 'the stakeholder rhetoric, by conceptually leveling the interests of individuals or groups with different qualities of affectedness, conceals that not all interests are necessarily equally legitimate' (Dingwerth, 2005, p. 75).

A third problem relates to the question of how stakeholder representatives are selected and how they can be made accountable to their stakeholder groups. A relatively small multi-stakeholder working group, for example, selected the commission members of the WCD. In addition, they were asked to serve in a personal capacity, rather than as representatives of their organisations. The commission members were therefore not accountable to broader stakeholder groups.[57] Another partnership with a multi-stakeholder board is the Global Fund. It has a fixed allocation of seats for various stakeholder groups. Each constituency is responsible for selecting its representative and can freely determine the process for doing so. Where stakeholder groups are well defined and well organised, this can create a democratically acceptable selection process. It is equally possible, however, that individual actors who have little accountability to the other members dominate stakeholder groups.

Considering these opportunities and potential pitfalls, partnerships including stakeholder representatives in their governing bodies should comply with the following standards:

- Provide stakeholder representatives with real decision-making power. Partnerships choosing to include stakeholder representatives in their governing bodies should involve them in the committees that take decisions relating to rules, norms and standards. If this is not the case and stakeholders are only included in consultative fora, partnerships have to deal with problems of stakeholder selection and representation without reaping the democratic benefit of granting stakeholders immediate control over outcomes.

- Adopt a considered definition of relevant stakeholder groups that remains open to review. Determining which groups should and which should not be represented in a partnership is always difficult. To optimise their approach, partnerships should go through a carefully designed stakeholder identification process. This involves mapping all those groups and individuals that have an important input to make and that are significantly affected by the partnership's work.[58] Representatives of these groups should be invited to participate. Crucially, partnerships should also have a transparent process for reconsidering their stakeholder composition. Thus non-participating stakeholders should be able to state their stake and demand representation. The partnership should have a clear process and criteria for deciding on such applications.
- Determine the relative weight of the different stakeholder groups depending on the legitimacy of their interests and their size. The task of determining how many votes or representatives each stakeholder group should have is even more difficult than the process of stakeholder identification. To ensure their democratic accountability, partnerships should not take this decision purely based on the degree of power held by the various groups. Instead, they should consider the groups' degree of affectedness, the legitimacy of their interests and the number of individuals they involve.
- Follow basic democratic principles when selecting stakeholder representatives. Another important aspect of democratic accountability relates to the method for choosing stakeholder representatives. An appropriate procedure needs to meet several requirements. Firstly, the stakeholder groups should be able to select their representatives themselves. Secondly, the groups should hold periodic elections with an open nomination process to choose their representatives.[59] Finally, the representatives should regularly report back to their constituencies and solicit their inputs on current issues and decisions.

A second possibility for enhancing participation is to conduct formal consultation processes with stakeholder groups. Irrespective of the composition of their governance bodies, partnerships can solicit the inputs of relevant stakeholders while devising their work procedures, when defining rules or standards or when revising them.

Of the case examples discussed above, ICANN has developed comparatively refined consultative techniques. Thus, for example, a task force usually oversees each process of rule development or revision. One of the principal missions of the task forces is to gather information on the positions of relevant constituencies. Once a draft version of the new regulation exists, ICANN routinely gives public notice and allows for a comments period. Whenever possible, it also holds public fora to discuss new policies. Moreover, special consultations are conducted with organised constituencies, like, for example, the Government Advisory Committee, which gets involved when issues relating to public policy are at stake.

Formal consultations have distinct advantages as tools to enhance participation. In contrast to the inclusion of stakeholder representatives in governing bodies, they allow for the involvement of a large group of individuals and organisations. This enables partnerships to design their participatory processes in an open manner. As a result, groups overlooked in the stakeholder identification process are not permanently excluded but can contribute to the partnership at a later stage. Moreover, individual stakeholders can voice their positions and interests directly. Any complications related to differences within stakeholder groups, the selection of stakeholder representatives and their accountability to their constituencies can thus be avoided.

But consultations also have their downsides. One set of problems is linked to the lack of control over who gets engaged in consultations. Important stakeholder groups may, for example, find it difficult to get access to the necessary information about the process.[60] In addition, strongly affected groups may lack the necessary skills and resources to articulate their concerns and interests effectively. The risk is that few powerful, well-organised and vocal actors dominate the process.[61]

Another set of potential problems stems from the uncertainty of how the inputs will be used. Organisations holding consultations may use them as a sham to create a semblance of democratic legitimacy. Rather than seriously considering all contributions, these organisations may be tempted to ignore inputs or to selectively use only those reaffirming their original positions.[62] Poorly designed consultative processes that lack credibility may therefore fail to create democratic accountability as well as the ownership among stakeholders that is necessary to achieve voluntary compliance with the proposed rules.

Rule-setting partnerships can opt for consultations as their preferred method of participation or complement the inclusion of stakeholder representatives in governance structures through formal consultations. To design consultative processes in an effective and legitimate way, partnerships should adhere to the following principles:

- Use an open consultation process. Partnerships can use a broad range of consultative techniques. They range from written questionnaires and comments procedures for new policies to online discussion fora and in-person meetings or workshops.[63] Irrespective of which technique is chosen, partnerships should design the process in an open manner, enabling the participation of all interested parties. Thus, for example, questionnaires used to gather information about the positions of different stakeholder groups should not only be sent to a predetermined set of stakeholders but should also be available for other interested parties.

- Disseminate information about the issues addressed as well as the possibilities for submitting contributions widely. This is an important precondition for ensuring broad participation. The dissemination effort should contain two elements. Firstly, partnerships should identify relevant stakeholders and contact them directly. Secondly, they should openly publish information through as many appropriate channels as possible. Depending on the circumstances and the types of stakeholders involved, this may include prominent postings on the partnership's website, on newsletters and websites of thematically related organisations, in relevant publications, the media or on local notice boards.[64]

- Open several consultation channels simultaneously to further increase the number of stakeholders involved. A range of different consultation techniques was mentioned above. These methods can reach diverse audiences and can encourage contributions of differing quality. By using several consultation channels at the same time, partnerships can broaden the scope of both participation and types of submissions. Thus, for example, a partnership may at first hold personal meetings to determine whether and where new standards or rules are necessary. It may then distribute questionnaires among a wider group of stakeholders in order to collect information about their positions. Finally, it may open drafts of the rules to public comments.

- Select consultation techniques suited to the needs and skills of key stakeholder groups. When selecting avenues for consultation, partnerships should bear in mind that stakeholder groups can have very different resources and skills at their disposal. Partnerships should tailor their consultation methods to the capacities of important stakeholder groups. This can become relevant, for example, for determining the languages used, for choosing between verbal or written and electronic or non-electronic means of communication.

- Ensure a balanced representation of interests by supporting disadvantaged groups. In addition to choosing their consultation methods according to the needs of important stakeholders, partnerships should take measures to facilitate the participation of disadvantaged groups or individuals. Disadvantaged stakeholders are those lacking the resources or skills needed to make their voices heard. NGOs in developing countries may, for example, not be able to cover the travel costs for participating in international meetings and may have difficulties in gaining access to relevant knowledge. Within communities, women or certain minorities may find it hard to speak out. Depending on the identity of the disadvantaged groups, assistance can range from financial support and capacity building to the use of facilitation tools designed to achieve equal participation.[65]

- Give contributions due and equal consideration and deal with them in a transparent manner. Once partnerships have achieved broad and balanced participation, they have to handle the inputs they receive appropriately.

This implies firstly that partnerships treat submissions as objectively as possible. Secondly, it entails that partnerships either integrate the proposals in their work or provide a justification and explanation for why they were not taken into account.[66] Thirdly, partnerships should be transparent in this process. A good way to create transparency is to create a collection or summary containing all contributions together with the partnership's reactions. This document should be freely accessible to all interested parties, for example by posting it on the partnership's website.

Finally, partnerships can strengthen participation by establishing permanent mechanisms that allow interested parties to raise issues or voice concerns. In this case, partnerships do not actively solicit inputs during the rule-making process. Instead, stakeholders can act on their own initiative and trigger debates or certain policy procedures. Permanent complaints and comments mechanisms are a good complement to the active involvement of stakeholders in partnership activities. On their own, however, they are not sufficient for creating an adequate level of democratic accountability for rule-setting partnerships.

There is a variety of tools and institutional features providing stakeholders with the opportunity to articulate their concerns and preferences. In addition to its other elaborate channels for participation, ICANN, for example, has instituted several mechanisms to deal with stakeholder complaints. This includes a reconsideration policy, an independent review policy and the office of an ombudsman.[67] Thus anybody materially affected by an ICANN action can request the ICANN board to reconsider this action. A special board committee decides within 30 days whether or not it accepts the request and is obliged to justify any rejections. Within 90 days, the committee should forward its final recommendation to the board. All reconsideration requests and subsequent decisions are published on ICANN's website. The independent review policy covers instances when actions by ICANN or its staff are deemed inconsistent with its articles of incorporation or by-laws. An independent international arbitrator handles these complaints. Finally, ICANN has an ombudsman who deals with any disputes not covered by the other two mechanisms. The mission of the ombudsman is to resolve conflicts informally, relying, for example, on negotiations, facilitation or 'shuttle diplomacy'. Other procedures common in many democratic polities, though not applied by any of the partnerships discussed as case examples here, include formal petitions as well as the possibility to introduce draft norms to the rule-setting process.[68]

Open comments and complaints procedures create important benefits in terms of democratic accountability: They are usually open to contributions from all interested parties and they allow stakeholders to decide when and on what they want to comment. Thus they complement both main alternatives for the inclusion of stakeholders well. They enhance the democratic accountability of partnerships including stakeholder representatives in their governing bodies because they enable all stakeholders, including those that may not have representation, to voice their interests and concerns directly. Partnerships relying on stakeholder consultations often have access to a broader group of interested parties, but they tend to solicit their inputs on very specific questions. Open comments and complaints procedures can strengthen democratic accountability here by broadening both the scope of issues open for comment and the time frame for submitting contributions. Due to these benefits, both ISO guide 59 and the ISEAL code of good practice for standard-setting organisations recommend the institutionalisation of comments and complaints mechanisms.[69]

At the same time, however, open comments and complaints procedures face strong limitations as instruments of democratic accountability. Firstly, the contributions received are very unlikely to provide a representative picture of the different stakeholder interests relating to any specific issue. Since interested parties submit comments on their own initiative, a systematic collection of viewpoints on a specific issue does not usually take place. Moreover, it is very likely that well-informed, well-resourced and vocal interests dominate these open comment mechanisms. Lack of control over who gets involved was already mentioned as a problem in stakeholder consultations. It is strongly exacerbated in open comments and complaints procedures, however, since they usually do not involve any process of stakeholder identification or proactive outreach to disadvantaged groups.

A second problem relates to the effectiveness of comments or complaints in generating changes. Many institutions inviting open comments do not clarify how these inputs are treated. And even where a procedure is defined, such as the right to receive a reply that is guaranteed by various European institutions, the influence of comments on the policy process may remain unclear. As a result, open comments and complaints procedures easily lack credibility and stakeholders may not have sufficient incentives for using these avenues for participation. Therefore, open comments and complaints procedures cannot generate appropriate democratic accountability if used on their own. In conjunction with other participatory techniques, however, they can be beneficial.

To reap the benefits of open comments and complaints procedures while avoiding their pitfalls, partnerships should adhere to the following related principles:

- Generate possibilities for submitting open comments and complaints as a complement to other procedures for participation. Rule-setting partnerships should allow for continuous comments relating to any aspect of their work. These comments and complaints procedures should, however, only be used as a complement and not as an alternative for other means of participation.

- Broadly disseminate information on how and when interested parties can comment or complain. Open comments and complaints procedures do not usually allow partnerships to actively identify and contact relevant stakeholder groups. To encourage widespread use of the mechanisms and increase the representative nature of submissions, partnerships should as a minimum explain clearly how the comments and complaints procedures work. This information should be made easily accessible to all interested parties.
- Use open comments and complaints to raise issues, rather than as a decision-making procedure. As discussed above, it is very difficult, if not impossible, to receive a representative sample of stakeholder views through open comments and complaints. The main function of comments and complaints procedures should therefore be agenda setting. Issues raised by interested parties should then be discussed and resolved with the help of other, more representative, participatory tools.
- Define a procedure for dealing with comments or complaints. To make their comments and complaints procedures credible, partnerships should have a clear process for handling contributions. This process should provide some guarantee that legitimate inputs are treated properly, while allowing partnerships to reject insincere or immaterial comments. As a minimum, everybody submitting a comment or complaint should be granted the right to receive a reply outlining how the partnership will deal with the submission or justifying why the contribution is rejected.
- Ensure transparency in dealing with comments and complaints. Finally, to further strengthen the credibility of the process, partnerships should handle comments and complaints in a transparent way. This entails firstly that the procedures for managing comments and complaints are clearly defined and easily accessible to all interested parties. Secondly, it involves collecting and regularly publishing the inputs received as well as the corresponding reactions.

5.2.2.2 *Provide stakeholders with relevant information, knowledge and skills*

Transparency has repeatedly been discussed in this book as an essential ingredient for any type of accountability. Following the basic model of accountability outlined in section 2.2.1, access to relevant information is crucial because it enables principals to evaluate the behaviour of their agents. For a different reason, transparency is once more key at this juncture. Democratic accountability, it was argued above, is to an important degree about giving those affected a say in the rule-making process. Effective stakeholder participation, however, cannot be guaranteed solely by instituting formal possibilities for participation. Stakeholders are only able to execute their rights and provide meaningful inputs if they are equipped with the necessary information, knowledge and skills.

In his frequently quoted and powerful words, James Madison describes the importance of knowledge for democratic government as follows:

> A popular Government, without popular information, or the means of acquiring it, is but a Prologue to a Farce or a Tragedy; or, perhaps both. Knowledge will forever govern ignorance: And a people who mean to be their own Governors, must arm themselves with the power which knowledge gives.
>
> (Hunt, 1900–10, Vol. 1, Chap. 18, Doc. 35)[70]

Organisations like Privacy International, which runs a major campaign for freedom of information legislation, emphasise the link between access to information and the ability to participate:

> Democracy is based on the consent of the citizens and that consent turns on the government informing citizens about their activities and recognizing the right to participate. The public is only truly able to participate in the democratic process when they have information about the activities and policies of the government.
>
> (Banisar, 2006, p. 6)

Because of its centrality to both accountability in general and to participation, transparency has become a very broadly recognised standard of democratic governance. Thus, for instance, the Universal Declaration of Human Rights and the International Covenant on Civil and Political Rights recognise the right to seek, receive and impart information.[71] Moreover, the UN Convention against Corruption requires governments to take measures to enhance the transparency of their public administration and the Rio Declaration demands access to environmental information to enable participation.[72] The importance of transparency is also increasingly reflected in government practice. Thus by 2006 70 countries from across the globe had adopted comprehensive freedom of information legislation, while another 50 were in the process of developing it.[73]

Consequently, the codes defining governance norms for standard-setting organisations also emphasise transparency. Both, ISO guide 59 and the ISEAL code of good practice, demand that standard-setting organisations publish their future work programmes or notify stakeholders of upcoming decisions, make available copies of the draft standards, publish approved standards promptly and document the process of standard development. Beyond that, ISEAL proposes that organisations publish all received comments, as well as the ensuing reactions and that they create a dedicated focal point for enquiries to facilitate the provision of information.[74]

As discussed in section 2.2.2.4, as well as in section 4.2.3, transparency can concern many different aspects of an organisation. Several of these areas are relevant in the context of participation. For stakeholders to be able to deliver meaningful inputs, they need sufficient information about the rule-setting process, including the schedule of planned activities and the procedures for submitting contributions, as well as the subject matter under consideration. To strengthen the credibility of the process, two further elements of transparency are instrumental. Firstly, organisations should handle submissions in a transparent way so that stakeholders know how their contributions influence the rule-setting process. Secondly, transparency on their financial sources can help address potential concerns about a partnership's independence and objectivity.

Organisations can take very different steps to create transparency. Which activities are required to generate an adequate level of transparency depends on the nature of the stakeholders involved. In the case of ICANN, for example, affected stakeholders are by definition engaged in activities related to the Internet. Therefore, it seems appropriate for ICANN to rely mainly on electronic means of communication to publish and disseminate relevant information. For partnerships dealing with well-organised and well-informed stakeholders, moreover, a relatively passive approach to information dissemination may be sufficient. EITI, for instance, predominantly addresses multinational companies active in the extractive industries that have a strong interest in and awareness of international norm-setting processes. The WCD, by contrast, faced different requirements. Among its key stakeholders were local communities affected by dam-building projects. To inform them and encourage their participation, on-site meetings, non-electronic communication, active outreach, capacity building and the use of local languages were essential.

This dependence on context makes it difficult to establish general standards relating to the concrete modalities necessary for generating appropriate levels of transparency. Nevertheless rule-setting partnerships should respect the following principles to create the conditions for effective participation:

- Provide and disseminate information about the rule-setting process, the procedures for participating, the subject matter under consideration, the way contributions are dealt with and the partnership's financial sources.
- Choose the format and language for providing and disseminating information depending on the needs and capacities of key stakeholders. A basic starting point for partnerships is to publish relevant information online. In many cases, however, information will have to be available in several languages and may require the use of non-electronic forms of communication.
- Where necessary, reach out actively to disadvantaged stakeholders and provide them with training and capacity building. As described in the previous section, measures to support disadvantaged stakeholder groups may include the organisation of separate meetings, capacity building, mandated representation or the use of levelling techniques in facilitation.

- Respond appropriately to inquiries from third parties. Partnerships should be prepared to make information available in response to inquiries from interested parties. To do so in an appropriate way, partnerships should have an agreed information policy, which defines, where necessary, legitimate confidentiality areas. They should also respond to inquiries in a timely manner.

5.2.3 Accountability to avoid the abuse of authority

Parliamentary accountability mechanisms, it was argued above, aim not only at allowing affected parties a say in the norm-setting process but also seek to prevent the abuse of legislative authority. For that purpose, democracies have devised a range of different mechanisms. Citizens can use their right to vote to replace parliaments abusing their authority. Constitutional rules limit parliamentary authority and protect basic rights. These rules can usually not be changed through a simple parliamentary act but require popular referenda or supermajorities. Systems of checks and balances, moreover, enable other governmental bodies to control legislative action. Most importantly, the judiciary can use the process of judicial review to determine the constitutionality and rule conformity of legislative acts. Depending on the political system, the executive can also play an important role in exercising political oversight, for example through its right of veto or its authority to dissolve the parliament.

Compared to the complex institutional set-up of democratic governments, the rule-setting partnerships analysed here have adopted only few similar accountability mechanisms. In many cases, partnership boards take the final decision on new or amended rules. The procedures for selecting partnership boards vary, but rarely include fully democratic elections. Thus, for example, the stakeholder council formally appoints the GRI board. The council, however, can only accept or reject a slate of candidates proposed by a nominating committee, which contains a majority of board members. ICANN used to conduct general elections for its board but now relies on a nominating committee and a fixed stakeholder composition.

In some of the case examples, the partnerships are also able to unilaterally change their mandates and authorities. GRI's board, for example, can amend the partnership's articles of association with a two-thirds majority. The WCD, by contrast, had its mandate clearly defined by an initial stakeholder workshop. Similarly, ICANN cannot autonomously change its constitutional documents, since they are contained in a contract with the US-American government.

The weakest point, however, relates to the partnerships' systems of checks and balances. In the case examples, power is often strongly concentrated. The authority to adopt rules, for example, is in most cases invested in a single body, be it the board, a meeting of partners or a multi-stakeholder committee. ICANN is the only exception here. It has a policy that is similar to judicial review. Through its independent review process, an external arbitrator can establish whether or not actions taken by the partnership are consistent with its by-laws and articles of incorporation.

Should it be a cause for concern if rule-setting partnerships do not match most institutional features of parliamentary accountability? In answering this question, we have to distinguish between various levels of accountability and between two kinds of rule-setting partnerships. Firstly, it was established in the first section of this chapter that all partnerships need to fulfil certain minimum requirements for their governance and internal control structures. These provide a basic protection against the abuse of authority and all rule-setting partnerships have to comply with them. Secondly, it was argued that the accountability arrangements espoused by rule-setting partnerships do not have to be identical, but should be functionally equivalent to democratic accountability mechanisms. What functional equivalence entails in this context, however, strongly depends on the potential of organisations to abuse their legislative authority. In this respect, there is a significant difference between institutions that can pass binding rules and those that can only propose voluntary rules. The standards defined in the following paragraphs therefore distinguish between these two cases.

5.2.3.1 *Partnerships proposing voluntary rules: No additional measures are necessary*

Parliaments have the authority to set rules that are binding for all those within the jurisdiction of the state. These rules are usually not only binding in theory but can be enforced by the judiciary and executive branches of government. Most rule-setting partnerships, by contrast, only have the authority to propose non-binding rules. They rely on voluntary compliance and are not linked to strong enforcement mechanisms. The Voluntary Principles on Security and Human Rights, for example, already contain their voluntary nature in their title. Both governments and companies can decide freely whether or not they want to join the initiative. Once they have subscribed to the principles, all participants commit to promoting the principles and to reporting publicly on the activities undertaken in their support. Similarly, the transparency principles and templates proposed by EITI are adopted voluntarily by governments and companies involved in the extractive industries. By comparison, the standards developed by the WCD enjoy greater authority. They have become a reference point for many debates and decisions relating to the construction of large dams.[75] The standards, however, derive their authority mainly from the comprehensive and inclusive process that led to their development. Formally, any acceptance of the standards is entirely voluntary.

Partnerships developing voluntary rules, though, can hardly abuse their legislative authority. Stakeholders concerned about the process of rule development or the content of the proposed rules can always reject them. Should, for example, GRI proclaim new standards in an area unrelated to sustainability reporting or should those norms violate basic rights, affected parties can withhold their ex-post authorisation and refuse to comply with the rules. The stakeholders of partnerships setting voluntary rules thus enjoy automatic protection against the abuse of legislative authority. Therefore, there is no need for these partnerships to adopt additional measures to achieve functional equivalence with parliamentary accountability.

5.2.3.2 Partnerships setting binding rules: Authorisation, mandate, judicial review

While most partnerships define voluntary rules, some are in a position to set norms with a binding character. This can be the case, for example, where stakeholders depend strongly on a partnership. The dependence can be created through financial links, strong power asymmetries or through the necessity of working with one common system of rules. Partnerships can also be authorised by the relevant authorities to take binding decisions. In classical corporatist arrangements, for instance, partnerships can define rules relating to labour.

Among the case examples, ICANN is the only partnership asserting that its rules are binding. As an analyst puts it:

> ICANN, in short, was both asserting control over the design of the name space and imposing constraints on people using that space. ICANN's exercise of authority looked, walked, and quacked like public regulatory power.
>
> (Weinberg, 2000, p. 217)

ICANN was created through an agreement with the US government. As such, it lacks appropriate authorisation for issuing policies and rules that are binding for the entire Internet community. Its stipulations also lack the backing of a compulsory enforcement system. But the nature of its task provides its decisions with strong authority. ICANN regulates the definition and assignment of Internet domain names and ensures that each name is linked to a unique IP address. This is a condition for the smooth functioning of the Internet.[76] In theory, other organisations could set up domain name registers outside the realm of ICANN. Yet this would undermine the functioning of the entire system. In actual practice, ICANN's policies and rules therefore enjoy a strongly binding character.[77]

Where partnerships set rules with a strongly binding character, stakeholders do not enjoy automatic protection from a potential abuse of legislative authority. Additional accountability measures akin to those used for parliaments or independent regulatory agencies are therefore necessary:[78]

- Achieve appropriate and revocable authorisation for the partnership. Partnerships with the power to set binding rules should derive their authority from appropriate external bodies. For partnerships active at the international level, appropriate authorisation can either be granted by intergovernmental bodies or by affected stakeholders. In either case, the delegating body should be in a position to revoke or renew its authorisation. For intergovernmental organisations this entails retaining the right to withdraw the authorisation and entrust another organisation with the task. Where stakeholders delegate the necessary authority directly, they should either make up the rule-setting body themselves or periodically elect its members.

- Define a clear mandate delimiting the partnership's authority. Rule-setting partnerships should have mandates that spell out clearly where the partnership has authority and where it does not. It is also important that the mandate cannot be changed unilaterally by the partnership. The first definition as well as any significant changes of the mandate should require the consent of the relevant authorising bodies.

- Partnership activities should be subject to a process of judicial review. Finally, allegations that a partnership violates its mandate or critical procedural rules should be subject to authoritative review by an independent body. All interested parties should be able to submit cases, at least if their concerns can be shown to be substantial. This also makes it necessary to devise a reasonable way to deal with the costs arising from the procedure so that they do not constitute a material barrier against bringing cases. To be effective, the independent arbitrator or review panel should also be in a position to pass final and binding decisions on the matters referred to it.

5.2.4 Summary of standards

Table 5.2 provides an overview of relevant accountability standards for rule setting and regulation partnerships.

Table 5.2 Accountability standards for rule setting and regulation partnerships

Accountability principles	Accountability standards	Practical steps
Democratic accountability through participation	Formal possibilities for participation alternative (a): include stakeholder representatives in decision-making bodies	Provide stakeholder representatives with real decision-making power
		Adopt a considered definition of relevant stakeholder groups that remains open to review
		Determine the weight of stakeholder groups depending on the legitimacy of their interests and their size
		Follow basic democratic principles when selecting stakeholder representatives

Table 5.2 Continued

Accountability principles	Accountability standards	Practical steps
	formal possibilities for participation alternative (b): conduct stakeholder consultation processes	Use an open consultation process Widely disseminate information about issues addressed and possibilities for submitting contributions Open several consultation channels simultaneously Select consultation techniques suited to the needs and skills of key stakeholder groups Ensure a balanced representation of interests by supporting disadvantaged groups Give contributions due and equal consideration and deal with them in a transparent manner
	Formal possibilities for participation supplement: establish permanent comments and complaints procedures	Establish comment and complaints procedures as a complement to other participatory mechanisms Broadly disseminate information on how and when to use the comment or complaints procedures Use comments and complaints to raise issues, rather than to settle them Specify a process for dealing with comments or complaints, including at least a guaranteed formal reply to all submissions Ensure transparency in dealing with comments and complaints
	Transparency	Create transparency relating to rule-setting process, the procedures for participating, the subject matter under consideration, the way contributions are dealt with and the partnership's financial sources Choose the format and language for providing and disseminating information depending on the needs and capacities of stakeholders Where necessary, reach out actively to disadvantaged stakeholders and provide them with training and capacity building Respond appropriately to inquiries from interested parties

(Continued)

Table 5.2 Continued

Accountability principles	Accountability standards	Practical steps
Democratic accountability to avoid the abuse of authority	Partnerships setting voluntary rules need no additional accountability	Stakeholders enjoy automatic protection against the abuse of legislative authority through their right to reject rules
	Partnerships setting binding rules do need additional accountability measures	Achieve appropriate and revocable authorisation for the partnership
		Define a clear mandate, delimiting the partnership's authority
		Subject partnership activities to a process of judicial review

5.3   Standards for implementation partnerships

A third group of partnerships identified among the case examples focuses directly on policy implementation. The term 'implementation partnership' sometimes generates confusion because almost all partnerships engage in some form of implementation. Partnerships typically set their agendas, develop policies and then seek to implement them. The label for this group of partnerships, however, does not refer to the partnerships' internal processes. Rather, it describes which part of the global policy cycle the partnerships seek to contribute to.[79] In this context, implementation partnerships differ from the partnerships described thus far. Advocacy and awareness-raising partnerships seek to influence how a policy problem is defined and how central it is on the political agenda. Rule-setting partnerships add to the decision and policymaking stage. Implementation partnerships, by contrast, seek to support the implementation of set policies by contributing necessary resources.

Implementation partnerships thus have to mobilise substantial resources beyond those needed to finance their own core operations. During the financial year 2006, for example, GAIN received over US$7.6 million in donations, GAVI received US$250 million, Stop TB had an income of US$42 million and for the Global Fund, pledges worth over two billion US dollars were due in 2006. These partnerships all focus on public health problems – a comparatively non-controversial and highly visible policy area. Their main donors are typically governments as well as large corporations or private philanthropic organisations. Governments, for instance, provide most of the resources for the Global Fund, whereas the Gates Foundation is the dominant donor for GAIN and GAVI.

This means that to be successful, implementation partnerships need to achieve the delegation of authority over resources at a very different scale than other partnerships. Donors interested in solving a public policy problem usually have many options on how to allocate their resources. Other things being equal, they are likely to spend their funds in the way that is seen as most effective in addressing the problem.[80] Therefore, implementation partnerships need to demonstrate their efficiency and effectiveness in achieving development outcomes. In addition to the basic forms of accountability required for all partnerships, implementation partnerships should thus emphasise accountability for outcomes. This accountability constellation is depicted in Figure 5.3.

This is not to say that outcome accountability cannot be relevant to other forms of partnerships as well. Since all partnerships depend to some extent on the delegation of authority over resources, it is always beneficial if they can demonstrate efficiency and effectiveness in their operations. Yet the discussion about financial accountability earlier has already shown that the scale of financial contributions matters for defining which accountability standards are appropriate. Creating accountability for outcomes is always costly and often very difficult. Implementation partnerships typically operate with greater resources than other types of partnerships. Moreover, they focus directly on effecting development outcomes so that their work tends to lend itself more easily to measurement and results-based evaluation. The ensuing principles of outcome accountability are therefore only defined as expected standards for implementation partnerships.

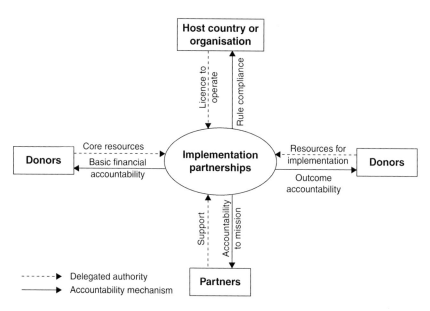

Figure 5.3 Accountability of implementation partnerships

5.3.1 Applying corporate accountability standards to partnerships

Attempts to create or increase accountability for outcomes can be observed in all sectors. The archetypal area of practice for outcome accountability, however, is the corporate sector. Therefore, this section briefly revisits the mechanisms at work in corporate accountability and discusses how these principles can be transferred to implementation partnerships.[81]

Accountability arrangements in corporations focus overwhelmingly on creating accountability for outcomes. This happens at several levels, only some of which an individual company can influence. Firstly, the classical tool for ensuring companies' efficient and effective operations is the market. A well-functioning market is characterised by competition between various providers of similar goods and services and the availability of adequate information about these goods and services. Under these conditions, consumers can choose the products that best suit their needs and that offer the best quality for the relatively lowest price. Since consumption behaviour decides on the economic survival of individual firms, the competition inherent in a functioning market puts companies under continuous pressure to optimise their processes and improve their performance as seen by consumers.

Secondly, the majority of larger companies today are run by professional managers. Owners, who delegate the authority over their resources to managers, have developed a range of mechanisms to make them accountable for performance. These aim either at aligning the interests of managers to those of the owners or at improving the monitoring of managers. The mechanisms include several forms of sanctions and incentives, such as hiring and firing policies, performance-related compensation and the option for owners to sell their stake in the company. They also include tools to improve monitoring by reducing the information asymmetry between owners and managers, for example through strict accounting, reporting and auditing standards as well as the institution of a supervisory board.

In many respects, implementation partnerships work under different circumstances than companies. Firstly, they often provide goods or services for which there is no or a very constrained market. The implementation partnerships among the case examples analysed here, for example, all address public health issues with a focus on developing countries. The partnerships' beneficiaries usually do not have to pay at all or at least not for the full cost of the goods or services they receive. Secondly, implementation partnerships usually do not face competition in the traditional sense. The partnerships were created to fill existing gaps in the provision of goods and services. Often, therefore, there are no or few alternative providers of similar goods and services. And even where various providers coexist, they do not tend to compete for 'customers'. Their ultimate goal is not to make a profit but to provide a public service, and their economic survival depends on the continued commitment of donors, rather than the individual choices of beneficiaries.

Finally, partnerships usually lack a clearly defined performance measure that would be comparable to a corporation's financial bottom line.

Given these differences, how can corporate accountability standards be applied to partnerships? Over recent years, both public and civil society organisations have experimented with introducing results-focused accountability mechanisms in their work. These experiences have shown that the translation of private sector principles for the public and non-profit sectors faces some inherent limitations. At the same time, however, a range of mechanisms were introduced to strengthen accountability for outcomes. These include a focus on performance evaluations, as well as the introduction of market elements in the provision of public goods and services.

5.3.2 Outcome accountability through performance evaluation

Creating accountability for outcomes entails assessing the performance of an organisation or individual against a certain yardstick or measure.[82] In the corporate sector, a clearly defined, common yardstick exists. No matter what product or service a company offers and no matter which additional objectives individual owners pursue, all companies share one goal. This goal is firstly to ensure the company's economic survival and secondly to maximise profits.

Government agencies, NGOs and partnerships, by contrast, work on a non-profit basis. They may share an interest in institutional survival. Beyond that, however, they have no common or equally clearly defined bottom line. In the words of an analyst commenting on the difficulties involved in assessing the organisational performance of NGOs:

> NGOs must contend with the fact that they belong to a category of organisation with no straightforward or uncontested measure of organisational, as distinct from project, effectiveness. In other words [...] non-profits have no readily acknowledged 'bottom line'.
>
> (Fowler, 1995, p. 147)[83]

To build accountability for outcomes, implementation partnerships should nevertheless try to assess their performance. As a first step, this necessitates setting clear goals and targets. As a second step, it requires monitoring performance and linking it to incentives for performance improvement.

5.3.2.1 Define clear objectives and performance targets

Organisations can only evaluate their performance if they have clearly defined organisational objectives that can be translated into measurable performance targets. The implementation partnerships among the case examples all emphasise the definition of goals and targets. Yet they differ both in the clarity of the targets chosen and the level at which performance is evaluated.

GAIN, for example, set itself the target of reaching one billion people at risk of malnutrition with fortified foods by 2008 and has defined several indicators for tracking organisational performance.[84] Similarly, Stop TB has committed itself to reaching time-bound targets relating to the diagnosis, treatment and prevention of TB. To date, however, it has not established performance criteria that would indicate how the partnership's activities contribute to reaching these goals.[85] Similarly, RBM emphasises quantified objectives in the overall fight against malaria without singling out its own contribution to that goal.[86] GAVI and the Global Fund, by contrast, have defined both overall outcome targets (reflected in performance agreements with recipient countries) and quantified, time-bound performance measures for their own activities.[87]

With the growing popularity of results-based management strategies over recent years, many government agencies and civil society organisations have made first experiences with quantified goals and performance targets. This is especially the case in countries with an Anglo-American background, including the UK, the US, Canada, Ireland, Australia and New Zealand. The introduction of performance measures is particularly popular in policy areas like public health, education, welfare and development.[88] The effects of these measures are controversial and have generated much academic and political debate.[89]

Analysts have identified several potential problems related to the definition of clear organisational objectives and their translation into measurable performance indicators in the public sector and in civil society organisations. Due to these problems, it is disputed whether or not performance indicators improve efficiency and strengthen accountability for outcomes.[90]

A first problem is that performance measures tend to be simple indicators that can easily fail to reflect the complexity of the issue addressed. Matthew Diller finds this to be the case with the indicators chosen during the welfare reform in the US and believes that the problem is not easy to remedy:

> In the new regime that focuses on results, the most visible and quantifiable of outcomes become the most important. [...] While performance-based government may be effective if the goal is defined in terms as simple and unequivocal as caseload reduction, the introduction of caveats and countervailing interests may render it ineffective as a means of establishing central control.
>
> (Diller, 2000, pp. 1183 and 1184)

Secondly, several analysts find that the indicators chosen to measure performance are often not sufficiently clearly related to the organisation's overall goals. Propper and Wilson, for example, cite a study on the effects of the performance measures introduced as part of the US Job Training and Partnership Act of 1982. The study finds that most performance indicators are evaluated on a short-term basis and that as a result, the long term added-value goals are not met. Instead, the short-term PMs [performance measures] that are used in their place are either uncorrelated with, or negatively correlated with, long-term value added.

(Propper and Wilson, 2003, p. 257)

Thirdly, as a result of poorly chosen indicators, managers and staff can face perverse incentives. Thus, for example, the focus on standardised school tests may force teachers who are genuinely interested in furthering their students' knowledge, ability to learn and think critically to 'teach to the test' and neglect their broader educational objectives.[91]

Implementation partnerships intent on strengthening their accountability for outcomes should learn from the controversial experiences made in the public sector and in civil society organisations and adhere to the following standards when defining their organisational objectives and performance targets:

- Invest significant efforts into the definition of organisational objectives and performance targets. Experiences with the introduction of performance measures in the public sector and in civil society organisations have shown that poorly chosen performance indicators can be counterproductive. Because of their strong focus on outcome accountability, implementation partnerships must evaluate their performance. In order to avoid the potential problems related to indicator selection, they should, however, be prepared to invest the necessary effort to establish a well-designed system for performance evaluation.
- Demonstrate how performance indicators are linked to and will lead to the achievement of broader organisational objectives. A first crucial requirement is that the indicators chosen are positively correlated to the partnership's goals. Where possible, the indicators should therefore include measures directly assessing changes in the intended outcomes. Moreover, partnerships should establish exactly how their own activities are intended to contribute to the desired goal and develop a strategy for evaluating these activities as well as their effects.
- Involve stakeholders in the definition of goals and indicators. Implementation partnerships typically seek to deliver a good or service to an underserved community. An important aspect of performance is thus to what degree and how partnership activities affect the position or welfare of their target groups. The affected individuals or groups themselves are best placed to establish which elements are most important for their well-being. They should therefore be strongly involved in the definition of performance indicators for implementation partnerships.[92]
- Combine objective and subjective, as well as quantitative and qualitative indicators. To avoid some of the potential counterproductive effects of the introduction of performance measures, partnerships should rely on

a mix of different kinds of indicators. Thus they should not only rely on objective data, such as a reduction in waiting times or the number of goods delivered, but also on subjective data, such as service satisfaction or individual welfare assessments. To avoid the misinterpretation of quantitative data, moreover, the inclusion of qualitative data collection methods can be very helpful.

5.3.2.2 Monitor performance and create incentives for performance improvement

By establishing clear objectives and performance indicators or targets, organisations create the basis for evaluating their activities and clarify expectations for their behaviour. Following the basic model of accountability proposed in section 2.2.1, creating accountability additionally requires collecting information about the agent's behaviour and defining sanctions and incentives to encourage compliance or improvement. To effectively strengthen their accountability for outcomes, implementation partnerships should therefore monitor performance and create incentives to improve it.

The corporate sector strongly emphasises the necessity of accurate performance measurement and reporting. Especially for publicly traded companies, most relevant aspects relating to accounting, reporting and auditing are strictly regulated. Thus, for example, accountants and auditors have to comply with strict professional norms concerning both their training and the principles they apply. Moreover, most governments have passed legal regulations determining what information has to be recorded, when and how it has to be reported and whether it has to receive independent confirmation. As mentioned earlier, companies and their managers also face manifold incentives for performing well.

In the public and civil society sectors, by contrast, only certain aspects relating to financial accounting and reporting are subject to regulations. For the monitoring and reporting of performance results, no similar rules exist. Those government agencies and NGOs, however, that have determined performance indicators for their work, are also often monitoring and reporting on their performance. Whether and how performance results are linked to sanctions or incentives differs strongly. In some instances, for example, performance data are made public and influence the organisation's reputation. Even if only used internally or shared with donors, though, performance results can have an impact on promotions, on budget developments and the conclusion of new contracts.

Again, analysts have pointed to a number of potential problems and complications that can arise in the context of performance measurement in the public and non-profit sectors.[93] A first risk is that staff and managers manipulate performance data to their own advantage. Courty and Marschke, for example, analyse the phenomenon of 'gaming' in government organisations. They find that when agents strategically report their performance outcomes to maximise their awards, this can have a negative impact on the real goals of the organisation (Courty and Marschke, 2004). In addition to gaming, Peter Smith describes how the publication of performance data in the UK tempts officials to misrepresent data (Smith, 1995).

Secondly, researchers have found that a strong focus on quantitative performance targets can inhibit organisational learning. Thus, for instance, Thomas Freeman finds that as performance indicators are used to create external accountability and verification, they can undermine the conditions necessary for quality improvement (Freeman, 2002). Similarly, Alnoor Ebrahim contends that too much accountability can hinder NGOs in achieving their missions. More specifically, his concern is 'about instances of too narrowly focused upward accountability – where donor demands for information are satisfied at the expense of longer-term processes of organizational learning' (Ebrahim, 2005, p. 81).

Finally, performance measurement in the public and non-profit sectors is often confronted with complex technical problems. Relevant reliable and valid data are often difficult to come by. Moreover, in complex policy areas, it can be very hard to establish cause and effect or to measure the impact of an individual organisation on the final outcome.[94] As Hugo Slim puts it for NGOs:

[T]he current art and science of social and environmental accounting is truly complex on occasion. Accounting for the impact or outcome of NGO work can be uncertain, is usually contested and can border on pure speculation at times as NGOs try to track cause and effect between their actions and the personal, social, economic, environmental and political change around their projects.

(Slim, 2002, p. 4)

For implementation partnerships, these experiences contain the following lessons:

• Consider issues relating to performance measurement already during the planning process and start collecting data early. To assess the impact of partnership (or other organisations') activities on a public policy problem, it is standard practice to compare the actual situation to a counterfactual, that is, to the hypothetical case in which the activities did not take place.[95] To construct a convincing counterfactual, data describing the situation prior to the intervention are of central importance. Therefore, implementation partnerships should ensure they have access to or should collect relevant data as early as possible.
• Ensure objectivity of data and their presentation. Implementation partnerships can take various steps to reduce the risk of data manipulation and misrepresentation. Firstly, they can try to rely on external sources

of data, such as independent opinion polls or official statistics. Secondly, they can task independent agencies of good reputation to collect data on their behalf. Thirdly, they should conform to relevant existing rules concerning accounting, reporting and auditing.[96]

- Encourage learning by emphasising positive incentives. Performance evaluations have long been seen to pursue two purposes: creating accountability and encouraging learning.[97] Where accountability, however, means punishment,[98] it encourages a risk-averse culture and thus undermines efforts to learn from past experience and improve performance. To overcome the apparent accountability–learning dichotomy, implementation partnerships should involve their staff and managers in the evaluation process and reward good performance rather than simply punishing bad performance.[99] Moreover, partnerships should avoid giving perverse incentives. This is the case, for example, when current performance is used to determine future performance targets, which effectively punishes good performers.

5.3.3 Outcome accountability through the introduction of market elements

In the private sector, functioning markets have two main effects on outcome accountability. Competition creates continuous pressure on companies to enhance the efficiency of their operations. In addition, consumer choice gives individuals a powerful means of expressing their preferences and of indicating which products best fit their needs.

In the public sector, various strategies have been used to introduce market elements in the provision of public goods and services. In some areas, full privatisation is possible. Many governments have privatised formerly public utilities such as the providers of gas, water, electricity or telecommunication services, which share many characteristics of private goods.[100] In many other areas, however, governments do not consider privatisation a desirable option.[101] Instead of full privatisation, many governments have tried to introduce alternative means for creating the two effects described above. In order to generate competition, many governments delegate important tasks to private providers, using competitive bidding processes for allocating contracts.[102] Outsourcing can subject private and public service providers to competitive pressures. Most often, however, beneficiaries cannot make 'consumption choices' on those products and therefore play little or no role in assessing the quality and efficiency of the services provided. To remedy the situation in this context as well as in cases where government agencies continue to act as service providers, governments often employ client satisfaction surveys, recipient focus groups or similar means to collect beneficiary feedback.[103]

What lessons do these experiences hold for implementation partnerships? Full privatisation is usually not a viable alternative for the partnerships under consideration here. Their objective is to contribute to the achievement of public policy goals and to deliver goods and services in areas not sufficiently served by governments or companies. On their own, markets are therefore unlikely to generate the desired outcomes. The options for partnerships to increase their outcome accountability through the introduction of market elements thus include outsourcing and the gathering of beneficiary feedback. In both areas, partnerships should take on board the lessons learnt from similar experiences made by the public sector and civil society organisations.

5.3.3.1 Outsource suitable tasks through competitive bidding processes

Implementation partnerships can introduce an element of competition in their work by outsourcing certain tasks to competing providers. Among the case examples, almost all implementation partnerships allocate a significant amount of their resources to third providers. The Global Fund has gone furthest in this respect. It exclusively operates as a financial instrument, providing grants enabling other organisations to implement policies to fight AIDS, tuberculosis and malaria. In its 'performance-based grant making', the Global Fund emphasises results. Thus funding proposals are evaluated by a technical review committee before the board takes decisions; local fund agents assess the financial management and administrative capacities of recipients; success indicators and reporting requirements are agreed with the recipient agency and included in the contract; regular progress reports and audits are conducted on programmes and ongoing disbursements depend on the results of these evaluations.[104]

Analysts and commentators have identified several potential problems related to outsourcing as practised in the public sector. Firstly, they have raised the general concern that the introduction of market-based reforms may undermine traditional forms of governmental legitimacy and accountability.[105] Partnerships, however, are not naturally endowed with similar levels and types of accountability and legitimacy as governments. It is for this very reason that partnerships have been strongly criticised as a form of public private governance. It has been argued throughout this book that to counter these challenges, partnerships should adopt appropriate accountability mechanisms. For implementation partnerships, it was determined that because of their use and allocation of significant resources, a focus on accountability for outcomes was appropriate. In an answer to this general critique of outsourcing, implementation partnerships should therefore adopt the measures for enhancing outcome accountability discussed in this chapter.

Secondly, empirical studies have found that outsourcing does not necessarily lead to enhanced competition. This can be due to several reasons. Public agencies may not use competitive bidding processes to allocate contracts; where competitive bids are used, they may not attract a sufficient number of submissions to create competition; bids may not be evaluated in a fair manner but be used as a sham for allocating nepotistic contracts; and contractors may not really fear sanctions such as losing their contracts as a result of bad performance.[106]

Thirdly, analyses of performance-based contracts used in outsourcing or in agreements with independent government agencies often criticise the way performance is evaluated. The contracts typically define the goals to be pursued by the contractor and specify which indicators will be used to assess performance. Since the chances of gaining future contracts and often the level of compensation for current activities depend on these performance evaluations, indicator targets have great importance for contractors. As discussed in the previous section of this chapter, there is a strong risk that the chosen performance indicators do not reflect all or even the most important aspects of the desired outcomes. Just as deciding on suitable performance indicators is key to establishing outcome accountability for partnership operations generally, it is also crucial for designing functioning performance-based contracts with subcontractors.

Building on the experiences of the public sector, implementation partnerships should pay heed to the following principles when outsourcing parts of their tasks:

- Use competitive and transparent bidding processes to allocate contracts. Outsourcing can only increase the efficiency of partnership operations and enhance accountability for outcomes if it introduces competition in the provision of goods and services. Only contract allocation practices in which potential providers submit offers competing on price as well as the type or quality of services offered are therefore suitable for implementation partnerships.
- Ensure that a sufficient number of bids are submitted. To achieve this partnerships should only consider activity areas for outsourcing in which a number of different potential providers exist. Partnerships should also specify a minimum number of bids (for example, 3) required before any contract can be concluded.
- Use a transparent and fair process for evaluating bids and allocating contracts. Where competitive bidding processes are opaque, staff may be influenced by factors not related to the bidding document, including instances of corruption. Partnerships should therefore ensure transparency in dealing with submissions and evaluate bids in an objective and fair manner.
- Define adequate performance indicators to be included in the outsourcing contracts. Implementation partnerships should choose those activity areas for outsourcing where it is comparatively easy to define good performance indicators. Beyond that, partnerships should follow the standards for setting performance indicators outlined in the previous section.
- Link contractor performance to sanctions and incentives. Competitive pressures are only real if contractors have to face the consequences of

their performance. Where contracts are relatively long-term, partnerships should disburse resources in stages and make further payments dependent on performance. The prospect of new future contracts can also work as a powerful incentive. Work areas requiring ongoing or repeated efforts therefore lend themselves more easily to outsourcing than one-off contracts.

5.3.3.2 Collect beneficiary feedback to assess performance

Another critical contribution of markets to outcome accountability is that they provide consumers with an automatic and powerful avenue for expressing their opinions about products and services. Implementation partnerships, even if they do not operate under market conditions, can simulate this effect by gathering feedback from their clients or beneficiaries. This information can be crucial for assessing the quality of the products and services delivered and for evaluating whether partnership activities meet the needs of their target groups.[107]

Among the case examples, some implementation partnerships are collecting beneficiary and stakeholder feedback when evaluating their own or their contractors' activities. Yet there is much scope for further expanding this practice. One positive example is RBM. When it conducted an intensive external evaluation of its activities in 2002, an important part of the process included interviews with stakeholders in affected countries.[108] Similarly, the external evaluation conducted for the Stop TB partnership included several interviews with stakeholders and beneficiaries in affected and targeted countries.[109]

Stakeholder interviews enable partnerships or external evaluators to gather focused in-depth information from a relatively broad range of participants. They are, however, comparatively expensive to conduct and are thus rarely used on an ongoing basis. A cheaper alternative with an even broader reach is using client or beneficiary satisfaction surveys. They are used by many companies as well as governments in countries where the introduction of results-based management techniques is advanced, such as Australia, the UK or the US.[110] Both interviews and surveys, however, have a range of shortcomings. Thus they do not encourage debate or the exchange of information between different stakeholders, they are not suitable for providing ongoing feedback and they tend to strongly predetermine which topics are dealt with.[111] Another option used by both governments and companies are focus groups. These smaller group discussions allow for a more intensive exchange and give stakeholders a stronger role in setting the agenda.[112] Finally, many companies and governments have set up permanent complaints mechanisms, such as complaints hotlines or complaints boxes. These encourage all clients or beneficiaries to voice their grievances but are often only used by strongly disaffected or engaged users.[113]

This brief discussion shows that each specific technique for gathering beneficiary feedback has its distinct advantages and problems. To provide useful input to an assessment of the partnership's performance, feedback mechanisms should include information from diverse relevant sources and generate an accurate picture of beneficiary perceptions and opinions.[114] To achieve this, implementation partnerships should adhere to the following principles when designing feedback mechanisms for beneficiaries:

- Routinely gather information about beneficiary satisfaction and preferences. The implementation partnerships analysed as case examples here have mainly conducted stakeholder interviews as one-off or very irregular exercises. To engage in continuous quality improvement and to adapt their products and services to the needs of beneficiaries, however, partnerships should collect beneficiary feedback on a regular basis.
- Combine several methods for collecting beneficiary feedback. When choosing a technique for gathering information from beneficiaries, partnerships usually face a trade-off between the reach of the chosen method, the depth and openness of the information it can generate and the duration and frequency with which it can be used. To optimise the supply of information, partnerships should therefore employ several methods at the same time.
- Ensure coverage of relevant sources of information. Partnerships should make sure they receive feedback from the most relevant sources. Depending on the activities of the partnership, this may include, for example, potential beneficiaries who chose not to participate in a programme or it may require the collection of feedback over a longer period of time.

5.3.4 Summary of standards

Table 5.3 provides an overview of relevant accountability standards for implementation partnerships.

Table 5.3 Accountability standards for implementation partnerships

Accountability principles	Accountability standards	Practical steps
Outcome accountability through performance evaluation	Define clear objectives and performance targets	Invest significant efforts into the definition of organisational objectives and performance indicators
		Demonstrate how performance indicators will contribute to the achievement of broader organisational objectives
		Involve stakeholders in the definition of goals and targets
		Combine objective and subjective, as well as quantitative and qualitative indicators

Table 5.3 Continued

Accountability principles	Accountability standards	Practical steps
	Monitor performance and create incentives for performance improvement	Plan performance measurement and start collecting data as early as possible
		Ensure objectivity of data and their presentation
		Encourage learning by emphasising positive incentives
Outcome accountability through the introduction of market elements	Outsource suitable tasks through competitive bidding processes	Use competitive bidding processes to allocate contracts
		Ensure submission of a sufficient number of bids
		Use a transparent and fair process for evaluating bids and allocating contracts
		Define adequate performance indicators for inclusion in the contracts
		Link contractor performance to sanctions and incentives
	Collect beneficiary feedback to assess performance	Routinely gather information about beneficiary satisfaction and preferences
		Combine several methods for collecting beneficiary feedback
		Ensure coverage of all relevant sources of information

5.4   Standards for information-generating partnerships

A final group of partnerships identified among the case examples is concerned with the generation of information. Typically, partnerships work with two different kinds of information. One set of partnerships develops factual or technical information and knowledge about certain, often controversial, issue areas. The WCD, for example, invested a major effort into the development of a 'knowledge base' to create a shared understanding among different stakeholder groups on the development effectiveness of dams.[115]

Another set of partnerships generates information with the aim of verifying or certifying to what degree other organisations are complying with specific rules. The MSC, for instance, has created standards for sustainable fisheries. Companies complying with these rules can have their performance verified by independent certification organisations and apply the MSC label to their products.[116] Similarly, the 4C initiative contains an element of compliance verification. Rather than certifying full compliance with its standards, however, 4C engages organisations in a performance improvement process. Thus the organisations themselves submit information relating to their compliance and draw up improvement plans for problematic areas. Implementation and the systems used for verification are subject to external audit or evaluation.[117]

As these examples show, partnerships rarely pursue the generation of information as their sole or even predominant goal. In the three cases just mentioned, information generation constitutes a major element of the partnerships' work. Even they, however, do not see information generation as a goal in itself but rather as a means to achieve other objectives. Thus, for the WCD, it was an instrument to prepare the ground for consensual rules; MSC uses certification as a lever for increasing compliance with its standards and the 4C initiative supports its advocacy work by evaluating the implementation and verification of improvement plans.

Irrespective of what broader objectives the partnerships pursue, their information-generating activities are linked to specific accountability requirements. When partnerships create information or knowledge, they do so with the intention that other actors use and rely on that information. In other words, they want to achieve ex-post authorisation by their user groups to produce information on their behalf. Potential users are likely to do that if they feel they can trust the delivered information. To achieve this, partnerships must be able to demonstrate that they are independent and unbiased and that their work stands up to high professional standards.

As illustrated in Figure 5.4, where partnerships focus on the generation of information, they should emphasise accountability for independence and professionalism.

5.4.1 Transferable accountability practices in universities and the judiciary and guidance from relevant international standards

Like the other types of partnerships, information-generating partnerships do not have to build their accountability practices in a void. Rather, they can draw lessons from other, functionally similar organisations with more established accountability traditions. As already mentioned, information generation can mean two different things to partnerships. They are usually either concerned with creating factual or technical information and knowledge or with assessing the compliance of other actors with certain standards or rules. These two kinds of information correspond to two different organisational functions. Information-generating partnerships can therefore draw on two types of institutions as role models for their accountability arrangements: universities and the judiciary. Moreover, they can orient themselves along international standards that have been developed for evaluation, compliance verification and accreditation organisations.

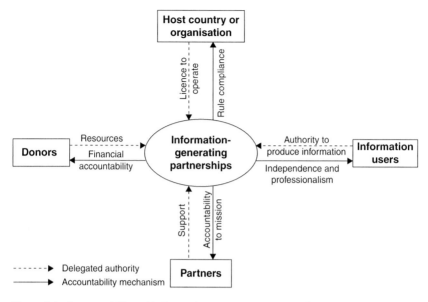

Figure 5.4 Accountability of information-generating partnerships

Universities form the classical institutional context for the creation of knowledge. Since the accountability arrangements of universities have not yet been discussed in this book, they warrant a slightly longer explanation at this stage. A crucial principle informing the governance characteristics of universities is the concept of academic freedom. Academic freedom describes the liberty of students, teachers and academic institutions to pursue their knowledge interests without undue interference. The unhampered search for truth is seen to confer benefits on society as a whole and the principle is closely linked to other precepts of liberal democratic thought. Today, academic freedom is broadly recognised as a normative ideal.[118] The principle is most strongly protected in Germany, where it enjoys the status of a fundamental right and is enshrined in the constitution: 'Kunst und Wissenschaft, Forschung und Lehre sind frei. Die Freiheit der Lehre entbindet nicht von der Treue zur Verfassung' (Deutscher Bundestag, 2007, Art. 5, § 3).[119]

In the US, to cite another national example, academic freedom is not directly referred to in the constitution. The Supreme Court has, however, consistently interpreted academic freedom as part of the first amendment right to free speech.[120] Moreover, most US-American academic institutions have endorsed the 1940 Statement of Principles on Academic Freedom and Tenure (American Association of University Professors and Association of American Colleges, 1940). By subscribing to this document, colleges and universities commit to protecting the freedom of their staff in teaching and research. Similarly, the academic freedom of university teachers is enshrined in the UK's 1988 Education Reform Act.[121]

To guarantee academic freedom, academic institutions and their staff need to enjoy a certain degree of independence. Two main mechanisms serve to ensure this independence. Firstly, universities are usually conceived as autonomous organisations. This means that even where universities are public institutions, they handle all issues relating to teaching and research internally.[122] Secondly, the independence of individual university teachers is secured through the institution of tenure. Tenure provides university teachers with a strong, though not unconditional, guarantee of employment. It ensures that they cannot be fired or financially penalised for pursuing a specific line of inquiry in research or teaching.[123]

The accountability arrangements of institutions of higher learning are, however, not only determined by the principle of academic freedom. Another strong concern for universities and their funders is to ensure a high quality of research and teaching. Ongoing mechanisms of quality control can easily undermine the independence of university teachers. Classically, universities have therefore defined very strict professional criteria for applicants to academic posts. These standards introduce formal criteria for academic staff and create strong peer control. To achieve a tenured position, scholars need to pass a range of formal exams, such as Bachelors', Masters' and get doctoral degrees. In addition, professors in the Anglo-American world can only receive tenure after a lengthy period of probation.[124] Germany and Austria, by contrast, still largely rely on the more formalistic quality assessment provided by an additional postdoctoral qualification, the habilitation. Academic peers play an important role in determining the qualification of their colleagues. Only the academic staff of recognised institutions of higher learning can decide whether individuals pass the formal tests and have the authority to award academic titles. Moreover, committees composed of fellow professors and other staff usually have a strong say in the selection of candidates for academic positions.

Through formal tests and strict appointment procedures, universities guarantee that their teachers and researchers are highly qualified. While these mechanisms are well suited for ensuring high professional standards when appointing new academic staff, they are less apt at vouching for good ongoing quality. Especially tenured professors, who enjoy job and income security, only face soft incentives for maintaining high standards. Many see the lure of prestige and a good reputation as an insufficient means of quality control. Over recent years, an increasing number of countries and universities have therefore increased their efforts at creating mechanisms for ongoing quality assurance. As consequence, promotion, tender and budget allocation decisions do now often take into account the results of performance assessments, based, for example, on student assessments or publication indices. In addition, university rankings focusing on the quality of teaching and research create more transparency and competition among institutions of higher learning.[125]

Ongoing mechanisms of quality control have become a popular element of academic accountability. Despite their popularity, however, they are frequently criticised for undermining academic freedom.[126] There is thus often a tension between the two pillars of accountability in academia, independence and high quality or professionalism.

If independence and professionalism are the two main principles underlying academic accountability, how does this compare to the other possible role model for information-generating partnerships, the judiciary? One author has likened the role of tenured professors to that of judges: 'In relation to tenure the position of the faculty member resembles that of the judge who holds office during good behavior to safeguard his fearlessness and objectivity in the performance of his duties' (Fuchs, 1963, p. 431). Indeed, typical judicial accountability arrangements show important similarities to these principles of academic accountability. In the liberal democratic tradition the judiciary is subject to few external controls. To ensure accountability, the judiciary instead relies mainly on independence and self-control.

Judicial independence entails firstly the formal autonomy of courts and judges. Accordingly, other state organs or external actors have no authority to change and reverse judgements or to interfere with judicial processes. Secondly, special measures serve to undergird the de facto independence of individual judges. Thus, for example, they usually enjoy long or life tenures as well as guaranteed salaries.

Again, independence is not the only relevant element of judicial accountability. To avoid the abuse of authority and ensure professionalism in the work of the judiciary, several mechanisms of self-control are typically in operation. The appeals process provides a bulwark against arbitrary individual decisions and promotes the consistent interpretation and application of legal principles. Compliance verification partnerships also pass judgement over whether or not individuals or organisations comply with specific sets of rules. Unlike the judiciary, however, partnerships mostly deal with voluntary norms and only have access to soft enforcement mechanisms. The institution of a full appeals process is therefore not required of information-generating partnerships.

Other measures adopted in the judiciary focus on the qualification and professionalism of legal staff. Thus most countries have defined very strict professional standards. They typically involve a formal education as well as official entry exams. In most cases, only the best-qualified individuals are eligible for the office of judge.

Both universities and the judiciary, then, stress independence and professionalism or quality control in their accountability arrangements. These principles are also reflected in international standards for inspection, certification and accreditation bodies. Relevant standards include, for example, the ISO guide 65 defining general requirements for bodies operating product certification systems (International Organization for Standardization, 1996), ISO standard 17011 for accreditation bodies (International Organization for Standardization, 2004) and ISO standard 19011 for quality and environmental management systems auditing (International Organization for Standardization, 2002). These standards vary in their focus and in some of the details of their recommendations. Overall, however, they all define criteria to safeguard the impartiality and independence, as well as the quality and professionalism of organisations and their staff.

5.4.2 Accountability for impartiality through independence

Other actors will only rely on the information generated by partnerships if they trust it. The results of studies or enquiries quickly lose their trustworthiness if suspected to be biased or influenced by specific interests. To create accountability for generating trustworthy information, partnerships must ensure their impartiality and independence.

The partnerships analysed as case examples above have chosen different strategies to guarantee that their information-generating activities are impartial. The WCD was itself ultimately responsible for compiling the report on the development effectiveness of dams. The commission was independent in so far as its findings were not subject to the control of any external party. The commission also enjoyed relative financial independence because it received support from a wide range of donors from all sectors and did not grant these donors any special role in its governance structure. Moreover, the commissioners were chosen to represent a balance among different stakeholder groups, they all enjoyed good international standing and reputation, were appointed for the entire duration of the process and were not financially dependent on their work as commissioners.

The 4C initiative, by contrast, has commissioned independent external organisations with the task of auditing and verifying the compliance of its members. Local verifiers have to be accredited by the Common Code Association. They are independent but can be subject to a systems verification, in turn conducted by an independent external organisation. Moreover, the 4C initiative demands that local verifiers disclose conflicts of interest. Similarly, MSC delegates compliance verification and certification to independent, accredited evaluators. The partnership goes a step further than the 4C initiative in that it even entrusts the accreditation process to an independent body. Explicitly following ISO standards 17011 and 19011, the agency (Accreditation Services International) accredits certification agencies, which in turn conduct certification assessments.

Which specific standards, then, should both kinds of information-generating partnerships fulfil relating to their impartiality and independence? The experiences of the judiciary and academia as well as the standards defined by ISO suggest that two complementary steps are necessary: Safeguarding the institutional independence of the bodies in charge of generating information and ensuring the personal independence of their staff members.

5.4.2.1 Ensure institutional independence

A first step to guarantee the impartiality of the knowledge or assessments developed by partnerships is to grant the bodies responsible for generating information institutional independence. Institutional independence has various dimensions.

Firstly, and most importantly, information-generating bodies should enjoy formal authority over their findings and results. Neither academia, nor the judiciary, for example, enjoys total autonomy. Thus universities are usually either public bodies or they need to be officially accredited. In many countries, moreover, the government formally appoints key academic staff. Similarly, judicial institutions are typically part of the government apparatus, rather than fully independent of it. Courts are public institutions and their judges are most often civil servants that are formally appointed by the government. Yet, both kinds of institutions are formally autonomous in the sense that no other institution has the right to interfere with their substantial results or decisions.

Thus academic freedom entails that universities can choose their focus in teaching and research and that research results are not subject to censorship.[127] Analogously, the verdicts of courts are considered binding and final and can only be reversed or changed through other judicial decisions.[128] According to ISO, the same standard should apply to certification bodies. It demands that the certification body be responsible for all decisions relating to the granting, maintaining, extending, suspending and withdrawing of certifications.[129]

Secondly, the financial position of the information-generating body can play an important role. Financial dependence on interested parties can undermine de facto institutional independence. The judiciary and academia, for example, typically receive the overwhelming majority of their resources from the public purse. But at the same time, the principles of judicial independence and academic freedom are grounded in public law. Public financial support can therefore not be tied to conditions relating to the substance of the work of these institutions.[130] Referring to the same question, the ISO standards stress that the bodies responsible for certification or accreditation should be free from undue commercial, financial or other pressures. They also emphasise that these bodies should describe their sources of income and avoid conflicts of interest.[131]

Finally, especially where complete independence from external interests cannot be guaranteed, institutional impartiality may entail the involvement of a balanced group of stakeholder representatives. In court, for example, judges are expected to be neutral and independent. At the same time, however, both the plaintiff and the defendant are represented through their legal counsels. Similarly, the ISO standards and guidelines request at several occasions that processes should be open to the participation of interested stakeholder groups.[132] Balanced multi-stakeholder arrangements may be particularly relevant for partnerships, which by definition are made up of different interest groups.

Following these examples, information-generating partnerships should adhere to a set of principles to ensure their impartiality and independence:

- Grant information-generating bodies formal and final authority over findings and results. To ensure that no external interests can manipulate the findings of the bodies in charge of generating information, they should have the last word on the subject. Correspondingly, no other institution should have the authority to correct, change, or otherwise amend their results.
- Seek unconditional, diverse and transparent institutional funding. The institutional entities responsible for generating information should enjoy as much financial security as possible. To avoid vulnerability to external pressure, information-generating partnerships should try to receive financial support that is not tied to any substantive results. Preferably, they should rely on diverse funding sources and they should always create maximum transparency concerning their sources of funds.
- Where complete independence from external interests is not possible, seek a balanced multi-stakeholder representation. As an alternative to full independence from external parties, partnerships can foster their impartiality by including a balanced number of representatives of diverse interests in their information-generating committees.

5.4.2.2 Foster personal independence

Institutional independence is only one side of the coin. To create a further bulwark against the manipulation of their findings, key staff members must be protected against external pressures and enjoy personal independence. Several factors can help to strengthen the independent position of key staff members.

Firstly, both academia and the judiciary rely on a high degree of job and income security for professors and judges to increase their immunity against external pressure. In the US, for example, life tenure and guaranteed salaries for judges are even enshrined in the constitution:

> The Judges, both of the supreme and inferior Courts, shall hold their Offices during good Behavior, and shall, at stated Times, receive for their Services a Compensation which shall not be diminished during their Continuance in Office.
>
> (United States of America, 1787, Art. III, section 1)[133]

Similarly, the academic world has a tradition of granting life tenure to professors.[134] The practice here, however, is not handled as strictly as in the judiciary. Following the criticism that tenure can have a negative impact on performance, an increasing number of teachers and researchers work off the tenure track. In addition, tenured professors can often be dismissed on the basis of a faculty decision.

Other organisations may find it difficult to create as much job and income security as the judiciary or academia. They may, for instance, not have the necessary financial security and planning horizon to offer lifetime appointments. In addition, the tasks they pursue may be of shorter duration. ISO has therefore proposed a more general formulation for the employees of accreditation bodies that can be transferred more easily to public policy partnerships:

> All accreditation body personnel and committees that could influence the accreditation process shall act objectively and shall be free from any undue commercial, financial and other pressures that could compromise impartiality.
>
> (International Organization for Standardization, 2004, clause 4.3.4.)

A second common step for ensuring the objectivity and independence of individual findings or assessments is to exclude conflicts of interest. Psychological research has found that financial interests create a self-serving bias in the perceptions and assessments of individuals. Interestingly, most test persons were unable to avoid this bias even when it would have been in their best interest to do so.[135] Institutions valuing objectivity therefore usually adopt practical measures to prevent or deal with conflicts of interest.

In the judiciary, impartiality is a core value. It is symbolised, for example, by Iustitia, the Roman Goddess of Justice, who in many depictions wears a blindfold to indicate that she assesses the merits of each case objectively. To ensure the impartiality of individual judges in practice, two measures are common in the judiciary. Firstly, the principle of impartiality and its practical implications are usually contained in the codes of ethics adopted by courts or professional associations.[136] Secondly, procedural rules of justice often contain elements protecting the impartiality of judgements. Thus, for example, some legal systems allow for the exclusion of judges from trials when they are reasonably suspected to be biased and others allow for appeals when bias can be demonstrated.[137]

In academia, an important control mechanism for ensuring the impartiality of research findings works on an informal level. Peer control, the public debate of research results and reputation effects create accountability for impartiality. In addition, however, universities, professional organisations and in some cases public authorities have also found more formal ways to deal with potential conflicts of interest. Thus the codes of ethics adopted by many professional associations and universities often contain principles relating to conflicts of interest.[138] In some countries, in addition, many professors enjoy the rank of civil servants. In that case, they are subject to more general regulations for civil servants, which often include the requirements to disclose financial interests or to obtain permission for engaging in additional occupations.[139]

The ISO standards and guidelines, finally, also make frequent reference to and propose concrete rules for dealing with conflicts of interest. Thus, for example, ISO guide 65 requests that certification bodies be free from external pressures and that they do not supply or design products of the type they certify, that they do not provide applicants with advice or consulting services related to the certification process and that they provide no other products or services which could compromise the confidentiality, objectivity and impartiality of their decisions (International Organization for Standardization, 1996, clauses 4.2.n and 4.2.o). Similarly, ISO standard 17011 prescribes that accreditation bodies shall not offer any service that may affect their impartiality and that they shall identify potential conflicts of interest that can arise from their or from related bodies' activities (International Organization for Standardization, 2004, clauses 4.3.6 and 4.3.7).

Thirdly, independence is not only a matter of objective circumstances but also of personal character. John Ferejohn, for example, explicitly introduces this aspect in his discussion of judicial independence: 'Independence, or impartiality, in this sense is a desirable aspect of a judge's character' (Ferejohn, 1999b, p. 353).

It is difficult to establish formal criteria and procedures for assessing an individual's character. In academia and the judiciary, however, the selection or election and appointment processes leave ample space for character considerations. ISO has attempted to define the desirable personal attributes of individuals conducting quality or environmental management systems audits. Accordingly, an auditor should be ethical, open-minded, diplomatic, observant, perceptive, versatile, tenacious, decisive and self-reliant (International Organization for Standardization, 2002, clause 7.2).

In designing their accountability arrangements focusing on the personal independence of key staff members, information-generating partnerships should orient themselves along these examples and observe the following principles:

- Ensure that staff members are free from undue commercial or financial pressures. To achieve this, institutions concerned with generating information can adopt two different strategies. One option is to work with financially independent experts that are not reliant on any income generated through their participation in the partnership. As an alternative, partnerships can offer reasonable job and income security for information-generating staff. This can involve, for example, fixed-term contracts as well as lump sum payments that are agreed upon at the outset and cannot be reduced based on the content of the results delivered.

• Adopt a written conflict of interest policy and require the disclosure of financial interests. Information-generating bodies should adopt explicit conflict of interest policies, outlining which external activities of key staff members are acceptable and which are not. Moreover, they should require all key personnel to indicate which other interests they hold.

• Appoint individuals of strong, independent character. To enhance the probability that individual researchers and evaluators are personally little susceptible to external pressure, information-generating partnerships can include a list of desired personal attributes in their job descriptions. Moreover, the selection and appointment process should enable a relatively large group of individuals to assess said personal characteristics alongside professional qualifications.

5.4.3 Accountability for accuracy and quality through professionalism

For information to be reliable and trustworthy, it does not only need to be unbiased. In addition, it needs to be accurate and of high quality. Next to safeguarding the independence of their information-generating bodies and staff, partnerships should therefore also ensure that they are professional and adhere to high quality standards.

The information-generating partnerships among the case examples rely on several strategies for ensuring the accuracy and quality of their results. For the creation of its knowledge base, the WCD, for example, selected commissioners of high repute representing different stakeholder interests. The commission then collected various kinds of inputs, including case studies of important dam projects, public submissions and debates with involved groups. Moreover, the commission relied on the WCD Forum to test the conclusions it drew from this evidence.

The 4C initiative also employs several parallel mechanisms to ensure the accuracy and quality of its assessment and verification schemes. Independent local verifiers verify the self-assessments submitted by local 4C units. These verifiers must fulfil specific conditions, be listed by the 4C Secretariat and receive special 4C training.[140] In addition, local verifications can be subject to a systems verification. These verifications are conducted by 'internationally recognised bodies' appointed by the executive board of the 4C association. The initiative also has several channels for dealing with disputes arising in the context of verification. Potential complaints are dealt with by the 4C secretariat, by the mediation board or by the independent ombudsman.

In a similar vein, MSC has various mechanisms in place to ensure the accuracy and quality of its certification processes. All certification bodies have to be accredited by an independent accrediting agency contracted by MSC. Moreover, MSC has defined standards relating to the professional expertise each assessment team must include.[141] In parallel to these standards, stakeholders and interested parties are given several opportunities to comment on the certification process.[142] If they are not satisfied with the final assessment, they can also lodge a formal objection. The certification body itself hears objections, but appeals to the MSC Objections Panel are also possible.

The practice of these information-generation partnerships, the experiences of the judiciary and academia and the standards defined by ISO suggest that partnerships should take two main steps to ensure that their results are accurate and of good quality: they should entrust the task of generating information to experts with relevant professional qualifications and they should create avenues for verifying results.

5.4.3.1 Recruit experts with formal qualification and good reputation

A crucial measure for fostering trust in a partnership's findings is to ensure that the individuals entrusted with generating information have appropriate professional qualifications and enjoy a good reputation.

Academia and the judiciary rely on similar practical steps to guarantee the professionalism of their staff. Both use specialised higher education programmes and professional training combined with official admissions tests as formal selection criteria. Thus only individuals that have successfully completed the relevant university education and that have passed the respective bar or state exams are eligible as candidates. In many cases, the ensuing selection and appointment process introduces an additional element of peer or popular evaluation. In academia, for example, the faculty usually plays a strong role in assessing and ranking potential new colleagues. In the judiciary, only some countries include peer or popular assessments in their selection procedures. In the US, for example, many judges are appointed following popular elections. Other judges are selected based on merit. In this case, a nomination committee comprising fellow lawyers as well as non-lawyers usually nominates them.[143]

The judiciary and different academic subjects each have their own dedicated higher education programmes as well as specialised qualification exams. Other institutions concerned with producing knowledge or assessing behaviour may be younger and may concentrate on much smaller thematic niches. For many, it is therefore difficult to resort to equally formalised and standardised selection practices. Instead, however, they can provide clear definitions of the formal qualifications and practical experiences they require of candidates. And they can offer additional specialised training to their staff.

ISO, for example, has defined such standards for quality and environmental management systems auditors.[144] In addition, ISO requires that auditors demonstrate their continual professional development and that they undergo regular evaluation.

To achieve similar levels of professionalism to the institutions discussed above, the partnership or independent bodies entrusted with generating information should comply with the following standards:

- Define necessary professional qualifications in terms of skills, education, work experience and training. For the recruitment of their researchers, evaluators or certifiers, information-generating partnerships should clearly outline formal qualification requirements. These should include a description of necessary generic skills as well as concrete conditions concerning the applicant's formal education, training and years and type of work experience.
- Include elements of peer or stakeholder assessment in the selection process of staff members. In addition to meeting formal criteria, it is important that candidates demonstrate the quality of their work. A proven practical way of achieving this is to involve peers or a broader group of stakeholder representatives in the nomination and selection of applicants.
- Where tasks are very specific, provide staff members with targeted training. Especially in partnerships engaged in compliance verification and certification, it is important that evaluators interpret and apply criteria consistently and follow comparable assessment strategies. To ensure staff members are able to do that, specialised training may be necessary.
- Encourage continuous professional development and periodically evaluate staff competences. Finally, information-generating partnerships should also be concerned with further developing the competences and experiences of their staff. They should therefore invest in the creation of professional development strategies. Regular evaluations of staff skills can, moreover, help to identify competence gaps and training needs.

5.4.3.2 Create possibilities for verifying or disputing results

Even the best-qualified and independent researchers and assessors can err in their analyses and judgements. A final important step for increasing the trustworthiness of the generated information therefore involves creating avenues for debating, disputing or verifying results.

In the academic world, open debate is a fundamental principle contributing to the advancement of science. The academic community is so big and structured in such a way that there are usually one or several groups of researchers focusing on the same or very similar topics. In this environment, new findings are subject to intense scrutiny and debate. And, without any formal rules governing this process, only widely accepted research results enter the canon of established knowledge. With the emergence of new approaches or contrary research results, however, even 'established knowledge' can be challenged at any time. Academia also acknowledges the importance of peer opinions in a more structured way. Thus, for example, the most respected scientific journals tend to be those involving a peer-review process. The reputation and influence of individual researchers, in turn, depends in part on how many articles they manage to publish in recognised journals.

A much more formal approach to debating or verifying results is dominant in the judiciary. Most judicial systems include a hierarchy of courts. Parties who feel wronged by a judgement can appeal to and have their case reheard by a court at a higher level.[145] Only the decisions of the highest court cannot be challenged within the judicial system. Appeals processes have been recognised as very effective means of recognising and rectifying judicial mistakes.[146]

For organisations involved in certification and accreditation activities at the international level, ISO has defined relevant standards. Accordingly, these organisations should have a – preferably independent – person or body to deal with complaints, appeals or disputes. The processes should include a decision on the validity of the appeal, the taking of appropriate action and a public documentation of all appeals, decisions and corresponding actions.[147]

For information-generating partnerships, these practices and rules can be translated into the following standards:

- Develop a procedure for soliciting public comments on drafts. Information generating partnerships should make copies of their preliminary findings available to the public. They should also adopt a formal procedure for dealing with comments received.
- Encourage and facilitate open debate about findings and results. Especially partnerships engaged in the creation of knowledge should actively promote debate on their findings. Depending on the context of the initiative, this may require holding local or regional discussion fora or establishing electronic debate platforms. Formal peer-review processes can further enhance the credibility of their results.
- Create a formal complaints or appeals processes. Partnerships engaged in verifying or certifying compliance with certain standards should, moreover, have formal and institutionalised complaints and appeals processes. This involves having a designated, preferably independent, person or body for hearing complaints and a clear process for deciding and taking action on appeals. In addition, the process should be made transparent by maintaining and publishing records of all complaints and appeals, as well as the corresponding decisions and actions.

5.4.4 Summary of standards

Table 5.4 provides an overview of relevant accountability standards for information-generating partnerships.

Table 5.4 Accountability standards for information-generating partnerships

Accountability principles	Accountability standards	Practical steps
Accountability for impartiality through independence	Ensure institutional independence	Grant information-generating bodies formal and final authority over their findings and results
		Seek unconditional, diverse and transparent financial support
		Where complete independence from external interests is not possible, seek balanced stakeholder representation
	Foster personal independence of key staff	Ensure that staff members are free from undue commercial and financial pressures
		Adopt a conflict of interest policy and require the disclosure of financial interests
		Appoint individuals of strong, independent character
Accountability for accuracy and quality through professionalism	Recruit experts with formal qualifications and good reputations	Define necessary professional qualifications in terms of skills, education, work experience and training
		Include elements of peer or stakeholder assessment in the selection process for staff members
		Where tasks are very specific, provide staff members with targeted training
		Encourage continuous professional development and periodically evaluate staff competences
	Create possibilities for debating, disputing and verifying results	Develop a procedure for soliciting public comments on drafts
		Encourage and facilitate open debate about findings and results (especially for partnerships generating knowledge)
		Create a formal complaints or appeals process (especially for partnerships verifying compliance)

6
Conclusion

6.1 Summary of findings

This book seeks to contribute to the debate and practice of partnerships by clarifying what accountability means, why partnerships should have more of it and what that entails in practice. It provides a detailed and theoretically well-founded account of why partnerships ought to have appropriate accountability arrangements and defines concrete accountability standards for different types of partnerships on that basis.

The study reaches its conclusions in four argumentative steps.[1] It begins by clarifying the concepts of 'partnership' and 'accountability'. The term partnership has many different uses. In the context of questions of governance, it can best be defined as a voluntary arrangement involving public, private and/or civil society organisations that is formalised, has common, non-hierarchical decision-making procedures and addresses a public policy issue. This definition has certain overlaps with the concepts of 'corporatism' and 'networks'. This study prefers to work with the term partnership, however, because it describes the empirical phenomenon under investigation more adequately and because it carries less theoretical baggage.

The core meaning of 'accountability' is deduced from the etymology of the term and from its theoretical foundations in principal–agent theory. Accountability can be understood as a mechanism designed to ensure that agents act in the best interest of their principals and do not abuse their authority. Based on this understanding, this book develops a model showing the general workings of accountability mechanisms.[2] The model suggests that different measures can contribute to a strengthening of accountability. Clarifying the agent's responsibilities and contributions to outcomes, improving the provision of information on the agent's behaviour, clarifying the principal's expectations and strengthening sanctions and incentives. A more concrete analysis of different accountability mechanisms reveals an accountability dilemma. Creating accountability can be costly and different kinds of accountability can contradict each other. Too much or the wrong

170

kind of accountability can therefore hamper organisational efficiency. From this, the study concludes that partnership accountability cannot simply be a case of 'the more, the better', but that partnerships need to choose carefully which accountability mechanisms are best suited to their situation.

Determining which accountability arrangements are necessary under what circumstances demands a clear understanding of the normative rationale underlying accountability. A second important step therefore is to analyse why we believe that organisations ought to be accountable. This study draws on well-established political, economic, legal and moral theories to argue that delegation creates the need for appropriate accountability arrangements. This argument intersects and overlaps in various ways with other justifications of accountability sketched earlier in Chapter 3. However, it provides a theoretical basis for accountability that at the same time creates a firmer normative basis and leads to more differentiated practical results.

The delegation of authority creates a duty for the agent to act in the best interest of the principal. Accountability mechanisms enable principals to monitor the behaviour of agents and to apply sanctions or incentives. In institutional settings, appropriate accountability mechanisms are necessary to ensure that agents fulfil their duties. Therefore, delegation creates an obligation to institute appropriate accountability arrangements, irrespective of whether it is explicit or implicit, ex-ante, ex-post or hypothetical. What kind of authority is delegated, in turn, determines which type of accountability is appropriate. The delegated or (in the case of ex-post or hypothetical delegation) assumed authority reflects itself in the function exercised by the organisation in question. Therefore, this study concludes that it is organisational function that defines which accountability arrangements are appropriate.

If organisational function determines accountability requirements, then a third important step is to establish which functions partnerships exercise. This study distinguishes between four relevant partnership functions: advocacy and awareness raising, rule setting and regulation, policy implementation and information generation (including both partnerships for knowledge creation and compliance verification).

In a fourth and final step, concrete accountability principles and standards are defined for each type of partnership. These standards are summarised in Table 6.1.

Advocacy and awareness-raising partnerships only require the delegation of basic forms of authority, including a licence to operate, authority over operational resources and support from partner or member organisations. Correspondingly, they need to espouse only basic forms of accountability, namely accountability for complying with relevant rules and regulations, basic financial accountability and accountability for working towards the partnership's mission. All types of partnerships need the forms of authority listed above to be able to operate. Therefore, the accountability standards defined for advocacy and awareness-raising partnerships apply to all partnerships.

172

Table 6.1 Summary of accountability standards for partnerships

Partnership type	Accountability principles	Accountability standards
Advocacy and awareness raising partnerships	Compliance with rules and regulations	Choose a well-governed host organisation
		Adopt clear internal rules
		Create an effective oversight body with the ability to apply sanctions
	Financial accountability	Adopt a system of internal financial controls
		Adopt accounting policies generating reliable, relevant, comparable and understandable information
		Adopt reporting practices generating reliable, relevant, comparable and understandable information and complying with donor demands
		Conduct independent audits for large partnerships
	Accountability for working towards the partnership's mission	Define a clear mission
		Orient activities along the mission
		Employ resources efficiently in pursuit of the mission
Rule-setting and regulation partnerships	Democratic accountability through participation	Formal possibilities for participation alternative (a): include stakeholder representatives in decision-making bodies
		Formal possibilities for participation alternative (b): conduct stakeholder consultation processes
		Formal possibilities for participation supplement: establish permanent comments and complaints procedures
		Create transparency
	Democratic accountability to avoid the abuse of authority	Partnerships setting voluntary rules need no additional accountability
		Partnerships setting binding rules should achieve appropriate authorisation, define a clear mandate and create a process of judicial review

Table 6.1 Continued

Partnership type	Accountability principles	Accountability standards
Implementation partnerships	Outcome accountability through performance evaluation	Define clear objectives and performance targets
		Monitor performance and create incentives for performance improvement
	Outcome accountability through the introduction of market elements	Outsource suitable tasks through competitive bidding processes
		Collect beneficiary feedback to assess performance
Information-generating partnerships	Accountability for impartiality through independence	Ensure institutional independence
		foster personal independence of key staff
	Accountability for accuracy and quality through professionalism	Recruit experts with formal qualifications and good reputations
		Create possibilities for debating, disputing and verifying results

Rule setting and regulation partnerships in addition assume or are granted the authority to set norms and rules. Therefore, they should adhere todemocratic standards of accountability. This involves creating formal possibilities for participation, generating a high degree of transparency and providing safeguards against the abuse of authority.

Implementation partnerships, in turn, have or seek authority over substantial resources. This triggers the need for creating accountability for outcomes. Outcome accountability can be strengthened, for example, through performance evaluations or through the introduction of market mechanisms.

Knowledge creation and compliance verification partnerships, finally, aspire to achieving ex-post authorisation by their user groups to generate information on their behalf. Similar to academia and the judiciary, they should therefore emphasise the trustworthiness of their information. Independence and professionalism should be the cornerstones of their accountability systems.

6.2 Lessons and applications

The preceding paragraphs have summarised the main results of this study in very brief terms. How, though, can we use those findings and what are their implications for the theory and practice of partnerships and accountability?

Firstly, the outcomes of this study have direct practical applications. Most obviously, the standards can be used to evaluate whether or not individual partnerships are sufficiently accountable. Practitioners can also use the accountability standards as guidelines for the institutional design of partnerships. By differentiating partnerships according to their function, the standards can help practitioners to identify priorities in designing accountability systems. They also indicate which practical measures can be taken to implement these priorities.

Secondly, this study contributes to the abstract debate on partnerships. The legitimacy of the partnership approach to governance is hotly debated. Can partnerships help the traditional nation state reassert its authority in an ever more complex world? Or do they, to the contrary, undermine democratic accountability standards that were hard fought for? The definition of different accountability requirements for different types of partnerships can render this discussion more differentiated. Moreover, the accountability standards defined in this study create the basis for systematic empirical research which could answer the question of whether or not partnerships are sufficiently accountable in practice.

Thirdly, the study adds to our conceptual and normative understanding of accountability since it proposes a generally applicable model of accountability. Most contributions to the theory of accountability to date are sector-specific, that is, they focus on accountability either in the context of the public sector, or the private sector or civil society. The reflections outlined here are more comprehensive because they deal with accountability at a more abstract level. At the same time, the argument proposed here not only accommodates but also proposes an explanation for the differences in accountability expectations and traditions between as well as within the various sectors of society.

Finally, this new understanding of accountability has important implications for the respective debates within the three sectors. The public sector, for example, currently faces a controversy over the new public management demand to create more accountability for outcomes. An application of the accountability concept generated here would suggest that this claim should neither be backed nor rejected in its entirety. Instead, it should be supported for all and only for those cases where public bodies operate as implementing agencies.

In the private sector, a current focus of discussion is on corporate social responsibility (CSR) and the related demand that companies should become more accountable in a democratic sense. The argument proposed here would reject this demand on normative grounds as long as companies do not get involved in setting rules for societies.

Relating to civil society organisations, finally, the results of this study would support those contributions suggesting different accountability arrangements depending on their functions. Rather than seeing this as a matter of strategic choice on the part of the NGOs, however, it would conceptualise this as a normative requirement.[3]

As the boundaries between the three sectors blur progressively and many organisations assume new functions, it is critical to operate with a comprehensive, yet differentiated concept of accountability. While this book cannot explore all its implications in detail, it lays the conceptual and normative foundations for subsequent studies to do so.

Notes

1 Introduction

1. CorpWatch, for example, is a US-American NGO investigating and exposing corporate violations of human rights, environmental crimes, fraud and corruption with the aim of holding these companies accountable for their actions. AccountAbility is an international NGO collecting and developing tools to increase accountability worldwide. The Campaign for Accountability of Our Media Voice seeks to increase the accountability of the media, especially of broadcast television. Corporate Accountability International is an NGO seeking to hold corporations accountable through lawsuits. These are just a few examples to illustrate the importance of 'accountability' as a political catchword. The list could be extended at will.

2. In the US Congress, for example, a large number of proposed bills even contain the term 'accountability' in their title. Melvin Dubnick lists 52 examples of legislation proposed by the 107th Congress including 'accountability' in their headings (Dubnick, 2002, p. 29).

3. A similar point is made by Richard Mulgan, who puts it in the following terms: 'That "accountability" is a complex and chameleon-like term is now a commonplace of the public administration literature. A word which a few decades or so ago was used only rarely and with relatively restricted meaning [...] now crops up everywhere performing all manner of analytical and rhetorical tasks and carrying most of the major burdens of democratic "governance" [...]. In the process, the concept of "accountability" has lost some of its former straightforwardness and has come to require constant clarification and increasingly complex categorization' (Mulgan, 2000a, p. 555).

4. In the political sciences, the term 'civil society' is disputed. Here, however, the purpose is not to contribute to that debate. In the following, the definition proposed by the London School of Economics Centre for Civil Society will be used: 'Civil society refers to the arena of uncoerced collective action around shared interests, purposes and values. In theory, its institutional forms are distinct from those of the state, family and market, though in practice, the boundaries between state, civil society, family and market are often complex, blurred and negotiated. Civil society commonly embraces a diversity of spaces, actors and institutional forms, varying in their degree of formality, autonomy and power. Civil societies are often populated by organisations such as registered charities, development non-governmental organisations, community groups, women's organisations, faith-based organisations, professional associations, trades unions, self-help groups, social movements, business associations, coalitions and advocacy groups' (Centre for Civil Society, 2004).

5. Since the possibilities for citizen control are limited, constitutional theorists have long argued for systems that control themselves. This is what is meant today by 'checks and balances' – independent political institutions that can check each other's power. In the words of Persson, Roland and Tabellini: 'Checks and balances work by creating conflict of interests between the executive and the

legislature, yet requiring both bodies to agree on public policy. In this way, the two bodies discipline each other at the voters' advantage' (Persson et al., 1997, p. 1163). Originally, the concept had a slightly different connotation and goes back to Aristotle's idea of mixed government. Walter Bagehot summarised this doctrine like this: 'A great theory, called the theory of "Checks and Balances," pervades an immense part of political literature, and much of it is collected from or supported by English experience. Monarchy, it is said, has some faults, some bad tendencies, aristocracy others, democracy, again others; but England has shown that a government can be constructed in which these evil tendencies exactly check, balance, and destroy one another – in which a good whole is constructed not simply in spite of, but by means of, the counteracting defects of the constituent parts' (Bagehot, 1873, p. 43).

In the current discourse on accountability, checks and balances are often referred to as 'horizontal accountability'. Guillermo O'Donnell, who has coined the term, defines it as 'the existence of state agencies that are legally enabled and empowered, and factually willing and able, to take actions that span from routine oversight to criminal sanctions or impeachment in relation to actions or omissions by other agents or agencies of the state that may be qualified as unlawful' (O'Donnell, 1999, p. 38). The claim that different state institutions relate to each other in a horizontal, that is, non-hierarchical way, has sparked much debate (see e.g. Kenney, 2000; Plattner, 1999; Schmitter, 1999; Schmitter, 2004; and Sklar, 1999). Despite the controversy, the spacial metaphor is frequently used in the discourse on public accountability.

6. Ebrahim (2005), for example, focuses on evaluations as accountability tools for non-profit organisations; Friedman and Phillips (2004) on the role of councils for professional organisations; Lee (2004) on public reporting for non-profit organisations; Young (2002) on accountability to mission of non-profit executives; Garn (2001) on the use of market-based accountability mechanisms in schools; Blasi (2002) on performance measurement for public service providers; and Schmitter (2004) on various mechanisms to create accountability for public officials.

7. See section 2.1.1 for a detailed discussion of the definition of 'partnership' used here.

8. Sources on GRI include Global Reporting Initiative (2002a), Global Reporting Initiative (2002b), Global Reporting Initiative (2002c), Global Reporting Initiative (2003), Global Reporting Initiative (2006a), http://www.globalreporting.org (last accessed 31 March 2010), Brown et al. (2007), Willis (2003), personal communication with Debbie Dickinson, Communications Coordinator, Global Reporting Initiative, 9 May 2007.

9. References on the Global Fund include The Global Fund to Fight AIDS, Tuberculosis and Malaria (2006), Technical Evaluation Reference Group (2006), Low-Beer et al. (2007), Fortier (2007), Wilkinson et al. (2006), http://www.theglobalfund.org (last accessed 31 March 2010), personal communication with Beatrice Bernescut of the Global Fund on 14 May 2007.

10. All partnerships discussed in this study engage in activities with an international or global reach. The context for accountability and legitimacy is very different at the national and the international level and this study espouses an international perspective.

11. These concerns are echoed, for example, in Ann-Marie Slaughter's reflections on transgovernmental networks, that is, cooperative arrangements between different governmental institutions: 'Transgovernmental networks that arise outside

the framework of international organizations and executive agreements are most likely to spawn fears of runaway technocracy. That a regulatory agency would reach out on its own account to its foreign counterparts, even in an effort to solve common problems, raises not only the possibilities of policy collusion, whereby transgovernmental support can be marshaled [*sic*] against domestic bureaucratic opponents, but also of the removal of issues from the domestic political sphere through deliberate technocratic de-politicization' (Slaughter, 2001, p. 18). Since accountability problems are even more complex and severe when networks involve not only governments but also civil society and business actors, her argument also applies to cross-sectoral partnerships.

12. Judith Richter, for example, describes public private partnerships as a tool used by industry to manipulate NGOs and steal their good image without making corporations more accountable. As a consequence, she argues that the term 'partnership' should be abolished. Cf. Richter, 2001, p. 170.

13. Activists have dubbed this 'greenwash' or 'bluewash', depending on whether corporations are accused of abusing the good environmental, 'green' reputation of NGOs or the 'blue' reputation of the United Nations. 'Greenwash' is defined as 'an attempt to achieve the appearance of social and environmental good without corresponding substance. Such greenwash is being used skilfully to manipulate public perceptions of corporations and diffuse public pressure to impose binding regulations. Through branding, corporate philanthropy, high-profile partnerships with NGOs and governments, and isolated but highly publicised "best practice" projects, corporations are making every effort to improve their image. All in order to avoid making the necessary changes to their core business practices demanded of them by civil society' (Corporate Europe Observatory, 2002, pp. 1–2).

14. Cf. e.g. Mallaby (2004).

15. An author who explicitly formulates his critique in terms of accountability is Robert Goodin, who warns that 'arrangements that straddle sectors (whether through partnership or competition) [...] undermine the accountability of each sector in its own terms and, hence, the interlocking system of social accountability overall' (Goodin, 2003, pp. 4–5). Similarly, Taylor and Warburton argue that as governments 'place an increasing emphasis on partnerships, the question of legitimacy and accountability is being blurred across the board' (Taylor and Warburton, 2003, p. 336).

16. The relationship between accountability and legitimacy, including the contribution made by accountability to input legitimacy, is discussed in greater detail in section 2.2.1.

17. The United Nations (UN) Commission on Sustainable Development (CSD), for example, is a crucial promoter of partnerships at the international level and within the UN system. It is also at the forefront of efforts to define criteria and guidelines for partnerships. One of its key demands is that 'Partnerships should be designed and implemented in a transparent and accountable manner' (Commission on Sustainable Development, 2003, Art. 22h). This is echoed by activists who state, for example, that 'Accountability is therefore key in delivering the legitimacy of partnerships required by a wider group of stakeholders' (Raynard and Cohen, 2003, p. 7).

18. A notable exception is the work of AccountAbility, an NGO promoting accountability. It has developed a concrete accountability standard called 'AA 1000'. This standard is designed to apply to all kinds of organisations, including all types of partnerships. AccountAbility explicitly states that 'AA 1000 is designed to

encompass the needs and requirements of adopters from all types of organisation. These include: (a) Large and small organisations. (b) Single site organisations, and multi-site, multinational organisations. (c) Public, private and non-profit organisations' (AccountAbility, 1999, p. 13). The definition of concrete criteria for accountability is a significant step forward. But their broad applicability also creates difficulties. As will be argued in this book, accountability requirements are determined by organisational function. Using the same criteria for assessing all types of partnerships, let alone organisations from the public, private and non-profit sectors, is therefore deeply problematic.

19. Over recent years, the discipline of political science has witnessed a rapidly growing debate on 'governance', both at the national and the international or global level of politics. For some of the many contributions to this debate see, for example, Albert and Kopp-Malek (2002), Bevir et al. (2003), Choudhury and Ahmed (2002), Finkelstein (1995), Hewson and Sinclair (1999), Hooghe and Marks (2003), Jordan et al. (2005), Keohane (2001), Knill and Lehmkuhl (2002), Kooiman (1993), Krahmann (2003), Nuscheler (2000), Nye and Donahue (2000), Pierre (2000), Rhodes (1996), Rosenau (1995), Stoker (1998), Vayrynen (1999). Key issues in this debate relate among others to the definition of the concept, empirical analyses of how governance works and the implications of new forms of governance for traditional government, its workings, legitimacy and account-ability. In many instances, the governance discourse relies on strong normative assumptions. This includes, for example, the assertion that it is necessary and good for governments to reassert their ability to shape policies by developing new ways of steering, but also that engagement in networks or partnerships can undermine traditional forms of democratic accountability, while at the same time creating new possibilities for citizen participation. Cf. Rhodes, 1997, Chapter 3.

Partnerships are a form of governance. By defining concrete accountability requirements for partnerships, this book thus makes an indirect and concrete contribution to the question of what implications new forms of governance can have for accountability.

2 The Concepts of Partnerships and Accountability

1. The term 'global public policy' was introduced in Reinicke (1998).
2. Thus, for example, major international partnership events in 2007 included the International Aid and Trade Event 'Building Partnerships for Relief and Development'; a partnerships fair held during the intergovernmental prepara-tory meeting for CSD 15; an OECD forum on improving cross-sector and multi-level cooperation; the Oslo conference on good governance and social and environmental responsibility titled 'Partnerships for Sustainable Development'; a partnerships fair held during the 15th CSD session; the 2007 conference on global health, 'Partnerships: Working Together for Global Health'; and a meet-ing of the Inter-American Water Resources Network, 'Strengthening Partnerships and Building the Basis for Meeting the Millennium Development Goals'. A list of relevant meetings is published, for example, by the United Nations Division for Sustainable Development (DESA) and is available at http://webapps01.un.org/dsd/partnerships/calendar/public/displayEvents.do (last accessed 27 August 2009).
3. Rodal and Mulder, for example, confirm this by writing: 'The word "partnership" has been over-used, misused, and often used imprecisely, to the point that it is

sometimes indistinguishable from other "good" management practices, such as consultations, either with external parties or internally with employees, or simply coordination of activities across an organization' (Rodal and Mulder, 1993, pp. 27–8). Even when focusing only on UN partnerships, Carmen Malena notes that 'Reviewing the literature and talking to UN and civil society representatives quickly reveals that there is little common understanding regarding the meaning of partnership' (Malena, 2004).

4. The 'ideal type' as a method for defining social scientific concepts is commonly ascribed to Max Weber. Social reality is usually so complex and varied that no conceptual apparatus can do it justice. Nevertheless, Weber argued, social scientists should define clear concepts that try to capture important similarities of phenomena and thus facilitate analysis and enquiry. Cf. for example, Käsler (1995), pp. 229–34.

5. Cf. the so-called Bali guiding principles (available at http://www.un.org/esa/sustdev/partnerships/bali_guiding_principles.htm, last accessed 27 August 2009) and the CSD 11 decision (Commission on Sustainable Development, 2003).

6. 'Unter "Public Private Partnerships" verstehen wir Entwicklungspartnerschaften mit der Privatwirtschaft: Die Partnerschaften bestehen aus gemeinsam finanzierten Projekten von Unternehmen und entwicklungspolitischen Institutionen' (Gesellschaft für Technische Zusammenarbeit, 2004).

7. The concept of corporatism has changed over time, sometimes creating confusion as to its exact meaning. Williamson (1985b), for example, provides a comprehensive discussion of the concept of corporatism and distinguishes three different usages of the term as a body of prescriptive economic and social thought, as a practice of a range of authoritarian regimes and as an analytical tool to examine the relations between organised groups and the state in liberal democracies.

8. Philippe S. Schmitter, a leading contemporary theorist on corporatism, for example, reflects the ambiguous connotations of the term when he states that 'Corporatism, either as a practice in political life or as a concept in political theory, has always been politically controversial. It has been heralded as a novel and promising way of ensuring harmony between conflicting social classes. It has also been condemned as a reactionary and antidemocratic formula for suppressing the demands of autonomous associations and movements' (Schmitter, 1995, p. 309).

9. This argument has been made most explicitly for partnerships operating at the international or transnational level by Marina Ottaway. To her, recent trends suggest that corporatist solutions at the global level are on the rise. Analysing the historical track record of corporatism, she comes to the conclusion that the main danger of corporatism as implemented in nation states, namely the emergence of authoritarianism, is not a risk at the global level. Yet she still concludes that corporatism's costs exceed it benefits: 'And this is what corporatism has always done: it absorbs groups that challenge the status quo in the political system, where they can have some impact on policy reform but are neutralized as vehicles for radical change' (Ottaway, 2001, p. 280).

   For the local level, Vivien Lowndes has emphasised that partnerships have the same shortcomings as the traditional corporatist model. Cf. Lowndes (2001).

10. Cf. Saul (1999).

11. The argument has been made most powerfully for NGOs operating at the transnational or international level. Thus, for example, Anderson and Rieff criticise the standard account of transnational NGOs as constituting 'global civil society' and

the connected claim that NGOs are representative and provide systems of global governance with legitimacy by giving ordinary people a voice. Instead, they argue that transnational and international NGOs are better seen as 'a revival of the post-religious of the earlier European and American missionary movements' or as 'a movement seeking to universalise the ultimately parochial model of European Union integration' (Anderson and Rieff, 2005, p. 26). Similarly, Martens (2001) argues that a corporatist framework is better suited than the predominant pluralist approaches for analysing and understanding the role played by NGOs in international organisations.

12. That large NGOs have a comparative advantage in engaging with partnerships was one of the points debated during the 2002 WSSD in Johannesburg. It is reflected, for example, in the summary of the Johannesburg debate provided by Witte and Streck: 'Moreover, there is a widespread perception that the small are losing out to the big once again. Whereas large NGOs – such as Greenpeace, IUCN-World Conservation Union or the World Wildlife Federation (WWF) – have the means and the leverage to design and develop partnerships according to their gusto, the voices of small NGOs or representatives of small businesses are often lost in the partnership hype' (Witte and Streck, 2003, p. 3).

13. Sources on the World Commission on Dams include World Commission on Dams (1999), World Commission on Dams (2000, 2001), Scudder (2001). Since the commission has been disbanded, there was no personal communication with the commission secretariat or individual commission members. Several intensive studies on the commission based on a large number of personal interviews with commission members, staff and stakeholders have been conducted by other researchers. They include Dubash et al. (2001), Khagram (1999), Dingwerth (2003) and Dingwerth (2005), who focuses on the legitimacy of the rule-setting process and includes a detailed analysis of the commission's governance structures and processes.

14. A notable exception to this is the International Labour Organization (ILO), which traditionally has a tripartite governance structure, involving national governments as well as employers and workers in all its bodies. For more information see http://www.ilo.org (last accessed 27 August 2009).

15. Cf. Scharpf (1993).

16. In 'Soziologie: Untersuchungen über die Formen der Vergesellschaftung' (1908), Simmel argued that the primary focus of sociology should be on the interactions between agents and analysed dyadic and triadic relationships. Cf. Rank (2003), p. 28.

17. See, for example, the edited volume by Boissevain and Mitchell (1973), in which a number of social anthropologists focus on interactions among people in order to remedy the perceived shortcomings of the hitherto dominant structural-functional approach to anthropological studies.

18. In the analysis of policy networks, for example, typologies have been developed that differentiate networks according to their degree of integration, membership, the distribution of resources among their members, their level of stability or the object of exchange involved. For a detailed discussion of a range of typologies for policy networks, see Thatcher (1998).

19. R. A. W. Rhodes even defines governance in terms of networks: 'So, *governance refers to self-organizing, interorganizational networks* characterized by interdependence, resource exchange, rules of the game and significant autonomy from the state' (Rhodes, 1997, p. 15, emphasis original). Other authors using the concept

of governance to describe non-hierarchical models of governing, relying on networks, include, for example, Bulmer (1994), Kooiman (1993) and Rosenau and
Czempiel (1992).

20. R. A. W. Rhodes in his influential writings has termed this the 'hollowing out of the
    state' which 'refers to the loss of functions upwards to the European Union, down-
    wards to special-purpose bodies and outwards to agencies' (Rhodes, 1997, p. 17).

21. For a similar definition of governance, as well as a critical analysis of the different
    and changing meanings of 'governance' by a long-term contributor to the debate,
    see, for example, Mayntz (2003). Cf. also Marin and Mayntz (1991).

22. Mark Thatcher, for example, finds that 'the concept of policy network appears
    so general that it is almost meaningless', and that the 'breadth of the concept of
    policy networks makes it difficult to operationalize and apply in empirical stud-
    ies' (Thatcher, 1998, p. 401). For a detailed description, application and critique
    of 'social network analysis', see Thompson (2003), Chapter 3. Rhodes (1997,
    pp. 10–13) also contains a summary of the criticisms levelled against the network
    approach.

23. Cf., for example, Thompson (2003), Chapters 2 and 3. For more references on
    transaction cost analysis and the New Institutional Economics, see section 2.2.1.

24. Cf. Rank (2003), p. 35.

25. In fact, the two terms are often used synonymously. See, for example, the article
    'Local Economic Development Partnerships: An Analysis of Policy Networks
    in EC-LEDA Local Employment Development Strategies' by Bennett and Krebs
    (1994); Bobrowsky's 'Creating a Global Public Policy Network in the Apparel
    Industry: The Apparel Industry Partnership' (Bobrowsky, 1999); Considine's 'The
    End of the Line? Accountable Governance in the Age of Networks, Partnerships,
    and Joined-up Services' (Considine, 2002); or Reinicke and Deng (2000).

26. Mark Thatcher, for example, describes as one extreme the 'issue network', which
    has broad membership but where 'participants are constantly changing, and the
    degree of mutual commitment and interdependence varies between them [...].
    No one is in control of the policies and issues covered by a network' (Thatcher,
    1998, pp. 391–2). At the other extreme, Grahame Thompson lists 'corporatism' as
    a possible network (Thompson, 2003, pp. 155–6). Anne-Marie Slaughter focuses
    on networks among national government officials, which she describes as either
    arising in the context of international organisations (such as the networks that
    have developed within the OECD), as created by executive agreement (e.g. the
    1998 Transatlantic Economic Partnership Agreement) or spontaneously (e.g. the
    Basle Committee working on banking regulation) (Slaughter, 2001, section 2).

27. Cf. Benner et al. (2004). The authors include flexibility and complementarity as
    additional network characteristics. Klijn and Koppenjan (2000) focus on mutual
    dependence, describe networks as interaction that arises around policy issues and
    resource clusters and emphasise that networks require active steering to manage
    the conflicting interests of participants.

28. For a more detailed discussion about solidarity, altruism, loyalty, trust and reci-
    procity as characteristic attributes of networks, see Thompson (2003), Chapter 2.

29. Cf. Douglas-Harper, entry for 'account'.

30. Cf. for example, some contributions to Arnull and Wincott (2002), Chaskin
    (2003), Genders (2002), Keohane (2002b), Naidoo (2004), Slim (2002) or Taiclet
    (2001).

31. Fritz Scharpf, probably the most influential contemporary contributor to the
    debate about legitimacy, has defined legitimacy as a 'socially sanctioned obligation

to comply with government policies even if these violate the actor's own interests or normative preferences, and even if official sanctions could be avoided at low cost' (Scharpf, 2003, p. 1). Thus legitimacy as a concept refers to a perceived quality of an institution or organisation, whereas accountability refers to a relationship between actors.

32. Weber (1976), p. 124, cf. Käsler (1995), pp. 207–15.
33. The widely accepted distinction between input and output legitimacy goes back to Fritz Scharpf. Cf. Scharpf (1970) and Scharpf (1999).
34. Thomas Risse, for example, writing on transnational, horizontal forms of governance, emphasises the connection between accountability and input legitimacy: 'If the agents involved in governance arrangements are both internally accountable to their "clients" – be it shareholders of firms or citizens of governments – and externally accountable to those who are affected by their decisions – the various "stakeholders" – input legitimacy should be insured' (Risse, 2006, p. 186).
35. The process of defining obligations and expectations can be very complex and can take various shapes in different situations. Thus, for example, obligations can be defined through contracts, as is the case in most economic interactions, from which the principal–agent theory was derived. Other situations, particularly in the political and social fields, however, are too complex and involve too many imponderables to be fixed in a contract. Here, obligations and expectations are defined socially and often remain diffuse. The various processes of defining obligations and expectations on the basis of which behaviour is evaluated are not included in Figure 2.3.
36. Again, Adam Smith provided a formulation of the problem of information asymmetry and information-cost for the principal hindering effective control of the agent that is still valid today: 'The trade of a joint stock company is always managed by a court of directors. This court, indeed, is frequently subject, in many respects, to the control of a general court of proprietors. But the greater part of those proprietors seldom pretend to understand any thing of the business of the company; and when the spirit of faction happens not to prevail among them, give themselves no trouble about it, but receive contentedly such half yearly or yearly dividend, as the directors think proper to make to them' (Smith, 1937, p. 699).
37. In an early and influential paper on the principal–agent relationship, Jensen and Meckling defined agency costs as follows: 'The principal can limit divergences from his interest by establishing appropriate incentives for the agent and by incurring monitoring costs designed to limit the aberrant activities of the agent. In addition in some situations it will pay the agent to expend resources (bonding costs) to guarantee that he will not take certain actions which would harm the principal or to ensure that the principal will be compensated if he does take such actions. However, it is generally impossible for the principal or the agent at zero cost to ensure that the agent will make optimal decisions from the principal's viewpoint. In most agency relationships the principal and the agent will incur positive monitoring and bonding costs (non-pecuniary as well as pecuniary), and in addition there will be some divergence between the agent's decisions and those decisions which would maximize the welfare of the principal' (Jensen and Meckling, 1976, p. 311). Total agency cost, then, is the sum of monitoring expenditures, bonding expenditures and residual loss.
38. As the definition of agency relationships by Ross used above suggests, principal–agent situations are not even restricted to contractual arrangements but include

any arrangement in which somebody acts for, on behalf of or as a representative of somebody else.

39. The 'father' of stakeholder theory, R. Edward Freeman, developed his concept as an alternative to existing theories of the firm. He proposed replacing the legal and moral fiduciary duty of managers to stockholders with a similar duty to different stakeholder groups: 'Corporations shall be managed in the interests of its stakeholders, defined as employees, financiers, customers, suppliers, and communities' (Freeman, 2001, p. 47).

40. These questions reflect in part those asked by Slim (2002) in relation to the accountability of NGOs.

41. Robert Keohane, for example, argues that 'it seems likely that [...] units will be able to evade accountability by blaming other units, or the operation of the system as a whole'. He describes different strategies to avoid accountability: 'Avoiding accountability relationships altogether', 'controlling the nominal principal', 'strategically limiting information to the principal' and 'creating so many principals that accountability is avoided' (Keohane, 2002b, pp. 12–14).

    A classic legal example is the M/S Herald of Free Enterprise case. In 1987, a passenger and car ferry capsized, leading to the death of 193 individuals. Although the behaviour of several crew members as well as the corporate culture were found seriously problematic, all crew members as well as the company itself were acquitted from the charge of manslaughter. For the official inquiry into the disaster, see Department of Transport (1987).

42. Thus, for example, a range of German companies are held accountable today through legal proceedings as well as public opinion pressure for activities they undertook during the Second World War, particularly relating to the use of forced labour in their factories.

43. Governments often operate with hierarchical models of accountability, when ministers are held to account for the conduct of their ministries. Yet when a minister can credibly claim she did not authorise or know about the activities in question, she might evade formalised sanctions, that is, resignation, and only suffer reputational damage. Thus the American secretary of defense, Donald Rumsfeld, experienced no formal personal consequences from the prisoner abuse scandal in Iraq's Abu Ghraib prison. At the same time, if a resignation is forced under similar circumstances, it is not clear how these sanctions contribute immediately to preventing similar misconduct in the future.

    In the aftermath of the Enron scandal in the US, the Sarbanes-Oxley Act also increased hierarchical accountability in public companies. Thus it specifies that chief executive officers and chief financial officers are responsible for the accuracy and validity of financial reports. Cf. One Hundred Seventh Congress of the United States of America (2002), title III.

44. Systems of collective accountability depend on strong collective identities. Societies based on a strong clan structure, for example, often experience blood feuds in which individual clan members are sanctioned for the behaviour of the family group as a whole. Similarly, in times of war national or ethnic identities tend to be strengthened and individuals can be attacked on the basis of their ethnic or national identity. With much less radical effects, the same mechanism is in effect when staff members of a company with bad reputation are shunned or criticised by other members of society.

45. A common case for the analysis of problems of multiple principals is a publicly traded company. Here, ownership does usually not reside with any one

individual or institution but is dispersed among a range of shareholders. The term 'fragmented principal' describes this situation. It differs from other situations involving multiple principals in so far as the interests of fragmented principals tend to be broadly similar, while multiple principals in other instances can have contradicting interests.

46. The economic literature on problems of control arising from fragmented principals is extensive. In a recent addition to this body of literature, Peter Gourevitch links corporate scandals such as Enron to collective action problems in situations with multiple principals. He describes the collective action problem as follows: 'no one has an incentive to pay the transactions [*sic*] costs required to monitor the managers' (Gourevitch, 2002, p. 3). Sean Gailmard uses a similar approach to analyse the problem of multiple principals in bureaucratic policymaking (Gailmard, 2002).

47. Edward Freeman in his important text 'A Stakeholder Theory of the Modern Corporation' described the conflicting claims of these stakeholders as follows: 'Owners want higher financial returns, while customers want more money spent on research and development. Employees want higher wages and better benefits, while the local community wants better parks and day-care facilities' (Freeman, 2001, p. 44).

48. Mark Bovens has termed this problem the 'problem of many eyes': 'From a sociological perspective, public managers face multiple accountabilities. They may have to account for various elements of their conduct to a variety of forums. To make things even more complicated, each of the forums may have different expectations, based on different sets of norms, about the propriety of the manager's conduct, and may therefore pass different judgments' (Bovens, 2005, p. 186).

49. Remember Keohane's argument that agents may deliberately multiply the number of principals they are accountable to in order to reduce their overall accountability: 'In a democratic era, it is difficult for an agent to say, 'the public be damned' and explicitly to dismiss accountability claims. It may be more feasible, and more clever, to multiply the number of principals to whom one is responsible – and principles on the basis of which one is responsible – that accountability is eroded in practice' (Keohane, 2002b, p. 14).

50. One notable exception is the United Nations. While its headquarters are located in the US, it enjoys extraterritorial status and its staff is protected from national legal procedures through diplomatic immunity. The ongoing dispute about unpaid parking tickets from UN diplomats illustrates the frustrations that can arise from such an exemption. The UN, though, seeks to counteract this accountability gap by designing its own internal rules and enforcement mechanisms. Similarly, diplomatic missions around the world, to which comparable exemptions apply, are bound by the laws and regulations of their home countries. Recent efforts to create international court systems, such as the establishment of the International Criminal Court (ICC), have to be seen as an attempt by the international community to close accountability gaps for grave abuses of human rights that arise when national legal systems fail.

51. Remember the close semantic proximity between 'accountability' and 'accounting' discussed above. Melvin Dubnick traces the origins of the word 'accountability' back to the old French 'comptes à rendre', which suggests a similar link to recording and explaining financial transactions (Dubnick, 2002, p. 3).

52. It is well known that the sources of funds and other resources are carefully watched in the public sector and for civil society organisations. More recently,

they have increasingly become an issue in the private sector as well. Private audit companies, for example, are easily exposed to a conflict of interest because they generate their income from the clients they are supposed to evaluate objectively. Collusion between auditors and fraudulent managers has been blamed as one of the reasons for spectacular corporate scandals such as Enron.

53. The term 'due diligence' comes from the discipline of economics. It is used in the context of mergers and acquisitions to designate the process of carefully evaluating all available evidence before taking the decision whether or not to invest in another business, cf. for example, Reed Lajoux and Elson (2000).

54. Both were accused of basing their decisions on faulty evidence. Greenpeace accused Shell of seriously underestimating the amount of chemicals left over in the oil buoy 'Brent Spar' and on this basis called for a boycott against Shell. Subsequent investigations proved that these allegations were wrong. The Bush administration made its original case for going to war against Iraq on the basis that it was producing weapons of mass destruction. The evidence leading to this assessment was found seriously flawed.

55. Transparency requirements are usually most far reaching for democratic governments and their agencies who have to publish detailed budgets, agendas and records of meetings as well as decisions. In the business sector, transparency demands by shareholders traditionally referred only to financial aspects. More recently, however, pressure by civil society groups and governments has led to increased social and environmental and, finally, sustainability reporting, that is, improved access to information about the non-financial aspects of a corporation's operations.

56. Financial reporting and auditing are highly regulated activities in most countries. There is also a widely accepted international set of standards, the International Financial Reporting Standards, which have been established by the International Accounting Standards Committee (IASC) Foundation, a private organisation. Standards for social, environmental or 'sustainability' reporting and accounting are only slowly emerging. Organisations leading the effort to design common standards include the US-American non-profit Social Accountability International (SAI) as well as the Global Reporting Initiative (GRI).

57. Cf. section 2.2.1.

58. This is Thompson's 'problem of many hands' which I referred to above: when various individuals or organisations contribute to a complex outcome, it is often difficult to establish whose behaviour had what impact on that outcome.

59. This approach differs, for example, from that espoused by Robert Keohane, who focuses on only one of these aspects, namely 'the *mechanisms used to sanction agents*' (Keohane, 2002b, p. 14, emphasis original). Based on these criteria for identification, he distinguishes hierarchical, supervisory, electoral, fiscal, legal, market, participatory and public reputational accountability.

60. This holds at least for what I have called 'proactive' or 'preventive accountability'. When we consider 'retroactive' accountability, that is, a situation where the principal actually employs sanctions to hold the agent to account for earlier wrongdoings, then unclear expectations of the principal might be an exception: particularly where sanctions are informal, for example, in the case of consumer reactions, they can be used even when there were no clearly defined expectations concerning the agent's behaviour.

61. The centrality of access to information for all kinds of accountability is reflected, for example, in criteria chosen by the One World Trust to evaluate the

accountability of intergovernmental organisations, NGOs and corporations: The 'Global Accountability Report' uses access to information as one of only two general criteria for determining an organisation's level of accountability (Kovach et al., 2003, p. iv). Many authors also include increased transparency prominently in their list of recommendations for making specific institutions more accountable. Anne-Marie Slaughter, for example, includes it as one of four measures to make government networks more accountable to citizens: 'A second step toward holding government networks as accountable as possible to domestic constituents is to make their activity as visible as possible to legislators, interest groups and ordinary citizens by ensuring that they operate in a real or virtual public space' (Slaughter, 2004, p. 172).

62. Alnoor Ebrahim discusses in greater detail the advantages and downsides of internal and external performance evaluations for NGOs (Ebrahim, 2003).

63. Cf. Pope (2000), Chapter 24.

64. Take, for example, the workings of a central bank, a highly formalised and easily quantifiable process. In democratic systems with independent central banks, the objectives of monetary policy are usually defined by law. In European systems, two goals are often mentioned: price stability and support for the economic policies of the government. Since this leaves it to the bank to determine how to balance these two objectives, de Haan, Amtenbrink and Eijffinger see an accountability gap: 'Where a central bank has both instrument and goal independence the body charged with holding the central bank accountable is not provided with an effective statutory yardstick to evaluate the performance of the bank, and thus to hold the bank accountable for its conduct of monetary policy' (de Haan et al., 1998, p. 4). But even where only price stability is defined as the objective of monetary policy, a bank has leeway since 'the objective of price stability has different interpretations: price level constancy versus zero inflation' (ibid.).

65. This brings us back to square one of principal–agent theory. One of the main assumptions of the original formulation of that theory was that the agent acts under conditions of uncertainty. Therefore, a complete definition of the agent's activities in a contract is not possible and the dilemma of control and accountability begins. Cf. Ross (1973).

66. Cf. Keohane (2002b), p. 14.

67. Since this dilemma is so difficult to solve, the Bible prescribes: 'No man can serve two masters: for either he will hate the one, and love the other; or else he will hold to the one, and despise the other. Ye cannot serve God and mammon' (Matthew 6:24, King James Version).

   In a more humoristic interpretation, Carlo Goldoni's play 'Il Servitore di Due Padroni' or 'The Servant of Two Masters' portrays the numerous problems that Truffaldino encounters when he attempts to serve to masters at the same time.

68. This list resembles, but is not entirely congruent with, the ones proposed among others by Benner et al. (2004), Keohane (2002b), Keohane and Nye (2001), Newell and Bellour (2002).

69. Despite the fact that elections are generally considered to be the main mechanism for creating democratic accountability, top politicians are often limited in the number of re-elections they can seek. James D. Fearon therefore argues that elections are not only used as mechanisms to create accountability through sanctions but also as a means of selecting 'good' politicians who will act in the citizens' best interest out of their own accord. Cf. Fearon (1999), p. 61.

70. This is what Albert O. Hirschman termed the option of 'exit' that actors can use if they cannot change elements they criticise through 'voice' (Hirschman, 1972).

71. Because reputation is hard to measure and often hard to influence, it often gets little consideration in debates and strategies. An indicator for the fact that the hard-nosed corporate sector is taking reputation more seriously as a factor for corporate success is the work of the Reputation Institute, which dedicates its work exclusively to this topic. For more information, see http://www.reputation institute.com (last accessed 27 August 2009).

72. These strategies are reflected, for example, in Anne-Marie Slaughter's recommendations on how to improve the accountability of government networks to domestic constituencies. Next to creating visibility and transparency, she advocates 'to ensure that government networks link legislators across borders as much as they do regulators and judges, to ensure that all three branches of government, with their relative strengths and weaknesses, are represented', that is, the inclusion of legislators in those networks, and 'to use government networks as the spines of larger policy networks, helping to mobilize transnational society', that is, facilitating collective action (Slaughter, 2004, p. 173).

73. Figure 2.4 is a very basic depiction of an 'accountability game', following the prescriptions on how to formalise a situation in the form of a game contained in Morrow (1994, Chapter 3).

74. John Ferejohn builds a formal model of political accountability and explains the agent's interest in strengthening accountability as follows: 'increasing the degree of accountability in an agency contract can increase the power of the agent, all things considered, and therefore [...] agents have an incentive to make themselves accountable'. Thus to 'the extent that the actions of elected officials can be monitored, citizens will be willing to invest more in government'. As a result, 'the increase in governmental authority has been brought about by the provision for increased agent observability' (Ferejohn, 1999a, pp. 140–1 and 148).

75. Cf. Jonathan Koppell who concludes: 'Accountability is good. There is little disagreement on this point. Complaints that an organization is "too accountable" are rarely heard' (Koppell, 2003, p. 174).

76. Thus, for example, Benner, Reinicke and Witte argue that 'While by now there is a sophisticated academic debate on the "democratic deficit" in global policy-making, all too often contributions to the debate fall short of operationalizing their findings for the daily practice of global governance: what approaches should we use to make global public policy-making more accountable?' (Benner et al., 2004, p. 191). More explicitly, the Global Accountability Report argues that institutions operating at the international level need more accountability: 'These institutions [international governmental organisations, transnational corporations and international NGOs] need to become more transparent and accountable to their stakeholders [...]. This will increase their legitimacy and lead to more effective decision-making' (Kovach et al., 2003, p. iv).

77. An indicator that this has been recognised as a problem in practice can be found in different attempts to limit the accountability of people or institutions. Thus the development of the limited liability company allowed entrepreneurs to take more risks and this contributed to economic growth over the last century. In the political sphere, the limitation of terms of office is often justified with enabling political leaders to pursue more long-term objectives, which can be hampered by electoral accountability.

78. The literature on the European Union's governance in general and its democratic deficit and accountability in particular is vast. For a few examples, see Amtenbrink (1999), Arnull and Wincott (2002), Asbach (2002), Chryssochoou et al. (1998), Coultrap (1999), Decker (2000), Grande (1996), Gustavsson (2000), Gusy (1998), Habermas (1998), Harlow (2002), Katz (2001), Kiernan (1997), Laffan (2003), Lemke (1999), Lindseth (1999), Lodge (1996, 2003), Lopez Coterilla and Vicente (1998), Lord (1998, 2001), Meadowcroft (2002), Misch (1996), Moravcsik (2002), Moussis (2000), Neunreither (1994), Norris (1997), Oberreuter (1999), Pasquino (2000), Pogge (1997), Rosanvallon (2002), Scharpf (1999), Tsebelis and Garrett (2000), Weiler et al. (1995), Wiener and Della-Sala (1997), Williams (1990), Wincott (1998), Wolf (2000), Zürn (2000), Zweifel (2002).
79. The operating framework for the Roll Back Malaria Partnership, for example, explicitly quotes increased accountability as a reason for choosing a partnership approach: 'A Partnership offers the prospect of a heightened level of accountability and responsibility of all partners, which is needed for achieving country agreed targets' (Roll Back Malaria Partnership, 2004, p. 2).
80. For a detailed discussion of the scandal, subsequent investigations and the changes introduced as a response, see Harlow (2002), Chapter 3.
81. For an analysis of the impacts of the Enron scandal on corporate governance, see Solomon and Solomon (2004) Chapter 2.
82. An important collection of the data on partnerships is the partnership database provided by the UN's Commission on Sustainable Development, which contains information on partnerships that register with CSD (see http://webapps01. un.org/dsd/partnerships/public/browse.do, last accessed 27 August 2009). Since CSD explicitly encouraged the creation and registration of new partnerships, the data is most likely biased with respect to partnership age. Yet the total number of partnerships listed is relatively large (319 at the time of the writing of the 2006 report of the secretary-general on partnerships for sustainable development to the Commission on Sustainable Development, 346 by 27 August 2009). Therefore, the following findings at least contain an indication as to how prevalent young partnerships are: 'A majority of the partnerships registered with the Commission secretariat were launched at or around the time of the World Summit. [...] Less than one tenth (9 per cent) of registered partnerships were in existence prior to 2002' (United Nations Economic and Social Council, 2006, p. 9).
83. Again, the business example clearly illustrates this. While Freeman claims that his 'stakeholder theory does not give primacy to one stakeholder group over another' (Freeman, 2001, p. 44), the reality looks different. Thus even the proponents of 'corporate social responsibility' (CSR) practices, that is, those who advocate taking responsibilities to stakeholder groups other than shareholders seriously, have had to recognise the predominance of owners and shareholders. As a consequence, most CSR advocates are now upholding the 'business case for CSR', that is, the argument that taking the concerns of other stakeholders into account is good for business. Among the many examples for 'business cases' for CSR, see, for example, Wieland and Conrad (2002), Hopkins and Cowe (2003) and Hartmann (2003).
84. Acar and Robertson emphasise this point: 'public–private partnerships are created in the first place to attain objectives that are jointly defined by individuals and organizations coming from public, private, and non-profit organizations. However, it is often the case that these actors' underlying values and operating goals vary to a great extent' (Acar and Robertson, 2004, p. 333).

3   Why Organisations Ought to be Accountable

1. And in fact, Brown and Moore take this step only reluctantly. Rather inconsistently, they argue that even though they abandon accountability as an 'abstract, fixed moral ideal', their account has accountability as 'both morally good and practically useful' (Brown and Moore, 2001, p. 2).

2. The notion of trust plays an important role in transaction cost economics. For an explicit discussion of trust in this context see, for example, Williamson (1993). For empirical studies analysing the influence of trust on transaction costs see, for example, Zaheer et al. (1998), Dyer and Chu (2003) and den Butter and Mosch (2003).

3. In a similar vein, Regina Herzlinger proposes that to restore trust in governmental agencies and non-profit organisations, one should 'Increase the *disclosure*, analysis, and *dissemination* of information on the performance of nonprofit and governmental organizations, and apply *sanctions* against those that do not comply with these requirements' (Herzlinger, 1996, p. 8, emphasis original). In other words, she concurs that stronger accountability can lead to increased trust. For similar arguments see, for example, Brody (2002), Fleishman (1999), Herzlinger (1996) or Kearns (1996).

   Onora O'Neill, by contrast, argues that accountability is ultimately insufficient to create trust: 'Elaborate measures to ensure that people keep agreements and do not betray trust must, in the end, be backed by – trust. At some point we just have to trust. There is no complete answer to the old question: "who will guard the guardians?" On the contrary, trust is needed precisely because all guarantees are incomplete' (O'Neill, 2002, p. 6).

4. Cf. the discussion on the relationship between 'legitimacy' and 'accountability' in section 2.2.1. Similarly, Klaus Dingwerth identifies 'three core concepts of democratic governance' which determine the democratic legitimacy of an institution or process: 'inclusiveness, transparency, and accountability' (Dingwerth, 2005, p. 72).

5. On consequentialist and principled justifications for authoritarianism see, for example, Mayer (2001). Most recently, people have defended authoritarianism as the more efficient form of government in the context of the Asian 'tiger states'. Their economic success, it was argued, was explained by their 'Asian values', which include strong paternalistic and authoritarian elements. Cf. for example, Sen (1999) or Thompson (2001).

6. When it comes to delivering public services, this is one of the arguments (apart from the one concerned with the effects of competition) for why the private sector might be more efficient than the public sector. Richard Mulgan states this explicitly: 'Contracting out has the potential to reduce the extent of public accountability by transferring the provision of public services to members of the private sector who are generally not subject to the same accountability requirements as public officials. Indeed, reduction in such accountability requirements may be one of the reasons for the greater efficiency of the private sector'(Mulgan, 1997, p. 1).

7. Stakeholders are also those who can influence a company. Advocates of stakeholder theory find it easy, though, to make the case for respecting those stakeholders' interests on prudential or instrumental grounds. A moral justification is necessary to justify why stakeholders who have no power over the company should be taken seriously and to determine whether or not any one stakeholder group should be treated preferentially.

Goodpaster claims that Freeman only includes groups that are affected by the company as stakeholders because they, too, could ultimately have an effect on the company (Goodpaster, 2002, p. 52). This claim is not convincing, however, since Freeman explicitly adopts a Kantian approach, that is, one in which the morality of actions is only judged by the motives underlying the action, not its consequences. Considering stakeholder claims only because they could have an impact on the company, by contrast, would be a consequentialist argument.

8. In fact, there were so many contributions to stakeholder theory over the last two decades, many asserting slightly different claims, that it is difficult to speak of one 'stakeholder theory'. Already in 1995, Donaldson and Preston counted 'about a dozen books and more than 100 articles' on stakeholder theory and found that 'Unfortunately, anyone looking into this large and evolving literature with a critical eye, will observe that the concepts *stakeholder, stakeholder model, stakeholder management* and *stakeholder theory* are explained and used by various authors in very different ways and supported (or critiqued) with diverse and often contradictory evidence and arguments' (Donaldson and Preston, 1995, pp. 65 and 66, emphasis original).

The aim here, however, is not to provide a full account of stakeholder theories with all their variations but to use them as an example of a normative theory that links the claim for accountability to power. Since Freeman originally articulated the theory and uses an explicit normative argument to justify his claims, this section refers mainly to his version of stakeholder theory.

9. An article written by Freeman and Evan even contains this normative basis in its title: 'A Stakeholder Theory of the Modern Corporation: Kantian Capitalism' (Evan and Freeman, 1988).

10. Immanuel Kant formulated this principle as follows: 'Es liegt also der moralische Wert einer Handlung nicht in einer Wirkung, die daraus erwartet wird […]. Es kann daher nichts anderes als die *Vorstellung des Gesetzes* an sich selbst, *die freilich nur im vernünftigen Wesen stattfindet*, so fern sie, nicht aber die verhoffte Wirkung, der Bestimmungsgrund des Willens ist, das so vorzügliche Gute, welches wir sittlich nennen, ausmachen' (Kant, 1996b, p. 185, emphasis original).

11. In Kant's words, 'Der praktische Imperativ wird also folgender sein: *Handle so, daß du die Menschheit, sowohl in deiner Person, als in der Person eines jeden anderen, jederzeit zugleich als Zweck, niemals bloß als Mittel brauchest*' (Kant, 1996c, p. 216, emphasis original).

12. Without going through the stakeholder concept, but by applying Kant's different formulations of the categorical imperative directly to businesses, Norman Bowie comes to a similar conclusion. According to his interpretation, the duty to treat others as ends in themselves creates a duty for managers among others to provide meaningful work (which is freely chosen, provides autonomy and furthers the rational development of workers) to employees. Since '[s]ome management attitudes and practices are more conducive toward meeting this obligation than others […] Kantian managers need to create a certain kind of organization'. The organisational requirements include that the company 'should have those affected by the firm's rules and policies participate in the determination of those rules and policies before they are implemented' (Bowie, 2002, p. 67).

13. Not least, much of the current hype surrounding partnerships themselves comes from the fact that they are 'multi-stakeholder' and are seen as one possible way of institutionalising stakeholder participation in political processes.

14. Friedman discusses the connection between economic and political freedom at much greater length in his seminal book 'Capitalism and Freedom'. He argues that 'Economic arrangements play a dual role in the promotion of a free society. On the one hand, freedom in economic arrangements is itself a component of freedom broadly understood, so economic freedom is an end in itself. In the second place, economic freedom is also an indispensable means toward the achievement of political freedom. [...] Viewed as a means to the end of political freedom, economic arrangements are important because of their effect on the concentration or dispersion of power. The kind of economic organization that provides economic freedom directly, namely, competitive capitalism, also promotes political freedom because it separates economic power from political power and in this way enables the one to offset the other' (Friedman, 1962, pp. 52–3).

15. The German 'Mitbestimmungsgesetz', for example, decrees that in companies with more than 2000 employees, half the seats of the supervisory board are reserved for employee representatives.

16. Freeman and Reed's definition applies to the stakeholders of corporations. According to them, stakeholders in the narrow sense include employees, customer segments, certain suppliers, key government agencies, shareowners and certain financial institutions. Stakeholders in the wider sense include in addition public interest groups, protest groups, government agencies, trade associations, competitors and unions. Cf. Freeman and Reed (1983) p. 91.

    For an application of the narrow stakeholder concept to non-profit organisations see, for example, Theuvsen (2001). For civil society groups, stakeholders in the narrow sense, who are important for the organisation's survival, would, for example, be donors, certain government regulators, beneficiaries who pay for the organisation's services or unpaid volunteers. Other beneficiaries or those marginalised groups on behalf of whom the NGO claims to speak, by contrast, would only count as stakeholders in the wider sense. An important contribution concerning the relative salience of stakeholder claims in this context is Mitchell et al. (1997).

17. This distinction between a normative and a strategic or instrumental version of stakeholder theory is also made, for example, by Ludwig Theuvsen. He writes: 'Das Stakeholder-Konzept kann zum einen normativ-ethisch orientiert sein. [...] Die Berücksichtigung der Anliegen aller Stakeholder einer Organisation wird bei dieser Ausrichtung als Wert als socher betrachtet; es wird davon ausgegangen, daß die Interessen aller Stakeholder einen Eigenwert besitzen und der gleichen Aufmerksamkeit bedürfen. Die zweite mögliche Ausrichtung eines Stakeholder-Managements gibt die Auffassung, daß alle Stakeholder dieselbe Beachtung verdienen, auf. [...] Im Mittelpunkt des Stakeholder-Managements steht vielmehr das Ziel, einen Beitrag zur langfristigen Überlebensfähigkeit einer Organisation zu leisten' (Theuvsen, 2001, p. 1).

18. Kenneth Goodpaster solves this problem by arguing for a 'stakeholder synthesis' that acknowledges the moral obligation of managers to stakeholders but does not treat them at the same level as shareholders. He writes that taking 'business ethics seriously need not mean that management bear *additional* fiduciary relationships to third parties (nonstockholder constituencies) [...]. It may mean that there are morally significant *nonfiduciary* obligations to third parties surrounding any fiduciary relationship. [... This] is *not* an expansion of the *list* of principals' (Goodpaster, 2002, pp. 57–8, emphasis original). By saying that stakeholders other than shareholders should not be recognised as principals, Goodpaster

effectively argues that there should be no accountability relationship between these stakeholders and managers.

19. David Held confirms this national focus. 'Throughout the twentieth century, especially, democratic theory has focused on the organizational and socioeconomic context of democratic procedures and the effects this context has on the operation of 'majority rule'. From the development of the theory of competitive elitism to the elaboration of classic pluralism, or to the critique of these ideas in the writing of contemporary radicals, the focus of modern democratic theory has been on the conditions which foster or hinder the democratic life of a nation' (Held, 1996, p. 335).

20. For powerful accounts of how states lose power due to economic globalisation see, for example, Strange (1996) or Sassen (1996).

21. For a detailed discussion of what constitutes the democratic deficit in the case of the European Union see, for example, Scharpf (1999). Other contributions to this debate include, for example, Chryssochoou et al. (1998), Coultrap (1999), Decker (2000), Giorgi et al. (2001), Grewal (2001), Guisan-Dickinson (1999), Gusy (1998), Judge (1995), Katz (2001), Kiernan (1997), Koenig-Archibugi (2002), Lindseth (1999), Lodge (1996), Lopez Coterilla and Vicente (1998), Lord (2001), Manzella (2002), Meadowcroft (2002), Misch (1996), Moravcsik (2002), Neunreither (1994), Norris (1997), Pasquino (2000), Pogge (1997), Williams (1990).

Over the last decade or two, analyses finding a democratic deficit in the EU's institutional design and proposing all kinds of solutions for it have proliferated. But the diagnosis is contested with an increasing number of authors questioning whether the EU really lacks democratic credentials. Probably the most vociferous critic of the democratic deficit hypothesis is Andrew Moravcsic. He argues 'that an assessment of the democratic legitimacy of a real-world international institution is as much social scientific as philosophical. If such an assessment is not to be an exercise in utopian thinking, then international institutions should not be compared to ideal democratic systems. Instead we must ask whether they approximate the "real world" democracy generally achieved by existing advanced democracies, which face constraints of limited public information and interest, regulatory capture, the credibility of commitments, and bounded consensus. [...] If we adopt these reasonable normative and empirical criteria for evaluating democracy, moreover, it is unclear that international institutions lack democratic legitimacy, as most analysts assume' (Moravcsik, 2004, p. 337). For a similar argument see, for example, Zweifel (2002).

22. Cf. for example, Howse (2003), Stiglitz (2002) or Woods (2003).

23. Reform proposals for the United Nations abound. For an overview see, for example, Ghebali (1997) or Hüfner and Martens (2000).

24. Stutzer and Frey, for example, analyse international (i.e. intergovernmental) organisations (Stutzer and Frey, 2005) and Ann-Marie Slaughter focuses on intergovernmental networks (Slaughter, 2004).

25. The proliferation of the democratic argument as a critique of international institutions has led to frustration for some scholars. Moravcsik, for example, writes, 'Is global governance – the structure of international institutions – democratically legitimate, or does it suffer from a "democratic deficit"? This is emerging as one of the central questions – perhaps the central question – in contemporary world politics. Whatever their underlying motivations, critics these days ranging from the extreme right to the extreme left, and at almost every point in between, couch criticisms of globalization in democratic rhetoric' (Moravcsik, 2004, p. 336).

26. Klaus Dingwerth goes even a step further by claiming: 'There appears to be a more or less broad consensus that the current system of global governance ought to be democratised. What the concept of democracy entails when it is transferred to the global level of decision-making, which structures would best satisfy the call for democratisation, and why exactly such a call deserves our support in the first place, is however far from clear' (Dingwerth, 2007, p. 14). As argued later, however, some analysts and activists propose to remedy the democratic deficit by limiting the influence of international institutions and by restoring national autonomy.

27. For a good overview over the thinking of 'the new sovereigntists' and a powerful rebuttal of their arguments see, for example, Spiro (2000).

28. Archibugi (2004) provides not only a good summary of the principles of 'cosmopolitan democracy' but also discusses the main criticisms levelled against this proposal and attempts to rebut them.

29. Cf. for example, Anheier et al. (2005), Arts (1998), Breitmeier and Rittberger (1998), Brunnengräber et al. (2001), Charnovitz (1997), Fox and Brown (1998), Keck and Sikkink (1998), Salamon et al. (1999) or Willetts (2000).

30. See, for example, Gereffi et al. (2001), Johns (2003), Mallaby (2004), Ottaway (2001) or Schmidt and Take (1997).

31. The control function of parliaments is less relevant at the international level since no formal executive exists. In addition, parliaments traditionally exercise their control function mainly through the budget. Currently, no direct taxes are levied internationally. The control requirement based on 'no taxation without representation' therefore also loses relevance.

32. Klaus Dingwerth, one of the very few authors explicitly analysing the democratic legitimacy of partnerships as instruments of global governance also focuses exclusively on their rule-making capacity (Dingwerth, 2007).

33. For a critique of this approach arguing that these two elements are incompatible see Patterson (1992).

34. Cf. DeMott (1988), p. 908.

35. Cf. Weinrib (1975), p. 3.

36. Regarding equivalent institutions in other jurisdictions, he states that 'There is great variety – mainly in civil law systems – among institutions that are functionally equivalent to trust or Treuhand; they serve similar purposes, but the technicalities of their juridical construction differ' (Grundmann, 1999, p. 402). For an overview see, for example, Dyer and van Loon (1982).

37. On the concept of *negotiorum gestio* in civil law countries see, for example, Sheehan (2006). He argues that a similar principle exists in English law.

38. Boucher and Kelly describe how social contract thinkers differ with respect to the purpose they use the contract for, the nature of the contract, the identity of the parties to the contract and the motivation for entering a contract: 'The choice may be to create society; civil society; a sovereign; procedural rules of justice; or morality itself. It may be a choice of contract that binds in perpetuity, or one renewed with each succeeding generation. The choice may be historical, ideal or hypothetical, its expression explicit or tacit, and the contractees may be each individual contracting with every other, individuals contracting with their rulers and God [...], the heads of families agreeing among themselves, corporations or cities contractually bound to a superior, or the people as a body contracting with a ruler or king. Furthermore, the motivation for the choice may be a religious duty, personal security, economic welfare, or moral self-righteousness' (Boucher and Kelly, 1994, p. 2).

39. In Thomas Hobbes' version, conflict is a direct consequence of the legitimate human longing for self-preservation and the roughly equal physical and mental capacity of humans: 'From this equality of ability, ariseth equality of hope in the attaining of our Ends. And therefore if any two men desire the same thing, which neverthelesse they cannot both enjoy, they become enemies; and in the way to their End, (which is principally their owne conservation, and sometimes their delectation only,) endeavour to destroy, or subdue one an other' (Hobbes, 1909, Chapter XIII).

40. Jean-Jacques Rousseau argues strongly against Hobbes' account of the state of nature. He contends that men lived in a peaceful original state, which was only corrupted by increasing interactions between humans: 'As soon as men began to value one another, and the idea of consideration had got a footing in the mind, every one put in his claim to it, and it became impossible to refuse it to any with impunity. Hence arose the first obligations of civility even among savages; and every intended injury became an affront; because, besides the hurt which might result from it, the party injured was certain to find in it a contempt for his person, which was often more insupportable than the hurt itself. Thus, as every man punished the contempt shown him by others, in proportion to his opinion of himself, revenge became terrible, and men bloody and cruel' (Rousseau, 1754, part II).

41. In Rousseau's words: 'Il faut remarquer encore que la délibération publique, qui peut obliger tous les sujets envers le souverain, à cause des deux différents rapports sous lesquels chacun d'eux est envisagé, ne peut, par la raison contraire, obliger le souverain envers lui-même, et que, par conséquent, il est contre la nature du corps politique que le souverain s'impose une loi qu'il ne puisse enfreindre. Ne pouvant se considérer que sous un seul et même rapport il est alors dans le cas d'un particulier contractant avec soi-même: par où l'on voit qu'il n'y a ni ne peut y avoir nulle espèce de loi fondamentale obligatoire pour le corps du peuple, pas même le contrat social' (Rousseau, 1762, Chapter VII).

42. Claude Ake, for example, confirms this dominance: 'This radical wing of the natural law school [following Locke in arguing for a right of revolution] was easily the strongest influence on the theoretical foundations of the Western "democracies." The great documents and theoreticians of the Western tradition – J. S. Mill, de Tocqueville, Jefferson, Paine, the Declaration of Independence, the American Constitution, the Federalist Papers, the Declaration of the Rights of Man and of the Citizen, and so on – speak the language of the radical wing. For example, men have rights which are inalienable; government depends on the consent of the governed; political obligation is limited by the end for which government was constituted' (Ake, 1969, p. 248).

43. The establishment of political authority in the liberal democratic tradition following John Locke is thus conditional. A corollary of this is that citizens no longer have an obligation to obey the government if the government does not fulfil its purpose. In Claude Ake's words: 'This theory of obligation posits that when a government ceases to fulfil the expectations which alone justified obedience to it, its citizens have a right to disobey it' (Ake, 1969, p. 245). Ake goes on to argue that citizens actually have a duty to disobey. Bernard Wand criticises Ake's justification for the duty to disobey, but offers another account that also results in the obligation to resist governments that violate individual rights (Wand, 1970).

44. It goes beyond the scope of this book to review the criticisms of the social contract theory and of liberal democratic thought. The communitarian, Marxist and

feminist critiques of the social contract, however, are briefly discussed in the section of this chapter dealing with hypothetical and ex-post consent and delegation. For a brief discussion of the major objections to democracy articulated today from an economic efficiency and a cultural diversity perspective see, for example, Sen (1999).

45. In fact, Max Weber argued that the emergence of representative democracy could only be explained by the historical and social peculiarities of 'the West': 'Sowohl die genuine parlamentarische Repräsentation mit voluntarisitischem Interessenbetrieb der Politik, wie die daraus entwickelte plebiszitäre Parteiorganisation mit ihren Folgen, wie der moderne Gedanke *rationaler* Repräsentation durch Interessenvertreter sind dem Okzident eigentümlich und nur durch die dortige Stände- und Klassen-Entwicklung erklärlich, welche schon im Mittelalter hier, und nur hier, die Vorläufer schuf' (Quoted in Käsler, 1995, p. 215, emphasis original).

46. Francis Fukuyama takes this as the point of departure for his much debated argument about the 'end of history'. One does not have to share Fukuyama's Hegelian argument, however, to agree with his assessment that after the fall of communism, liberal democracy and free-market capitalism have become the dominant models for organising society across the globe. Cf. Fukuyama (1992). How many countries have actually embraced democracy remains controversial. The American organisation Freedom House, using a substantive rather than formal definition of democracy, has been assessing the degree of civil liberties and political rights across the world since 1972 and has found a steady increase in freedom. Thus, in 1972, 68 countries were classified as 'not free', 35 as 'partially free' and 44 as 'free'. In 1990, 49 were 'not free', 50 'partially free' and 65 'free'. In 2006, 45 were found 'not free', 57 'partially free' and 91 'free'. Cf. Freedom House (2007).

47. Smith's original formulation of the invisible hand theorem relates to foreign trade. It is apparent throughout his work, though, that he sees self-interest giving rise to positive economic effects. When discussing the effects of commercial towns, for example, he writes: 'A revolution of the greatest importance to the public happiness was in this manner brought about by two different orders of people who had not the least intention to serve the public. To gratify the most childish vanity was the sole motive of the great proprietors. The merchants and artificers, much less ridiculous, acted merely from a view to their own interest, and in pursuit of their own pedlar principle of turning a penny wherever a penny was to be got. Neither of them had either knowledge or foresight of that great revolution which the folly of the one, and the industry of the other, was gradually bringing about. It is thus that through the greater part of Europe the commerce and manufactures of cities, instead of being the effect, have been the cause and occasion of the improvement and cultivation of the country' (Smith, 1904, Book III, Chapter 4, §17–18). Similarly, he writes on the choice of employment: 'Every individual is continually exerting himself to find out the most advantageous employment for whatever capital he can command. It is his own advantage, indeed, and not that of the society, which he has in view. But the study of his own advantage naturally, or rather necessarily, leads him to prefer that employment which is most advantageous to the society' (Smith, 1904, Book IV, Chapter 2, §4).

48. The basis of utilitarian moral philosophy is 'the principle of utility', also known as the 'greatest happiness' or 'greatest felicity' principle. In the words of its founder, Jeremy Bentham, it is 'that principle which approves or disapproves of

every action whatsoever, according to the tendency which it appears to have to augment or diminish the happiness of the party whose interest is in question' (Bentham, 2005, p. 11). There is considerable debate among utilitarians concerning the application of the principle of utility. Firstly, there is disagreement as to what kind of utility should be considered. Bentham emphasised pleasure and pain, while his follower John Stuart Mill put greater weight on cultural, intellectual and spiritual pleasure (Mill, 1863). Secondly, there is disagreement concerning whose utility should be considered, the utility of the members of a society, as Bentham and Mill claimed, or those of all sentient beings, including animals (Singer, 1979) and future generations (Sidgwick, 1907). Thirdly, there are different proposals on how to calculate the biggest utility, especially whether total aggregate utility or average utility should count. Finally, utilitarians debate whether the consequences of individual acts (Bentham, 2005) or of rules (Mill, 1863) should be evaluated. Despite these differences, most utilitarians would probably agree that, other things being equal, greater social wealth means greater happiness.

49. Economists may also emphasise the contractual obligations of agents. Principals buy the services of managers or other agents and the terms of their mutual agreement are laid down in a contract. Contract keeping is essential for enabling market-based exchanges and is therefore justified as a norm on a utilitarian basis. This argument, however, does nothing to specify what the content of any given contract should be or whether it should contain accountability mechanisms.

50. In their textbook on economic theories of organisation, Picot, Dietl and Franck, for example, describe this normative element of principal agent theory. They argue that humans seek to satisfy their needs under conditions of scarcity. An efficient use of resources is desirable because it increases the well-being of individuals. The division of labour, specialisation, trade and coordination are key mechanisms to ensure the efficient use of resources. Under optimal conditions of perfect information (so-called first-best solutions), agents always promote the interests of their principals and welfare is maximised. Since conditions in reality are not optimal, accountability mechanisms are desirable because, and in so far as, they reduce the losses incurred from delegation (Picot et al., 2004, pp. 1–3 and 72–4).

51. Cf. Jensen and Meckling (1976), p. 6 and section 2.2.1.

52. For a detailed discussion of the constitutional implications of liberal thought see, for example, Herz (1999).

53. This is not the place to offer a comprehensive overview over the comparative political science literature, which is vast and includes both descriptive and normative contributions. A few selected examples must suffice: a good collection of articles focusing on different ways to control public agencies is contained, for example, in Kaufman et al. (1986). Jabbra and Dwivedi provide a compendium that compares the accountability arrangements of governments across the world (Jabbra and Dwivedi, 1988). A more recent collection exploring how elections and different governmental structures influence accountability is Przeworski et al. (1999).

54. Important texts of the New Public Management literature include Osborne and Gaebler (1992), Barberis (1998), Borins (1995), Box et al. (2001) or Hood (1991). Behn, who criticises the New Public Management approach for overly reducing political accountability (Behn, 1998), proposes a comprehensive account of a new accountability system that is compatible with the values and goals of New Public Management (Behn, 2001).

55. A similar definition is offered by Schmitter and Karl: 'Modern political democracy is a system of governance in which rulers are held accountable for their actions in the public realm by citizens, acting indirectly through the competition and cooperation of their elected representatives' (Schmitter and Karl, 1991, p. 76).

56. Manin, Przeworski and Stokes emphasise this special feature of government accountability: 'The peculiarity of the principal-agent relation entailed in the relation of political representation is that our agents are our rulers' (Manin et al., 1999b, pp. 23–4).

57. Other organisations like associations are also subject to governance and accountability requirements. These tend to be much less strict. Associations under German law, for example, are only required to have a board of directors that is elected by an assembly of all members (§§ 21–79 BGB). Registered charities usually have to promote certain public goods and have to provide transparency concerning the sources and use of funds (cf. e.g. the UK Charities Act of 1993).

58. The list is available at http://www.independentsector.org/issues/accountability/standards2.html (last accessed 27 August 2009).

59. Prominent examples of corporate governance codes include the OECD Principles of Corporate Governance (Organisation for Economic Co-operation and Development, 2004), the Cadbury (1992), Greenbury (1995), Hampel (1998) and Higgs (2003) reports of the UK government, the French Report (Vienot, 1999) and many more. Important codes for the non-profit sector include the report of the Canadian Panel on Accountability and Governance in the Voluntary Sector (1999), the Standards for Charity Accountability of the BBB Wise Giving Alliance (available at http://www.bbb.org/us/Charity-Standards/ last accessed 27 August 2009), or the report of the US-American Panel on the Nonprofit Sector (2005).

60. Andrew Mason also distinguishes these two components of autonomy and argues that they give rise to various different conceptions of autonomy. Cf. Mason (1990), p. 435.

61. This second aspect of autonomy is often referred to as 'moral autonomy'. It has its roots in Immanuel Kant's approach to ethics, which was already referred to above in the context of stakeholder theories. Kant writes: 'Autonomie des Willens ist die Beschaffenheit des Willens, dadurch derselbe ihm selbst (unabhängig von aller Beschaffenheit der Gegenstände des Wollens) ein Gesetz ist. Das Prinzip der Autonomie ist also: nicht anders zu wählen als so, daß die Maximen seiner Wahl in demselben Wollen zugleich als allgemeines Gesetz mit begriffen seien' (Kant, 1996/1786, p. 95). In other words, autonomous is who chooses to follow the categorical imperative, using his rationality to derive the rules conforming to this principle.

62. Referring to Joel Feinberg, Susan Brison describes the different variations of the concept of autonomy as follows: 'Although everyone agrees that the word "autonomy", true to its etymological roots, refers in some way to self-government, some consider it to denote a capacity to govern oneself, while others think it refers to an achieved state of self-government, a right to govern oneself, or an ideal of virtue, that is, a value to be pursued' (Brison, 1998, p. 323).

63. Andrew Mason, for example, has identified three different versions of what it means to be independent of the will of others. Most far reaching is the 'independent-minded' conception of autonomy (supported e.g. by Robert Wolff and Thomas Scanlon), which posits that people need to reflect every time before they act and never do anything just because someone else tells them to. A slightly less demanding variety is the 'critical reflection' conception (proposed

e.g. by John Stuart Mill, Stanley Benn and Richard Lindley), which demands that people re-evaluate their conception of the good from time to time. A formal conception of autonomy (backed e.g. by Gerald Dworkin) finally accepts anybody as autonomous who acts on a conception of the good which is based on an unmanipulated analysis of situations and available options. On this account, neither constant reflection, nor periodic re-evaluation is necessary for autonomy. Cf. Mason (1990), pp. 435–40.

64. Philosophers using an autonomy argument against paternalism – which involves forcing individuals to do something against their will for their own good – include, for example, Arneson (1980), Brock (1983), Dworkin (1971), Feinberg (1971), Rawls (1971), Scoccia (1990), VanDeVeer (1986).

65. For an extensive list of authors, including detailed references see, for example, Brison (1998), p. 312.

66. For a critique of the autonomy argument against paternalism see, for example, Husak (1981). Brison (1998), for example, argues that unrestricted free speech cannot be justified on the basis of autonomy.

67. The core assumption of rational choice or rational action models is that individuals have a consistent system for ranking alternative choices or courses of action and that they act to maximise their marginal utility. The foundational texts for this important strand of economic thought include Pareto (1909) and Hicks and Allen (1934).

68. George Stigler and Gary Becker characterise the mainstream position held by economists as follows: 'Tastes are the unchallengeable axioms of a man's behavior: he may properly (usefully) be criticized for inefficiency in satisfying his desires, but the desires themselves are *data*' (Stigler and Becker, 1977, p. 76, emphasis original). The same authors propose an alternative approach, suggesting that preferences should be seen as stable and similar between people. The vast majority of economic theories and models, however, continue to operate on the assumption that preference functions vary both between people and over time. Accordingly, any preference function that is consistent, that is, complete and transitive, is generally accepted as 'rational'. For a good overview of other approaches challenging the intrinsic rationality of preference functions see, for example, Hansson and Grüne-Yanoff (2006). The authors also show convincingly why these alternative arguments have remained marginal to the discipline of economics.

69. Some see this as deeply problematic. They argue that because elections have a dual role, neither of the two functions is exercised well. Manin, Przeworski and Stokes, for example, write that 'voters have only one instrument to reach two goals: to select better policies and politicians, and to induce them to behave well while in office. [... But] the system that Madison and his colleagues designed makes it possible to strive for one goal only at the expense of the other'. It is partly because of this that they conclude: 'citizens' control over politicians is at best highly imperfect in most democracies. Elections are not a sufficient mechanism to insure that governments will do everything they can to maximise citizens' welfare' (Manin et al., 1999a, pp. 45–6 and 50).

70. Focusing on the delegation of legislative authority, Peter Lindseth, for example, also espouses a broad concept of delegation. He argues that governance in the European Union in reality is polyarchical and that many sources of normative power exist. While delegation from national parliaments is therefore not useful as an empirical-analytical concept for understanding regulatory power in the EU,

Lindseth argues that it should be maintained as a normative yardstick because the EU exercises the norm-setting functions that originally belong to parliaments. Cf. Lindseth (2002).

71. Sources on RBM include Roll Back Malaria Partnership (2004), Roll Back Malaria Partnership (2005), Roll Back Malaria Partnership (2006), Korenromp et al. (2005), Malaria Consortium (2002), van Ballegoyen (1999), Low-Beer et al. (2007), Narasimhan and Attaran (2003), Waddington et al. (2005), http://www. rollbackmalaria.org (last accessed 30 March 2010), personal communication with Pru Smith, Senior Communication Advisor, Roll Back Malaria Partnership Secretariat, 9 May 2007.

72. Cf. for example, Einhorn, (2001) or Babb and Buira (2005). The term 'mission creep' is also frequently used in a military context to describe the unintended expansion of military missions. Another international organisation that has seen the continuous expansion of its authorities is the EU. Rather than applying the negative term of 'mission creep', however, analysts mainly rely on (neo-)functional theories of integration to explain how the delegation of one set of authorities creates functional pressures demanding the delegation of additional authorities so that the original tasks can be fulfilled properly. A major reason why 'mission creep' has not become a rallying cry for EU critics is that member states continually update the formal mandate of the EU. For important neo-functionalist texts on regional integration see, for example, Haas (1961), Lindberg (1963), Lindberg and Scheingold (1971), Nye (1965), Schmitter (1969).

73. Sources on the 4C initiative include Common Code of the Coffee Community (2004), Common Code of the Coffee Community (2006), Common Code of the Coffee Community (2007c), Hamm (2004), Kolk (2005), Vallejo and Hauselmann (2005), personal communication with Carsten Schmitz-Hoffmann, Senior Project Manager Common Code for the Coffee Community, 25 April 2007.

74. Outside the European Union, most international organisations are intergovernmental in nature. The United Nations General Assembly, for example, is the institution that comes closest to being a 'global parliament'. It can take decisions by majority vote, but these only have moral authority. To become binding, they have to be ratified by the member states – a form of ex-post delegation.

75. To many, it seems puzzling that in the absence of an international legislature, executive and system of courts, a great and complex body of international law exists and is obeyed by most states most of the time. As defined in Article 38 (1) of the Statute of the International Court of Justice, international conventions, international custom and the general principles of law recognised by civilised nations are recognised as the main sources of international law. Cf. Shaw (1997), pp. 54–6. International conventions are often drafted and originally signed by a small number of states and subsequently joined by more. Even the Statute of the International Court of Justice, for example, which is an integral part of the Charter of the United Nations, was originally signed by only 51 states. Today, it has 192 members and has thus received significant ex-post consent. Custom as the second most important source of international law, by definition relies on implicit consent.

76. Cynthia Stark, for example, discusses the connection between legitimacy and the obligation to comply. She proposes a view where 'legitimacy is a necessary, but not a sufficient, condition for obligation'. Only principles and norms that are considered legitimate are therefore likely to be complied with by individuals: 'the requirement that principles be justifiable to everyone is based upon the need for

compliance. If principles are not justifiable to all, then those to whom they are not will have no reason to comply' (Stark, 2000, pp. 326 and 329).

77. Wer ein Geschäft für einen anderen besorgt, ohne von ihm beauftragt oder ihm gegenüber sonst dazu berechtigt zu sein, hat das Geschäft so zu führen, wie das Interesse des Geschäftsherren mit Rücksicht auf dessen wirklichen oder mutmaßlichen Willen es erfordert. [...] Im Übrigen finden auf die Verpflichtungen des Geschäftsführers die für einen Beauftragten geltenden Vorschriften der §§ 666 bis 668 entsprechende Anwendung.

78. Cf. BGB (2006), § 683.

79. Cf. for example, Sheehan (2006).

80. Cf. section 3.2.1.

81. For a summary of some of the main arguments against contract theory see, for example, Boucher and Kelly (1994) pp. 17–29.

82. Cf. Filmer (1991).

83. For an analysis of Locke's two seemingly conflicting stories about the emergence of political societies, see Waldron (1994). Waldron concludes that Locke uses the social contract story in order to establish criteria and interprets history with their help.

84. Translation by James W. Ellington (1785): 'Act only according to that maxim whereby you can at the same time will that it should become a universal law.'

85. On Kant's political teachings, which are often contained in his writing about law or his philosophy of history see, for example, Hassner (1987).

86. Das höchste Oberhaupt soll aber gerecht für sich selbst, und doch ein Mensch sein. Diese Aufgabe ist daher die schwerste unter allen; ja ihre vollkommene Auflösung ist unmöglich: aus so krummem Holze, als woraus der Mensch gemacht ist, kann nichts ganz Gerades gezimmert werden. Nur die Annäherung zu dieser Idee ist uns von der Natur auferlegt.

87. Hanna Pitkin makes this argument in her influential essay 'Obligation and Consent': 'Legitimate government acts within the limits of authority rational men would, abstractly and hypothetically, have to give to a government they are founding. Legitimate government is government which *deserves* consent' (Pitkin, 1965, p. 999, emphasis original).

88. For an analysis of Hegel's critique of the social contract see, for example, Boucher and Kelly (1994), pp. 23–6 or Haddock (1994). For a summary of communitarian arguments against liberalism more generally see, for example, Buchanan (1989).

89. An overview over the Marxist critique of the social contract is contained in Wilde (1994).

90. Cf. for example, Pateman (1988), Coole (1994). For a race-conscious critique of the social contract tradition see, for example, Mills (1997).

91. John Rawls set out to rescue the Kantian contract from its communitarian critics. He invented the original position and the veil of ignorance to abstract individuals from their social positions and create impartial judgements. This, however, failed to convince communitarian philosophers like Michael Sandel (Sandel, 1982). In his later book 'Political Liberalism', Rawls maintains the contract argument to justify why people would choose a liberal political regime. But he also makes significant concessions to the communitarians by recognising that individuals are socially embedded: 'All those who affirm the political conception start from within their own comprehensive view and draw on the religious, philosophical, and moral grounds it provides' (Rawls, 1993, p. 147). Cf. Kelly (1994). Thomas

Scanlon runs into similar difficulties explaining how the criteria for his 'reasonable' and 'rational' individuals can be justified.

92. Cf. Stark (2000), p. 314. Similar arguments are made by Daniel Brudney, Jean Hampton, Henry Phelps-Brown, John Simmons and Jonathan Wolff.

93. Cf. Stark (2000), p. 314.

94. Thomas Lewis makes a similar argument. He questions whether the hypothetical consent of citizens is sufficient to ground a theory of obligation. But he argues that what he terms 'subjective hypothetical consent' 'can be used as a standard for the exercise of political authority. This standard specifies that a political authority must treat subjects as if they had consented, even though they have not consented' (Lewis, 1989, p. 798).

95. A case in point is, for example, the Global Reporting Initiative. Without appropriate prior authorisation, it proposes rules and guidelines for sustainability reports of organisations. While organisations may face some pressure from external groups to submit sustainability reports and to conform to the GRI guidelines while doing so, compliance with the guidelines can in most cases be seen as voluntary. While GRI does therefore not violate the rights of other organisations if it does not adopt appropriate accountability mechanisms, it may well jeopardise its chances of voluntary adoption.

96. The One World Trust regularly applies the principles defined in its index and publishes a 'global accountability report' that rates the accountability of important governmental, corporate and civil society organisations. Cf. Blagescu and Lloyd (2006). Another organisation proposing principles applicable to all types of organisations is AccountAbility. Its AA1000 Series defines process standards relating to planning, accounting, auditing and reporting, embedding and stakeholder engagement to ensure organisations operate in an accountable and inclusive way. Cf. AccountAbility (1999).

97. Chapter 5 repeatedly refers to important accountability standards that were defined for other sectors, but have implications for specific types of partnerships.

98. In section 2.2.2, four questions were used to define any concrete accountability relationship: Who is accountable, to whom, for what and how? Delegation offers answers to the first three of those questions. Agents are defined as those who exercise authority on somebody else's behalf. Principals are those who originally or rightfully hold the authority and who – explicitly, implicitly, hypothetically or after the fact – delegate it to the agent. This definition establishes who is or should be accountable to whom. Agents ought to be accountable to principals. Delegation also explains what the agents are accountable for: for exercising their authority in a way that corresponds to the interests of the principals. Delegation does not directly answer the fourth question of how accountability is or should be created. But, as this section argues, it provides a general criterion for evaluating accountability arrangements.

99. These examples are used here to illustrate that there are basic differences in the interests of principals and the corresponding accountability mechanisms. For this purpose, the examples are strongly simplified to uncover the core mechanisms at work. For the business and public sector examples, Dennis Young roughly confirms this interpretation: 'In the grossest terms, businesses are accountable to their owners for making money. Government is accountable to its citizens for carrying out the public's will, as ultimately reflected in voting, legislation, and judicial interpretation' (Young, 2002, p. 3).

100. 'Form follows function' is a principle that was espoused by modern architecture and important design schools like the Bauhaus movement. The original formulation is attributed to the architect Louis Henry Sullivan (1856–1924). Cf. Encyclopaedia Britannica (2007).

4   Partnerships in Practice

1. The terms 'class', 'category', 'type', 'group' and 'kind' can all have more specific meanings in different contexts. Within a biological taxonomy, for example, a class of animals occupies a clearly defined position in the hierarchy of groups, subgroups and further subdivisions. Likewise, categories in their original Aristotelian use denote a limited number of fundamental classes that together encompass all phenomena. Despite these differences, and corresponding to their common usage, the terms are used as rough equivalents here.

2. For the purposes of a review of the literature and research on partnerships addressing social issues, Selsky and Parker, for example, organise partnerships in four 'arenas': non-profit – business partnerships; government – business partnerships; government – non-profit partnerships; and partnerships involving actors from all three sectors (Selsky and Parker, 2005, p. 854).

3. The Business Partners for Development (BPD), for example, orient their work along partnership clusters, including partnerships working on natural resources, on water and sanitation, on youth development and road safety. For more information on BPD's work, see http://www.bpdweb.com (last accessed 27 August 2009).

4. Anne-Marie Slaughter, for example, categorises transnational regulatory networks based on their institutional characteristics. Thus she distinguishes networks of national government officials that develop and operate within international organisations from networks that are based on executive agreements between governments and those that arise 'spontaneously' outside existing institutional arrangements. These three types of transnational networks have significant differences in their accountability (Slaughter, 2001, pp. 9–14).

5. Börzel and Risse, though operating with a definition of partnerships that is much wider than the one employed here, use this criterion for classifying partnerships between public institutions and private organisations. They identify four types of partnerships: the regular consultation or cooptation of private partners; the delegation or 'outsourcing' of public functions to private institutions; co-regulation, where private actors hold at least a veto over outcomes; and publicly encouraged self-regulation of private actors. Cf. Börzel and Risse (2005) p. 200.

   Similarly, Murphy and Bendell (1997) categorise partnerships between businesses and NGOs according to the degree to which NGOs are involved in business operations. They distinguish involvement in business processes, in business projects or relating to a product.

6. Klaus Dieter Wolf analyses the contribution of private actors to governance. To determine different levels of de-governmentalisation, he measures both the scope of involvement (from agenda setting to monitoring compliance) and its intensity (marking hierarchical, cooperative, complementary or intervening models). Cf. Wolf (2001), pp. 7–11.

   Long and Arnold (1995) characterise environmental partnerships by the degree of conflict prevailing between partner organisations and distinguish between preemptive, coalescing, exploration and leverage partnerships.

7. Rodal and Mulder (1993), for example, distinguish partnerships according to what they achieve for the principal partner. Their partnership types include consultative or advisory partnerships, contributory or support sharing partnerships, operational or work sharing partnerships and collaborative or decision-making partnerships.

Löffler (2000) analyses partnerships between different governmental institutions and distinguishes partnerships that serve to jointly produce products or services from those that are created to jointly manage a common resource and partnerships for planning and implementing joint investment projects.

8. Categorising or classifying phenomena into groups is fundamental for human understanding, communication and analysis. Many classical philosophers tried to devise systems of classification that would encompass the entire universe of things or ideas. Thus, for example, Aristotle provided a list of ten highest order categories, which could each be further subdivided and would include all forms of being (Aristotle, 1975). Immanuel Kant criticised Aristotle for not using a clear method for arriving at these last categories and proposed an alternative attempt (Kant, 1968). In both cases, categories and subclasses were meant to be mutually exclusive and collectively exhaustive at each level of a system of classification.

As the work of the cognitive psychologist Eleanor Rosch and her colleagues has shown, however, humans in reality rely much more strongly on prototypes than abstract criteria for grouping phenomena. This understanding acknowledges that the boundaries between categories are not always sharp and accounts for the fact that most categories are graded, that is, some objects belong more clearly to a category than others (Cf. Rosch (1983) and Rosch and Lloyd (1978)). As a result, categories do not necessarily have to be mutually exclusive and collectively exhaustive to be useful. Nevertheless they should be based on clear, consistent and relevant criteria for distinguishing between phenomena.

An example for an inconsistent categorisation is the one proposed by Ann Zammit for descriptive purposes: She distinguishes a number of partnerships according to their field of activity (partnerships to facilitate foreign investment and private sector development, partnerships to assist and promote SMEs, partnerships on environmental issues and partnerships for health) and includes the category of 'Global Compact partnerships' in the same classification (Zammit, 2003, pp. 56–62).

9. Thus, for example, partnerships encouraging innovation are either advocacy and awareness raising or implementation partnerships, depending on whether or not they invest resources in research and development. 'Trading comparative advantage' and 'pulling together all available forces' is a feature of most partnerships, independent of what authority they assume, and whether partnerships contribute to 'closing the participatory gap' depends on what accountability arrangements they choose, not on what authority they assume.

10. Sources on PCFV include Partnership for Clean Fuels and Vehicles (2002), Partnership for Clean Fuels and Vehicles (2003), Partnership for Clean Fuels and Vehicles (2005a), Partnership for Clean Fuels and Vehicles (2005b), Partnership for Clean Fuels and Vehicles (2005c), Valve Seat Working Group (2004) and http://www.unep.org/pcfv (last accessed 30 March 2010).

11. Sources on the Global Public-Private Partnership for Handwashing with Soap include Health in Your Hands (2005), Health in Your Hands (2007), The London School of Hygiene & Tropical Medicine (2002), Curtis (2002), Curtis et al. (2007), Thomas and Curtis (2003), Witte and Reinicke (2005), http://www.globalhandwashing.org

(last accessed 30 March 2010), personal communication with contact person for the partnership at the World Bank, Lene Jensen, 21 April 2007.

12. Sources on EITI include Extractive Industries Transparency Initiative (2003), Extractive Industries Transparency Initiative (2005a), Extractive Industries Transparency Initiative (2005b), EITI International Advisory Group (2006), Global Witness (2004), Haufler (2004), Leipprand and Rusch (2007), Ocheje (2006), Palley (2003), Schumacher (2004), Williams (2004), http://www.eitransparency. org (last accessed 30 March 2010).

13. Partnerships could also take a different approach to coordination, which would require the delegation or assumption of much more far-reaching authority. They could try to play the role of a central coordinating institution determining which tasks need to be fulfilled and allocating roles across various agencies. None of the partnerships analysed as part of the case examples as well as during the scoping exercise conducted for case selection, however, has such a far-reaching mandate or ambition.

14. Sources on GWP include Kirby and Spedding (2006), Global Water Partnership (2003), Global Water Partnership Technical Committee (2004), Global Water Partnership (2006a), Global Water Partnership (2006b), Global Water Partnership (2006c), Global Water Partnership (2006d), http://www.gwpforum. org (last accessed 31 March 2010), personal communication with James Lenahan, Communications Head, Secretariat, Global Water Partnership on 7 May 2007.

15. Sources on ICANN include ICANN (2006), NGO and Academic ICANN Study (2001), Froomkin (2003), Hofmann (2002), Hunter (2003), Klein (2002), Kleinwaechter (2003), Koppell (2005), Leib (2002), One World Trust (2007), Weinberg (2000), http://www.icann.org (last accessed 31 March 2010).

16. Sources on GAIN include Global Alliance for Improved Nutrition (2004), Global Alliance for Improved Nutrition (2007), United Nations (2002), Ashraf (2003), Bekefi (2006), Carriere (2003), Sangvi et al. (2007), Witte and Reinicke (2005), http://www.gainhealth.org (last accessed 31 March 2010), personal communication with Floriane Marquis, Communication Department of the Global Alliance for Improved Nutrition, 10 May 2007.

17. Sources on GAVI include GAVI Alliance (2006), GAVI Alliance Secretariat (2006a), GAVI Alliance Secretariat (2006b), http://www.gavialliance.org (last accessed 31 March 2010), Brugha et al. (2002), Lu et al. (2006), Muraskin (2004).

18. Sources on GVEP include Global Village Energy Partnership (2006), Global Village Energy Partnership (2005a), Global Village Energy Partnership (2005b), Energy and Security Group and Sustainable Energy Solutions (2007), Morales and Bergqvist (2002), http://www.gvepinternational.org (last accessed 31 March 2010), personal communication with Sarah Adams, CEO of GVEP, 21 April 2007.

19. Sources on REEEP include Renewable Energy and Energy Efficiency Partnership (2005), Renewable Energy and Energy Efficiency Partnership (2006), The Expert Group on Renewable Energy (2005), Nilsson et al. (2003), http://www.reep.org (last accessed 31 March 2007).

20. Sources on MSC include Marine Stewardship Council (2006), Marine Stewardship Council (2007a), Marine Stewardship Council (2007b), Marine Stewardship Council (2007c), Cummins (2004), Food and Agriculture Organization of the United Nations (2005), Peacey (2000), Phillips et al. (2003), http://www.msc.org (last accessed 31 March 2007), personal communication with Alli Barnes, information officer at the Marine Stewardship Council on 9 May 2007.

21. Following the explicit wish of DFID to internationalise the initiative, presumably to increase its international legitimacy, the EITI Secretariat has been hosted by the Norwegian Government since 2007.

22. Sources on Stop TB include Stop TB Partnership (2001a), Stop TB Partnership (2001b), Stop TB Partnership (2006a), Stop TB Partnership (2006b), Stop TB Partnership (2007), Institute for Health Sector Development (2003), World Health Organization and Stop TB Partnership (2006), World Health Organization (2007), Kumaresan et al. (2004), Raviglione and Uplekar (2006), http://www.stoptb.org (last accessed 31 March 2010), personal conversation with Louise Baker, Principal Officer at the Stop TB Partnership Secretariat, 29 May 2007.

23. Sources on the Voluntary Principles include The Information Working Group of the Voluntary Principles (2006), Bennett (2002), Freeman and Hernández Uriz (2003), http://www.voluntaryprinciples.org (last accessed 31 March 2010), personal communication with Katie Swinerton, Business for Social Responsibility, 25 April 2007, and conversation with Amanda Gardiner, Manager, Voluntary Principles Secretariat, International Business Leaders Forum, 29 May 2007.

24. Cf. Renewable Energy and Energy Efficiency Partnership (2005), p. 8.

25. The results of this review are published in Curtis (2002).

26. Cf. Roll Back Malaria Partnership (2005), p. 42.

5   Concrete Partnership Accountability Standards

1. David Moore articulates the connection between tax exemption and increased demands for accountability as follows: 'By granting public benefit status, the decision-maker lays the foundation for distinct regulatory treatment – treatment that entails both benefits (usually tax exemptions) and obligations (more stringent accountability requirements)' (Moore, 2006, p. 4).

2. For an overview over 'global civil society' and its activities see, for example, Anheier et al. (2005). Brown and Moore distinguish between NGOs delivering welfare and services, building capacity for self-help and influencing policy and institutions (Brown and Moore, 2001, p. 16). Korten (1989) distinguishes different generations of NGOs, emphasising relief and welfare, community organisation and capacity building, the creation of sustainable development systems and the catalysation of large-scale social movements.

3. Recent literature has stressed, for example, the increasing advocacy and policy work by NGOs focusing on development issues. Cf. for example, Bryer and Magrath (1999), Hudson (2002), de Senillosa (1998).

4. To derive commonly applicable rules, the International Center for Not-for-Profit Law has compiled a list of 'generally accepted international practices regarding legislation governing civil society organisations'. According to it, minimum governance requirements prescribed by law include the definition of a governing body that receives and approves reports on finances and operations and the specification of duties of the members of the governing board, including the duty to be loyal to the organisation, the duty of care and diligence and the obligation to respect confidentiality agreements. In addition, laws define reporting requirements, such as annual financial and activity reports, special reports demanded by tax authorities, combined with the authority of the supervisory organ to conduct audits. For organisations with significant activities or assets, moreover, public reporting is usually required. Cf. International Center for Not-for-Profit Law (2006).

5. A study on registration practices in the US revealed that this instrument is rarely used. Thus, in 1994, only 520 of 46,887 applications were rejected. Cf. Hawks (1997).
6. Cf. World Health Organization (2000), regulation 12.1.
7. For the Global Fund's policy on ethics and conflict of interest, see The Global Fund to Fight AIDS, Tuberculosis and Malaria (2003), annex 3. For the by-laws, see The Global Fund to Fight AIDS, Tuberculosis and Malaria (2005).
8. Cf. International Center for Not-for-Profit Law (2006), §§ 2.1 and 2.4.
9. Cf. Wyatt (2004), p. 8a.
10. Herman and Renz (1997), for example, identify the following list of commonly recommended good governance practices for non-profit boards: having a board nominating or board development committee, using a board profile when recruiting new members, conducting interviews with nominees, relying on written selection criteria for board members, providing members with a board manual, conducting orientation sessions for new members, adopting a policy concerning the attendance of meetings, dismissing members for absenteeism, giving all board members office or committee responsibilities, distributing agendas prior to meetings, organising an annual board retreat, establishing an executive committee with written roles and powers, conducting collective and individual evaluations and providing feedback on them, formulating expectations on giving and soliciting in writing, establishing a board process for appraising the CEO, limiting the number of possible consecutive terms and providing board members with recognition for their services after retirement. For lists or codes including similar criteria see, for example, Bradshaw et al., (1992), Canadian Comprehensive Audit Foundation (1996), Drucker (1998), Gill et al. (2005), Silk (2004). For a good overview over relevant codes of corporate governance proposing similar measures see, for example, Gregory and Simmelkjaer (2002).
11. Many, but not all partnership boards, coordinating committees or meetings of core partners have these authorities. For the governance of non-profit organisations, however, they are standard practice. Thus, for example, the Accountability Charter of International Non Governmental Organisations, which lists 'only minimal governance requirements, states that an NGO's governing body should oversee the organisation's CEO, budget and programmes (International Non Governmental Organisations, 2006, p. 4). The Panel on Accountability and Governance in the Voluntary Sector stipulates that boards need to exercise their fiduciary responsibilities, including approving the budget, monitoring expenditures and approving annual reports (Panel on Accountability and Governance in the Voluntary Sector, 1999, p. 27). And the International Center for Not-for-Profit Law sees it as a generally accepted practice that NGO governing bodies are required by law to receive and approve reports on finances and operations (International Center for Not-for-Profit Law, 2006, § 2.3).
12. The Nonprofit Overhead Cost Project, a research project analysing non-profit overhead costs and their effects, for example, found that restricted contributions often limit the resources charities can spend on fund-raising and administration and lead to a reduced effectiveness of programmes. Cf. Nonprofit Overhead Cost Project (2004a).
13. For their recommendations, see Charity Commission for England and Wales (2003), Mango (2005), Cuomo (2005). For governments, relatively similar basic internal control measures are standard. The main standard setter for government agencies in the US, the General Accounting Office, for example, also demands

a clear segregation of duties, a restriction of access to resources and records, the appropriate documentation of transactions and physical control over assets (United States General Accounting Office, 1999, pp. 11–16). At the international level, almost identical standards have been published by the International Organization of Supreme Audit Institutions (INTOSAI) (INTOSAI, 2004).

14. For IASB's main website, see http://www.iasb.org (last accessed 27 August 2009).
15. Another important international standard-setting body for the accounting profession is the International Federation of Accountants (IFAC). It concentrates mainly on accounting policies for businesses, but also develops norms for public sector accountants, through its International Public Sector Accounting Standards Board (IPSASB). The respective websites of IFAC and IPSASB are http://www.ifac.org and http://www.ifac.org/PublicSector/ (last accessed 27 August 2009).
16. Both SSAPs and FRSs can be downloaded from http://www.frc.org.uk/asb/technical/standards/accounting.cfm (last accessed 27 August 2009). SSAP 4, for example, deals with the accounting treatment and disclosure of government grants and other forms of government assistance. The provisions also apply to grants and assistance from other sources. Cf. The Institute of Chartered Accountants in England and Wales (1990). For smaller charities (defined as organisations that do not exceed two or more of the following criteria: annual turnover of £2,800,000, balance sheet of £1,400,000 and a maximum of 50 employees) the Financial Reporting Standards for Smaller Entities (FRSSE) find application (Accounting Standards Board, 2001).
17. The American Institute of Certified Public Accountants (AICPA) is an important standard setter for the accounting profession. It has recently published an updated audit and accounting guide for non-profit organisations, including guidance from the latest relevant FASB statements (American Institute of Certified Public Accountants, 2006).
18. According to the UK Charity Commission's SORP, non-profits should account separately for unrestricted funds, be they general or designated, and restricted funds. It further recommends that NGOs distinguish their restricted funds between income and endowments, while further differentiating expendable and permanent endowments. Moreover, it asks charities to account for donated services or facilities as incomes if they are reasonably quantifiable and measurable (Charity Commission for England and Wales, 2005, pp. 11 and 21). In its statement 116, the US-American FASB demands that non-profits distinguish between permanently restricted, temporarily restricted and unrestricted contributions. It also requires that services are accounted for as contributions if they create or enhance non-financial assets or require specialised skills that would normally have to be purchased (Financial Accounting Standards Board, 1993a).
19. While the principle of differentiation is shared, the recommendations again differ in their details. Thus the charity commission wants charities to distinguish between the costs of generating funds, expenses for charitable activities, governance costs and other expenses (Charity Commission for England and Wales, 2005, p. 27). The FASB, in statement 117, merely requires non-profits to account separately for their expenses on mission-related programme activities and all other costs, including, for example, management, fund-raising, membership development and general activities (Financial Accounting Standards Board, 1993b, p. 11).
20. Thus the charity commission states that realised or unrealised gains or losses on assets as well as depreciation or a permanent fall in the value of assets have to

be accounted for (Charity Commission for England and Wales, 2005, p. 11). The FASB deals with the same topic in its statement 124. Accordingly, investments in equity securities with readily determinable fair values and all investments in debt securities must be reported at fair value (Financial Accounting Standards Board, 1995). Following statement 93, non-profits have to recognise the costs of using up long-lived tangible assets in their financial statements (Financial Accounting Standards Board, 1987).

21. According to the Global Civil Society Report 2004/5, a total of 17,952 international or internationally oriented NGOs were counted in 2003. Of those, 3305 had their headquarters and secretariats located in the US. The second biggest host country was the UK with 1923 headquarters or secretariats, followed by Belgium (1855) and France (1405). Cf. Anheier et al. (2005), pp. 297–302.

22. IRS form 990 is available for download at http://www.irs.gov/pub/irs-pdf/f990.pdf (last accessed 27 August 2009).

23. Cf. Keating and Frumkin (2000), p. 1.

24. For more information about GuideStar, see the organisation's website: http://www.guidestar.org (last accessed 27 August 2009). Another important non-profit evaluator is Charity Navigator. It rates charities according to their organisational efficiency and capacity. It also relies mainly on data drawn from IRS form 990. For more information, see the organisation's website: http://www.charitynavigator.org (last accessed 27 August 2009).

    While IRS form 990 is thus increasingly used for creating non-profit accountability, both the form and typical reporting practices have been strongly criticised. Elizabeth Keating and Peter Frumkin, for example, extensively discuss the merits and problems of the information provided by IRS form 990. They summarise the problems as follows: 'First, filings are not useful because they are often one to two years out of date. [...] Second, the typical Form 990 is riddled with mistakes and goes unverified. [...] Third, the Form 990 fails to conform to GAAP' (Keating and Frumkin, 2000, pp. 10–11).

25. For the annual return form of the charity commission, including versions for organisations with revenues between £10,000 and £250,000, those exceeding £250,000 and the summary information return, see http://www.charity-commission.gov.uk/investigations/ccmonlinks.asp (last accessed 27 August 2009).

26. The charity registry can be accessed and searched online at http://www.charity-commission.gov.uk/registeredcharities/first.asp. GuideStar UK can be accessed at http://www.guidestar.org.uk. Other non-profit rating or evaluation agencies in the UK relying strongly on data provided in annual returns include Development Ratings (http://www.developmentratings.com, all sites last accessed 27 August 2009), as well as the Voluntary Sector Almanac published by the National Council for Voluntary Organisations (NCVO) (Reichardt et al., 2007).

27. Knack and Rahman, for example, emphasise that 'Transaction costs associated with numerous and diverse donor rules and procedures for managing aid projects and programs [...] can also be viewed as detracting from aid's value' (Knack and Rahman, 2004, p. 2).

28. Another important standard setter for public reports is GRI, portrayed above as an example for rule-setting partnerships. GRI's reporting framework, its principles and guidance, protocols, standard disclosures and sector supplements can be used by 'organizations of any size, sector, or location' (Global Reporting Initiative, 2006b, p. 2). As such, the guidelines are also applicable to partnerships. The focus of the guidelines, however, is on so-called sustainability reporting. Sustainability

reporting is 'the practice of measuring, disclosing, and being accountable to internal and external stakeholders for organizational performance towards the goal of sustainable development' (Global Reporting Initiative, 2006b, p. 3). In contrast to regular activity and financial reporting, sustainability reporting is not a generally accepted and expected practice for NGOs and other organisations.

29. Financial audits are the classical form of audit. More recently, however, organisations also have other aspects of their work scrutinised by auditors. This can include internal structures and processes, for example through an audit of an organisation's internal control systems. It can also concern particular aspects of the organisation's performance, for example its environmental impact. Michael Power, for example, observes an 'audit explosion' in the UK, which he describes as follows: 'In addition to financial audits, there are now environmental audits, value for money audits, management audits, forensic audits, data audits, intellectual property audits, medical audits, teaching audits, technology audits, stress audits, democracy audits and many other besides' (Power, 1994, p. 1).

30. Within the European Union, for example, the minimum professional and registration requirements for auditors are regulated in a directive issued by the European Parliament and the council. Accordingly, only officially recognised and approved auditors may exercise the profession. For official approval, both auditing firms and individual auditors need to be of good repute. Moreover, auditors need to undergo adequate training, including university-level theoretical education and practical training. Auditors need to demonstrate their professional competence in a special exam. Cf. European Parliament and Council (2006a), §§ 3–13.

31. United Way of America conducted an informal survey on audit costs among its members. Its findings indicate that while absolute audit costs increase with the size of the organisation, relative costs decrease. Organisations with annual revenues below 500,000 US$ were found to spend an average of 0.93 per cent of annual revenues on audits, organisations with revenues between 2 million and 2.8 million US$ spent 0.37 per cent and organisations with budgets between 4 and 9 million US$ spent 0.26 per cent. Quoted in Panel on the Nonprofit Sector (2005), p. 36.

32. Throughout the EU, for example, audit requirements are regulated by directive 78/660/EEC of 1978. It decrees that all European member states must require companies to have their annual accounts audited by authorised auditors. It allows member states to grant exemptions from this rule for small companies (European Parliament and Council, 1978, Art. 51 and 11). In 2006, the relevant thresholds were redefined in directive 2006/46/EC. Exemptions are possible for companies that do not exceed the limits of two or more of the following criteria: a net turnover of 8.8 million €, a total balance sheet of 4.4 million € and an average of 50 employees (European Parliament and Council, 2006b, Art. 1). Many European countries grant these exemptions only to private and not to publicly traded companies.

In the US, the regulations for audits have been tightened through the 2002 Sarbanes-Oxley Act, adopted in the wake of the Enron scandal. The act only applies to publicly traded companies. It demands that public companies rotate their audit company or its lead partner at least every five years, that conflicts of interest between the auditor and the audited organisation be avoided, that auditors are not used for non-auditing services, except the preparation of tax forms, and that critical accounting policies and practices be disclosed. Cf. One Hundred Seventh Congress of the United States of America (2002). Most of these elements were already contained in the recommendations for corporate governance of the British 1992 Cadbury Report (Cadbury, 1992).

33. Thomas Silk, for example, who works with an important law firm specialising in non-profit law, predicts that as one of ten major developments and trends in the governance of non-profit organisations, '[e]very nonprofit corporation with substantial assets or annual revenue should be audited annually by an independent auditing firm' (Silk, 2004, p. 78).

34. This regulation applies to accounting periods starting on or after 27 February 2007. The charity commission has published these changes in its spring newsletter (Charity Commission for England and Wales, 2007).

35. This threshold has been in force for the fiscal years ending after 31 December 2003. The requirement is defined in circular A-133 of the Office of Management and Budget of the Executive Office of the President (OMB), (Office of Management and Budget, 2003, § 200).

36. The Panel on the Nonprofit Sector was convened by the NGO Independent Sector. It presented its conclusions to the US Congress in 2005. Its recommendations concerning audits and reviews can be found at (Panel on the Nonprofit Sector, 2005, pp. 35–6).

37. A broad range of other evaluation criteria and self-imposed NGO governance standards also contains audit requirements for NGOs. They include the Code of Conduct for Non Government Development Organisations of the Australian Council for International Development, which does not differentiate between internal and external audits (Australian Council for International Development, 2004); the Code of Ethics of the Canadian Council for International Co-operation, which, like the Australian code, does not indicate a financial threshold for audits (Canadian Council of International Co-operation, 2002/1995); the Code of Ethics and Conduct for NGOs of the World Association of Non-Governmental Organizations, which only demands audits for organisations with 'substantial annual revenues' (World Association of Non-Governmental Organizations, 2004); the 'minimum norms of good governance' of India's Credibility Alliance, which asks all voluntary organisations to make signed, audited financial statements available (http://www.credall.org.in/norms/norms.htm last accessed 27 August 2009); the Checklist for Accountability of the Independent Sector endorses the 1 million US$ threshold (Independent Sector, 2005); the NPO Certification Model of the Pakistan Centre for Philanthropy prescribes different levels of audit depending on organisational size (Pakistan Centre for Philanthropy, 2004); the Private Voluntary Organization Standards of InterAction, the American Council for Voluntary International Action demands independent audits for all NGOs exceeding 100,000 US$ in revenues (http://www.interaction.org/pvostandards/index.html, last accessed 30 June 2007). For an annotated list of NGO codes and standards see, for example, http://www.oneworldtrust.org/?display=ngoinitiatives#o, last accessed 27 August 2009.

38. ISA 200 states explicitly that 'Irrespective of whether an audit is being conducted in the private or public sector, the basic principles of auditing remain the same' (International Federation of Accountants, 2007, p. 228).

39. As mentioned above, the Sarbanes-Oxley Act of 2002 introduced additional audit standards in the US. Some commentators and analysts recommend that non-profit organisations comply with these additional rules, cf. for example, Silk (2004), Graham (2004). This opinion, however, has not been broadly accepted and there are even claims that these rules impose undue burden on companies listed in the US.

40. Witte and Reinicke (2005), p. 63, for example, analyse the following motives for companies to engage in partnerships in decreasing order of importance: showing good corporate citizenship, increasing reputation, individual leadership, improving the investment market and meeting government requirements. According to Reich (2002), governments mainly engage in partnerships because they recognise that they need partners to address crucial public policy problems. Companies, by contrast, are suspected to pursue various objectives including future profits and markets, control over international agendas, tax deductions or subsidies for new products. For a more detailed account of the motives of governments, including local governments see, for example, Collin (1998).

41. As mentioned earlier, accountability to mission is a fuzzier concept than accountability for complying with rules or financial accountability. As a result, there are no strict 'standards' governing the development of mission statements, neither for partnerships, nor for NGOs. There are, however, numerous handbooks providing relevant advice. Radtke (1998), for example, advises that mission statements should describe the purpose of the organisation, its contribution to that goal and the values guiding its work. Bryce (1992) recommends that missions should be so clearly defined that they can be applied to all NGO activities. Drohan (1999) emphasises that mission statements are working documents that require continued attention. Ingrim (1990) stresses that all those connected with the organisation should understand its mission and that the mission statement should serve as a guide for planning. For a more detailed annotated bibliography relating to NGO missions and visions see, for example, http://www.centerpointforleaders. org/toolkit_biblio_vision.html, last accessed 27 August 2009.

42. Logical frameworks and results chains are crucial elements of results-based management strategies. These management strategies are broadly applied in bilateral and multilateral development agencies and are increasingly adopted by other organisations working in the field of development. Results chains link short-term outputs to medium-term outcomes and long-term impacts. Thereby, they show how individual activities contribute to the achievement of broader development goals. The logical framework is a tool to help results-based planning which links the different levels of objectives and goals to information on how the objective can be measured, how relevant information can be obtained and what external factors could intervene. The handbook and 'how-to' literature on results-based management is vast. For a brief bibliography on logical frameworks see, for example, den Heyer (2001). UNDP has compiled a short bibliography on results-based management (Evaluation Office, 2002, pp. 110–11), as has the Canadian International Development Agency (Results-Based Management Division, 2000, pp. 135–8).

43. Edwards and Hulme, for example, emphasise the difficulty of measuring the performance of NGOs: 'A great part of the dilemma faced by GROs [grassroots organisations] and NGOs lies in the nature of the work they do and the messy and complex world in which they do it – measuring performance in relation to the kind of development subscribed to by most NGOs is an extraordinarily difficult task, particularly in relation to "empowerment" and other qualitative changes' (Edwards and Hulme, 1995, p. 11). Similarly, Slim (2002) stresses the difficulties of implementing social and environmental accounting practices in NGOs.

  For the public sector, Göran Arvidsson has articulated the problems of efficiency and effectiveness-focused performance evaluations as follows: 'Public activities have intrinsic values which cannot be expressed in terms of economic

effectiveness or rationality' (Arvidsson, 1986, p. 629). Similarly, Oliver and
Drewry (1996) mention that the use of performance indicators in the public service can be counterproductive; Harlow (2002) shows how value for money audits
can lead to an abdication of ministerial responsibility; Neal (1995) and Sirotnik
(2004) criticise the practice of performance measurement in higher education;
and Dahl (1994) as well as Behn (2001) highlight the trade-offs involved in creating greater accountability for performance.

44. For an introduction to benchmarking as a technique see, for example, Spendolini
(1992). The dedicated journal, *Benchmarking: An International Journal*, discusses
technical aspects as well as the application of benchmarking techniques in different sectors.

45. The importance of using the mission as a guide for setting programme priorities
has been emphasised, for example, by Ingrim (1990).

46. The BBB Wise Giving Alliance, for example, uses this standard as one of its rating criteria for NGOs. In addition, it requires organisations to spend no more
than 35 per cent of funds raised on fund-raising activities (BBB Wise Giving
Alliance, 2003). The US Office of Personnel Management also requires non-profit
organisations to have combined fund-raising and administrative costs of less than
35 per cent. For NGOs receiving funds raised through its Combined Federal
Campaign, these costs have to remain below 25 per cent of total revenues.
Cf. Office of Personnel Management (2006). Charity Navigator has more differentiated score for 'organisational efficiency', including different thresholds
for different types of charities. The thresholds are, though, in the same order of
magnitude. Cf. http://www.charitynavigator.org/index.cfm/bay/content.view/
cpid/48.htm (last accessed 27 August 2009). GuideStar, by contrast, rejects the
use of financial ratios as criteria for organisational efficiency. Cf. http://www.
guidestar.org/news/features/ratios.jsp (last accessed 27 August 2009). For a discussion about the merits and problems of imposing limits on overhead costs see, for
example, Nonprofit Overhead Cost Project (2004b).

47. International law can have a variety of sources. Art. 38 (1) of the Statute of the
International Court of Justice is widely recognised as the most authoritative
statement on the sources of international law. It includes international conventions, international custom, the general principles of law recognised by civilised
nations, as well as judicial decisions and teachings as subsidiary means for determining the law. Cf. Brownlie (1995), p. 448. For a good introduction into the
sources of international law see, for example, Shaw (1997), pp. 54–98.

48. Klaus Dingwerth in his analysis of the democratic legitimacy of rule-making
partnerships also considers the implications of the mostly non-binding nature of
the proposed rules. While employing a different reasoning, he also concludes that
rule making partnerships ought to have democratic legitimacy: 'Thus, a further
distinctive feature of public-private rule making is that it cannot establish legally
binding rules. However, the observation that nonbinding guidelines and norms
set by public-private bodies are being observed by states, and the experience that
norms of soft law may serve as the foundation for later efforts to establish *internationally binding* rules – as, for instance, in the case of the OECD guidelines on the
trade in hazardous waste and the Basel convention – provide strong reasons for
examining the democratic legitimacy of the processes by which they are generated' (Dingwerth, 2005, p. 80, emphasis original).

49. As two researchers of the World Bank's Development Research Group who have
a critical attitude towards the benefits of participation put it: 'Participation is

expected to lead to better designed projects, better targeted benefits, more cost-effective and timely delivery of project inputs, and more equitably distributed project benefits with less corruption and other rent-seeking activity' (Mansuri and Rao, 2004, p. 11).

50. The principles contained in the ISO guide include, for example, the requirement that written procedures should exist and be made available for standard-setting processes, that an appeals mechanism should exist, that notice should be given to enable contributions, that materially and directly interested persons and organisations should be able to participate in the process and that the representation of interest categories in the standard-setting process should be balanced. Cf. International Organization for Standardization (1994).

51. The ISEAL code recommends, for example, to include stakeholders in the development of procedures for the standard-setting process, the publication of the standard-setting organisation's work programme, the provision for two rounds of public comments of at least 60 days for new standards or amendments, participation reflecting a balance of interests among interested parties and of geographic scope and the proactive involvement of disadvantaged groups. Cf. International Social and Environmental Accreditation and Labelling Alliance (2004), as well as the more detailed guidance document (International Social and Environmental Accreditation and Labelling Alliance, 2006).

52. The Centre for Global Studies of the University of Victoria, for example, has published *Rethinking Governance Handbook*, which describes and assesses numerous initiatives of international organisations that are designed to strengthen their accountability, the participation of affected stakeholders and their transparency (Centre for Global Studies, 2001); the World Bank's *Participation Sourcebook* includes an analytical discussion of the concept of participation, examples of participatory projects from around the globe and practical guidance on how to design and implement participation (The World Bank, 1996); the *OECD Handbook on Information, Consultation and Public Participation in Policy-Making* focuses on government officials. It explains the rationale for participation and provides practical guidance on how governments can strengthen their relations with citizens (Gramberger, 2001); FAO's participation handbook focuses on the involvement of local communities in development programmes and the creation of sustainable livelihoods (Wilde, 2001). Studies analysing the effects of participation on development policies include, for example, Isham et al. (1995), Mansuri and Rao (2004) and Khwaja (2004).

53. This categorisation of relevant stakeholder groups is contained in the report of the World Commission on Dams (World Commission on Dams, 2000, p. viii).

54. While nation states usually have a clear definition of who does and who does not count as a citizen, these definitions are often hotly contested. This includes, for example, the question of who can apply under what conditions for nationality, whether the right to vote should be extended to minors, whether foreign residents should have the right to participate in certain elections or whether prisoners should be allowed to exercise their citizen rights. For a feminist perspective on the concept of citizenship see, for example, Lister (1997). For a general debate about the contested nature of the concept of citizenship, especially outside the national context see, for example, Bosniak (2000).

55. The World Bank Participation Sourcebook states the difficulty of developing general rules for stakeholder identification powerfully: 'Much still needs to be learned about how to identify and involve stakeholders. No hard or fast rules

exist to tell us whom to involve and how. What we do know is that stakeholder involvement is context-specific' (The World Bank, 1996, p. 126).

56. Cf. Dingwerth (2005), pp. 73–4.

57. The limited representative nature of the commission and the lack of accountability of its members to broader stakeholder groups were, however, compensated by other features. Thus stakeholder groups were directly involved in the creation of the knowledge base and could be included in the WCD Stakeholder Forum.

58. For a rough practical guide outlining issues to be considered during a stakeholder identification process see, for example, Hemmati (2002), pp. 217–20.

59. These points are also emphasised, for example, by Hemmati (2002), pp. 220–2.

60. The WCD complemented its multi-stakeholder composition through consultations. Lack of information has been referred to as one of the shortcomings of that process: 'it has been argued that in the early phase of the WCD process, the necessary publicity was missing in order to widen the discussion about the work program to a larger number of stakeholders' (Dingwerth, 2005, p. 75).

61. This risk is addressed by both ISO and ISEAL. ISO guide 59 demands that consensus-building procedures should provide for a balanced representation of interest categories (International Organization for Standardization, 1994, art. 4.5). The ISEAL code of good practice requires that standard-setting organisations proactively seek the contributions of directly affected parties. Moreover, it recommends that the constraints on disadvantaged groups (including financial hurdles as well as lack of expertise and knowledge) be addressed in the standard-setting process. Cf. International Social and Environmental Accreditation and Labelling Alliance (2004), p. 6.

62. ISEAL's code of good practice addresses this problem directly. It demands that standard-setting organisations take the received comments into account. It specifies that this entails considering all inputs on an equal and objective basis, giving justifications if an issue is not incorporated, as well as preparing and publishing a written synopsis on how each material issue has been addressed. Cf. International Social and Environmental Accreditation and Labelling Alliance (2004), pp. 4–5 and International Social and Environmental Accreditation and Labelling Alliance (2006), p. 5.

63. For a collection of different participatory tools currently employed by international organisations see, for example, Centre for Global Studies (2001). The handbook contains examples on capacity-building activities for participating organisations, the establishment of dedicated units or channels for engaging NGOs, community-based methods of participation, online fora, independent multi-stakeholder commissions and the involvement of private actors in advisory bodies. For a description of additional participatory techniques, see also The World Bank (1996), Appendix 1. It includes workshop-based methods, community-based methods, methods for stakeholder consultation and methods for social analysis.

64. *The World Bank Participation Sourcebook*, for example, emphasises the importance of a wide dissemination of information, including the two elements of identifying stakeholders and publishing information openly. Cf. The World Bank (1996), p. 128.

65. For practical strategies on how to involve less powerful and less vocal groups or figures at the local level see, for example, Wilde (2001), pp. 32–3. *The World Bank Participation Sourcebook* describes the following strategies to involve the voiceless: build capacity, mandate representation, organise separate events, use 'levelling

techniques' in facilitation or involve surrogates if it proves impossible to engage a certain stakeholder group. Cf. The World Bank (1996), pp. 132–4.

66. Good democratic practice of dealing with open comments entails at least the right to receive an answer, preferably in a publicly transparent way. European citizens submitting comments to European institutions, for example, have the right to receive a reply in the language of their submission. Cf. European Communities (2002), p. 45.

67. All three complaints mechanisms are enshrined in ICANN's by-laws, cf. ICANN (2006), Articles IV and V.

68. Various Bundesländer in Germany, for example, allow citizens to introduce draft legislation to parliament if they reach a minimum number of signatures, cf. for example, Jung (1997). In Poland, 100,000 signatures are necessary to introduce draft legislation to the Sejm. For an overview of elements of direct democracy in various transition countries see, for example, Frey (2003).

   Among the case examples, MSC has relatively open procedures for initiating new standard-setting procedures. Thus any MSC body can propose the development of new consultations, whereupon the MSC board conducts consultations and takes the decision on whether or not to develop new norms. Since stakeholders are represented in the Stakeholder Forum, they too can initiate new standards. Cf. Marine Stewardship Council (2007c), p. 2.

69. Cf. International Organization for Standardization (1994), Art. 2.2 and International Social and Environmental Accreditation and Labelling Alliance (2004), Art. 5.1.

70. In his text, Madison describes the benefits of a general system of education. Since his point rings true more generally, however, various authors and institutions have adopted the quote to argue for the importance of transparency in governments. Transparency International, for example, uses the quote in support of a 'right to information' (Pope, 2000, p. 235), as does the NGO Privacy International (cf. its theme page on freedom of information, available on the organisation's website http://www.privacyinternational.org, last accessed 28 August 2009).

71. Cf. United Nations General Assembly (1948), Art. 19 and United Nations General Assembly (1966), Art. 19. Organisations like Article 19 or Privacy International interpret this norm as including a general right to freedom of information. This interpretation remains, however, disputed.

72. Cf. United Nations General Assembly (2003), Art. 10 and United Nations Conference on Environment and Development (1992), Principle 10.

73. Cf. Banisar (2006), p. 6.

74. Cf. International Organization for Standardization (1994) and International Social and Environmental Accreditation and Labelling Alliance (2004).

75. Thus despite their criticisms concerning the contents of the report, 'dam builders and operators, whether actually or rhetorically, have already begun to use the recommendations of the commission as a point of reference' (Dingwerth, 2005, p. 69).

76. For a very accessible description of the technical requirements of the Internet see, for example, Weinberg (2000).

77. The binding nature of ICANN's policies and regulations has given rise to an intense debate. The Internet Governance Project, for example, summarises the problem as follows in its proposal for structural reform: 'Today ICANN exercises quasi-governmental powers. However, it lacks corresponding mechanisms for accountability, oversight, and representation' (Klein and Mueller, 2005, p. 2).

78. Partnerships setting rules with a strongly binding character can be compared to domestic regulatory agencies. Klein (2005), for example, bases his proposals for a reform of ICANN on the argument that ICANN is de facto a regulatory agency. The practice of delegating rule setting and regulatory tasks to independent agencies has been on the rise throughout the developed world for over two decades. For an analysis of the rise of regulatory agencies in Europe see, for example, Majone (1994), and for an analysis of the reasons for their diffusion see, for example, Gilardi (2005).

    Authors vary in the precise elements they define as central to the good governance and accountability of regulatory agencies. The standards are, however, usually related to the internal governance of regulatory agencies (which is more strongly linked to accountability through participation than to accountability to prevent the abuse of legislative authority), the authorisation and mandate of the agency, as well as to judicial review and, at times, political oversight. De Haan et al. (1998), for example, focus on the definition of a clear mandate and goals, on transparency and on the ability of parliament to authorise regulatory agencies and to change or withdraw that authorisation. Klein (2005) includes the elements of political authorisation, legislative mandate, internal processes, judicial review and political oversight in his list of 'good regulatory practices'.

79. The policy cycle is a standard way in political science of conceptualising the process by which public policy is developed and implemented. Authors vary in the labels and the exact number of stages they use in their models of the policy cycle. Typically, however, they include a form of problem definition and agenda setting, decision or policymaking, policy implementation and evaluation. For an introduction to the policy cycle including a description of the various models proposed over time see, for example, Jann and Wegrich (2003).

80. Donors, be they government agencies, private organisations or individuals, can have a range of motives for engaging in philanthropic activities, ranging from a genuine interest in addressing a problem to personal gratification and reputational benefits. For an analysis of different altruistic and selfish motivations of public donors and their influence on donor policies see, for example, Canavire Bacarreza et al. (2005). On the motives of private donors see, for example, Harbaugh (1998). Even for deriving prestige and reputation, however, it is important that the charitable activities a donor engages in are seen as useful and effective.

81. Proposals for increased outcome accountability in other sectors also often refer to corporate sector standards. In the public sector, for example, the dominant school of thought pushing for more outcome accountability is the New Public Management. Proponents of New Public Management reforms advocate the creation of greater efficiency in the public sector by introducing accountability mechanisms derived from the private sector.

82. This follows the basic definition of performance evaluation proposed by Göran Arvidsson: 'performance evaluation means to find out and appraise how well an activity, a program or an agency fulfills or has fulfilled its objectives' (Arvidsson, 1986, p. 627).

83. Fowler actually contrasts NGOs in this respect from governments, arguing that governments have 'political support' as their bottom line. Political support, however, mainly expresses itself in relation to parties and elected politicians. Many public agencies, by contrast, are today under strong (political) pressure to demonstrate their efficiency and effectiveness. When attempting to evaluate their performance, these government agencies face very similar problems to NGOs and other non-profit organisations in defining performance criteria.

84. Cf. Global Alliance for Improved Nutrition (2007).
85. Cf. Stop TB Partnership (2006b).
86. Cf. Roll Back Malaria Partnership (2005).
87. Cf. GAVI Alliance Secretariat (2006c) and Low-Beer et al. (2007).
88. On the widespread introduction of performance measures in the public sector in the US and the UK see, for example, Propper and Wilson (2003), pp. 250–1.
89. The literature concerning this subject is much too broad to be reviewed comprehensively here. Several contributions, however, contain literature reviews or summaries of arguments. Freeman (2002), for example, provides a synthesis and review of the literature on the use of performance indicators to improve public health services in the UK; Marshall et al. (2000) summarise the empirical evidence on the effects of publishing performance data in the US-American health sector; Hepworth (1998) focuses on the use of the balanced score card in the US and the UK; Smith (1995) collects the unintended consequences related to the use of performance indicators in the UK; and Dorsch and Yasin (1998) provide a literature review on benchmarking in the public sector.
90. With respect to the public sector, one study concludes, for example, that 'PMs are now widely used within public sector organizations, but there is a lack of evidence regarding their usefulness. Hence, it is still not clear to what extent PMs help agencies achieve the goals that have been set by policy-makers' (Propper and Wilson, 2003, p. 264). Another study focusing on non-profit organisations concludes that 'In theory, outcomes assessment can be a helpful tool for realizing publicly valued ends such as fiscal accountability, program integration, and citizen empowerment. However, our findings suggest that achieving these ends in practice will be rare rather than routine' (Campbell, 2002, p. 254). By contrast, Boyne and Chen (2006) find that performance targets do improve the performance of English schools.
91. For the 'teaching to the test' phenomenon see, for example, Pollitt (1995), p. 215 and for a more general analysis of the problem of 'measure fixation' see, for example, Smith (1995).
92. In the literature on performance evaluation in the public and non-profit sectors, there is broad consensus on the importance of involving stakeholders in the definition of performance criteria. Cf. for example, Herman and Renz (1998), Fowler (1995), Edwards and Hulme (1995), Freeman (2002), Kravchuk and Schack (1996).
93. The British Royal Statistical Society concludes that 'PM [performance measurement] done well is broadly productive for those concerned. Done badly, it can be very costly and not merely ineffective but harmful and indeed destructive' (Bird et al., 2005, p. 1).
94. Wolfgang Wirth, for example, list the following necessary conditions for creating effective output control: 'output control is feasible, if there are unambiguous, reliable and generally accepted measures of desired results available; if these measures capture all significant dimensions of performance and contain all the information required for full evaluation; if single or individual contributions to final outputs can be measured separately in case of complex, joint or interdependent activities; and if results that are due to chance can be distinguished from those which can be attributed to foresight' (Wirth, 1986a, p. 603).
95. All classical methods for conducting social cost-benefit analyses concur that projects should be evaluated relative to a counterfactual. Cf. for example, Devarajan et al. (1997), pp. 35–6.

96. For a discussion of relevant accounting, reporting and auditing rules for NGOs, see section 5.1.2.2.
97. These two purposes are emphasised, for example, by an analyst of performance evaluations in the development sector: 'Ever since the evaluation of development aid first began in the early 1960s in the USA, there has been a tension between the two competing objectives of evaluation, namely, accountability on the one hand, and lesson-learning on the other' (Cracknell, 2000, p. 54).
98. This refers to Robert Behn's formulation that 'Those whom we want to hold accountable have a clear understanding of what accountability means: Accountability means punishment' (Behn, 2001, p. 3).
99. On the importance of staff involvement and communication for learning see, for example, Forss et al. (1994).
100. Private goods are those usually traded on markets. Their characteristics include that they are excludable, that is, they have a clearly identifiable owner, and that they are rival, that is, one person's use or consumption of the good precludes another person's use. Pure public goods exhibit the opposite attributes and are non-excludable as well as non-rival. Seen from an economic perspective, these traits give individuals benefiting from public goods a strong incentive to free-ride. As a result, public goods tend to be underprovided and economists accord governments an important role in providing public goods. For a brief explanation of the concept of public good as well as its extension into the global realm see, for example, Kaul (2000).
101. This can be based on the fact that the goods and services in question display some public good characteristics, that they create strong externalities or that they are linked to a natural monopoly. It can also be based on ideological preferences or equity concerns.
102. This technique is often used for the provision of social services. Diller (2000), for example, analyses attempts by the US-American government to introduce performance-based accountability in welfare services. The task of providing welfare services at the ground level was delegated either to government agencies enjoying broad discretion or to private providers, relying on performance-based contracts. Klingner et al. (2002) scrutinise a similar case of outsourcing in the context of the Kansas foster care reform. For a more detailed discussion of outsourcing and what it entails for federal and local governments see, for example, O'Looney (1998).
103. Carr-Hill (1992), for example, analyses the use of patient satisfaction surveys in the health sector and compares this method of gathering beneficiary feedback to qualitative methods. A study on outcome measurement in NGOs reports that client satisfaction surveys are relatively frequently used by service providing non-profit organisations, with over half of the surveyed organisations in one study collecting such information from clients, indirect customers or other stakeholder (Morley et al., 2001, p. 6).
104. For a description of the Global Fund's policies on allocating resources, as well as an analysis of the results of this strategy see, for example, Low-Beer et al. (2007), esp. Chapter 4.
105. Blanchard, Hinnant and Wong, for example, have described the introduction of market-based reforms as a move from the social contract to a 'social sub-contract'. They summarise their assessment as follows: 'Although economic efficiency may be gained from market-based reforms, many questions related to the accountability and legitimacy of such arrangements have gone unanswered' (Blanchard et al., 1998, pp. 508–9).

106. Gerald Blasi, for instance, has analysed human service contracts issued by various government entities in the US. He found that most, but not all, of the contracts were based on competitive bidding processes. Even where competitive bidding processes were used, he concludes that '[i]n reality, it is difficult to say whether this is a viable accountability method as the competitive aspect is questionable in that many human service contracts do not have multiple bidders' (Blasi, 2002, pp. 526–7). Therefore, Blasi doubts whether the threat of losing a contract to the competition is a valid reality.

107. When accountability standards for rule setting and regulation partnerships were developed, the importance of formal consultation processes with stakeholders was discussed (cf. section 5.2.2.1). While there is some overlap between the mechanisms employed, as well as the standards for using them, there are also significant differences. This is due to the fact that the consultation processes pursue different objectives in both cases. For rule-setting partnerships, stakeholder consultations are designed to enable stakeholders to participate in the policymaking process of the partnership. For implementation partnerships, by contrast, stakeholder feedback is 'only' one means of several to collect information for assessing partnership performance.

108. For the report and a summary of the results of these stakeholder interviews, see Green (2002).

109. For a list of interviewees for the Stop TB evaluation, see Institute for Health Sector Development (2003), Annex B.

110. For an analysis of the importance of customer satisfaction in the US, as well as a guide on how to develop, implement and analyse corporate customer satisfaction surveys see, for example, Hayes (1998). For a discussion about the use of satisfaction surveys in the public sector see, for example, Swindell and Kelly (2000).

111. For an analysis of the shortcomings of surveys and stakeholder interviews, especially in areas requiring much technical information see, for example, Darnall and Jolley (2004).

112. There is a broad literature on focus groups as a research method. For a discussion on the advantages of open-ended interview techniques and especially the use of focus groups in research see, for example, Krueger and Casey (2000), Morgan (1997) or Stewart et al. (2007).

113. Batchelor et al. (1994), for example, analyse the use of complaints boxes and telephone hotlines in addition to client satisfaction surveys and interviews in health care.

114. A study on outcome accountability in NGOs, for example, recommends that organisations collecting data for outcome measurement provide incentives to achieve adequate response rates in surveys, that surveys be tested and kept simple and that information be collected over a long period of time (12 months) (Morley et al., 2001, p. 8). Similarly, Blasi (2002) criticises that surveys do often not reach individuals who are not or no longer involved in the programme, that response rates are low and that outcomes are rarely measured on a long-term basis (p. 533).

115. The main product of the WCD was its report 'Dams and Development: A New Framework for Decision-Making'. Part I of the report, 'Global Review of Large Dams', presents the results of the various studies on economic, environmental and social performance of dams. Cf. World Commission on Dams (2000), pp. 35–194.

116. For a description of the progress made by MSC in certifying fisheries and fish producers and suppliers until March 2006, see the partnership's annual report (Marine Stewardship Council, 2006).

117. 4C describes the processes used for compliance verification, for example, in Common Code of the Coffee Community (2007a).

118. For a history of the concept of academic freedom, the underlying rationale, its increasing acceptance throughout the world and different interpretations, for example, in the UK and the US see, for example, Fellman (1973–4).

119. 'Art and scholarship, research, and teaching shall be free. The freedom of teaching shall not release any person from allegiance to the constitution' (translation by Inter Nationes).

120. Cf. for example, the 1985 decision 'Regents of the University of Michigan v. Ewing' (US Supreme Court, 1985).

121. It states that university commissioners need to ensure that 'academic staff have freedom within the law to question and test received wisdom, and to put forward new ideas and controversial or unpopular opinions, without placing themselves in jeopardy of losing their jobs or privileges they may have at their institutions' (United Kingdom Parliament, 1988, §202, 2a).

122. On the concept of university autonomy, its different traditions, developments over time and institutional implications see, for example, Berg (1993), Tapper and Salter (1995) or Pechar (2005).

123. On the principle of tenure and its relationship to academic freedom see, for example, Brown and Kurland (1990) or Haskell (1997).

124. According to the 1940 Statement of Principles on Academic Freedom and Tenure, the probation period should not exceed seven years. Cf. American Association of University Professors and Association of American Colleges (1940), p. 4.

125. Evaluations and performance assessments first became popular in the US and the UK. One analyst describes the fondness for assessments of American universities and colleges as follows: 'Practically everybody in the academic community gets assessed these days, and practically everybody assesses somebody else' (Astin, 2003, p. 1). More recently, similar practices have also spread to Europe and other countries. For a discussion of the increasing use of evaluations in German universities and their reception by faculty and students see, for example, Wellhöfer et al. (2002).

126. Haskell (1997), for example, finds that student evaluations of faculty members can seriously impinge on their academic freedom, leading teachers to lower their teaching and exam standards, lower their classroom requirements and adjusting courses to popular beliefs and notions. Berdahl (1990) criticises the introduction of competition as a method of quality control because it risks undermining the academic integrity of universities.

127. The details of regulations for universities and other institutions of higher learning vary between countries. In most cases, public and private universities coexist and are subject to different kinds of government influence. Thus, for example, public universities are usually predominantly publicly financed and the government often has a say in the appointment of the institution's leadership and professors. Private universities can enjoy greater autonomy in their finances and appointment procedures but have to be publicly accredited to be able to award academic titles. To take an example from Germany, the State of Bavaria, for instance, regulates these aspects in its Hochschulgesetz (Landtag des Freistaates Bayern, 2006, esp. Art. 5, 13, 76). At the same time, this legal framework – as

well as many others – stresses the principle of academic freedom and the right of these institutions to regulate their internal matters autonomously (Landtag des Freistaates Bayern, 2006, Art. 3 and 11).

128. In the US, for example, the constitution assigns the authority to appoint the judges of the Supreme Court to the president. Article II, section 2 reads: 'he [the President] shall nominate, and by and with the Advice and Consent of the Senate, shall appoint [...] Judges of the Supreme Court, and all other Officers of the United States, whose Appointments are not herein otherwise provided for, and which shall be established by Law: but the Congress may by Law vest the Appointment of such inferior Officers, as they think proper, in the President alone, in the Courts of Law, or in the Heads of Departments'. Article III, section 1, at the same time, places judicial power exclusively in the hands of the courts: 'The judicial Power of the United States, shall be vested in one supreme Court, and in such inferior Courts as the Congress may from time to time ordain and establish.'

129. Cf. International Organization for Standardization (1996), Clause 4.2 b.

130. A World Bank background paper provides a good global overview over university finance. It finds that recent reform trends include various strategies to supplement governmental with non-governmental revenues. Despite these reforms, the paper finds that 'The financing of most higher education will remain substantially dependent on public revenues. Even in countries, like the United States, where private higher education is very developed, both private and public universities receive public aid' (Johnstone, 1998, p. 20). For more precise statistics on public and private spending on higher education in OECD countries see, for example, Organisation for Economic Co-operation and Development (2003). Increasingly, public contributions to university budgets are also tied to performance criteria. Common criteria include, for example, 'degrees awarded, degrees awarded in particular fields, average time to degree completion, performance of graduates on post graduate or licensure examinations, success of faculty in winning competitive research grants, or peer-based scholarly reputation of the faculty' (Johnstone, 1998, p. 22). By contrast, performance criteria cannot include issues such as which research questions or methods are pursued, which results are achieved or which contents are taught.

    Regarding the influence of public finance on the independence of the courts, Douglas and Hartley (2001) find no evidence that the government uses its power of the purse to influence judicial decisions and undermine judicial independence.

131. Cf. for example, International Organization for Standardization (2004), Clauses 4.3.4 and 4.5.2 and International Organization for Standardization (1996), Clause 4.2.m.

132. Cf. for example, International Organization for Standardization (2004), Clause 4.3.2 or International Organization for Standardization (1996), Clause 4.2.e.

133. The only way to remove a US judge from office against her will is through an impeachment procedure. The concerned judge has to be impeached by the House of Representatives and convicted by the Senate, deciding with a two-thirds majority. In Germany, federal judges, including judges serving on the constitutional court (who are appointed for a non-renewable term of 12 years), can only be removed from office by a decision of the federal constitutional court, which also requires a two-thirds majority. Cf. Deutscher Bundestag (1993), §105 BVerfGG.

134. Cf. for example, the 1940 Statement of Principles on Academic Freedom and Tenure (American Association of University Professors and Association of American Colleges, 1940) or the German Hochschulrahmengesetz (Deutscher Bundestag, 1999, § 46).
135. The relevant research is summarised, for example, in Dana and Loewenstein (2003).
136. Cf. for example, the Code of Judicial Ethics adopted by the International Criminal Court, which states: 'Judges shall be impartial and ensure the appearance of impartiality in the discharge of their judicial functions. Judges shall avoid any conflict of interest, or being placed in a situation which might reasonably be perceived as giving rise to a conflict of interest' (International Criminal Court, 2005, Article 4). Similarly, the International Association of Judges in its Universal Charter of the Judge demands among others that 'In the performance of the judicial duties the judge must be impartial and must so be seen' and that 'The judge must not carry out any other function, whether public or private, paid or unpaid, that is not fully compatible with the duties and status of a judge' (International Association of Judges, 1999, Articles 5 and 7). Similarly, the International Bar Association, a federation of national bar associations and legal societies (most of which have their own codes of ethics) has adopted an International Code of Ethics. It dedicates several paragraphs to conflicts of interest. Cf. International Bar Association (1988), especially Articles 3, 12, 13.
137. The exclusion of judges from trials in cases of reasonably suspected bias is, for example, strongly anchored in the German procedural rules of justice. Regulations on 'Befangenheit' of judges are laid down in § 42 ZPO and § 24 StPO.
138. The Statement on Professional Ethics of the American Association of University Professors, for example, contains the clause: 'Although professors may follow subsidiary interests, these interests must never seriously hamper or compromise their freedom of inquiry' (American Association of University Professors, 1987, Article I). A statement of the Harvard University Policy on Conflicts of Interest and Commitment, including a disclosure form, for example, can be accessed at http://www.ogc.harvard.edu/documents/conflict_policy-senior_officials.doc. The Statement of Policy and Procedure on Conflict of Interest of Oxford University is available at http://www.admin.ox.ac.uk/rso/integrity/conflict_interest_policy.shtml (all sites last accessed 27 August 2009).
139. In Germany, for example, where the overwhelming majority of professors are civil servants, the Länder are responsible for defining the details of rules relating to civil servants as well as to universities. The federal guidelines for university laws ('Hochschulrahmengesetz'), however, decree that professors have to disclose all external activities for which they receive remuneration. Cf. Deutscher Bundestag (1999), § 52.
140. The 4C initiative describes the listing criteria for local verifiers as 'experience in social and/or environmental standards' auditing, background knowledge in the coffee sector as well as a positive track record. [...] In addition to the 4C criteria, either ISO9000 or ISO14000 accredited auditors as well as auditors active in sustainable coffee certification qualify for listing by the 4C Association subject to attending an initial training' (Common Code of the Coffee Community, 2007b, §§ 135 and 136).
141. Thus each assessment team must have appropriate demonstrated technical expertise in fish stock assessment, fish stock biology/ecology (with at least five

years research expertise in target or similar species), fishing impacts on aquatic ecosystems (at least five years experience), fishery management and operations (at least ten years experience as practicing aquatic natural resource manager) and appropriate current knowledge of the country, language and local fishery context. Cf. Marine Stewardship Council (2004), section 2.2.3.

142. This includes the possibility to comment on the composition of the assessment team, on the preparation of the assessment hierarchy (which determines critical thresholds for certification) and on the draft findings. For a more detailed description of the assessment process see, for example, Leadbitter and Grieve (2004).

143. For a summary of the debate and historical evolution relating to the method for appointing judges in the US, as well as its implications for judicial accountability see, for example, Hanssen (1999) or Webster (1995).

144. ISO defines the following benchmarks for the education, work experience and training of auditors: An auditor should have completed secondary education, at least five years of total work experience, at least two years of work experience in quality or environmental management, at least 40 hours of audit training and should have completed at least four complete audits as an auditor-in-training. Cf. International Organization for Standardization (2002), Table 1. More generically, ISO guide 65 demands that verification bodies define minimum criteria for the competence of staff and that they maintain and update records on the training and experience of their staff (International Organization for Standardization, 1996, Clauses 5.2.1 and 5.2.3).

145. Platto (1992), for example, describes the appeals processes in over 25 jurisdictions. As Shapiro (1981) explains in his comparative analysis of court systems, most types of jurisdictions allow for appeals. Appeals processes are, however, limited under Islamic law.

146. For an analysis of various possible rationales underlying the appeals process see, for example, Shavell (1995). Shavell concludes that appeals are a very cost effective way to correct errors.

147. These standards are contained in International Organization for Standardization (2004), Clauses 5.9 and 7.10 and International Organization for Standardization (1996), Clauses 4.5.3.m, 7.1 and 7.2. Only the former, ISO standard 17011, demands that the person or body investigating the appeal be independent of the subject of the appeal.

6 Conclusion

1. Cf. Figure 1.1.
2. Cf. Figure 2.2.
3. This comment refers to a paper by Brown and Moore. It distinguishes desirable accountability arrangements for NGOs depending on their main function, but sees the issue as an issue of strategy, rather than a question of norms and values. Cf. Brown and Moore (2001).

Bibliography

Acar, M., and Robertson, P. J. (2004). 'Accountability Challenges in Networks and Partnerships: Evidence from Educational Partnerships in the United States'. *International Review of Administrative Sciences*. 70(2): 331–44.

AccountAbility. (1999). AccountAbility 1000 (AA1000) Framework. London.

Accounting Standards Board. (2001). Financial Reporting Standard for Smaller Entities. London.

Aghion, P., and Bolton, P. (1992). 'An Incomplete Contracts Approach to Financial Contracting'. *Review of Economic Studies*. 59: 473–94.

Ake, C. (1969). 'Political Obligation and Political Dissent'. *Canadian Journal of Political Science/Revue Canadienne de Science Politique*. 2(2): 245–55.

Akerlof, G. (1970). 'The Market for "Lemons": Quality Uncertainty and the Market Mechanism'. *Quarterly Journal of Economics*. 84: 488.

Albert, M., and Kopp-Malek, T. (2002). 'The Pragmatism of Global and European Governance: Emerging Forms of the Political "Beyond Westphalia"'. *Millennium: Journal of International Studies*. 31(3): 453–71.

Alesina, A., and Summers, L. H. (1993). 'Central Bank Independence and Macroeconomic Performance: Some Comparative Evidence'. *Journal of Money, Credit and Banking*. 25(2): 151–62.

Almazan, A., and Suarez, J. (2003). 'Entrenchment and Severance Pay in Optimal Governance Structures'. *The Journal of Finance*. LVIII (2): 519–47.

Almond, G., and Genco, S. (1977). 'Clouds, Clocks, and the Study of Politics'. *World Politics*. 29(4): 489–522.

American Association of University Professors. (1987). Statement on Professional Ethics. Washington.

American Association of University Professors and Association of American Colleges. (1940). 1940 Statement of Principles on Academic Freedom and Tenure. Washington: American Association of University Professors.

American Institute of Certified Public Accountants. (2006). Not-For-Profit Organizations – AICPA Audit and Accounting Guide. With Conforming Changes as of 1 May 2006. Ewing.

Amtenbrink, F. (1999). *The Democratic Accountability of Central Banks: A Comparative Study of the European Central Bank*. Oxford: Hart.

Anderson, K., and Rieff, D. (2005). '"Global Civil Society": A Sceptical View', in H. K. Anheier, M. Glasius, and M. Kaldor (Eds), *Global Civil Society 2004/5*. 26–39. London, Thousand Oaks, New Delhi: Sage.

Andonova, L. (2005). 'International Institutions, Inc: The Rise of Public-Private Partnerships in Global Governance', *Conference on the Human Dimensions of Global Environmental Change*. Berlin.

Andonova, L., and Levy, M. A. (2003). 'Franchising Global Governance: Making Sense of the Johannesburg Type Two Partnerships', in O. S. Stokke and Ø. B. Thommessen (Eds), *Yearbook of International Cooperation on Environment and Development 2003/2004*. 19–31. London: Earthscan.

Anheier, H., Glasius, M., Kaldor, M., and Holland, F. (Eds) (2005). *Global Civil Society 2004/5*. London, Thousand Oaks, New Delhi: Sage.

Archer, M., Bhaskar, R., Collier, A., Lawson, T., and Norrie, A. (Eds) (1998). *Critical Realism: Essential Readings*. London: Routledge.

Archibugi, D. (2004). 'Cosmopolitan Democracy and its Critics: A Review'. *European Journal of International Relations*. 10(3): 437–73.

Aristotle. (1975). *Categories and De Interpretatione: Translated with Notes by J. L. Ackrill*. Oxford: Clarendon Press.

Arneson, R. (1980). Mill vs. Paternalism. *Ethics*. 90: 470–80.

Arnull, A., and Wincott, D. (Eds) (2002). *Accountability and Legitimacy in the EU*. Oxford: Oxford University Press.

Arrow, K. J. (1963). 'Uncertainty and the Welfare Economics of Medical Care'. *American Economic Review* 53(5): 941–73.

Arts, B. (1998). *The Political Influence of Global NGOs: Case Studies on the Climate Change and Biodiversity Conventions*. Utrecht: International Books.

Arvidsson, G. (1986). 'Performance Evaluation', in F.-X. Kaufmann, G. Majone, and V. Ostrom (Eds), *Guidance, Control, and Evaluation in the Public Sector*. 625–44. Berlin, New York: de Gruyter.

Asbach, O. (2002). 'Verfassung und Demokratie in der Europaschen Union: Zur Kritik der Debatte um eine Konstitutionalisierung Europas'. *Leviathan*. 30(2): 267–97.

Ashraf, H. (2003). 'Alliance Offers Healthy Diet'. *The Lancet*. 361(9374): p. 2051.

Astin, A. W. (2003). *Assessment for Excellence: The Philosophy and Practice of Assessment and Evaluation in Higher Education*. Greenwood: The Oryx Press.

Atchison, A. B., Liebert, L. T., and Russell, D. K. (1999). 'Judicial Independence and Judicial Accountability: A Selected Bibliography'. *Southern California Law Review*. 72(3): 723–810.

Aucoin, P., and Heintzman, R. (2000). 'The Dialectics of Accountability for Performance in Public Management Reform'. *International Review of Administrative Sciences*. 66(1): 45–55.

Australian Council for International Development. (2004). ACFID Code of Conduct For Non Government Development Organisations. Deakin.

Babb, S., and Buira, A. (2005). 'Mission Creep, Mission Push and Discretion: The Case of IMF Conditionality', in A. Buira (Ed.), *The IMF and the World Bank at Sixty*. London: Anthem Press.

Bagehot, W. (1873). *The English Constitution*, e-book.

Banisar, D. (2006). Freedom of Information Around the World 2006: A Global Survey of Access to Government Information Laws. London: Privacy International.

Barberis, P. (1998). 'The New Public Management and a New Accountability'. *Public Administration*. 76(3): 451–70.

Baron de Montesquieu, C.d.S. (1748). *De L'Esprit des Lois*. Genève: Barillot.

Baron de Montesquieu, C.d.S. (1914). *The Spirit of Laws*. Translated by Thomas Nugent, revised by J. V. Prichard. London: G. Bell & Sons.

Batchelor, C., Owens, D. J., Read, M., and Bloor, M. (1994). 'Patient Satisfaction Studies: Methodology, Management and Consumer Evaluation'. *International Journal of Health Care Quality Assurance*. 7(7): 22–30.

BBB Wise Giving Alliance. (2003). Standards for Charitable Accountability. Arlington.

Bebchuk, L. A., and Fried, J. M. (2003). 'Executive Compensation as an Agency Problem'. *Journal of Economic Perspectives*. 17(3): 71–92.

Becht, M., Bolton, P., and Röell, A. (2003). 'Corporate Governance and Control', in G. M. Constantinides, M. Harris, and R. M. Stulz (Eds), *Handbook of the Economy of Finance*. Amsterdam, Boston: Elsevier.

Behn, R. D. (1998). 'The New Public Management Paradigm and the Search for Democratic Accountability'. *International Public Management Journal.* 1(2): 131–64.

Behn, R. D. (2001). *Rethinking Democratic Accountability.* Washington: Brookings Institution Press.

Bekefi, T. (2006). *Business as a Partner in Tackling Micronutrient Deficiency: Lessons in Multisector Partnership.* Cambridge: Corporate Social Responsibility Initiative, John F. Kennedy School of Government, Harvard University.

Bendell, J. (2006). *Debating NGO Accountability.* New York, Geneva: United Nations.

Benner, T., Reinicke, W. H., and Witte, J. M. (2004). 'Multisector Networks in Global Governance: Towards a Pluralistic System of Accountability'. *Government and Opposition.* 39(2): 191–210.

Bennett, J. (2002). 'Multinational Corporations, Social Responsibility and Conflict'. *Journal of International Affairs.* 55(2): 393–410.

Bennett, R. J., and Krebs, G. (1994). 'Local Economic Development Partnerships: An Analysis of Policy Networks in EC-LEDA Local Employment Development Strategies'. *Regional Studies.* 28: 119–40.

Bentham, J. (2005). *An Introduction to the Principles of Morals and Legislation: An Authoritative Edition by J. H. Burns and H. L. A. Hart.* Oxford: Clarendon Press.

Berdahl, R. (1990). 'Academic Freedom, Autonomy and Accountability in British Universities'. *Studies in Higher Education.* 15(2): 169–80.

Berg, C. (1993). 'University Autonomy and Quality Assurance'. *Higher Education in Europe.* 18(3): 18–26.

Berle, A. A., and Means, G. C. (1932). *The Modern Corporation and Private Property.* New York: Macmillan Publishing Co.

Bernstein, S., Lebow, R. N., Stein, J. G., and Weber, S. (2000). 'God Gave Physics the Easy Problems: Adapting Social Science to an Unpredictable World'. *European Journal of International Relations.* 6(1): 43–76.

Beutz, M. (2003). 'Functional Democracy: Responding to Failures of Accountability'. *Harvard International Law Journal.* 44: 387–431.

Bevir, M., Rhodes, R. A. W., and Weller, P. (2003). 'Traditions of Governance: Interpreting the Changing Role of the Public Sector'. *Public Administration.* 81(1): 1–17.

BGB. (2006). *Bürgerliches Gesetzbuch. BeurkundungsG, BGB–Informationspflichten–VO, ProdukthaftungsG, WohnungseigentumsG, ErbbauVO, GleichbehandlungsG.* München: DTV-Beck.

Biggs, S., and Neame, A. (1995). 'Negotiating Room for Manoeuvre: Reflections Concerning NGO Autonomy and Accountability Within the New Policy Agenda', in M. Edwards and D. Hulme (Eds), *Non-Governmental Organisations: Performance and Accountability Beyond the Magic Bullet.* 31–40. London: Earthscan.

Bird, S. M., Cox, D., Farewell, V. T., Goldstein, H., Holt, T., and Smith, P. C. (2005). 'Performance Indicators: Good, Bad, and Ugly'. *Journal of the Royal Statistical Society: Series A (Statistics in Society).* 168(1): 1–27.

Blagescu, M., and Lloyd, R. (2006). *2006 Global Accountability Report.* London: One World Trust.

Blanchard, L. A., Hinnant, C. C., and Wong, W. (1998). 'Market-Based Reforms in Government: Toward a Social Subcontract?' *Administration and Society.* 30(5): 483–512.

Blasi, G. J. (2002). 'Government Contracting and Performance Measurement in Human Services'. *International Journal of Public Administration.* 25(4): 519–38.

Bluemel, E. (2005). 'Overcoming NGO Accountability Concerns in International Governance'. *Brooklyn Journal of International Law*. 31(1): 139–206.

Bobrowsky, C. (1999). Creating a Global Public Policy Network in the Apparel Industry: The Apparel Industry Partnership: Case Study for the UN Vision Project on Global Public Policy Networks. Available at http://www.gppi.net/publications/gpp_cases/.

Boissevain, J., and Mitchell, J. C. (Eds). (1973). *Network Analysis: Studies in Human Interaction*. The Hague, Paris: Mouton.

Borins, S. (1995). 'The New Public Management is Here to Stay'. *Canadian Public Administration*. 38(1): 122–32.

Börzel, T. A., and Risse, T. (2005). 'Public-Private Partnerships: Effective and Legitimate Tools of International Governance?' in E. Grande and L. W. Pauly (Eds), *Complex Sovereignty: Reconstituting Political Authority in the Twenty-First Century*. 195–216. Toronto, Buffalo, London: University of Toronto Press.

Bosniak, L. (2000). 'Citizenship Denationalized'. *Indiana Journal of Global Legal Studies*. 7: 447–509.

Boucher, D., and Kelly, P. (1994). 'The Social Contract and Its Critics: An Overview', in D. Boucher and P. Kelly (Eds), *The Social Contract from Hobbes to Rawls*. 1–34. London, New York: Routledge.

Bovens, M. (1998). *The Quest for Responsibility: Accountability and Citizenship in Complex Organisations*. Cambridge, New York: Cambridge University Press.

Bovens, M. (2005). 'Public Accountability', in E. Ferlie, L. E. Lynne, and C. Pollitt (Eds), *The Oxford Handbook of Public Management*. 182–208. Oxford, New York: Oxford University Press.

Bowie, N. E. (2002). 'A Kantian Approach to Business Ethics', in T. Donaldson, P. H. Werhane, and M. Cording (Eds), *Ethical Issues in Business: A Philosophical Approach*. 61–71. Upper Saddle River: Prentice Hall.

Box, R. C., Marshall, G. S., Reed, B. J., and Reed, C. M. (2001). 'New Public Management and Substantive Democracy'. *Public Administration Review*. 61(5): 608–19.

Boyne, G. A., and Chen, A. A. (2006). 'Performance Targets and Public Service Improvement'. *Journal of Public Administration Research and Theory* 17(3): 455–77.

Bradshaw, P., Hayday, B., Armstrong, R., Levesque, J., and Rykert, L. (1998). 'Nonprofit Governance Models: Problems and Prospects', *ARNOVA Conference*. Seattle, Washington.

Bradshaw, P., Murray, V., and Wolpin, J. (1992). 'Do Nonprofit Boards Make a Difference? An Exploration of the Relationships Among Board Structure, Process, and Effectiveness'. *Nonprofit and Voluntary Sector Quarterly*. 21(3): 227–49.

Bratton, W. W., and McCahery, J. A. (1999). 'Comparative Corporate Governance and the Theory of the Firm: The Case Against Global Cross Reference'. *Columbia Journal of Transnational Law*. 38: 213–97.

Breitmeier, H., and Rittberger, V. (1998). 'Environmental NGOs in an Emerging Global Civil Society', in Center for International Relations/Peace and Conflict Studies (Ed.), *Tübinger Arbeitspapiere zur Internationalen Politik und Friedensforschung Nr. 32*. Tübingen: University of Tübingen.

Brison, S. J. (1998). 'The Autonomy Defense of Free Speech'. *Ethics*. 108(2): 312–39.

Brock, D. (1983). 'Paternalism and Promoting the Good', in R. Sartorius (Ed.), *Paternalism*. Minneapolis: University of Minnesota Press.

Brody, E. (2002). 'Accountability and Public Trust', in L. M. Salamon (Ed.), *The State of Nonprofit America*. 471–98. Washington: Brookings Institution Press.

Brown, H. S., de Jong, M., and Lessidrenska, T. (2007). 'The Rise of the Global Reporting Initiative (GRI) as a Case of Institutional Entrepreneurship'. *Working Paper No. 36.*

Cambridge: Corporate Social Responsibility Initiative, John F. Kennedy School of Government, Harvard University.

Brown, L. D., and Moore, M. H. (2001). 'Accountability, Strategy, and International Non-Governmental Organizations'. *Nonprofit and Voluntary Sector Quarterly.* 30(3): 569–587.

Brown, R. S., and Kurland, J. E. (1990). 'Academic Tenure and Academic Freedom'. *Law and Contemporary Problems.* 53(3): 325–55.

Brownlie, I. (Ed.). (1995). *Basic Documents in International Law.* Oxford: Clarendon Press.

Brugha, R., Starling, M., and Walt, G. (2002). 'GAVI, the First Steps: Lessons for the Global Fund'. *The Lancet.* 359(9304): 435–8.

Brunnengräber, A., Klein, A., and Walk, H. (Eds). (2001). *NGOs als Legitimationsressource. Zivilgesellschaftliche Partizipationsformen im Globalisierungsprozess.* Opladen: Leske+Budrich.

Bruno, K. (2002). *Greenwash + 10. The UN's Global Compact, Corporate Accountability and the Johannesburg Earth Summit.* San Francisco: CorpWatch/Tides Center.

Bryce, H. (1992). *Financial and Strategic Management for Nonprofit Organizations.* Englewood Cliffs: Prentice-Hall.

Bryer, D., and Magrath, J. (1999). 'New Dimensions of Global Advocacy'. *Nonprofit and Voluntary Sector Quarterly.* 28(4): 168–77.

Buchanan, A. E. (1989). 'Assessing the Communitarian Critique of Liberalism'. *Ethics.* 99(4): 852–82.

Bulmer, S. J. (1994). 'The Governance of the European Union: A New Institutionalist Approach'. *Journal of Public Policy.* 13(4): 351–80.

Burbank, S. B. (1999). 'The Architecture of Judicial Independence'. *Southern California Law Review.* 72(3): 315–51.

Cadbury, A. (1992). *Report of the Committee on the Financial Aspects of Corporate Governance.* London: The Committee on the Financial Aspects of Corporate Governance and Gee and Co. Ltd.

Campbell, D. (2002). 'Outcomes Assessment and the Paradox of Nonprofit Accountability'. *Nonprofit Management & Leadership.* 12(3): 243–59.

Canadian Comprehensive Audit Foundation. (1996). Governance Information – Strategies for Success: A Governance Information Check-Up. Ottawa.

Canadian Council of International Co-operation. (2002/1995). Code of Ethics. Ottawa.

Canavire Bacarreza, G. J., Nunnenkamp, P., Thiele, R., and Triveno, L. (2005). 'Assessing the Allocation of Aid: Developmental Concerns and the Self-Interest of Donors'. *Kiel Working Paper No. 1253.* Kiel: Kiel Institute for World Economics.

Carmichael, H. L., and MacLeod, W. B. (2000). 'Worker Cooperation and the Ratchet Effect'. *Journal of Labor Economics.* 18(1): 1–19.

Carr-Hill, R. A. (1992). 'The Measurement of Patient Satisfaction'. *Journal of Public Health.* 14: 236–49.

Carriere, R. (2003). 'Public-Private Sector Alliances for Food Fortification: Time for Optimism'. *Food and Nutrition Bulletin.* 24(4): 155–9.

Carter, T. S., and Cooper, K. J. (2006). 'The Legal Context of Nonprofit Management', in V. Murray (Ed.), *The Management of Non-Profit and Charitable Organizations in Canada.* 127–71. Toronto: LexisNexis Butterworths.

Cendón, A. B. (2000). 'Accountability and Public Administration: Concepts, Dimensions, Developments', in M. Kelle (Ed.), *Openness and Transparency in Governance: Challenges and Opportunities.* 22–61. Maastricht, Bratislava: EIPA, NISPAcee.

Centre for Civil Society. (2004). Definition of Civil Society. London: London School of Economics and Political Science.

Centre for Global Studies. (2001). Rethinking Governance Handbook: An Inventory of Ideas to Enhance Participation, Transparency and Accountability. Victoria: University of Victoria.

Charity Commission for England and Wales. (2003). CC8 – Internal Financial Controls for Charities. Liverpool.

Charity Commission for England and Wales. (2005). Accounting and Reporting by Charities: Statement of Recommended Practice. Liverpool.

Charity Commission for England and Wales. (2007). Charity Commission News 26 – Spring 2007. Liverpool.

Charnovitz, S. (1997). 'Two Centuries of Participation: NGOs and International Governance'. *Michigan Journal of International Law*. 18(2): 183–286.

Chaskin, R. J. (2003). 'Fostering Neighborhood Democracy: Legitimacy and Accountability Within Loosely Coupled Systems'. *Nonprofit and Voluntary Sector Quarterly*. 32(2): 161–89.

Chaves, M., Stephens, L., and Galaskiewicz, J. (2004). 'Does Government Funding Suppress Nonprofits' Political Activity?' *American Sociological Review*. 69(2): 292–316.

Cheibub, J. A., and Limongi, F. (2002). 'Democratic Institutions and Regime Survival: Parliamentary and Presidential Democracies Reconsidered'. *Annual Review of Political Science*. 5: 151–79.

Choudhury, E., and Ahmed, S. (2002). 'The Shifting Meaning of Governance: Public Accountability of Third Sector Organizations in an Emergent Global Regime'. *International Journal of Public Administration*. 25(4): 561–88.

Chryssochoou, D. N., Stavridis, S., and Tsinisizelis, M. J. (1998). 'European Democracy, Parliamentary Decline and the "Democratic Deficit" of the European Union'. *Journal of Legislative Studies*. 4(3): 109–29.

Coase, R. H. (1937). 'The Nature of the Firm'. *Economica, New Series*. 4(16): 386–405.

Collier, D., and Mahoney, J. (1996). 'Insights and Pitfalls: Selection Bias in Qualitative Research'. *World Politics*. 49(1): 56–91.

Collin, S.-O. (1998). 'In the Twilight Zone: A Survey of Public-Private Partnerships in Sweden'. *Public Productivity & Management Review*. 21(3): 272–83.

Commission on Global Governance. (1995). *Our Global Neighbourhood: The Report of the Commission on Global Governance*. Oxford: Oxford University Press.

Commission on Sustainable Development. (2003). The Implementation Track for Agenda 21 and the Johannesburg Plan of Implementation: Future Programme, Organisation and Methods of Work of the Commission on Sustainable Development. New York: CSD 11.

Common Code of the Coffee Community. (2004). The Common Code for the Coffee Community. Bonn.

Common Code of the Coffee Community. (2006). The Common Code for the Coffee Community Annual Report 2005. Eschborn, Amsterdam: Deutsche Gesellschaft für Technische Zusammenarbeit (GTZ), European Coffee Federation.

Common Code of the Coffee Community. (2007a). 4C Update Information January 2007. Bonn.

Common Code of the Coffee Community. (2007b). 4C Verification Scheme. Bonn.

Common Code of the Coffee Community. (2007c). Statutes of the Common Code for the Coffee Community Association. Geneva.

Considine, M. (2002). 'The End of the Line? Accountable Governance in the Age of Networks, Partnerships, and Joined-up Services'. *Governance: An International Journal of Policy, Administration, and Institutions*. 15(1): 21–40.

Conyon, M. J., and Florou, A. (2002). 'Top Executive Dismissal, Ownership and Corporate Performance'. *Accounting and Business Research*. 32: 209–25.

Coole, D. (1994). 'Women, Gender and Contract: Feminist Interpretations', in D. Boucher and P. Kelly (Eds), *The Social Contract from Hobbes to Rawls*. 191–210. London, New York: Routledge.

Core, J. E., Holthausen, R. W., and Larcker, D. F. (1999). 'Corporate Governance, Chief Executive Officer Compensation, and Firm Performance'. *Journal of Financial Economics*. 51(3): 371–406.

Corporate Europe Observatory. (2002). Girona Declaration: From Rio to Johannesburg. Amsterdam.

Coultrap, J. (1999). 'From Parliamentarism to Pluralism: Models of Democracy and the European Union's "Democratic Deficit"'. *Journal of Theoretical Politics*. 11(1): 107–35.

Council on Foreign Relations. (2004). An Update on the Global War on Terror with Donald Rumsfeld. New York.

Courty, P., and Marschke, G. (2004). 'An Empirical Investigation of Gaming Responses to Explicit Performance Incentives'. *Journal of Labor Economics*. 22: 23–56.

Cracknell, B. E. (2000). *Evaluating Development Aid*. New Delhi, Thousand Oaks, London: Sage.

Cudd, A. (2006). 'Contractarianism', in E. N. Zalta (Ed.), *The Stanford Encyclopedia of Philosophy*. Stanford: The Metaphysics Research Lab, Center for the Study of Language and Information, Stanford University.

Cummins, A. (2004). 'The Marine Stewardship Council: A Multi-Stakeholder Approach to Sustainable Fishing'. *Corporate Social Responsibility and Environmental Management*. 11(2): 85–94.

Cunningham, J. (1998). Next Steps Report 1998. London: The Stationary Office.

Cuomo, A. (2005). Internal Controls and Financial Accountability for Not-for-Profit Boards. New York: Office of the Attorney General, Charities Bureau.

Curtis, V. (2002). Health in Your Hands: Lessons from Building Public-Private Partnerships for Washing Hands with Soap. Washington: Water and Sanitation Program, The World Bank.

Curtis, V., Garbrah-Aidoo, N., and Scott, B. (2007). 'Ethics in Public Health Research: Masters of Marketing: Bringing Private Sector Skills to Public Health Partnerships'. *American Journal of Public Health*. 97(4): 634–41.

D'Agostino, F. (2006). 'Contemporary Approaches to the Social Contract', in E. N. Zalta (Ed.), *The Stanford Encyclopedia of Philosophy*. Stanford: The Metaphysics Research Lab, Center for the Study of Language and Information, Stanford University.

Dahl, R. A. (1994). 'A Democratic Dilemma: System Effectiveness versus Citizen Participation'. *Political Science Quarterly*. 109(1): 23–34.

Dahl, R. A. (1999). 'Can International Organizations be Democratic? A Skeptic's View', in I. Shapiro and C. Hacker-Cordón (Eds), *Democracy's Edges*. 19–36. Cambridge: Cambridge University Press.

Dana, J., and Loewenstein, G. (2003). 'A Social Science Perspective on Gifts to Physicians From Industry'. *The Journal of the American Medical Association*. 290(2): 252–5.

Danermark, B., Ekström, M., Jakobsen, L., and Karlsson, J. C. (2002). *Explaining Society: Critical Realism in the Social Sciences.* London: Routledge.

Darnall, N., and Jolley, G. J. (2004). 'Involving the Public: When Are Surveys and Stakeholder Interviews Effective?' *Review of Policy Research.* 21(4): 581–93.

Davidson, W. N., Pilger, T., and Szakmary, A. (1998). 'Golden Parachutes, Board and Committee Composition, and Shareholder Wealth'. *The Financial Review.* 33(4): 17–32.

De Haan, J., Amtenbrink, F., and Eijffinger, S. C. W. (1998). 'Accountability of Central Banks: Aspects and Quantification'. Tilburg: Center for Economic Research, Tilburg University.

De Senillosa, I. (1998). 'A New Age of Social Movements: A Fifth Generation of Non-Governmental Development Organisations (NGDOs) in the Making'. *Development in Practice.* 8(1): 40–53.

Dechow, P., and Sloan, R. (1991). 'Executive Incentives and the Horizon Problem'. *Journal of Accounting and Economics.* 14(1): 51–89.

Decker, F. (2000). 'Demokratie und Demokratisierung jenseits des Nationalstaats: das Beispiel der Europäischen Union'. *Zeitschrift für Politikwissenschaft.* 10(2): 558–629.

DeMott, D. A. (1988). 'Beyond Metaphor: An Analysis of Fiduciary Obligation'. *Duke Law Journal* (5): 879–924.

Den Butter, F. A. G., and Mosch, R. H. J. (2003). 'Trade, Trust, and Transaction Costs'. *Tinbergen Institute Discussion Papers.* Amsterdam: Tinbergen Institute.

Den Heyer, M. (2001). *A Bibliography for Program Logic Models/Logframe Analysis.* Ottawa: International Development Research Centre.

Department for International Development. (2007). *Statistics on International Development 2002/03 – 2006/07.* East Kilbride.

Department of Transport. (1987). *Sheen Report: The Merchant Shipping Act 1984, M V Herald of Free Enterprise – Report of Court No 8074.* London: HMSO.

Deutscher Bundestag. (1993). *Gesetz über das Bundesverfassungsgericht.* Berlin.

Deutscher Bundestag. (1999). *Hochschulrahmengesetz.* Berlin.

Deutscher Bundestag. (2007). *Grundgesetz für die Bundesrepublik Deutschland.* Berlin.

Devarajan, S., Squire, L., and Suthiwart-Narueput, S. (1997). 'Beyond Rate of Return: Reorienting Project Appraisal'. *The World Bank Research Observer.* 12(1): 35–46.

Diller, M. (2000). 'The Revolution in Welfare Administration: Rules, Discretion & Entrepreneurial Government'. *New York University Law Review.* 75(5): 1121–220.

Dingwerth, K. (2003). 'Globale Politiknetzwerke und ihre demokratische Legitimation: Analyse der World Commission on Dams'. *Global Governance Working Paper No. 6.* Potsdam, Berlin, Oldenburg: The Global Governance Project.

Dingwerth, K. (2005). 'The Democratic Legitimacy of Public-Private Rule-Making: What Can We Learn From the World Commission on Dams?' *Global Governance.* 11(1): 65–83.

Dingwerth, K. (2007). *The New Transnationalism: Private Rule-Making & Democracy.* Basingstoke: Palgrave Macmillan.

Domingo, P. (1999). 'Judicial Independence and Judicial Reform in Latin America' in A. Schedler, L. Diamond, and M. F. Plattner (Eds), *The Self-Restraining State: Power and Accountability in New Democracies.* 151–75. Boulder, London: Lynne Rienner Publishers.

Donaldson, T., and Preston, L. E. (1995). 'The Stakeholder Theory of the Corporation: Concepts, Evidence, and Implications'. *The Academy of Management Review.* 20(1): 65–91.

Dorsch, J., and Yasin, M. (1998). 'A Framework for Benchmarking in the Public Sector: Literature Review and Directions for Future Research'. *International Journal of Public Sector Management*. 11(23): 91–115.

Douglas-Harper. Online Etymology Dictionary.

Douglas, J. W., and Hartley, R. E. (2001). 'State Court Budgeting and Judicial Independence. Clues from Oklahoma and Virginia'. *Administration & Society*. 33(1): 54–78.

Drohan, W. M. (1999). *Board Primer: Writing a Mission Statement*. Washington: American Society of Association Executives.

Drucker, P. F. (1998). *The Drucker Foundation Self-Assessment Tool: Participant Workbook*. San Francisco: Jossey-Bass.

Dubash, N. K., Dupar, M., Kathasi, S., and Lissi, T. (2001). *A Watershed in Global Governance? An Independent Assessment of the World Commission on Dams*. Washington: World Resources Institute.

Dubnick, M. J. (2002). 'Seeking Salvation for Accountability'. *Annual Meeting for the American Political Science Association*. Boston.

Dubnick, M. J. (2003). 'Accountability and the Promise of Performance: In Search of the Mechanisms'. *Annual Meeting of the American Political Science Association*. Philadelphia.

Dunn, J. (1999). 'Situating Democratic Public Accountability', in A. Przeworski, S. C. Stokes, and B. Manin (Eds), *Democracy, Accountability, and Representation*. 329–44. Cambridge, New York: Cambridge University Press.

Dworkin, G. (1971). 'Paternalism', in R. Wasserstrom (Ed.), *Morality and the Law*. 107–26. Belmont: Wadsworth Publishing Co.

Dworkin, R. (1973). 'The Original Position'. *The University of Chicago Law Review*. 40(3): 500–33.

Dyer, A., and van Loon, H. (1982). *Report on Trusts and Analogous Institutions*. The Hague: United Nations.

Dyer, J. H., and Chu, W. (2003). 'The Role of Trustworthiness in Reducing Transaction Costs and Improving Performance: Empirical Evidence from the United States, Japan, and Korea'. *Organization Science*. 14(1): 57–68.

Ebrahim, A. (2003). 'Accountability in Practice: Mechanisms for NGOs'. *World Development*. 31(5): 813–829.

Ebrahim, A. (2005). 'Accountability Myopia: Losing Sight of Organizational Learning'. *Nonprofit and Voluntary Sector Quarterly*. 34(1): 56–87.

Ebrahim, A., and Weisband, E. (Eds). (2007). *Global Accountabilities. Participation, Pluralism, and Public Ethics*. Cambridge, New York: Cambridge University Press.

Eckstein, H. (1975). 'Case Study and Theory in Political Science', in F. Greenstein and N. Polsby (Eds), *Handbook of Political Science*. Vol. 7. 79–138. Reading: Addison-Wesley.

Edwards, M., and Hulme, D. (1995). 'NGO Performance and Accountability: Introduction and Overview', in M. Edwards and D. Hulme (Eds), *Non-Governmental Organisations: Performance and Accountability Beyond the Magic Bullet*. 3–16. London: Earthscan.

Edwards, M., and Hulme, D. (1998). 'Too Close for Comfort? The Impact of Official Aid on Nongovernmental Organizations'. *Current Issues in Comparative Education*. 1(1): 1–21.

Eichenberger, R., and Frey, B. S. (2002). 'Democratic Governance for a Globalized World'. *Kyklos*. 55: 265–87.

Einhorn, J. (2001). 'The World Bank's Mission Creep'. *Foreign Affairs*. 80(5): 22–35.

EITI International Advisory Group. (2006). Final Report International Advisory Group. London: Extractive Industries Transparency Initiative.

Encyclopaedia Britannica. (2007). Sullivan, Louis, *Encyclopaedia Britannica Online*.

Energy and Security Group, and Sustainable Energy Solutions. (2007). GVEP International: Partnership in Action. London: GVEP International.

Epstein, M. J., and Hanson, K. O. (Eds). (2006). *The Accountable Corporation*. Westport, London: Praeger.

European Communities. (1992). 'Protocol on the Statute of the European System of Central Banks and of the European Central Bank'. *Official Journal of the European Communities*. C191/68.

European Communities. (2002). 'Consolidated Version of the Treaty Establishing the European Community'. *Official Journal of the European Communities*. C325: 33–184.

European Parliament and Council. (1978). 'Directive 78/660/EEC'. *Official Journal of the European Communities*. 21(L222).

European Parliament and Council. (2006a). 'Directive 2006/43/EC of the European Parliament and of the Council of 17 May 2006, on Statutory Audits of Annual Accounts and Consolidated Accounts, Amending Council Directives 78/660/EEC and 83/349/EEC and Repealing Council Directive 84/253/EEC'. *Official Journal of the European Union*. 49(L157): 87–107.

European Parliament and Council. (2006b). 'Directive 2006/46/EC of the European Parliament and Council'. *Official Journal of the European Communities*. (L224): 1–7.

Evaluation Office. (2002). *Handbook on Monitoring and Evaluating for Results*. New York: United Nations Development Programme.

Evan, W. M., and Freeman, R. E. (1988). 'A Stakeholder Theory of the Modern Corporation: Kantian Capitalism', in T. L. Beauchamp and N. Bowie (Eds), *Ethical Theory and Business*. 75–93. Englewood Cliffs: Prentice Hall.

Extractive Industries Transparency Initiative. (2003). Statement of Principles and Agreed Actions. London: Department for International Development.

Extractive Industries Transparency Initiative. (2005a). EITI Factsheet. London: Department for International Development.

Extractive Industries Transparency Initiative. (2005b). *Extractive Industries Transparency Initiative Source Book*. London: Department for International Development.

Falk, R., and Strauss, A. (2001). 'Toward Global Parliament'. *Foreign Affairs*. 80(1): 212–20.

Fearon, J. D. (1999). 'Electoral Accountability and the Control of Politicians: Selecting Good Types versus Sanctioning Poor Performance', in A. Przeworski, S. C. tokes, and B. Manin (Eds), *Democracy, Accountability, and Representation*. 55–97. Cambridge, New York: Cambridge University Press.

Feinberg, J. (1971). 'Legal Paternalism'. *Canadian Journal of Philosophy*. 1: 105–24.

Fellman, D. (1973–4). 'Academic Freedom', in P. P. Wiener (Ed.), *Dictionary of the History of Ideas: Studies of Selected Pivotal Ideas*. Vol. 1. 9–17. New York: Charles Scribner's Sons.

Ferejohn, J. (1999a). 'Accountability and Authority: Toward a Theory of Political Accountability', in A. Przeworski, S. C. Stokes, and B. Manin (Eds), *Democracy, Accountability, and Representation*. 131–53. Cambridge, New York: Cambridge University Press.

Ferejohn, J. (1999b). 'Independent Judges, Dependent Judiciary: Explaining Judicial Independence'. *Southern California Law Review*. 72(3): 353–84.

Filmer, S. R. (1991). *Patriarcha and Other Writings*. Cambridge: Cambridge University Press.

Financial Accounting Standards Board. (1987). Statement No. 93: Recognition of Depreciation by Not-for-Profit Organizations. Norwalk.

Financial Accounting Standards Board. (1993a). Statement No. 116: Accounting for Contributions Received and Contributions Made Norwalk.

Financial Accounting Standards Board. (1993b). Statement No. 117: Financial Statements of Not-for-Profit Organizations. Norwalk.

Financial Accounting Standards Board. (1995). Statement No. 124: Accounting for Certain Investments Held by Not-for-Profit Organizations. Norwalk.

Finkelstein, L. S. (1995). 'What is Global Governance?' *Global Governance*. 1(3): 367–71.

Fleishman, J. (1999). 'Public Trust in Not-for-Profit Organizations and the Need for Regulatory Reform', in C. Clotfelter and T. Ehrlich (Eds), *Philanthropy and the Nonprofit Sector in a Changing America*. Bloomington, Indianapolis: Indiana University Press.

Florini, A. M. (Ed.). (2000). *The Third Force: The Rise of Transnational Civil Society*. Washington: Carnegie Endowment for International Peace.

Foley, M. (1999). *The Politics of the British Constitution*. Manchester, New York: Manchester University Press.

Fombrun, C. J. (1996). *Reputation: Realizing Value from the Corporate Image*. Boston: Harvard Business School Press.

Food and Agriculture Organization of the United Nations. (2005). Guidelines for the Ecolabelling of Fish and Fishery Products from Marine Capture Fish. Rome.

Forss, K., Cracknell, B., and Samset, K. (1994). 'Can Evaluation Help an Organization to Learn?' *Evaluation Review*. 18(5): 574–91

Fortier, E. (2007). *An Evolving Partnership: The Global Fund and Civil Society in the Fight Against AIDS, Tuberculosis and Malaria*. Vernier: The Global Fund to Fight AIDS, Tuberculosis and Malaria.

Fowler, A. (1995). 'Assessing NGO Performance: Difficulties, Dilemmas and a Way Ahead', in M. Edwards and D. Hulme (Eds), *Non-Governmental Organisations: Performance and Accountability Beyond the Magic Bullet*. 143–56. London: Earthscan.

Fox, J. A., and Brown, L. D. (Eds). (1998). *The Struggle for Accountability: The World Bank, NGOs, and Grassroots Movements*. Cambridge: MIT Press.

Freedom House. (2007). Freedom in the World Country Ratings 1972–2007. Washington, New York.

Freeman, B., and Hernández Uriz, G. (2003). 'Managing Risk and Building Trust. The Challenge of Implementing the Voluntary Principles on Security and Human Rights', in R. Sullivan (Ed.), *Business and Human Rights. Dilemmas and Solutions*. 243–59. Sheffield: Greenleaf Publishing.

Freeman, R. E. (1984). *Strategic Management: A Stakeholder Approach*. Boston: Pitman Publishing.

Freeman, R. E. (2001). 'Stakeholder Theory of the Modern Corporation (Reprint)', in T. Donaldson, P. H. Werhane, and M. Cording (Eds), *Ethical Issues in Business: A Philosophical Approach*. 38–48. Upper Saddle River: Prentice-Hall.

Freeman, R. E., and Reed, D. L. (1983). 'Stockholders and Stakeholders: A New Perspective on Corporate Governance'. *California Management Review*. (25): 88–106.

Freeman, T. (2002). 'Using Performance Indicators to Improve Health Care Quality in the Public Sector: A Review of the Literature'. *Health Services Management Research*. 15(2): 126–37.

Frey, B. S. (1994). 'How Intrinsic Motivation is Crowded Out and In'. *Rationality and Society*. 6(3): 334–52.

Frey, B. S. (2003). 'Direct Democracy for Transition Countries'. *Journal for Institutional Innovation, Development and Transition.* 7: 42–59.

Frey, B. S., and Osterloh, M. (2005). 'Yes, Managers Should Be Paid Like Bureaucrats'. *Journal of Management Inquiry* 14: 96–111.

Friedman, A., and Phillips, M. (2004). 'Balancing Strategy and Accountability: A Model for the Governance of Professional Associations'. *Nonprofit Management & Leadership.* 15(2): 187–204.

Friedman, M. (1962). *Capitalism and Freedom.* Chicago: University of Chicago Press.

Friedman, M. (2002). 'The Social Responsibility of Business is to Increase its Profits', in T. Donaldson, P. H. Werhane, and M. Cording (Eds), *Ethical Issues in Business. A Philosophical Approach.* 33–8. Upper Saddle River: Prentice Hall.

Froomkin, M. (2003). 'ICANN 2.0: Meet the New Boss'. *Loyola of Los Angeles Law Review.* 36: 1087–101.

Fuchs, R. F. (1963). 'Academic Freedom: Its Basic Philosophy, Function, and History'. *Law and Contemporary Problems.* 28(3): 431–46.

Fukuyama, F. (1992). *The End of History and the Last Man.* Harmondsworth: Penguin.

Gagnon, S. (1996). 'Promises vs Performance: Pay Devolution to Next Steps Executive Agencies in the British Civil Service'. *Employee Relations.* 18(3): 25–47.

Gailmard, S. (2002). *Multiple Principals and Outside Information in Bureaucratic Policy Making.* Chicago: The Harris School.

Garn, G. (2001). 'Moving From Bureaucratic to Market Accountability: The Problem of Imperfect Information'. *Educational Administration Quarterly.* 37(4): 571–99.

GAVI Alliance. (2006). Overview Over the GAVI Alliance Governance Structures. Geneva.

GAVI Alliance Secretariat. (2006a). GAVI Alliance Board Meeting 20 June 2006: Background Document: Resource Report. Geneva.

GAVI Alliance Secretariat. (2006b). GAVI Alliance Board Meeting 20 June 2006: GAVI Evaluation Framework. Review of GAVI Phase 1. Geneva.

GAVI Alliance Secretariat. (2006c). GAVI Alliance Strategy (2007–10). Geneva.

Geddes, B. (1990). 'How the Cases You Choose Affect the Answers You Get: Selection Bias in Comparative Politics'. *Political Analysis.* 2(1): 131–50.

Genders, E. (2002). 'Legitimacy, Accountability and Private Prisons'. *Punishment & Society.* 4(3): 285–303.

Gereffi, G., Garcia-Johnson, R., and Sasser, E. (2001). 'The NGO-Industrial Complex'. *Foreign Policy.* 125: 56–65.

Gesellschaft für Technische Zusammenarbeit. (2004). 'PPP Report'. Magazin für Entwicklungspartnerschaften mit der Wirtschaft 13/Juni 2004. Eschborn.

Ghebali, V.-Y. (1997). 'United Nations Reform Proposals Since the End of the Cold War: An Overview', in M. Bertrand and D. Warner (Eds), *A New Charter for a Worldwide Organisation?* 79–111. The Hague: Kluwer Law International.

Gibbons, R., and Murphy, K. J. (1992). 'Optimal Incentive Contracts in the Presence of Career Concerns: Theory and Evidence'. *Journal of Political Economy.* 100: 468–505.

Gilardi, F. (2003). 'Delegation to Independent Regulatory Agencies in Western Europe: A Cross-Sectional Comparison'. *ECPR Joint Sessions of Workshops.* Edinburgh.

Gilardi, F. (2005). 'The Institutional Foundations of Regulatory Capitalism: The Diffusion of Independent Regulatory Agencies in Western Europe'. *Annals of the American Academy of Political and Social Sciences.* 598: 84–101.

Gill, M., Flynn, R. J., and Reissing, E. (2005). 'The Governance Self-Assessment Checklist: An Instrument for Assessing Board Effectiveness'. *Nonprofit Management & Leadership.* 15(3): 271–94.

Giorgi, L., Crowley, J., and Ney, S. (2001). 'Surveying the European Public Space – A Political and Research Agenda'. *Innovation*. 14(1): 73–83.

Global Alliance for Improved Nutrition. (2004). The Global Alliance for Improved Nutrition (GAIN) Statutes. Geneva.

Global Alliance for Improved Nutrition. (2007). Annual Report 2005–2006. Geneva.

Global Reporting Initiative. (2002a). Deed of Incorporation of Stitching Global Reporting Initiative: Amsterdam.

Global Reporting Initiative. (2002b). Introducing the 2002 Sustainability Reporting Guidelines. Amsterdam.

Global Reporting Initiative. (2002c). Sustainability Reporting Guidelines. Amsterdam.

Global Reporting Initiative. (2003). Business Plan 2003–2005. Amsterdam.

Global Reporting Initiative. (2006a). Annual Review of Activities 2005. Amsterdam: Global Reporting Initiative.

Global Reporting Initiative. (2006b). Sustainability Reporting Guidelines 3.0. Amsterdam.

Global Village Energy Partnership. (2005a). Proceedings from the First Global Village Energy Partnership Partner Assembly in Blue Tree Hotel, Brasilia. 20–21 October 2005.

Global Village Energy Partnership. (2005b). Technical Secretariat Work Programme July–December 2005. Washington: ESMAP, The World Bank.

Global Village Energy Partnership. (2006). 2005 Annual Report. GVEP: Harnessing Energy for Poverty Reduction. Warwickshire: Technical Secretariat, Global Village Energy Partnership.

Global Water Partnership. (2003). Effective Water Governance. Stockholm.

Global Water Partnership. (2006a). Annual Report for the Financial Year 2005. Stockholm.

Global Water Partnership. (2006b). The Global Water Partnership's Consulting Partners' Meeting. GWP's First Ten Years: Reflecting Back and Looking Forward. Stockholm.

Global Water Partnership. (2006c). GWP in Action 2006. Stockholm.

Global Water Partnership. (2006d). Setting the Stage for Change. Second Informal Survey by the GWP Network Giving the Status of the 2005 WSSD Target on National Integrated Water Resources Management and Water Efficiency Plans. Stockholm.

Global Water Partnership Technical Committee. (2004). Catalyzing Change: A Handbook for Developing Integrated Water Resources Management (IWRM) and Water Efficiency Strategies. Stockholm: Global Water Partnership.

Global Witness. (2004). Time for Transparency. Coming Clean on Oil, Mining and Gas Revenues. Washington: Global Witness Publishing.

Goodin, R. E. (2003). Democratic Accountability: The Third Sector and All. Cambridge: Hauser Center for Nonprofit Organizations, John F. Kennedy School of Government, Harvard University.

Goodpaster, K. E. (2002). 'Business Ethics and Stakeholder Analysis', in T. Donaldson, P. H. Werhane, and M. Cording (Eds), *Ethical Issues in Business. A Philosophical Approach*. Upper Saddle River: Prentice Hall.

Gordon, M. T. (2000). 'Public Trust in Government: The US Media as an Agent of Accountability?' *International Review of Administrative Sciences*. 66(2): 297–310.

Gormley, W. T., and Balla, S. J. (2003). *Bureaucracy and Democracy : Accountability and Performance*. Washington: CQ Press.

Gourevitch, P. (2002). 'Collective Action Problems in Monitoring Managers: The Enron Case as a Systemic Problem'. *Economic Sociology: European Electronic Newsletter*. 3(3): 3–16.

Graham, J. H. (2004). 'The Crisis Facing Associations and Other Nonprofits in the United States'. *The International Journal of Not-for-Profit Law*. 6(3).

Gramberger, M. (2001). *Citizens as Partners: OECD Handbook on Information, Consultation and Public Participation in Policy-Making*. Paris: OECD.

Grande, E. (1996). 'Demokratische Legitimation und europäische Legitimation'. *Leviathan*. 24: 339–60.

Green, C. (2002). *External Evaluation of Roll Back Malaria: Report of RBM Stakeholder Interviews*. Liverpool: Malaria Consortium.

Greenbury, R. (1995). 'Directors' Remuneration'. Report of a Study Group chaired by Sir Richard Greenbury.

Gregory, H. J. (2001). *International Comparison of Corporate Governance Guidelines and Codes of Best Practice: Developed Markets*. New York: Weil, Gotshal & Manges LLP.

Gregory, H. J., and Simmelkjaer, R. T. (2002). *Comparative Study of Corporate Governance Codes Relevant to the European Union and its Member States*. New York: Weil, Gotshal & Manges LLP on behalf of the European Commission, Internal Market Directorate General.

Grewal, S. S. (2001). 'The Paradox of Integration: Habermas and the Unfinished Project of European Union'. *Politics*. 21(2): 114–23.

Grundmann, S. (1999). 'Trust and Treuhand at the End of the 20th Century: Key Problems and Shift of Interests'. *The American Journal of Comparative Law*. 47(3): 401–28.

Guba, E. G., and Lincoln, Y. S. (1994). 'Competing Paradigms in Qualitative Research', in N. K. Denzin, and Y. S. Lincoln (Eds), *Handbook of Qualitative Research*. 105–17. Newbury Park: Sage.

Guisan-Dickinson, C. (1999). 'The Common European Heritage'. *World Affairs (New Delhi)*. 3(4): 26–35.

Gustavsson, S. (2000). 'Reconciling Suprastatism and Democratic Accountability'. *Harvard Jean Monnet Working Paper, 11/99*. 21. Cambridge: Harvard Law School.

Gusy, C. (1998). 'Demokratiedefizite postnationaler Gemeinschaften unter Berücksichtigung der EU'. *Zeitschrift für Politikwissenschaft*. 45(3): 267–81.

Haas, E. B. (1961). 'International Integration: The European and the Universal Process'. *International Organization* 15(3): 366–92.

Habermas, J. (1998). 'Die Postnationale Konstellation und die Zukunft der Demokratie'. *Blätter für Deutsche und Internationale Politik*. 43(7): 804–17.

Haddock, B. (1994). 'Hegel's Critique of the Theory of the Social Contract', in D. Boucher and P. Kelly (Eds), *The Social Contract from Hobbes to Rawls*. 147–63. London, New York: Routledge.

Hale, T. (2003). 'Managing the Disaggregation of Development: How the Johannesburg "Type II" Partnerships Can Be Made Effective'. *Working Paper*. Princeton: Woodrow Wilson School of Public and International Affairs, Princeton University.

Hale, T., and Mauzerall, D. L. (2004). 'Thinking Globally and Acting Locally: Can the Johannesburg Partnerships Coordinate Action on Sustainable Development?' *Journal of Environment & Development*. 13(3): 220–39.

Hall, B. J., and Liebman, J. B. (1998). 'Are CEOs Really Paid Like Bureaucrats?' *The Quarterly Journal of Economics*. 113(3): 653–91.

Hall, P. L., and Anderson, D. C. (1997). 'The Effect of Golden Parachutes on Shareholder Wealth and Takeover Probabilities'. *Journal of Business Finance & Accounting*. 24(3): 445–63.

Hamilton, A., Madison, J., and Jay, J. (1992). *The Federalist Papers*. Campaign, IL: Project Gutenberg.

Hamm, B. (2004). Evaluation des Multistakeholderprozesses des Common Code for the Coffee Community (4-C) aus zivilgesellschaftlicher Sicht. Duisburg: INEF.

Hampel, R. (1998). Committee on Corporate Governance. Final Report. London: The Committee on Corporate Governance, Gee Publishing Ltd.

Hanssen, F. A. (1999). 'The Effect of Judicial Institutions on Uncertainty and the Rate of Litigation: The Election Versus Appointment of State Judges'. *Journal of Legal Studies*. 28: 205–32.

Hansson, S. O., and Grüne-Yanoff, T. (2006). 'Preferences', in E. N. Zalta (Ed.), *The Stanford Encyclopedia of Philosophy*. Stanford: The Metaphysics Research Lab, Center for the Study of Language and Information, Stanford University.

Harbaugh, W. T. (1998). 'The Prestige Motive for Making Charitable Transfers'. *The American Economic Review*. 88(2): 277–82.

Harlow, C. (2002). *Accountability in the European Union*. Oxford, New York: Oxford University Press.

Hartmann, J. (2003). 'The "License to Co-Operate". A Business Case for Engagement in Sustainability Reporting and Cross-Sector Partnerships'. *Partnership Matters: Current Issues in Cross-Sector Collaboration*. (1): 20–2.

Haskell, R. E. (1997). 'Academic Freedom, Tenure, and Student Evaluation of Faculty: Galloping Polls in the 21st Century'. *Education Policy Analysis Archives* 5(6).

Hassner, P. (1987). 'Immanuel Kant', in L. Strauss and L. Cropsey (Eds), *History of Political Philosophy*. 581–621. Chicago, London: The University of Chicago Press.

Haufler, V. (2004). 'Conflict Prevention, Norm Development, and Multinational Corporations'. *100th Annual Meeting of the American Political Science Association*. Chicago.

Hawks, J. (1997). *For a Good Cause? How Charitable Institutions Became Powerful Economic Bullies*. Secaucus: Carol Publishers.

Hayes, B. E. (1998). *Measuring Customer Satisfaction. Survey Design, Use, and Statistical Analysis Methods*. Milwaukee: ASQ Quality Press.

Health in Your Hands. (2005). The Handwashing Handbook: A Guide for Developing a Hygiene Promotion Program to Increase Handwashing with Soap. Washington: World Bank Group.

Health in Your Hands. (2007). SoapBox: The Public Private Partnership for Handwashing Newsletter July 2007. Washington: Public-Private Partnership for Handwashing with Soap.

Healy, P. (1985). 'The Effect of Bonus Schemes on Accounting Decisions'. *Journal of Accounting and Economics*. 7: 85–107.

Held, D. (1996). *Models of Democracy*. Cambridge: Polity Press.

Held, D. (2004). 'Democratic Accountability and Political Effectiveness from a Cosmopolitan Perspective'. *Government and Opposition*. 39(2): 364–91.

Held, D., and Koenig-Archibugi, M. (2004). 'Introduction'. *Government and Opposition*. 39(2): 125–31.

Hemmati, M. (2002). *Multi-Stakeholder Processes for Governance and Sustainability: Beyond Deadlock and Conflict*. London: Earthscan.

Hepworth, P. (1998). 'Weighing It Up – A Literature Review for the Balanced Scorecard'. *The Journal of Management Development*. 17(8): 559–63.

Hermalin, B. E., and Weisbach, M. S. (2003). 'Boards of Directors as an Endogenously Determined Institution: A Survey of the Economic Literature'. *FRBNY Economic Policy Review* (April): 7–26.

Herman, R. D., and Renz, D. O. (1997). 'Board Practices of Especially Effective and Less Effective Local Nonprofit Organizations'. *Annual Meeting of the Association for Research on Nonprofit Organizations and Voluntary Action*. Indianapolis.

Herman, R. D., and Renz, D. O. (1998). 'Nonprofit Organizational Effectiveness: Contrasts Between Especially Effective and Less Effective Organizations'. *Nonprofit Management and Leadership*. 9(1): 23–38.

Herz, D. (1999). *Die wohlerwogene Republik: Das konstitutionelle Denken des politisch-philosophischen Liberalismus*. Paderborn, München, Wien, Zürich: Schöningh.

Herzlinger, R. (1996). Can Public Trust in Nonprofits and Governments be Restored? *Harvard Business Review*. (March–April): 97–107.

Hewson, M., and Sinclair, T. J. (Eds). (1999). *Approaches to Global Governance Theory*. Albany: State University of New York Press.

Hicks, J. R., and Allen, R. G. D. (1934). 'A Reconsideration of the Theory of Value: Part I'. *Economica, New Series*. 1(1): 52–76.

Higgs, D. (2003). *Review of the Role and Effectiveness of Non-Executive Directors*. London: The Department of Trade and Industry.

Hirschman, A. O. (1972). *Exit, Voice, or Loyalty Responses to Decline in Firms, Organizations, and States*. Cambridge: Harvard University Press.

Hobbes, T. (1909). *Hobbes's Leviathan reprinted from the edition of 1651 with an Essay by the Late W. G. Pogson Smith* Oxford: Clarendon Press.

Höffe, O. (1999). *Demokratie im Zeitalter der Globalisierung*. München: C. H. Beck.

Hofmann, J. (2002). Verfahren der Willensbildung und Selbstverwaltung im Internet: Das Beispiel ICANN und die At-Large-Membership. Berlin: Wissenschaftszentrum Berlin für Sozialforschung.

Hood, C. C. (1991). 'A Public Management for All Seasons'. *Public Administration*. 69: 3–19.

Hood, C. C. (1995). 'The "New Public Management" in the 1980s: Variations on a Theme'. *Accounting, Organizations and Society*. 20(3): 93–109.

Hooghe, L., and Marks, G. (2003). 'Unraveling the Central State, but How? Types of Multi-Level Governance'. *American Political Science Review*. 97(2): 233–43.

Hopkins, M., and Cowe, R. (2003). *Corporate Social Responsibility: Is There a Business Case?* Glasgow: The Association of Chartered Certified Accountants (ACCA).

Hopt, K., Kanda, H., Roe, M. J., Wymeersch, E., and Prigge, S. (Eds) (1998). *Comparative Corporate Governance: The State of the Art and Emerging Research*. Oxford, New York: Claredon Press.

Howse, R. (2003). 'How to Begin to Think About the "Democratic Deficit" at the WTO', in S. Griller (Ed.), *International Economic Governance and Non-Economic Concerns: New Challenges for the International Legal Order*. Wien: Springer.

Huber, J. D., and Shipan, C. R. (2006). 'Politics, Delegation, and Bureaucracy', in B. R. Weingast and D. Wittman (Eds), *The Oxford Handbook of Political Economy*. 256–72. Oxford: Oxford University Press.

Hudson, A. (2002). 'Research Note: Advocacy by UK-Based Development NGOs'. *Non-Profit and Voluntary Sector Quarterly*. 31(3): 402–18.

Hüfner, K., and Martens, J. (2000). *UNO-Reform zwischen Utopie und Realität: Vorschläge zum Wirtschafts- und Sozialbereich der Vereinten Nationen*. Frankfurt a.M.: Lang.

Hulme, D., and Edwards, M. (Eds). (1997). *NGOs, States and Donors: Too Close for Comfort?* New York: St. Martin's Press.

Hume, D. (1969). *A Treatise on Human Nature*. London: Penguin.

Hume, D. (1994). 'Of the Original Contract', in K. Haakonssen (Ed.), *Hume, Political Essays*. 186–201. Cambridge: Cambridge University Press.

Hunt, G. (Ed.) (1900–10). *The Writings of James Madison*. New York: G. P. Putnam's Sons.

Hunter, D. (2003). 'ICANN and the Concept of Democratic Deficit'. *Loyola of Los Angeles Law Review*. 36: 1149–83.

Husak, D. N. (1981). 'Paternalism and Autonomy'. *Philosophy and Public Affairs*. 10(1): 27–46.

ICANN. (2006). Bylaws for Internet Corporation for Assigned Names and Numbers. A California Nonprofit Public-Benefit Corporation, as amended effective 28 February 2006. Marina del Rey.

Independent Sector. (2005). Checklist for Accountability. Washington.

Ingrim, R. T. (1990). *Ten Basic Responsibilities of Nonprofit Boards*. Washington: National Center for Nonprofit Boards.

Institute for Health Sector Development. (2003). Independent External Evaluation of the Global Stop TB Partnership. London.

International Association of Judges. (1999). The Universal Charter of the Judge. Rome.

International Bar Association. (1988). International Code of Ethics. London.

International Center for Not-for-Profit Law. (2006). Checklist for CSO Laws. Washington.

International Centre for Trade and Sustainable Development. (1999). Accreditation Schemes and Other Arrangements for Public Participation in International Fora. A Contribution to the Debate on WTO and Transparency. Geneva.

International Committee of the Red Cross. (2005). Annual Report 2004. Geneva.

International Criminal Court. (2005). Code of Judicial Ethics. Vol. ICC-BD/ 02-01-05.

International Federation of Accountants' Ethics Committee. (2005). *Code of Ethics for Professional Accountants*. New York: International Federation of Accountants.

International Federation of Accountants. (2007). *Handbook of International Auditing, Assurance, and Ethics Pronouncements*. New York.

International Non Governmental Organisations. (2006). Accountability Charter. Johannesburg.

International Organization for Standardization. (1994). ISO Guide 59: Code of Good Practice for Standardization. Geneva.

International Organization for Standardization. (1996). ISO/IEC Guide 65: General Requirements for Bodies Operating Product Verification Systems. Geneva.

International Organization for Standardization. (2002). ISO 19011: Guidelines for Quality and/or Environmental Management Systems Auditing. Geneva.

International Organization for Standardization. (2004). ISO/IEC 17011: Conformity Assessment – General Requirements for Accreditation Bodies Accrediting Conformity Assessment Bodies Geneva.

International Social and Environmental Accreditation and Labelling Alliance. (2004). ISEAL Code of Good Practice for Setting Social and Environmental Standards. Bonn.

International Social and Environmental Accreditation and Labelling Alliance. (2006). Guidance on the Application of the ISEAL Code of Good Practice for Setting Social and Environmental Standards. London.

INTOSAI. (2004). Guidelines for Internal Control Standards for the Public Sector. Brussels.

Irvin, R. A. (2005). State Regulation of Nonprofit Organizations: Accountability Regardless of Outcome. *Nonprofit and Voluntary Sector Quarterly*. 34(2): 161–78.

Isham, J., Narayan, D., and Pritchett, L. (1995). 'Does Participation Improve Performance? Establishing Causality with Subjective Data'. *The World Bank Economic Review*. 9: 175–200.

Ismayr, W. (Ed.) (1999). *Die politischen Systeme Westeuropas*. Opladen: Leske und Budrich.

Ivanova, M. H. (2003). 'Partnerships, International Organizations, and Global Environmental Governance', in J. M. Witte, C. Streck, and T. Benner (Eds), *Progress or Peril? Partnerships and Networks in Global Environmental Governance: The Post-Johannesburg Agenda*. 9–36. Washington, Berlin: Global Public Policy Institute.

Jabbra, J. G., and Dwivedi, O. P. (Eds). (1988). *Public Service Accountability: A Comparative Perspective*. West Hartford: Kumarian Press.

Jann, W., and Wegrich, K. (2003). 'Phasenmodelle und Politikprozesse: Der Policy Cycle' in K. Schubert and N. C. Bandelow (Eds), *Lehrbuch der Politikfeldanalyse*. 71–104. München, Wien: R. Oldenbourg Verlag.

Jensen, M. C., and Meckling, W. H. (1976). 'Theory of the Firm: Managerial Behavior, Agency Costs and Ownership Structure'. *Journal of Financial Economics*. 3(4): 305–60.

Jensen, M. C., and Murphy, K. J. (1990). 'CEO Incentives: It's not How Much You Pay, but How'. *Harvard Business Review*. 68(3): 138–53.

Jepson, P. (2005). 'Governance and Accountability of Environmental NGOs'. *Environmental Science & Policy*. 8: 515–524.

Johns, G. (2003). 'The NGO Challenge: Whose Democracy is it Anyway?' *We're Not From the Government, But We Are Here to Help You: Nongovernmental Organizations: The Growing Power of an Unelected Few*. Washington: American Enterprise Institute for Public Policy Research.

Johnston, M. (1999). 'A Brief History of Anticorruption Agencies', in A. Schedler, L. Diamond, and M. Plattner (Eds), *The Self-Restraining State: Power and Accountability in New Democracies*. Boulder, London: Lynne Rienner.

Johnstone, D. B. (1998). *The Financing and Management of Higher Education: A Status Report on Worldwide Reforms*. Washington: The World Bank.

Jordan, A., Wurzel, R. K. W., and Zito, A. (2005). 'The Rise of "New" Policy Instruments in Comparative Perspective: Has Governance Eclipsed Government?' *Political Studies*. 53(3): 477–96.

Jordan, L. (2005). 'Mechanisms for NGO Accountability'. *GPPi Research Paper Series*. Berlin: Global Public Policy Institute.

Judge, D. (1995). 'The Failure of National [European] Parliaments?' *West European Politics*. 18(3): 79–100.

Jung, O. (1997). 'Direkte Demokratie im Grundgesetz und den Landesverfassungen der Bundesrepublik Deutschland', in W. Kremp and G. Mielke (Eds), *Amerikanische Einflüsse auf Verfassungsdenken und Verfassungspraxis in Deutschland*. 71–93. Kaiserslautern: Atlantische Akademie Rheinland-Pfalz e.V.

Kaiser, K. (1971). 'Transnational Relations as a Threat to the Democratic Process'. *International Organization*. 25(3): 706–20.

Kamhi, A. (2006). 'The Russian NGO Law: Potential Conflicts with International, National, and Foreign Legislation'. *The International Journal of Not-for-Profit Law*. 9(1): 34–57.

Kant, I. (1968). *Kritik der reinen Vernunft*. Berlin: Walter de Gruyter.

Kant, I. (1996a). 'Idee zu einer allgemeinen Geschichte in weltbürgerlicher Absicht (1784)', in G. Schulte (Ed.), *Kant: Ausgewählt und vorgestellt von Günter Schulte*. 309–25. München: Diederichs.

Kant, I. (1996b). 'Übergang von der gemeinen sittlichen Vernunfterkenntnis zu philosophischen (Aus der Grundlegung der Metaphysik der Sitten, 1786)', in G. Schulte (Ed.), *Kant: Ausgewählt und vorgestellt von Günter Schulte*. 176–90. München: Diederichs.

Kant, I. (1996c). 'Übergang von der populären sittlichen Weltweisheit zur Metaphysik der Sitten (Aus der Grundlegung der Metaphysik der Sitten, 1786)', in G. Schulte (Ed.), *Kant: Ausgewählt und vorgestellt von Günter Schulte*. 191–219. München: Diederichs.

Kant, I. (1996/1786). *Grundlegung zur Metaphysik der Sitten*. Stuttgart: Reclam.

Käsler, D. (1995). *Max Weber: Eine Einführung in Leben, Werk und Wirkung*. Frankfurt a.M., New York: Campus Verlag.

Katz, R. S. (1980). *A Theory of Parties and Electoral Systems*. Baltimore: Johns Hopkins University Press.

Katz, R. S. (2001). 'Models of Democracy: Elite Attitudes and the Democratic Deficit in the European Union'. *European Union Politics*. 2(1): 53–79.

Kaufman, F.-X., Majone, G., and Ostrom, V. (Eds). (1986). *Guidance, Control and Evaluation in the Public Sector*. Berlin, New York: de Gruyter.

Kaul, I. (2000). 'What is a Public Good?' *Le Monde Diplomatique* (June).

Kaul, I. (2006). 'Exploring the Space Between Markets and States: Global Public-Private Partnerships', in I. Kaul and P. Conceição (Eds), *The New Public Finance. Responding to Global Challenges*. 219–68. New York, Oxford: Oxford University Press.

Kearns, K. P. (1996). *Managing for Accountability: Preserving the Public Trust in Public and Nonprofit Organizations*. San Francisco: Jossey-Bass Publishers.

Keating, E. K., and Frumkin, P. (2000). Reeingineering Nonprofit Financial Accountability: Toward a More Reliable Foundation for Regulation. Hauser Center for Nonprofit Organizations, John F. Kennedy School of Government, Harvard University.

Keck, M. E., and Sikkink, K. (1998). *Activists Beyond Borders: Advocacy Networks in International Politics*. Ithaca: Cornell University Press.

Kelly, P. (1994). 'Justifying "Justice". Contractarianism, Communitarianism and the Foundations of Contemporary Liberalism', in D. Boucher and P. Kelly (Eds), *The Social Contract from Hobbes to Rawls*. 226–44. London, New York: Routledge.

Kenney, C. D. (2000). 'Reflections on Horizontal Accountability: Democratic Legitimacy, Majority Parties and Democratic Stability in Latin America'. *Institutions, Accountability, and Democratic Governance in Latin America*. Notre Dame: Kellogg Institute for International Studies, University of Notre Dame.

Keohane, R. O. (2001). 'Governance in a Partially Globalized World'. *American Political Science Review*. 95(1): 1–13.

Keohane, R. O. (2002a). 'Global Governance and Democratic Accountability'. Mimeo. Durham.

Keohane, R. O. (2002b). 'Political Accountability'. *Conference on Delegation to International Organizations*. Park City, Utah.

Keohane, R. O., and Nye, J. S., Jr. (2001). *Democracy, Accountability and Global Governance*. Cambridge: John F. Kennedy School of Government, Harvard University.

Khagram, S. (1999). Beyond Temples and Tombs: Towards Effective Governance for Sustainable Development Through the World Commission on Dams. Case Study for the UN Vision Project on Global Public Policy Networks.

Khwaja, A. I. (2004). 'Is Increasing Community Participation Always a Good Thing?' *Journal of the European Economic Association* 2(2–3): 427–36.

Kiernan, A. K. (1997). 'Citizenship – The Real Democratic Deficit of the European Union?' *Citizenship Studies*. 1(3): 323–34.

Kilby, P. (2004). 'Accountability for Empowerment: Dilemmas Facing Non-Governmental Organisations'. *Discussion Papers*. Canberra: Asia and Pacific School of Economics and Government, Australian National University.

King, G., Keohane, R. O., and Verba, S. (1994). *Designing Social Inquiry. Scientific Inference in Qualitative Research*. Princeton: Princeton University Press.

Kirby, A., and Spedding, V. (2006). *The Boldness of Small Steps. Ten Years of the Global Water Partnership*. Stockholm: Global Water Partnership.

Kjaer, L. (Ed.). (2003). *Local Partnerships in Europe: An Action Research Project*. Copenhagen: Copenhagen Centre.

Klein, H. (2002). 'ICANN and Internet Governance: Leveraging Technical Coordination to Realize Global Public Policy'. *The Information Society*. 18: 193–207.

Klein, H. (2005). 'ICANN Reform: Establishing the Rule of Law'. *The World Summit on the Information Society (WSIS)*. Tunis.

Klein, H., and Mueller, M. (2005). *What to Do About ICANN: A Proposal for Structural Reform*. Syracuse: Internet Governance Project.

Kleinwaechter, W. (2003). 'From Self-Governance to Public-Private Partnership: The Changing Role of Governments in the Management of the Internet's Core Resources'. *Loyola of Los Angeles Law Review*. 36: 1103–26.

Klijn, E.-H., and Koppenjan, J. F. M. (2000). 'Public Management and Policy Networks: Foundations of a Network Approach to Governance'. *Public Management*. 2(2): 135–58.

Klingner, D. E., Nalbandian, J., and Romzek, B. S. (2002). 'Politics, Administration, and Markets: Conflicting Expectations and Accountability'. *American Review of Public Administration*. 32(2): 117–44.

Knack, S., and Rahman, A. (2004). 'Donor Fragmentation and Bureaucratic Quality in Aid Recipients'. *Policy Research Paper*. Washington: World Bank.

Knill, C., and Lehmkuhl, D. (2002). 'Private Actors and the State: Internationalization and the Changing Patterns of Governance'. *Governance: An International Journal of Policy, Administration, and Institutions*. 15(1): 41–63.

Koenig-Archibugi, M. (2002). 'The Democratic Deficit of EU Foreign and Security Policy'. *The International Spectator*. 4: 61–73.

Kolk, A. (2005). 'Corporate Social Responsibility in the Coffee Sector: The Dynamics of MNC Responses and Code Development'. *European Management Journal*. 23(2): 228–36.

Kooiman, J. (Ed.). (1993). *Modern Governance: New Government-Society Interactions*. London, Thousand Oaks, New Delhi: Sage.

Koppell, J. G. (2003). *The Politics of Quasi-Government. Hybrid Organizations and the Dynamics of Bureaucratic Control*. Cambridge: Cambridge University Press.

Koppell, J. G. (2005). 'Pathologies of Accountability: ICANN and the Challenge of "Multiple Accountabilities Disorder"'. *Public Administration Review*. 65(1): 94–108.

Korenromp, E., Miller, J., Nahlen, B., Wardlaw, T., and Young, M. (2005). World Malaria Report 2005. Geneva, New York: World Health Organization Roll Back Malaria Department, United Nations Children's Fund.

Korten, D. (1989). *Getting to the 21st Century: The Role of the Voluntary Sector*. West Hartford: Kumarian Press.

Kovach, H., Neligan, C., and Burall, S. (2003). 'Power Without Accountability?' *Global Accountability Report*. London: One World Trust.

Krafchik, W., and Wehner, J. (1999). The Role of Parliament in the Budget Process. Pretoria, Cape Town: Budget Information Service, Institute for Democracy.

Krahmann, E. (2003). 'National, Regional, and Global Governance: One Phenomenon or Many?' *Global Governance*. 9(3): 323–346.

Kravchuk, R., and Schack, R. (1996). 'Designing Effective Performance Measurement Systems under the Government Performance and Results Act 1993'. *Public Administration Review*. 56(4): 348–58.

Kreps, D. M., and Wilson, R. (1982). 'Reputation and Imperfect Information'. *Journal of Economic Theory*. 27: 253–79.

Krueger, R. A., and Casey, M. A. (2000). *Focus Groups: A Practical Guide for Applied Research*. Thousand Oaks, London, New Delhi: Sage.

Kumaresan, J., Heitkamp, P., Smith, I., and Billo, N. (2004). 'Global Partnership to Stop TB: A Model of an Effective Public Health Partnership'. *The International Journal of Tuberculosis and Lung Disease*. 8(1): 120–9.

Laffan, B. (2003). 'Auditing and Accountability in the European Union'. *Journal of European Public Policy*. 10(5): 762–77.

Landtag des Freistaates Bayern. (2006). *Bayerisches Hochschulgesetz*. Vol. 2210-1-1-WFK. 245-284: Bayerisches Gesetz- und Verordnungsblatt Nr. 10/2006.

Leadbitter, D., and Grieve, C. (2004). *Integrated Fisheries Assessments – the Marine Stewardship Council's Methodology*. London: Marine Stewardship Council.

LeDuc, L. (2003). *The Politics of Direct Democracy: Referendums in Global Perspective*. Peterborough, Orchard Park: Broadview Press.

Lee, M. (2004). 'Public Reporting: A Neglected Aspect of Nonprofit Accountability'. *Nonprofit Management & Leadership*. 15(2): 169–85.

Leib, V. (2002). ICANN und der Konflikt um die Internet-Ressourcen: Institutionenbildung im Problemfeld Internet Governance zwischen multinationaler Staatstätigkeit und globaler Selbstregulierung. Konstanz: Universität Konstanz.

Leipprand, T., and Rusch, P. (2007). Advancing the Extractive Industries Transparency Initiative (EITI). Cambridge: John F. Kennedy School of Government, Harvard University.

Lemke, C. (1999). 'Europa als politischer Raum: Konzeptionelle Überlegungen zur aktiven Bürgerschaft und zur Demokratie in der Europäischen Union'. *Kritische Justiz*. 32(1): 1–14.

Levy, D. (1995). 'Does an Independent Central Bank Violate Democracy?' *Journal of Post Keynesian Economics*. 18: 189–210.

Levy, M. A., and Chernyak, M. (2006). 'Bytes of Note: Sustainable Development Partnerships'. *Environment*. 48: 3–4.

Lewis, T. J. (1989). 'On Using the Concept of Hypothetical Consent'. *Canadian Journal of Political Science/Revue Canadienne de Science Politique*. 22(4): 793–807.

Lijphart, A. (1984). *Democracies. Patterns of Majoritarian and Consensus Government in Twenty-One Countries*. New Haven, London: Yale University Press.

Lijphart, A. (1994). *Electoral Systems and Party Systems: A Study of Twenty-Seven Democracies, 1945–1990*. Oxford: Oxford University Press.

Lijphart, A. (2002). 'Introduction', in A. Lijphart (Ed.), *Parliamentary Versus Presidential Government*. 1–30. Oxford, New York: Oxford University Press.

Lindberg, L. N. (1963). *The Political Dynamics of European Economic Integration*. Stanford, London: Stanford University Press, Oxford University Press.

Lindberg, L. N., and Scheingold, S. A. (Eds). (1971). *Regional Integration*. Cambridge: Harvard University Press.

Linder, S. H., and Rosenau, P. V. (2000). 'Mapping the Terrain of the Public-Private Policy Partnership', in P. V. Rosenau (Ed.), *Public-Private Policy Partnerships*. 1–18. Cambridge: MIT Press.

Lindseth, P. (2002). 'Delegation is Dead, Long Live Delegation: Managing the Democratic Disconnect in the European Market-Polity', in C. Joerges and R. Dehousse (Eds), *Good Governance in Europe's Integrated Market*. 139–63. Oxford: Oxford University Press.

Lindseth, P. L. (1999). 'Democratic Legitimacy and the Administrative Character of Supranationalism: The Example of the European Community'. *Columbia Law Review*. 99(3): 628–738.

Lipsky, M., and Smith, S. R. (1989–90). 'Nonprofit Organizations, Government, and the Welfare State'. *Political Science Quarterly*. 104(4): 625–48.

Lister, R. (1997). *Citizenship: Feminist Perspectives*. Basingstoke: Macmillan.

Locke, J. (1690). *Two Treatises of Government*. London: The Constitution Society.

Lodge, J. (1996). 'Democratic Legitimacy and the EC: Crossing the Rubicon'. *International Journal of Public Administration*. 18(10): 1595–637.

Lodge, J. (2003). 'Transparency and EU Governance: Balancing Openness with Security'. *Journal of Contemporary European Studies*. 11(1): 95–117.

Löffler, E. (2000). 'Managing Accountability in Intergovernmental Partnerships', in K. König and E. Löffler (Eds), *Accountability Management in Intergovernmental Partnerships*. 3–38. Paris: Organisation for Economic Co-operation and Development, Forschungsinstitut für Öffentliche Verwaltung bei der Deutschen Hochschule für Verwaltungswissenschaften Speyer.

Long, F., and Arnold, M. (1995). *The Power of Environmental Partnerships*. Fort Worth: The Dryden Press.

Lopez Coterilla, B., and Vicente, J. (1998). 'El Parlamento Europeo y el Deficit Democratico de la Union Europea'. *Relaciones Internacionales*. 78: 99–111.

Lord, C. (1998). *Democracy in the European Union*. Sheffield: Academic Press.

Lord, C. (2001). 'Assessing Democracy in a Contested Polity'. *Journal of Common Market Studies*. 39(4): 641–61.

Low-Beer, D., Banati, P., and Komatsu, R. (2007). *Partners in Impact: Results Report*. Vernier: The Global Fund to Fight AIDS, Tuberculosis and Malaria.

Lowndes, V. (2001). *Local Partnerships and Public Participation*. London: IPPR Partnerships Commission.

Lu, C., Michaud, C., Gakidou, E., Khan, K., and Murray, C. (2006). 'Effect of the Global Alliance for Vaccines and Immunisation on Diphtheria, Tetanus, and Pertussis Vaccine Coverage: An Independent Assessment'. *The Lancet*. 368(9541): 1088–95.

Macan-Markar, M. (2005). *NGOs Can Add to Disasters*. New York: Global Policy Forum.

Magnette, P. (2003). 'Between Parliamentary Control and the Rule of Law: The Political Role of the Ombudsman in the European Union'. *Journal of European Public Policy*. 10(5): 677–94.

Majone, G. (1994). 'The Rise of the Regulatory State in Europe'. *West European Politics*. 17(3): 77–101.

Malaria Consortium. (2002). Final Report of the External Evaluation of Roll Back Malaria. Achieving Impact: Roll Back Malaria in the Next Phase. Liverpool.

Malena, C. (2004). 'Strategic Partnership: Challenges and Best Practices in the Management and Governance of Multi-Stakeholder Partnerships Involving UN and Civil Society Actors'. Background paper prepared for the Multi-Stakeholder Workshop on Partnerships and UN-Civil Society Relations in Pocantico, New York, February 2004.

Mallaby, S. (2004). 'Fighting Poverty, Hurting the Poor'. *Foreign Policy*. (September/October 2004): 51–8.

Mallin, C. A. (2004). *Corporate Governance*. Oxford: Oxford University Press.

Mango. (2005). Introduction to Internal Controls. Available at www.mango.org.uk.

Manin, B., Przeworski, A., and Stokes, S. C. (1999a). 'Elections and Representation', in A. Przeworski, S. C. Stokes, and B. Manin (Eds), *Democracy, Accountability, and Representation*. 29–54. Cambridge, New York: Cambridge University Press.

Manin, B., Przeworski, A., and Stokes, S. C. (1999b). 'Introduction', in A. Przeworski, S. C. Stokes, and B. Manin (Eds), *Democracy, Accountability, and Representation*. 1–26. Cambridge, New York: Cambridge University Press.

Mansuri, G., and Rao, V. (2004). 'Community-Based and -Driven Development: A Critical Review'. *World Bank Policy Research Working Paper*. Washington: The World Bank.

Manzella, A. (2002). 'The Convention as a Way of Bridging the EU's Democratic Deficit'. *The International Spectator*. 1: 47–58.

Maravall, J. M. (1999). 'Accountability and Manipulation', in A. Przeworski, S. C. Stokes, and B. Manin (Eds), *Democracy, Accountability, and Representation*. 154–96. Cambridge, New York: Cambridge University Press.

Marin, B., and Mayntz, R. (Eds). (1991). *Policy Networks: Empirical Evidence and Theoretical Considerations*. Boulder: Westview.

Marine Stewardship Council. (2004). Marine Stewardship Council Fisheries Certification Methodology. London.

Marine Stewardship Council. (2006). Annual Report 2005/06. London.

Marine Stewardship Council. (2007a). Annual Report 2006/07. London.

Marine Stewardship Council. (2007b). Developing an Integrated Strategic Plan for the MSC. London.

Marine Stewardship Council. (2007c). MSC Standard Setting Procedure: The Development and Approval of MSC International Standards. London.

Marshall, M. N., Shekelle, P. G., Leatherman, S., and Brook, R. H. (2000). 'The Public Release of Performance Data: What Do We Expect to Gain? A Review of the Evidence'. *The Journal of the American Medical Association*. 283: 1866–74.

Martens, K. (2001). 'Non-Governmental Organisations as Corporatist Mediator? An Analysis of NGOs in the UNESCO System'. *Global Society*. 15(4): 387–404.

Mason, A. D. (1990). 'Autonomy, Liberalism and State Neutrality'. *The Philosophical Quarterly*. 40(161): 433–52.

Mayer, R. (2001). 'Strategies of Justification in Authoritarian Ideology'. *Journal of Political Ideologies* 6(2): 147–68.

Mayntz, R. (2003). 'New Challenges to Governance Theory', in H. P. Bang (Ed.), *Governance as Social and Political Communication*. 27–40. Manchester, New York: Manchester University Press.

McCrary, S. V., Anderson, C. B., Jakovljevic, J., Khan, T., McCullough, L. B., Wray, N. P., and Brody, B. A. (2000). 'A National Survey of Policies on Disclosure of Conflicts of Interest in Biomedical Research'. *The New England Journal of Medicine*. 343(22): 1621–6.

Meadowcroft, J. (2002). 'The European Democratic Deficit, the Market and the Public Space: A Classical Liberal Critique'. *Innovation*. 15(3): 181–92.

Ménard, C., and Shirley, M. M. (Eds). (2005). *Handbook of New Institutional Economics*. Dordrecht, Berlin, Heidelberg, New York: Springer.

Meny, Y. (1998). *Government and Politics in Western Europe. Britain, France, Italy, Germany*. Oxford: Oxford University Press.

Merriam-Webster. (2004). Online Dictionary: Merriam-Webster.

Mershon, C. (1996). 'The Costs of Coalition: Coalition Theories and Italian Governments'. *The American Political Science Review*. 90(3): 534–54.

Mill, J. S. (1861). *Consideration on Representative Government*. e-book.

Mill, J. S. (1863). *Utilitarianism*. London: Parker, Son, and Bourn.

Mills, C. W. (1997). *The Racial Contract*. Ithaca, London: Cornell University Press.

Minow, N. (2000). CEO Contracts 1999: Introduction. Portland: The Corporate Library.

Misch, A. (1996). 'Legitimation durch Parlamentarisierung? Das Europaische Parlament und das Demokratiedefizit der EU'. *Zeitschrift für Politikwissenschaft*. 6(4): 969–95.

Mitbestimmungsgesetz. Available at http://www.gesetze-im-internet.de/mitbestg/index.html.

Mitchell, R. K., Agle, B. R., and Wood, D. J. (1997). 'Toward a Theory of Stakeholder Identification and Salience: Defining the Principle of Who and What Really Counts'. *Academy of Management Review*. 22(4): 853–86.

Moore, D. (2006). 'The Public Benefit Commission: A Comparative Overview'. *The International Journal of Not-for-Profit Law*. 8(2): 4–6.

Morales, M. M., and Bergqvist, A. (2002). 'Outcomes from the WSSD: The Case of the Global Village Energy Partnership'. *Renewable Energy for Development*. 15(1/2): 8.

Moravcsik, A. (2002). 'In Defence of the "Democratic Deficit": Reassessing Legitimacy in the European Union'. *Journal of Common Market Studies*. 40(4): 603–24.

Moravcsik, A. (2004). 'Is there a "Democratic Deficit" in World Politics? A Framework for Analysis'. *Government and Opposition*. 39(2): 336–63.

Morgan, D. L. (1997). *Focus Groups as Qualitative Research*. Thousand Oaks, London, New Delhi: Sage.

Morley, E., Vinson, E., and Hatry, H. P. (2001). *Outcome Measurement in Nonprofit Organizations: Current Practices and Recommendations*. Washington: Independent Sector.

Morrow, J. D. (1994). *Game Theory for Political Scientists*. Princeton: Princeton University Press.

Moulton, L., and Anheier, H. K. (2001). 'Public-Private Partnerships in the United States: Historical Patterns and Current Trends'. *Civil Society Working Paper*. London: The Centre for Civil Society, London School of Economics and Political Science.

Moussis, N. (2000). 'La Construction Européenne et le Citoyen: Déficit Démocratique ou Déficit d'Information? *Revue du Marché Commun et de l'Union Européenne*. 436: 153–9.

Mulgan, R. (1997). 'Contracting Out and Accountability'. *Discussion Paper 51*. Canberra: Australian National University.

Mulgan, R. (2000a). '"Accountability": An Ever Expanding Concept?' *Public Administration*. 78(3): 555–73.

Mulgan, R. (2000b). 'Comparing Accountability in the Public and Private Sectors'. *Australian Journal of Public Administration*. 59(1): 87–97.

Mulgan, R., and Uhr, J. (2000). 'Accountability and Governance'. *Discussion Paper 71*. Canberra: The Australian National University.

Mulgan, R. G. (2003). *Holding Power to Account: Accountability in Modern Democracies*. Basingstoke, Hampshire, New York: Palgrave Macmillan.

Muraskin, W. (2004). 'The Global Alliance for Vaccines and Immunization: Is It a New Model for Effective Public–Private Cooperation in International Public Health?' *American Journal of Public Health*. 94(11): 1922–5.

Murphy, D. F., and Bendell, J. (1997). *In the Company of Partners: Business, Environmental Groups and Sustainable Development Post-Rio*. Bristol: The Policy Press.

Murphy, K. J. (1999). 'Executive Compensation', in O. Ashenfelter and D. Card (Eds), *Handbook of Labor Economics*. Vol. III. 2485–563. Amsterdam: Elsevier.

Naidoo, K. (2004). 'The End of Blind Faith? Civil Society and the Challenge of Accountability, Legitimacy and Transparency'. *Accountability Forum*. 2: 14–25.

Narasimhan, V., and Attaran, A. (2003). 'Roll Back Malaria? The Scarcity of International Aid for Malaria Control'. *Malaria Journal*. 2(8): 1–8.

National Conference of Commissioners on Uniform State Laws. (1997). Uniform Partnership Act. San Antonio.

Neal, J. E. (1995). 'Overview of Policy and Practice: Differences and Similarities in Developing Higher Education Accountability', in G. H. Gaither (Ed.), *Assessing Performance in an Age of Accountability: Case Studies*. 3–10. San Francisco: Jossey-Bass.

Nelson, J. (2002). *Building Partnerships. Cooperation Between the United Nations System and the Private Sector*. New York: United Nations.

Nelson, J., and Zadek, S. (2000). *Partnership Alchemy. New Social Partnerships in Europe*. Copenhagen: The Copenhagen Centre.

Neunreither, K. (1994). 'The Democratic Deficit of the European Union: Towards Closer Cooperation Between the European Parliament and the National Parliaments'. *Government and Opposition*. 29(3): 299–314.

Newell, P., and Bellour, S. (2002). *Mapping Accountability: Origins, Contexts and Implications for Development*. Brighton: Institute of Development Studies.

NGO and Academic ICANN Study. (2001). ICANN, Legitimacy, and the Public Voice: Making Global Participation and Representation Work.

Nilsson, L. J., Arvidson, A., and Eberhard, A. (2003). *Public Benefits and Power Sector Reform. Report from an International Workshop*. Stockholm: Stockholm Environment Institute, Climate and Energy Programme.

Nohlen, D. (1978). *Wahlsysteme der Welt*. München: Piper.

Nohlen, D. (2004). *Wahlrecht und Parteiensystem*. Opladen: Leske und Budrich.

Nolan, C., and Schaling, E. (1996). 'Monetary Policy Uncertainty and Central Bank Accountability'. *Bank of England Working Paper No. 54*. London: Bank of England.

Nonprofit Overhead Cost Project. (2004a). Getting What We Pay For: Low Overhead Limits Nonprofit Effectiveness. Washington, Bloomington: Center on Nonprofits and Philanthropy, Urban Institute and Center on Philanthropy, Indiana University.

Nonprofit Overhead Cost Project. (2004b). The Pros and Cons of Financial Efficiency Standards. Washington, Bloomington: Center on Nonprofits and Philanthropy, Urban Institute and Center on Philanthropy, Indiana University.

Norris, P. (1997). 'Representation and the Democratic Deficit'. *European Journal of Political Research*. 32(2): 273–82.

North, D. C. (1982). *Structure and Change in Economic History*. New York, London: W. W. Norton.

North, D. C. (1990). *Institutions, Institutional Change and Economic Performance*. Cambridge: Cambridge University Press.

Nuscheler, F. (2000). 'Kritik der Kritik am Global Governance-Konzept'. *Prokla*. 30(1): 151–6.

Nye, J. S. (1965). 'Patterns and Catalysts in Regional Integration'. *International Organization* 19(4): 870–84.

Nye, J. S., and Donahue, J. D. (Eds). (2000). *Governance in a Globalizing World*. Washington: Brookings Institution Press.

O'Donnell, G. (1999). 'Horizontal Accountability in New Democracies', in A. Schedler, L. Diamond, and M. Plattner (Eds), *The Self-Restraining State: Power and Accountability in New Democracies*. 29–51. Boulder, London: Lynne Rienner.

O'Donnell, G. (2004). 'Why the Rule of Law Matters'. *Journal of Democracy*. 15(4): 32–46.

O'Looney, J. A. (1998). *Outsourcing State and Local Government Services: Decision–Making Strategies and Management Methods*. Greenwood: Quorum.

O'Neill, O. (2002). *A Question of Trust: The BBC Reith Lectures 2002*. Cambridge: Cambridge University Press.

Oberreuter, H. (1999). 'Demokratiedefizite in der EU'. *Politische Studien*. 368: 54–8.

Ocheje, P. D. (2006). 'The Extractive Industries Transparency Initiative (EITI): Voluntary Codes of Conduct, Poverty and Accountability in Africa'. *Journal of Sustainable Development in Africa*. 8(3): 222–39.

Odell, J. S. (2001). 'Case Study Methods in International Political Economy'. *International Studies Perspective*. 2(2): 161–76.

Office of Management and Budget. (2003). Circular No. A-133, Revised to Show Changes Published in the Federal Register June 27, 2003. Washington: Executive Office of the President.

Office of Personnel Management. (2006). Solicitation of Federal Civilian and Uniformed Service Personnel for Contributions to Private Voluntary Organizations – Eligibility and Public Accountability Standards. Final Rule. Vol. FR Doc. E6 – 19628: Federal Register.

Oliver, D., and Drewry, G. (1996). *Public Service Reforms: Issues of Accountability and Law*. London, New York: Pinter.

Olson, M. (1965). *The Logic of Collective Actions: Public Goods and the Theory of Groups*. Cambridge: Harvard University Press.

One Hundred Seventh Congress of the United States of America. (2002). Sarbanes-Oxley Act of 2002. Washington.

One World Trust. (2007). Independent Review of ICANN's Accountability and Transparency – Structures and Practices. London.

Organisation for Economic Co-operation and Development. (2003). Education at a Glance: OECD Indicators 2003. Paris.

Organisation for Economic Co-operation and Development. (2004). OECD Principles of Corporate Governance. Paris.

Osborne, D. T., and Gaebler, T. (1992). *Reinventing Government: How the Entrepreneurial Spirit is Transforming the Public Sector*. Reading: Addison-Wesley.

Ottaway, M. (2001). Corporatism Goes Global: International Organizations, Nongovernmental Organization Networks, and Transnational Business. *Global Governance*. 7(3): 265–292.

Pakistan Centre for Philanthropy. (2004). NPO Certification Model. Islamabad.

Palley, T. I. (2003). 'Lifting the Natural Resource Curse'. *Foreign Service Journal*. 80: 54–61.

Panel on Accountability and Governance in the Voluntary Sector. (1999). Building on Strength: Improving Governance and Accountability in Canada's Voluntary Sector. Washington: Independent Sector.

Panel on the Nonprofit Sector. (2005). Strengthening Transparency, Governance, Accountability of Charitable Organizations. A Final Report to Congress and the Nonprofit Sector. Washington: Independent Sector.

Pareto, V. (1909). *Manual of Political Economy, English translation by A. S. Schwier, 1971*. New York: Augustus M. Kelley.

Partnership for Clean Fuels and Vehicles. (2002). Mission Statement. Nairobi: United Nations Environment Programme.

Partnership for Clean Fuels and Vehicles. (2003). Governance Rules. Nairobi: United Nations Environment Programme.

Partnership for Clean Fuels and Vehicles. (2005a). Programme of Work of the PCFV Clearing House for 2006 & 2007. Nairobi: United Nations Environment Programme.

Partnership for Clean Fuels and Vehicles. (2005b). Report Back from Clearing House: 2005 Activities. Nairobi: United Nations Environment Programme.

Partnership for Clean Fuels and Vehicles. (2005c). Summary of the Fourth Meeting of the Global Partnership for Clean Fuels and Vehicles in UNEP Headquarters, Nairobi. 14–15 December 2005.

Pasquino, G. (2000). 'Deficit Democratico e Leadership Nell' Unione Europea'. *Teoria Politica.* 16(1): 3–23.

Pastor, R. A. (1999). 'A Brief History of Electoral Commissions', in A. Schedler, L. Diamond, and M. Plattner (Eds), *The Self-Restraining State: Power and Accountability in New Democracies.* Boulder, London: Lynne Rienner.

Pateman, C. (1988). *The Sexual Contract.* Stanford: Stanford University Press.

Patterson, D. M. (1992). 'The Value of a Promise'. *Law and Philosophy.* 11(4): 385–402.

Peacey, J. (2000). 'The Marine Stewardship Council Fisheries Certification Program: Progress and Challenges', paper presented at *2000 Conference of the International Institute for Fisheries Economics and Trade* in Corvallis.

Pechar, H. (2005). 'University Autonomy in Austria'. *HOFO Working Paper Series.* Vienna: Fakultät for Interdisziplinäre Forschung und Fortbildung.

Persson, T., Roland, G., and Tabellini, G. (1997). 'Separation of Powers and Political Accountability'. *Quarterly Journal of Economics.* 112(4): 1163–202.

Phillips, B., Ward, T., and Chaffee, C. (2003). *Eco-Labelling in Fisheries: What is it All About?* Oxford: Blackwell.

Picot, A., Dietl, H., and Franck, E. (2004). *Organisation: Eine ökonomische Perspektive.* Stuttgart: Schaeffer Poeschel.

Pierre, J. (Ed.) (2000). *Debating Governance.* Oxford: Oxford University Press.

Pitkin, H. (1965). 'Obligation and Consent – I'. *American Political Science Review.* 59: 990–9.

Plattner, M. (1999). 'Traditions of Accountability', in A. Schedler, L. Diamond, and M. Plattner (Eds), *The Self-Restraining State: Power and Accountability in New Democracies.* Boulder, London: Lynne Rienner.

Platto, C. (Ed.) (1992). *Civil Appeal Procedures Worldwide.* London, Boston: Graham & Trotman.

Pogge, T. W. (1997). 'Creating Supra-National Institutions Democratically: Reflections on the European Union's "Democratic Deficit"'. *Journal of Political Philosophy.* 5(2): 163–82.

Pollitt, C. (1995). 'Management Techniques for the Public Sector: Pulpit and Practice', in B. G. Peters and D. J. Savoie (Eds), *Governance in a Changing Environment.* 203–38. Montréal & Kingston, London, Buffalo: Canadian Centre of Management Development/McGill-Queen's University Press.

Pope, J. (2000). *Confronting Corruption. The Elements of a National Integrity System.* Berlin: Transparency International.

Power, M. (1994). *The Audit Explosion.* London: Demos.

Propper, C., and Wilson, D. (2003). 'The Use and Usefulness of Performance Measures in the Public Sector'. *Oxford Review of Economic Policy.* 19: 250–67.

Przeworski, A., Stokes, S. C., and Manin, B. (Eds). (1999). *Democracy, Accountability, and Representation.* Cambridge, New York: Cambridge University Press.

Qvortrup, M. (2002). *A Comparative Study of Referendums: Government by the People.* Manchester, New York: Manchester University Press.

Radtke, J. M. (1998). *Strategic Communications for Nonprofit Organizations: Seven Steps to Creating a Successful Plan.* New York: John Wiley & Sons.

252 *Bibliography*

Rank, O. N. (2003). *Formale und informelle Organisationsstrukturen: Eine Netzwerkanalyse des strategischen Planungs- und Entscheidungsprozesses multinationaler Unternehmen.* Wiesbaden: Gabler.

Raviglione, M. C., and Uplekar, M. W. (2006). 'WHO's New Stop TB Strategy'. *The Lancet.* 367(9514): 952–5.

Rawls, J. (1971). *A Theory of Justice.* Oxford: Oxford University Press.

Rawls, J. (1993). *Political Liberalism.* New York: Columbia University Press.

Raynard, P., and Cohen, J. (2003). 'Partnerships: the Accountability Dimension'. *AccountAbility Quarterly.* (20): 4–9.

Reed Lajoux, A., and Elson, C. M. (2000). *The Art of M&A Due Diligence: Navigating Critical Steps and Uncovering Crucial Data.* New York, San Francisco, Washington D.C., Auckland, Bogotá, Caracas, Lisbon, London, Madrid, Mexico City, Milan, Montreal, New Delhi, San Juan, Singapore, Sydney, Tokyo, Toronto: McGraw-Hill Professional.

Reich, M. R. (2002). 'Introduction: Public-Private Partnerships for Public Health', in M. R. Reich (Ed.), *Public-Private Partnerships for Public Health.* 1–18. Cambridge: Harvard University Press.

Reichardt, O., Wilding, K., and Kane, D. (2007). *The UK Voluntary Sector Almanac: The State of the Sector 2007.* London: NCVO.

Reinicke, W. H. (1998). *Global Public Policy: Governing Without Government?* Washington: Brookings Institution Press.

Reinicke, W. H., and Deng, F. (2000). *Critical Choices: The United Nations, Networks, and the Future of Global Governance.* Ottawa: International Development Research Centre.

Renewable Energy and Energy Efficiency Partnership. (2005). Strategy and Work Programme 2005/2006. Vienna.

Renewable Energy and Energy Efficiency Partnership. (2006). REEEP: A Partnership that Delivers. Annual Report 2005/6. Vienna.

Renz, L., and Atienza, J. (2006). *International Grantmaking Update: A Snapshot of US Foundation Trends.* New York: Foundation Center.

Results-Based Management Division. (2000). RBM Handbook on Developing Results Chains: The Basics of RBM as Applied to 100 Project Examples. Quebec: Canadian International Development Agency.

Rhodes, R. A. W. (1996). 'The New Governance: Governing Without Government'. *Political Studies.* 44(4): 652–67.

Rhodes, R. A. W. (1997). *Understanding Governance: Policy Networks, Governance, Reflexivity and Accountability.* Maidenhead: Open University Press.

Richter, J. (2001). *Holding Corporations Accountable. Corporate Conduct, International Codes, and Citizen Action.* London, New York: Zed Books.

Riker, W. H. (1992). 'The Justification of Bicameralism'. *International Political Science Review/Revue Internationale de Science Politique.* 13(1): 101–16.

Risse, T. (2006). 'Transnational Governance and Legitimacy', in Y. Papadopoulos and A. Benz (Eds), *Governance and Democracy: Comparing National, European and International Experiences.* 179–99. London, New York: Routledge.

Rodal, A., and Mulder, N. (1993). 'Partnerships, Devolution and Power-Sharing: Issues and Implications for Management'. *Optimum: The Journal of Public Sector Management.* 24(3): 27–48.

Roll Back Malaria Partnership. (2004). The Roll Back Malaria Partnership's Operating Framework September 2004. Geneva.

Roll Back Malaria Partnership. (2005). Roll Back Malaria Global Strategic Plan 2005–2015. Geneva.

Roll Back Malaria Partnership. (2006). *Roll Back Malaria Partnership By Laws*, July 2006. Geneva.

Rosanvallon, P. (2002). 'Le Déficit Démocratique Européen'. *Esprit*. (10): 87–100.

Rosch, E. (1983). 'Prototype Classification and Logical Classification: The Two Systems', in E. F. Scholnick (Ed.), *New Trends in Conceptual Representation: Challenges to Piaget's Theory?* Hillsdale: Erlbaum.

Rosch, E., and Lloyd, B. B. (Eds). (1978). *Cognition and Categorization*. Hillsdale: Erlbaum.

Rosenau, J. N. (1995). 'Governance in the Twenty-First Century'. *Global Governance*. 1(1): 13–43.

Rosenau, J. N., and Czempiel, E. O. (Eds). (1992). *Governance Without Government: Order and Change in World Politics*. Cambridge: Cambridge University Press.

Ross, S. (1973). 'The Economic Theory of Agency: The Principal's Problem'. *The American Economic Review*. 63(2): 134–9.

Rourke, F. E. (1984). *Bureaucracy, Politics and Public Policy*. Boston: Little, Brown.

Rousseau, J.-J. (1754). *A Discourse on a Subject Proposed by the Academy of Dijon: What is the Origin of Inequality Among Men, and is it Authorised by Natural Law?* Translated by G. D. H. Cole. Austin: The Constitution Society.

Rousseau, J.-J. (1762). *Du Contrat Social. Ou, Principes du Droit Politique*. Amsterdam: Marc Michel Rey.

Rudzio, W. (2000). *Das politische System der Bundesrepublik Deutschland*. Opladen: Leske und Budrich.

Runciman, D. (2003). 'Partnering the State'. *Partnership Matters. Current Issues in Cross-Sector Collaboration* (1): 8–15.

Salamon, L. M., and Anheier, H. K. (Eds). (1997). *Defining the Nonprofit Sector: A Cross-National Analysis*. Manchester, New York: Manchester University Press.

Salamon, L. M., Anheier, H. K., List, R., Toepler, S., and Sokolowski, S. W. (1999). *Global Civil Society: Dimensions of the Nonprofit Sector*. Bloomfield: Kumarian Press.

Salamon, L. M., Hems, L. C., and Chinnock, K. (2000). 'The Non-Profit Sector: For What and For Whom?' *Working Papers of the Johns Hopkins Comparative Non-Profit Sector Project*. Baltimore: The Johns Hopkins Center for Civil Society Studies.

Sandel, M. J. (1982). *Liberalism and the Limits of Justice*. Cambridge: Cambridge University Press.

Sangvi, T., Van Ameringen, M., Baker, J., and Fiedler, J. (2007). 'Vitamin and Mineral Deficiencies Technical Situation Analysis: A Report for the Ten Year Strategy for the Reduction of Vitamin and Mineral Deficiencies'. *Food and Nutrition Bulletin*. 28 (1, supplement): 155–219.

Sassen, S. (1996). *Losing Control? Sovereignty in an Age of Globalization*. New York: Columbia University Press.

Saul, J. R. (1999). *The Unconscious Civilization*. New York: Simon & Schuster.

Scanlon, T. (1990). Promises and Practices. *Philosophy and Public Affairs*. 19(3): 199–226.

Scanlon, T. M. (1998). *What We Owe to Each Other*. Cambridge, London: The Belknap Press of Harvard University Press.

Scharpf, F. W. (1970). *Demokratietheorie zwischen Utopie und Anpassung*. Konstanz: Universitätsverlag.

Scharpf, F. W. (1993). 'Coordination in Hierarchies and Networks', in F. W. Scharpf (Ed.), *Games in Hierarchies and Networks: Analytical and Empirical Approaches to the Study of Governance Institutions*. Boulder: Westview.

Scharpf, F. W. (1999). *Regieren in Europa: Effektiv und Demokratisch?* Frankfurt a.M.: Campus.

Scharpf, F. W. (2003). 'Problem-Solving Effectiveness and Democratic Accountability in the EU'. *MPIfG Discussion and Working Papers 1.* Cologne: Max Planck Institute for the Study of Societies.

Schedler, A. (1999). 'Conceptualizing Accountability', in A. Schedler, L. Diamond, and M. Plattner (Eds), *The Self-Restraining State: Power and Accountability in New Democracies.* 13–28. Boulder, London: Lynne Rienner.

Schmidt, H., and Take, I. (1997). 'Demokratischer und besser? Der Beitrag von Nichtregierungsorganisationen zur Demokratisierung internationaler Politik'. *Aus Politik und Zeitgeschichte.* (43–44): 12–20.

Schmitter, P. C. (1969). 'Three Neo-Functional Hypotheses About International Integration'. *International Organization* 23(1): 161–6.

Schmitter, P. C. (1995). 'Corporatism', in S. M. Lipset (Ed.), *The Encyclopedia of Democracy.* Vol. I. 308–10. London: Routledge.

Schmitter, P. C. (1999). 'The Limits of Horizontal Accountability', in A. Schedler, L. Diamond, and M. Plattner (Eds), *The Self-Restraining State: Power and Accountability in New Democracies.* 59–62. Boulder, London: Lynne Rienner.

Schmitter, P. C. (2004). 'The Ambiguous Virtues of Accountability'. *Journal of Democracy.* 15(4): 47–60.

Schmitter, P. C., and Karl, T. L. (1991). 'What Democracy Is and Is Not'. *Journal of Democracy.* 2(3): 75–88.

Scholte, J. A. (2002). 'Civil Society and Democracy in Global Governance'. *Global Governance.* 8(3): 281–304.

Schöneburg, V. (1998). 'Nullum Crimen, Nulla Poena Sine Lege. Rechtsgeschichtliche Anmerkungen'. *Utopie Kreativ.* 94: 60–70.

Schultz, J. (2003). *Reviving the Fourth Estate.* Cambridge: Cambridge University Press.

Schumacher, J. A. (2004). 'Introducing Transparency into the Oil Industry. The Quest for EITI. *Global Jurist Advances.* 4(3): 1–41.

Scoccia, D. (1990). 'Paternalism and Respect for Autonomy'. *Ethics.* 100(2): 318–34.

Scott-Joynt, J. (2003). *Charities in Terror Fund Spotlight.* New York: Global Policy Forum.

Scudder, T. (2001). 'The World Commission on Dams and the Need for a New Development Paradigm'. *International Journal of Water Resources Development.* 17(3): 343–52.

Selsky, J. B., and Parker, B. (2005). 'Cross-Sector Partnerships to Address Social Issues: Challenges to Theory and Practice'. *Journal of Management.* 31(6): 849–73.

Sen, A. K. (1999). 'Democracy as a Universal Value'. *Journal of Democracy* 10(3): 3–17.

Seventh United Nations Congress on the Prevention of Crime and the Treatment of Offenders. (1985). *Basic Principles on the Independence of the Judiciary.* Milan: Office of the High Commissioner for Human Rights.

Shah, P., and Shah, M. K. (1995). 'Participatory Methods for Increasing NGO Accountability: A Case Study from India', in M. Edwards and D. Hulme (Eds), *Non-Governmental Organisations: Performance and Accountability Beyond the Magic Bullet.* 183–191. London: Earthscan.

Shapiro, M. M. (1981). *Courts: A Comparative and Political Analysis.* Chicago, London: University of Chicago Press.

Shavell, S. (1995). 'The Appeals Process as a Means of Error Correction'. *The Journal of Legal Studies.* 24(2): 379–426.

Shaw, M. N. (1997). *International Law.* Cambridge: Cambridge University Press.

Sheehan, D. (2006). 'Negotiorum Gestio: A Civilian Concept in the Common Law?' *International and Comparative Law Quarterly*. 55(2): 253–80.

Shetreet, S., and Deschênes, J. (Eds). (1985). *Judicial Independence: The Contemporary Debate*. Dordrecht, Boston, Lancaster: Martinus Nijhoff Publishers.

Shleifer, A., and Vishny, R. W. (1997). 'A Survey of Corporate Governance'. *The Journal of Finance*. 52(2): 737–83.

Sidgwick, H. (1907). *The Method of Ethics*. London: Macmillan.

Silk, T. (2004). 'Ten Emerging Principles of Governance of Nonprofit Corporations and Guides to a Safe Harbor'. *International Journal of Not-for-Profit Law* 7(1): 76–84.

Singer, P. (1979). *Practical Ethics*. Cambridge: Cambridge University Press.

Sirotnik, K. A. (2004). 'Introduction: Critical Concerns About Accountability Concepts and Practices', in K. A. Sirotnik (Ed.), *Holding Accountability Accountable. What Ought to Matter in Public Education*. 1–17. New York and London: Teachers College Press.

Sklar, R. L. (1999). 'Democracy and Constitutionalism', in A. Schedler, L. Diamond, and M. Plattner (Eds), *The Self-Restraining State. Power and Accountability in New Democracies*. 53–8. Boulder: Lynne Rienner.

Slaughter, A.-M. (2001). 'Global Government Networks, Global Information Agencies, and Disaggregated Democracy'. *Harvard Law School Public Law Working Paper No. 018*. Cambridge: Harvard Law School.

Slaughter, A.-M. (2004). 'Disaggregated Sovereignty: Towards the Public Accountability of Global Government Networks'. *Government and Opposition*. 39(2): 159–90.

Slim, H. (2002). 'By What Authority? The Legitimacy and Accountability of Non-Governmental Organisations', paper presented at *International Meeting on Global Trends and Human Rights – Before and After September 11* in Geneva.

Smith, A. (1904). *An Inquiry Into the Nature and Causes of the Wealth of Nations (first published 1776)*. London: Methuen and Co.

Smith, H. M. (1997). 'Paradox of Promising'. *The Philosophical Review*. 106(2): 153–96.

Smith, P. (1995). 'On the Unintended Consequences of Publishing Performance Data in the Public Sector'. *International Journal of Public Administration*. 18(2&3): 277–310.

Solomon, J., and Solomon, A. (2004). *Corporate Governance and Accountability*. Chichester: John Wiley & Sons Ltd.

Spendolini, M. J. (1992). *The Benchmarking Book*. Washington: Amacom.

Spiro, P. J. (2000). 'The New Sovereigntists: American Exceptionalism and Its False Prophets'. *Foreign Affairs* (November–December).

Spiro, P. J. (2002). 'Accounting for NGOs'. *Chicago Journal of International Law* (3): 161–9.

Stark, C. A. (2000). Hypothetical Consent and Justification. *The Journal of Philosophy*. 97(6): 313–334.

Steets, J. (2006). *Partnerships for Sustainable Development: On the Road to Implementation*. Berlin: Werkverlag AG.

Steinberg, G. M. (2005). 'The Unhelpful Hand: Time to Free the Palestinians from NGOs'. *Wall Street Journal Europe*. New York: Global Policy Forum.

Stepan, A., and Skach, C. (1993). 'Constitutional Frameworks and Democratic Consolidation: Parliamentarism and Presidentialism'. *World Politics*. 46: 1–22.

Stewart, D. W., Shamdasani, P. N., and Rook, D. W. (2007). *Focus Groups: Theory and Practice*. Thousand Oaks, London, New Delhi: Sage.

Stigler, G. J., and Becker, G. S. (1977). 'De Gustibus Non Est Disputandum'. *The American Economic Review*. 67(2): 76–90.

Stiglitz, J. (2002). *Globalization and Its Discontents*. London: Penguin.

Stiglitz, J. E. (2006). *Making Globalization Work*. New York, London: W. W. Norton & Company.

Stoker, G. (1998). 'Governance as Theory: Five Propositions'. *International Social Science Journal*. 155: 17–28.

Stop TB Partnership. (2001a). Global Plan to Stop TB. Phase 1: 2001–2005. Geneva: World Health Organization.

Stop TB Partnership. (2001b). Global TB Drug Facility. Prospectus. Geneva: World Health Organization.

Stop TB Partnership. (2006a). Annual Report 2005. Geneva: World Health Organization.

Stop TB Partnership. (2006b). The Global Plan to Stop TB 2006–2015. Actions for Life. Towards a World Free of Tuberculosis. Geneva: World Health Organization.

Stop TB Partnership. (2007). Annual Report 2006. A Portrait of Progress. Geneva: World Health Organization.

Strange, S. (1996). *The Retreat of the State. The Diffusion of Power in the World Economy*. Cambridge: Cambridge University Press.

Strøm, K. (2000). 'Delegation and Accountability in Parliamentary Democracies'. *European Journal of Political Research*. 37: 261–89.

Stutzer, A., and Frey, B. S. (2005). 'Making International Organizations More Democratic'. *Review of Law and Economics*. 1(3): 305–30.

Swindell, D., and Kelly, J. M. (2000). 'Linking Citizen Satisfaction Data to Performance Measures: A Preliminary Evaluation'. *Public Performance & Management Review*. 24(1): 30–52.

Taiclet, A.-F. (2001). 'Legitimacy and Accountability in Multi-Level Games: An Empirical Assessment Through Local Economic Development Policies in France', paper presented at *ECPR Joint Sessions 'Governance and Democratic Legitimacy'* in Grenoble. 6–11 April 2001.

Tamanaha, B. Z. (2004). *On the Rule of Law: History, Politics, Theory*. Cambridge: Cambridge University Press.

Tapper, E. R., and Salter, B. G. (1995). 'The Changing Idea of University Autonomy'. *Studies in Higher Education*. 20(1): 59–71.

Taylor, M., and Warburton, D. (2003). 'Legitimacy and the Role of UK Third Sector Organizations in the Policy Process'. *Voluntas: International Journal of Voluntary and Nonprofit Organizations*. 14(3): 321–38.

Technical Evaluation Reference Group. (2006). Framework Document on the Scale and Scope of the Five-Year Evaluation. Geneva: The Global Fund to Fight AIDS, Tuberculosis and Malaria.

Tennyson, R. (2003). *The Partnering Toolbook*. London, Geneva: International Business Leaders Forum, Global Alliance for Improved Nutrition.

Thatcher, M. (1998). 'The Development of Policy Network Analyses. From Modest Origins to Overarching Frameworks'. *Journal of Theoretical Politics*. 10(4): 389–416.

The Expert Group on Renewable Energy. (2005). Increasing Global Renewable Energy Market Share: Recent Trends and Perspectives. New York: The United Nations Department of Economic and Social Affairs.

The Global Fund to Fight AIDS, Tuberculosis and Malaria. (2003). Fourth Board Meeting: Report of the Governance and Partnership Committee. Geneva.

The Global Fund to Fight AIDS, Tuberculosis and Malaria. (2005). The Global Fund to Fight AIDS, Tuberculosis & Malaria By-Laws, as Amended September 30, 2005. Geneva.

The Global Fund to Fight AIDS, Tuberculosis and Malaria. (2006). Annual Report 2005. Vernier.

The Information Working Group of the Voluntary Principles. (2006). Five-Year Overview of the Voluntary Principles on Security and Human Rights: Company Implementation Progress and Lessons Learned. London, Paris: Voluntary Principles on Security and Human Rights.

The Institute of Chartered Accountants in England and Wales. (1990). Statement of Standard Accounting Practice No. 4. London.

The London School of Hygiene & Tropical Medicine. (2002). The Global Market for Soaps. A Market Research Report for the Public-Private Partnership on Handwashing with Soap. London.

The National Council For Public-Private Partnerships. (2003). Critical Choices: The Debate Over Public-Private Partnerships and What it Means for America's Future. Washington.

The World Bank. (1996). *The World Bank Participation Sourcebook*. Washington.

The World Bank. (1999). 'Using an Ombudsman to Oversee Public Officials'. *World Bank PREM Notes No. 19*. Washington.

Theuvsen, L. (2001). 'Stakeholder Management – Möglichkeiten des Umgangs mit Anspruchsgruppen'. *Münsteraner Diskussionspapiere zum Nonprofit Sektor*. 1–27. Münster: Arbeitsstelle Aktive Bürgerschaft an der Westfälischen Wilhelms-Universität Münster.

Thomas, A., and Curtis, V. (2003). *Public-Private Partnerships for Health. A Review of Best Practices in the Health Sector*. Washington: Water and Sanitation Program, the World Bank.

Thompson, D. F. (1980). 'Moral Responsibility of Public Officials: The Problem of Many Hands'. *American Political Science Review* (74): 905–16.

Thompson, G. F. (2003). *Between Hierarchies and Markets: The Logic and Limits of Network Forms of Organization*. Oxford: Oxford University Press.

Thompson, M. R. (2001). 'Whatever Happened to "Asian Values?"' *Journal of Democracy* 12(4): 154–65.

Tirole, J. (1996). 'A Theory of Collective Reputations (with Applications to the Persistence of Corruption and to Firm Quality)'. *The Review of Economic Studies*. 63(1): 1–22.

Tsebelis, G. (1995). 'Decision Making in Political Systems: Veto Players in Presidentialism, Parliamentarism, Multicameralism and Multipartyism'. *British Journal of Political Science*. 25(3): 289–325.

Tsebelis, G., and Garrett, G. (2000). 'Legislative Politics in the European Union'. *European Union Politics*. 1(1): 9–36.

US Supreme Court. (1803). William Marbury v. James Madison, Secretary of State of the United States. Vol. 5 US 137: Cranch.

US Supreme Court. (1985). Regents of University of Michigan v. Ewing. Vol. 474 US 214.

United Kingdom Parliament. (1988). Education Reform Act. London: Her Majesty's Stationary Office.

United Nations. (2002). Press Conference on Global Alliance on Improved Nutrition. New York.

United Nations Conference on Environment and Development. (1992). Rio Declaration on Environment and Development, *GA/A/CONF.151/26 (Vol. I)*. Rio.

United Nations Economic and Social Council. (1996). Consultative Relationship Between the United Nations and Non-Governmental Organizations *Resolution 1996/31*. New York.

United Nations Economic and Social Council. (2004). Partnerships for Sustainable Development. Report of the Secretary General, *E/CN.17/2004/16*. New York: Commission on Sustainable Development.

United Nations Economic and Social Council. (2006). Partnerships for Sustainable Development. Report of the Secretary General., *E/CN.17/2006/6*. New York: Commission on Sustainable Development.

United Nations General Assembly. (1948). Universal Declaration of Human Rights, *GA/RES/217 A (III) of 10 December 1948*. New York.

United Nations General Assembly. (1966). International Covenant on Civil and Political Rights, *GA/RES/2200A (XXI) of 16 December 1966*. New York.

United Nations General Assembly. (2003). United Nations Convention Against Corruption, *GA/RES/58/4 of 31 October 2003*. New York.

United States Food and Drug Administration. (2004). FDA Public/Private Partnership Program. Rockville.

United States General Accounting Office. (1999). Standards for Internal Control in the Federal Government. Washington.

United States of America. (1787). United States Constitution.

Vaillancourt Rosenau, P. (1999). 'The Strengths and Weaknesses of Public-Private Policy Partnerships'. *American Behavioral Scientist*. 43(1): 10–34.

Vaillancourt Rosenau, P. (Ed.) (2000). *Public-Private Policy Partnerships*. Cambridge: MIT Press.

Vallejo, N., and Hauselmann, P. (2005). *Multi-Stakeholder Governance: A Brief Guide*. Pully: Pi Environmental Consulting.

Valve Seat Working Group. (2004). Eliminating Lead from Gasoline: Report on Valve Seat Recession. Nairobi: Partnership for Clean Fuels and Vehicles.

Van Ballegoyen, A. F. (1999). Roll Back Malaria: A Who Initiated Network in the Fight Against Malaria. Case Study for the UN Vision Project on Global Public Policy Networks.

Van Slyke, D. M. (2002). 'The Public Management Challenges of Contracting with Nonprofits for Social Services'. *International Journal of Public Administration*. 25(4): 489–517.

VanDeVeer, D. (1986). *Paternalistic Intervention*. Princeton: Princeton University Press.

Vayrynen, R. (1999). *Globalization and Global Governance*. New York: Rowman & Littelfield Publishers.

Vienot, M. (1999). Recommendations of the Committee on Corporate Governance Chaired by Mr. Mark Vienot. Paris: Association Francaise des Entreprises Privées, Mouvement des Entreprises de France.

Voigt, S., and Salzberger, E. M. (2002). 'Choosing Not To Choose: When Politicians Choose To Delegate Powers'. *Kyklos*. 55(2): 289–310.

Von der Crone, H. C. (2000). 'Verantwortlichkeit, Anreize und Reputation in der Corporate Governance der Publikumsgesellschaft'. *Zeitschrift für schweizerisches Recht*. 119: 239–75.

Waddington, C., Martin, J., and Walford, V. (2005). *Trends in International Funding for Malaria Control*. London: HLSP Institute.

Waldron, J. (1994). 'John Locke. Social Contract Versus Political Anthropology', in D. Boucher and P. Kelly (Eds), *The Social Contract from Hobbes to Rawls*. 51–72. London, New York: Routledge.

Wallerstein, I. (1984). *The Politics of the World-Economy. The States, the Movements, and the Civilizations*. Cambridge, New York, Melbourne, Paris: Editions de la Maison des Sciences de l'Homme and Cambridge University Press.

Wand, B. (1970). 'Ake on Political Obligation and Political Dissent: A Gloss'. *Canadian Journal of Political Science/Revue Canadienne de Science Politique*. 3(1): 158–61.

Wapner, P. (2002). 'Defending Accountability in NGOs'. *Chicago Journal of International Law* (3): 197–205.

Weber, M. (1964). *The Theory of Social and Economic Organization*. New York: Free Press.

Weber, M. (1976). *Grundriss der Sozialökonomik. III. Abteilung. Wirtschaft und Gesellschaft.* Tübingen: Mohr-Siebeck.

Webster, P. D. (1995). 'Selection and Retention of Judges: Is There One "Best" Method?' *Florida State University Law Review*. 23: 1–39.

Weiler, J. H. H., Haltern, U. R., and Mayer, F. C. (1995). 'European [Union] Democracy and its Critique'. *West European Politics*. 18(3): 4–39.

Weinberg, J. (2000). 'ICANN and the Problem of Legitimacy'. *Duke Law Journal*. 50: 187–260.

Weinrib, E. J. (1975). 'The Fiduciary Obligation'. *The University of Toronto Law Journal*. 25(1): 1–22.

Wellhöfer, P. R., Rothgang, G.-W., and Busse, J. (2002). 'Evaluation der Evaluation: Resonanz auf die Einführung der Evaluation der Lehre bei Lehrenden und Studierenden'. *Sonderdruck Schriftenreihe Nr. 15*. 1–32. Nürnberg: Georg-Simon-Ohm-Fachhochschule.

Wendt, A. (2003). 'Why a World State is Inevitable'. *European Journal of International Relations*. 9(4): 491–542.

Wieland, J., and Conrad, W. (2002). *Corporate Citizenship. Gesellschaftliches Engagement – unternehmerischer Nutzen*. Marburg: Metropolis.

Wiener, A., and Della-Sala, V. (1997). 'Constitution-Making and Citizenship Practice – Bridging the Democracy Gap in the EU?' *Journal of Common Market Studies*. 35(4): 595–614.

Wilde, L. (1994). 'Marx Against the Social Contract', in D. Boucher and P. Kelly (Eds), *The Social Contract from Hobbes to Rawls*. 164–74. London, New York: Routledge.

Wilde, V. (2001). *Field Level Handbook*. Rome: Socio-Economic and Gender Analysis Programme, Food and Agriculture Organization of the United Nations.

Wilkinson, D., Brugha, R., Hewitt, S., Trap, B., Eriksen, J., Nielsen, L., and Weber, W. (2006). Assessment of the Proposal Development and Review Process of the Global Fund to Fight AIDS, Tuberculosis and Malaria: Assessment Report. Søborg: Euro Health Group.

Willetts, P. (2000). 'From "Consultative Arrangements" to "Partnership": The Changing Status of NGOs in Diplomacy at the UN'. *Global Governance*. 6(2): 191–212.

Williams, C. A. (2004). 'Civil Society Initiatives and "Soft Law" in The Oil and Gas Industry'. *International Law and Politics*. 36: 457–502.

Williams, S. (1990). 'Sovereignty and Accountability in the European Community'. *Political Quarterly*. 61(3): 299–317.

Williamson, O. E. (1985a). *The Economic Institutions of Capitalism*. New York: The Free Press.

Williamson, O. E. (1993). 'Calculativeness, Trust, and Economic Organization'. *Journal of Law and Economics*. 36(1): 453–86.

Williamson, O. E., and Winter, S. G. (Eds). (1991). *The Nature of the Firm. Origins, Evolutions, and Development*. New York and Oxford: Oxford University Press.

Williamson, P. J. (1985b). *Varieties of Corporatism: A Conceptual Discussion*. Cambridge: Cambridge University Press.

Willis, A. (2003). 'The Role of the Global Reporting Initiative's Sustainability Reporting Guidelines in the Social Screening of Investments'. *Journal of Business Ethics*. 43(3): 233–7.

Wincott, D. (1998). 'Does the European Union Pervert Democracy? Questions of Democracy in New Constitutionalist Thought on the Future of Europe'. *European Law Journal*. 4(4): 411–28.

Wirth, W. (1986a). 'Control in Public Administration: Plurality, Selectivity and Redundancy', in F.-X. Kaufmann, G. Majone, and V. Ostrom (Eds), *Guidance, Control, and Evaluation in the Public Sector*. 595–624. Berlin, New York: de Gruyter.

Wirth, W. (1986b). 'Public Administration and Publics: Control of Bureacratic Performance by Affected Cititzens', in F.-X. Kaufmann, G. Majone, and V. Ostrom (Eds), *Guidance, Control, and Evaluation in the Public Sector* 739–64. Berlin, New York: de Gruyter.

Witte, J. M., and Reinicke, W. H. (2005). *Business UNusual: Facilitating United Nations Reform Through Partnerships*. New York: United Nations Global Compact Office.

Witte, J. M., and Streck, C. (2003). 'Introduction: Progress or Peril? Partnerships and Networks in Global Environmental Governance', in J. M. Witte, C. Streck, and T. Benner (Eds), *Progress or Peril? Partnerships and Networks in Global Environmental Governance: The Post-Johannesburg Agenda*. Washington, Berlin: Global Public Policy Institute.

Witte, J. M., Streck, C., and Benner, T. (2003). 'The Road From Johannesburg: What Future for Partnerships in Global Environmental Governance?' in J. M. Witte, C. Streck, and T. Benner (Eds), *Progress or Peril? Partnerships and Networks in Global Environmental Governance. The Post-Johannesburg Agenda*. Washington, Berlin: Global Public Policy Institute.

Wolf, K. D. (2000). *Die Neue Staatsräson – Zwischenstaatliche Kooperation als Demokratieproblem in der Weltgesellschaft*. Baden-Baden: Nomos.

Wolf, K. D. (2001). 'Private Actors and the Legitimacy of Governance Beyond the State', paper presented at *ECPR Joint Sessions of Workshops 'Governance and Democratic Legitimacy'* in Grenoble. 6–11 April 2001.

Woods, N. (2003). 'Holding Intergovernmental Institutions to Account'. *Ethics & International Affairs*. 17(1): 69–80.

Woods, N., and Narlikar, A. (2001). 'Governance and the Limits of Accountability: the WTO, the IMF and the World Bank'. *International Social Science Journal*. 53(4): 569–83.

World Association of Non-Governmental Organizations. (2004). Code of Ethics and Conduct for NGOs Tarrytown.

World Commission on Dams. (1999). WCD Work Programme. Cape Town.

World Commission on Dams. (2000). *Dams and Development: A New Framework for Decision-Making: The Report of the World Commission on Dams*. London: Earthscan.

World Commission on Dams. (2001). Project and Financial Report: May 1998–April 2001. Cape Town.

World Health Organization. (2000). Financial Regulations of the World Health Organization, *WHA 53.6*. Geneva: 53rd World Health Assembly.

World Health Organization. (2007). Global Tuberculosis Control: Surveillance, Planning, Financing, *WHO Report 2007*. Geneva.

World Health Organization, and Stop TB Partnership. (2006). The Stop TB Strategy. Building on and Enhancing DOTS to Meet the TB-Related Millennium Development Goals. Geneva.

World Summit on Sustainable Development. (2002a). From Our Origins to the Future, *Johannesburg Declaration on Sustainable Development*. Johannesburg.

World Summit on Sustainable Development. (2002b). Plan of Implementation. Johannesburg.

World Vision International. (2005). 2004 Annual Review. Monrovia, Geneva.

Wyatt, M. (2004). *A Handbook of NGO Governance*. Budapest: The Central and Eastern European Working Group on Nonprofit Governance.

Yin, R. K. (1994). *Case Study Research. Design and Methods*. Thousand Oaks: Sage.

Young, D. R. (2002). 'The Influence of Business on Nonprofit Organizations and the Complexity of Nonprofit Accountability: Looking Inside as Well as Outside'. *American Review of Public Administration*. 32(1): 3–19.

Zaheer, A., McEvily, B., and Perrone, V. (1998). 'Does Trust Matter? Exploring the Effects of Interorganizational and Interpersonal Trust on Performance'. *Organization Science*. 9(2): 141–59.

Zammit, A. (2003). *Development at Risk: Rethinking UN-Business Partnerships*. Geneva: South Centre.

Zürn, M. (2000). 'Democratic Governance Beyond the Nation-State: The EU and Other International Institutions'. *European Journal of International Relations*. 6(2): 183–221.

Zweifel, T. D. (2002). 'Who is Without Sin Cast the First Stone: The EU's Democratic Deficit in Comparison'. *Journal of European Public Policy*. 9(5): 812–40.

Index